7TH EDITION

THE
ENGLISH
LEGAL SYSTEM

JACQUELINE MARTIN

HODDER
EDUCATION

HACHETTE UK COMPANY

Orders: please contact Bookpoint Ltd, 130 Milton Park, Abingdon, Oxon OX14 4SB.
Telephone: (44) 01235 827720. Fax: (44) 01235 400454. Lines are open from 9.00–5.00,
Monday to Saturday, with a 24-hour message answering service. You can also order through our
website www.hoddereducation.co.uk.

British Library Cataloguing in Publication Data

A catalogue record for this title is available from the British Library

ISBN: 978 1 4441 8306 1

First edition Published 1997
Second edition Published 2000
Third edition Published 2002
Fourth edition Published 2005
Fifth edition Published 2007
Sixth edition Published 2010
This Edition Published 2013

Impression number   10 9 8 7 6 5 4 3 2 1

Year   2016 2015 2014 2013

Hachette UK's policy is to use papers that are natural, renewable and recyclable products and
made from wood grown in sustainable forests. The logging and manufacturing processes are
expected to conform to the environmental regulations of the country of origin.

Cover photo © Dinga/iStockphoto

Typeset by Aptara, Inc.

Printed in Italy for Hodder Education, an Hachette UK company, 338 Euston Road, London,
NW1 3BH.

CONTENTS

PREFACE

The book is intended for any first-time student of the English Legal System. In particular, the coverage of topics is suitable for the AS specifications in Law for OCR and WJEC and is aimed at candidates at the higher end of the ability range. The book is also suitable for those starting degree or similar courses. The book does not assume any prior knowledge and starts with an introduction to types of law, in particular the critical distinction between civil and criminal law. The first chapter also introduces jurisprudential concepts and discusses law and morality and law and justice using recent cases. This section has been deliberately kept fairly brief as I have always felt that an 'in depth' study of jurisprudence at an early stage of a legal course is not desirable.

The order of topics is then fairly traditional, starting with the sources of law and going on to look at the criminal justice system, the civil justice system and legal personnel. The chapters on criminal justice take the student through the entire process starting with the commission of crimes and police powers, covering prosecution, both pre-trial and the process in the courts, and finishing with sentencing. The civil justice chapters also endeavour to give comprehensive coverage including pre-litigation matters, the courts, tribunals, arbitration and ADR, remedies and enforcement of judgments. The chapters on legal personnel cover both the professionals and lay participation and the problem of financing litigation. The final chapter is a brief one on human rights.

I have tried to keep to the principles of explaining legal points simply and clearly, but at the same time providing sufficient depth for the more able students. Articles, cases and other 'live' material are used to illustrate points and to provide examples of the legal system at work today. Many of these items have also been used to give students the opportunity to do activities and exercises to help their understanding of topics. Key fact charts on many topics are included.

At the end of chapters, examination questions from recent WJEC and OCR papers are included. In addition, an extension essay title is provided for each chapter. These are suitable for those on access or degree courses and can provide the opportunity to stretch and challenge AS students.

This 7th edition includes recent changes to the legal system, including the changes to sentencing and legal aid made by the Legal Aid, Sentencing and Punishment of Offenders Act 2012.

The law is stated as I believe it to be on 1 January 2013.

Jacqueline Martin

ACKNOWLEDGEMENTS

The author and publishers would like to thank the following for the use of photographic material in this volume:

Page 44 © rnl – Fotolia.com; page 48 © SIMON WALKER/Rex Features; page 61 © Richard Sowersby/Rex Features; page 71 © VINCENT KESSLER/Reuters/Corbis; page 112 © ALEX SEGRE/Rex Features; page 138 © Rex Features; page 172 © Photofusion Picture Library/Alamy; page 194 © Dan Atkin/Alamy; page 207 © Stockdisc/Corbis; page 211 © Peter Dazeley/ Photographer's Choice/Getty Images; page 223 © TOBY MELVILLE/Reuters/Corbis; page 228 © Gareth Fuller/PA Wire/Press Association Images; page 241 © Oli Scarff/Getty Images; page 283 © Citizen's Advice Bureau; page 293 © John Edward Linden/Arcaid/Corbis.

The author and publishers would like to thank the following for the use of copyright material in this volume:

OCR for the use of OCR examination questions; Welsh Joint Education Committee for WJEC examination questions; © Daily Mail, p180, p197; © Guardian News & Media Ltd 1995, p46; © The Huffington Post, p4/5; © The Independent: www.independent.co.uk, p4, p135; © The Mailing Chronicle, p5; © Mersey Police website, p63; © Telegraph Media Group Limited 2009, p4; © The Times/nisyndication.com, p4, p6, p83, p214, p232, p260/1; © Crown copyright material is reproduced with permission of the Controller of HMSO.

Every effort has been made to trace and acknowledge the ownership of copyright material. The publishers apologise if any inadvertently remain unacknowledged and will be glad to make suitable arrangements to rectify this at the earliest opportunity.

TABLE OF ACTS OF PARLIAMENT

TABLE OF CASES

CHAPTER 1

THE RULE OF LAW

1.1 What is law?

Law can affect many aspects of our lives, yet most people living in England and Wales have little understanding of the legal system that operates in these countries. For many their main awareness comes from newspaper articles with headlines such as 'Murderer jailed for life'; 'Young offender goes free'; 'Burglar caught'. This type of headline appears so frequently that it is not surprising that, when law is mentioned, many people only think of the criminal law and the courts that deal with this type of case. In reality the law covers an enormous range of situations and the legal system in England and Wales has a variety of courts and methods for dealing with different types of cases.

1.1.1 Different types of law

Since the law does cover such a wide variety of matters it can be helpful to divide it into different categories. The first distinction is that between international and national (municipal) law; national law can then be classified into public and private law; finally these classifications can be subdivided into a number of different categories. These divisions are explained below.

International and national law

International law is concerned with disputes between nations; much of this law comes from treaties which have been agreed by the governments of the countries.

National law is the law which applies within a country: each country will have its own national law and there are often wide differences between the law of individual countries. This can be shown by the fact that Scotland has its own law and legal system which are quite separate from the law and legal system which operate in England and Wales. For example, while serious criminal cases are tried by jury in both systems, the Scottish jury has 15 members and the decision can be made by a simple majority of 8–7. In contrast the jury in England and Wales has 12 members, at least 10 of whom must agree on the decision.

Public and private law

Within national law there is usually a clear distinction between public and private law. Public law involves the state or government in some way, while private law is concerned with disputes between private individuals or businesses. Both public and private law can be subdivided into different categories.

Public law

There are three main types of law in this category. These are:

1. **Constitutional law**
   This controls the method of government and any disputes which arise over such matters as who is entitled to vote in an election, or who is allowed to become a Member of Parliament, or whether an election was carried out by the correct procedure.
2. **Administrative law**
   This controls how ministers of state and public bodies such as local councils should operate. An important part of this is the right to judicial review of certain decisions. Judicial review allows

judges to consider whether a decision (or a refusal to make a decision) is reasonable. If it is not, then the decision is reconsidered.

3. Criminal law

This sets out the types of behaviour which are forbidden at risk of punishment. A person who commits a crime is said to have offended against the state, and so the state has the right to prosecute them. This is so even though there is often an individual victim of a crime as well. For example, if a defendant commits the crime of burglary by breaking into a house and stealing, the state prosecutes the defendant for that burglary, although it is also possible for the victim to bring a private prosecution if the state does not take proceedings. However, if there is a private prosecution, the state still has the right to intervene and take over the matter. At the end of the case, if the defendant is found guilty, the court will punish the defendant for the offence, because he or she has broken the criminal law set down by the state. The victim will not necessarily be given any compensation, since the case is not viewed as a dispute between the burglar and the householder. However, the criminal courts have the power to order that the offender pays the victim compensation and can make such an order, as well as punishing the offender.

Private law

This is usually called civil law and has many different branches. The main ones are contract, tort, family law, law of succession, company law and employment law. This book does not deal with the actual legal rules of any of these areas, only with the system for dealing with disputes. However, it is sensible to have some idea of what types of dispute may be involved in these areas of law, so look at the following situations:

- A family complain that their package holiday did not match what was promised by the tour operator and that they were put into a lower-grade hotel than the one they had paid for.
- A woman has bought a new car and discovers the engine is faulty.
- A man who bought a new car on hire purchase has failed to pay the instalments due to the hire-purchase company.

All these situations come under the law of contract. There are, of course, many other situations in which contracts can be involved. Now look at the next list of situations; they are also civil matters, but of a different type.

- A child passenger in a car is injured in a collision (the tort of negligence).
- A family complain that their health is being affected by the noise and dust from a factory which has just been built near their house (the tort of nuisance).
- A woman is injured by faulty machinery at work (the tort of negligence, but may also involve occupiers' liability and/or employer's duty under health and safety regulations).
- A man complains that a newspaper has written an untrue article about him, which has affected his reputation (the tort of defamation).

All these cases come under the law of tort. A tort occurs where the civil law holds that, even though there is no contract between them, one person owes a legal responsibility of some kind to another person, and there has been a breach of that responsibility. There are many different types of tort, and the above examples demonstrate only some of them. Many cases arise from road traffic crashes, since drivers owe a duty of care to anyone who might be injured by their negligent driving.

Other divisions of private (civil) law concentrate on particular topics. Family law covers such

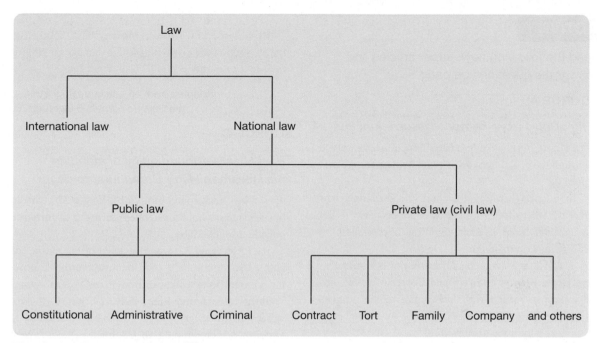

Figure 1.1 *Summary of the different categories of law*

matters as whether a marriage is valid, what the rules are for divorce and who should have the day-to-day care of any children of the family. The law of succession is concerned both with regulating who inherits property when a person dies without making a will, and also what the rules are for making a valid will. Company law is very important in the business world: it regulates how a company should be formed, sets out formal rules for running companies, and deals with the rights and duties of shareholders and directors. Employment law covers all aspects of employment, from the original formation of a contract of employment to situations of redundancy or unfair dismissal. As well as these areas of private law, there are also laws relating to land, to copyright and patents, to marine law and many other topics, so it can be seen that civil law covers a wide variety of situations.

Distinguishing between civil and criminal law

It is important to realise that civil law is very different from criminal law. The first point is shown in Figure 1.1 above. Criminal law is part of public law while civil law is the separate category of private law. The reason that criminal law is part of public law is that crime is regarded as an action against the state and society as a whole. Civil law is called private law because the issues it deals with are between two individuals. The two types of law have different aims and are dealt with in different courts.

On the next two pages there are five newspaper articles. Some are about civil law and some are about criminal law. Do the activity based on these and then read section 1.1.2 to get a clearer understanding of the differences between the two.

ACTIVITY

Read the following newspaper articles and answer the questions on page 5.

SOURCE A

High Court uses Twitter to issue injunction

The High Court has ordered an injunction to be served through the social networking site Twitter for the first time.

In yesterday's ruling, the court said issuing the writ over the micro-blogging site was the best way to get to an anonymous tweeter who was impersonating a right-wing commentator.

The Twitter account, blaneysbarney, was impersonating Donal Blaney, a lawyer and Conservative blogger. The account, which was opened last month, features a photograph of Mr Blaney followed by a number of messages purporting to be by him.

The Court said that the unknown imposter should stop their activities and that they should reveal themselves to the court. The owner of the fake account will receive the writ next time they enter the site.

Taken from an article in *The Times*, 2 October 2009
© The Times 2009/nisyndication.com

SOURCE B

Couple sue wedding photographer

A newly married couple have successfully sued their wedding photographer after paying £1,450 for a 'woefully inadequate' service.

Marc and Sylvia Day were presented with a disc full of pictures from the big day with heads chopped off, inattentive guests and random close-ups of vehicles. The cutting of the cake was missed and of the 400 images they were sent, only 22 met with their approval.

They have now been awarded compensation by a judge after winning a case for breach of contract against the photographer.

Deputy District Judge Keith Nightingale found in favour of the Days at Pontefract County Court and criticised the photographer Gareth Bowers for providing 'inappropriate' photos and a 'woefully inadequate' service.

He ordered him [Bowers] to pay back £500 from the £1,450 to the Days with £450 in damages, £100 for their loss of earnings and £170 in court fees.

Adapted from an article by Paul Stokes in the *Daily Telegraph,* 5 October 2009

SOURCE C

Paul McAteer found guilty of stabbing businessman Harry Broadhurst to death

A man has been found guilty of killing a 22-year-old businessman who was stabbed during a disturbance outside a social club.

Paul McAteer, 32, was convicted of the murder of Harry Broadhurst by a 10–2 majority verdict following a month-long trial at Birmingham Crown Court.

Jurors also found Liam Cole, 29, guilty of conspiracy to cause grievous bodily harm in relation to violence which erupted in Chelmsley Wood, West Midlands, on November 20 last year.

McAteer, of Kitts Green, and Cole, of Shard End, both Birmingham, will be sentenced tomorrow.

Adapted from an article by Matthew Cooper in the *Independent*, 17 July 2012, www.independent.co.uk

SOURCE D

Milly Evans, 11, wins £10.8m medical negligence award from Lincolnshire Hospital trust

A girl who suffered devastating injuries at birth is to receive compensation worth £10.8 million.

The sum awarded to 11-year-old Milly Evans at London's High Court is thought to be one of the highest – if not the highest – clinical negligence awards.

After Milly's birth at Lincoln County Hospital, on 1 March 2001, she was transferred to the neo-natal unit, where she underwent resuscitation and suffered a seizure.

Her parents claimed that if the baby's heart had been properly monitored, the midwife would have spotted her foetal distress sooner, and Milly would have been delivered earlier without suffering catastrophic injury.

Milly is confined to a wheelchair and unable to speak, although her intellect has remained fairly well intact and she communicates through sophisticated eye-gaze equipment. She sat smiling in court as the judge approved a settlement involving a lump sum of £5.866 million and lifelong periodic payments rising to £204,000 a year.

The judge had heard that United Lincolnshire Hospital NHS Trust admitted liability in March 2010 but had contested the amount of damages until the parties recently reached agreement.

Taken from an online article in
the *Huffington Post*, 1 May 2012

SOURCE E

'Cab-jacker' given suspended sentence

A man who assaulted a taxi driver in Shoreham and tried to drive off with his cab has been handed a suspended sentence.

Ian Archer, 47, had already pleaded guilty to a string of offences against the cab driver, including assault and damaging his car and mobile phone, when he appeared before Sevenoaks magistrates.

He also admitted driving off with the car, a Vauxhall Zafira, in addition to driving whilst uninsured and over the drink-driving limit.

Archer's sentence, suspended for a year, was 90 days for the assault, 14 days for criminal damage and 28 days for excess alcohol, all to run concurrently.

In addition he was disqualified from driving for 18 months, handed a supervision requirement, will be made to undergo alcohol treatment and was fined £500.

Adapted from an article in
Mailing Chronicle, 12 November 2009

Questions

1. Identify which of these articles is referring to civil cases and which to criminal cases. (If you wish to check that you are right before continuing with the rest of the questions, turn to the start of Appendix 1 at the back of the book.)
2. Look at the articles which you have identified as criminal cases and state in which courts the defendants were tried.
3. Look at the articles which you have identified as civil cases and state which courts are mentioned.
4. One of the defendants in the criminal cases pleaded guilty. Which one was this?
5. The defendants in the other criminal case were found guilty. Who made this decision?
6. In the criminal cases one defendant was sentenced on the day. List the different punishments used in the case. What was going to happen about sentencing the defendants in the other case?
7. In the civil cases two different types of remedy are mentioned. What are they?

1.1.2 Differences between criminal cases and civil cases

There are many differences between criminal cases and civil cases (you should already have noticed some from the articles):

● **The cases take place in different courts.**
In general, criminal cases will be tried in either the Magistrates' Court or the Crown Court, while civil cases are heard in the High Court or the County Court. (Note that some civil matters, especially family cases, can be dealt with in the Magistrates' Court – see sections 13.1.1 and 17.6 for further details.)

● **The person starting the case is given a different name.**
In criminal cases they are referred to as the prosecutor, while in civil cases they are called the

claimant (pre-1999, the plaintiff). As already stated, the criminal case is taken on behalf of the state and there is a Crown Prosecution Service responsible for conducting cases, though there are other state agencies that may prosecute certain types of crime; for example, the Environment Agency or Customs and Excise. Civil cases are started by the person (or business) who is making the claim.

- **The terminology used is different.**
A defendant in a criminal case is found guilty or not guilty (an alternative way of putting it is to say the defendant is convicted or acquitted), whereas a defendant in a civil case is found liable or not liable. At the end of a criminal case those who are found guilty of breaking the law may be punished, while at the end of a civil case anyone found liable will be ordered to put right the matter as far as possible. This is usually done by an award of money in compensation, known as damages, though the court can make other orders such as an injunction to prevent similar actions in the future, or an order for specific performance where the defendant who broke a contract is ordered to complete that contract.

- **The standard of proof is different.**
Criminal cases must be proved 'beyond reasonable doubt'. This is a very high standard of proof, and is necessary since a conviction could result in a defendant serving a long prison sentence. Civil cases have only to be proved 'on the balance of probabilities', a lower standard in which the judge decides who is most likely to be right. This difference in the standard to which a case has to be proved means that even though a defendant in a criminal case has been acquitted, a civil case based on the same facts against that defendant can still be successful. Such situations are not common, but one is illustrated in the article below.

Other situations in which a civil action may follow a successful criminal case are road accident cases. A defendant may be found guilty of a driving

EXAMPLE

Judgment overtakes Brink's-Mat accused 11 years later

Eleven years after a man was acquitted of the £26 million Brink's-Mat bullion robbery, a High Court judge ruled that he was involved and must repay the value of the gold.

Anthony White, acquitted at the Old Bailey in 1984 of taking part in Britain's biggest gold robbery, was ordered to repay the £26,369,778 value and £2,188,600 in compensation. His wife Margaret was ordered to pay £1,084,344. Insurers for Brink's-Mat had sued the couple for the value of the proceeds.

Mr Justice Rimmer told Mr White that his acquittal did not mean that the Old Bailey jury had been satisfied he was innocent; only that he was not guilty according to the standard of proof required in criminal cases . . .

The case against the Whites is the latest and almost the last in a series of actions since the 1983 robbery brought by insurers for Brink's-Mat against people either convicted or suspected of taking part in the robbery and of handling the proceeds.

Using the lower standards of proof in civil courts and in actions for seizure of assets, lawyers believe that they will recoup at least £20 million.

Taken from an article by Stewart Tendler in *The Times*, 2 August 1995 © The Times 1995/nisyndication.com 1995

	CIVIL CASES	CRIMINAL CASES
Purpose of the law	To uphold the rights of individuals	To maintain law and order; to protect society
Person starting the case	The individual whose rights have been affected	Usually the state through the Crown Prosecution Service
Legal name for that person	County Court or High Court Some cases dealt with in tribunals	Magistrates' Court or Crown Court
Standard of proof	The balance of probability	Beyond reasonable doubt
Person/s making the decision	Judge Very rarely a jury	Magistrates OR jury
Decision	Liable or not liable	Guilty or not guilty
Powers of the court	Usually an award of damages, also possible: injunction, specific performance of a contract, rescission or rectification	Prison, fine, community order, discharge, etc. (see Chapter 14)

Figure 1.2 *Distinctions between civil and criminal cases*

offence, such as going through a red traffic light or driving without due care and attention; this is a criminal case. Anyone who was injured or had property damaged as a result of the incident could bring a civil action to claim compensation. The fact that the defendant had already been convicted of a driving offence will make it easier to prove the civil case.

In the English legal system an understanding of these basic distinctions between civil and criminal cases is important. To help you, a chart of the main differences is provided in Figure 1.2.

1.1.3 Definition of 'law'

So far we have considered only some divisions of law, and briefly introduced the system which applies in England and Wales. It is now necessary to look more widely at, and to discuss what is meant by, law in general terms and to compare it with concepts of morality and justice.

It is not easy to give a simple one-sentence definition of law – however, legal theorists have tried to provide such a definition. John Austin, writing in the early 19th century, defined law as being a command issued from a superior (the state) to an inferior (the individual) and enforced by sanctions. This definition, however, does not truly apply to regulatory law such as that setting out how a will should be made; nor does it cover the concept of judicial review, where individuals may challenge the 'command' made by a minister of state. Austin was writing at a time when the law was much less developed than it is today, so it is not surprising that his definition does not cover all types of law today.

Sir John Salmond defined law as being 'the body of principles recognised and applied by the state in the administration of justice'. This is a much broader definition than Austin's and is probably the nearest that one can get to a workable 'one-sentence' definition. Law could also be described as a formal mechanism of social control. It is formal because the rules set down in the law can be enforced through the courts and legal system, while in a broad sense all law could be said to be involved in some area of social control.

Law and rules

Law applies throughout a country to the people generally. There are other rules that apply only to certain groups or in limited situations: for example, all sports have a set of rules to be followed, and the sanction applied for breaking the rules may be that a free kick is given to the other side, or that a player is sent off, or in serious cases a player is banned from competing for a certain number of weeks or months.

There are also unwritten 'rules' within communities. These come from local custom or practice, or they may be connected to religious beliefs. They enforce what is regarded by the community as the norm for behaviour. If you break such rules, others in the community may disapprove of your behaviour, but there is no legal sanction to force you to comply or to punish you if you refuse to do so. Such normative values are often connected with sexual behaviour and the concept of morality. The relationship of law and morality is explored in the next section of this chapter.

Codes of law

In some civilisations or countries, an effort has been made to produce a complete set of rules designed to deal with every possible situation that might arise. Some of the early major civilisations attempted this, notably the code of Justinian in Roman times. In the 18th century, Frederick the Great of Prussia compiled a code of 17,000 'rules' which he saw as a complete and ideal set of laws. In France, Napoleon also codified the law, and this Napoleonic Code is still the basis of French law today. In theory this idea of a complete code is attractive. It makes the law more accessible so that everyone knows exactly what their rights and duties are; however, law needs to be able to change and develop with the needs of society, and a fully codified system would prevent any such change.

1.2 Law and morality

The moral values of communities lay down a framework for how people should behave. Concepts of morality differ from culture to culture, although most will outlaw extreme behaviour such as murder. Often morality is based on religious ideas: the Bible teachings provide a moral code for Christian communities and the teachings in

the Koran for Muslims. The law of a country will usually reflect the moral values accepted by the majority of the country, but the law is unlikely to be exactly the same as the common religious moral code. One example is adultery: this is against the moral code for both Christians and Muslims but is not considered a crime in Christian countries; however, in some Muslim countries (though not all) it is against the criminal law.

The moral standards of a community are recognised as having a profound influence on the development of law, but in complex societies, morality and law are never likely to be co-extensive. Major breaches of a moral code (such as murder and robbery) will also be against the law, but in other matters there may not be consensus.

In England and Wales there has been a move away from religious belief and the way that the law has developed reflects this. Abortion was legalised in 1967, yet many people still believe it is morally wrong. A limited form of euthanasia has been accepted as legal with the ruling in *Airedale NHS Trust v Bland* (1993), where it was ruled that medical staff could withdraw life-support systems from a patient who could breathe unaided, but who was in a persistent vegetative state. This ruling meant that they could withdraw the feeding tubes of the patient, despite the fact that this would inevitably cause him to die. Again, many groups believe that this is immoral as it denies the sanctity of human life.

ACTIVITY

In *Re A (conjoined twins)* (2000) the Court of Appeal had to decide whether doctors should operate to separate Siamese twins when it was certain that the operation would kill one twin as she could not exist without being linked to her twin.

a) Search on the Internet for a report of this case. Try www.bailii.org and look under the England and Wales reports – the Court of Appeal (Civil Division) for September 2000. The case is likely to be indexed as A (children), Re with a reference of EWCA (Civ) 254.

b) Discuss:
1. Whether this sort of decision should be made by judges.
2. Whether you think that, knowing one child would die, it was right for the operation to go ahead.

Differences between law and morality

There are also differences between law and morality in the way the two develop and the sanctions imposed. The following is a suggested list of such differences.

1. Morality cannot be deliberately changed; it evolves slowly and changes according to the will of the people. Law can be altered deliberately by legislation: this means that behaviour which was against the law can be 'decriminalised' overnight. Equally, behaviour which was lawful can be declared unlawful.
2. Morality is voluntary with consequences, but generally carrying no official sanction (though some religions may 'excommunicate'); morality relies for its effectiveness on the individual's sense of shame or guilt. Law makes certain behaviour obligatory with legal sanctions to enforce it.
3. Breaches of morality are not usually subject to formal adjudication; breaches of law will be ruled on by a formal legal system.

1.3 Law and justice

It is often said that the law provides justice, yet this is not always so. Justice is probably the ultimate goal towards which the law should strive, but it is unlikely that law will ever produce 'justice' in every case.

First there is the problem of what is meant by 'justice'. The difficulty of defining justice was commented on by Lord Wright, who said:

'the guiding principle of a judge in deciding cases is to do justice; that is justice according to the law, but still justice. I have not found any satisfactory definition of justice . . . what is just in a particular case is what appears just to the just man, in the same way as what is reasonable appears to be reasonable to the reasonable man.'

In some situations people's concept of what is justice may not be the same. Justice can be seen as applying the rules in the same way to all people, but even this may lead to perceived injustices – indeed rigid application of rules may actually produce injustice.

An area in which there has been a lot of discussion is the amount of force that a householder can use on a burglar who enters that person's home. What is fair and just for both parties? Should the householder be allowed to seriously injure, or even kill, the burglar? Should the burglar be able to claim compensation for any injuries suffered?

The activity on page 10 is based on a similar situation.

Conclusion

From sections 1.2 and 1.3 it is clear that the three concepts of law, morality and justice are quite distinct. There is, however, a large overlap between law and morality, law and justice and also morality and justice. This idea of the overlapping of the three is illustrated in diagram form in Figure 1.3.

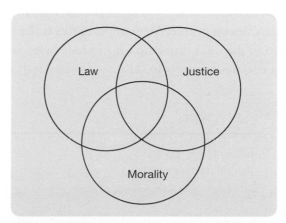

Figure 1.3 *Diagram of the relationship of law, morality and justice*

1.4 Rights and duties

The law gives rights to individuals and methods of enforcing those rights. Quite often the law is involved in a balancing act, trying to ensure that one person's rights do not affect another person's rights. In order to keep the balance the law also imposes duties on people.

This is more easily understood by looking at examples. In the law of contract, where one person buys a digital television from a shop each party will have rights and duties under this contract. For example, the shop has the right to be paid the agreed price for the TV, while the buyer has the right to have a set which is in working order.

The idea of rights and duties can also be seen clearly in employment law. An employer has a duty to pay wages to the employee, while the employee has the right to sue for any wages which are owed. An employee has a duty to obey reasonable lawful orders while an employer has a right to expect this and may be able to dismiss the employee if there is a serious breach. An employer has a duty to provide a safe system of work for all employees, while an employee has the right to claim compensation if he is injured because the employer has broken this duty. These are just a few of the rights and duties of employers and employees and this balancing of their rights and duties is also shown in Figure 1.4.

Even where there is no contract or agreement between the parties, the law can impose rights and duties on people. An example of this is the right to use one's own land (this includes a house or a flat) as one wants to. The law recognises that people have the right to enjoy the use of their own property, but this right is balanced by the right of other land users to enjoy the use of their properties. So the tort of nuisance allows a claim to be made if one's enjoyment of land is affected by too much noise, smoke, smells or other nuisances coming from another person's land.

Even in the criminal law this idea of rights and duties can be seen. The criminal law imposes a duty on all citizens to obey the law or face possible punishment. This duty is imposed to protect other citizens or society as a whole. In this way the law upholds the rights of people not to be assaulted or to have their possessions stolen or whatever else the particular crime involves.

ACTIVITY

Read the facts of the following case and use the questions below as the basis of a discussion on the concept of justice.

CASE *REVILL V NEWBERY* (1996)
Facts: Mark Revill, aged 21, with another man attempted to break into a brick shed on William Newbery's allotment at about 2 o'clock in the morning. Mr Revill and his companion had already that night stolen cars and caused criminal damage elsewhere, and intended to steal items from the shed. Mr Newbery, who was aged 76, was sleeping in the shed in order to protect his property after earlier thefts and vandalism. He had with

---

EMPLOYER	EMPLOYEE
Duty to pay employee ⟶	Right to claim for unpaid wages
Right to dismiss employee for serious misconduct ⟵	Duty to obey reasonable orders
Duty to provide safe system of work ⟶	Right to claim if injured because of unsafe system

Figure 1.4 *Balancing rights and duties in employment law*

him an air rifle and a single-barrelled 12-bore shotgun and ammunition for both guns. When he was awakened by the noise of the two men trying to break in, he loaded the shotgun, poked it through a small hole in the door and fired. The shot hit Mr Revill on the right upper arm and chest.

Criminal proceedings: Mr Revill was prosecuted for various criminal offences he had committed that night, pleaded guilty and was sentenced. Mr Newbery was prosecuted for wounding Mr Revill, but was found not guilty by the jury at the Crown Court.

Civil proceedings: Mr Revill then brought a civil case against Mr Newbery claiming damages for the injuries he had suffered from the shotgun blast. In this case the judge awarded Mr Revill damages of £12,100 but reduced the amount to £4,033 because the judge held that Mr Revill was two-thirds to blame for what had happened. This meant that Mr Newbery was ordered to pay Mr Revill £4,033.

Mr Newbery appealed against this order but the Court of Appeal dismissed his appeal saying that his conduct was 'clearly dangerous and bordered on the reckless'. One of the judges pointed out that: 'Violence may be returned with necessary violence but the force used must not exceed the limits of what is reasonable in the circumstances.'

Questions

1. Should a criminal be able to use the legal rules to claim for injuries caused by another person? Is it justice to award damages to someone who was injured while carrying out criminal activities?
2. Bearing in mind the fact that Mr Newbery had fired without warning, was the decision in the civil case brought by Mr Revill, that Mr Newbery should pay a reduced amount of damages to Mr Revill for the injuries, a just one?
3. Mr Newbery was found not guilty of a criminal charge of wounding Mr Revill. Was this a 'just' decision?

1.5 The rule of law

The 'rule of law' is a symbolic idea. It is difficult to give a precise meaning to the concept. The best-known explanation of the 'rule of law' was given by Dicey in the 19th century, but there have been other important writers on the topic since. These include FA von Hayek and Joseph Raz.

1.5.1 Dicey

Dicey thought that the rule of law was an important feature that distinguished English law from law in other countries in Europe. He held that there were three elements that created the rule of law.

These were:

- an absence of arbitrary power on the part of the state
- equality before the law
- supremacy of ordinary law.

An absence of arbitrary power of the state

The state's power must be controlled by the law. The law must set limits on what the state can or cannot do. In our legal system actions of, and decisions by, government ministers can be challenged by judicial review. One of the main aims of the rule of law is to avoid the state having wide discretionary powers. Dicey recognised that discretion can be exercised in an arbitrary way and this should be avoided to comply with the rule of law.

Everyone must be equal before the law

No person must be above the law. It does not matter how rich or powerful a person is, the law must deal with them in the same way as it would anyone else. Another side of this part of the rule of law is that those who carry out functions of state must be accountable under the law for their actions.

The law must be supreme

This is particularly true in the law of England and Wales in the time of Dicey, as many of the main developments up to that time were through judicial decisions rather than being created by the executive. Today most laws are through legislation, that is Acts of Parliament and delegated legislation, though judicial decisions do still create law.

Problems with Dicey's views

A major problem with Dicey's view of the rule of law is that it conflicts with another fundamental principle, that of Parliamentary supremacy. This concept holds that an Act of Parliament can overrule any other law. The concept also holds that no other body has the right to override or set aside an Act of Parliament. (See 4.7 for fuller details of the concept of Parliamentary supremacy.) So under the rule of law there should be no arbitrary power on the part of the state, yet under Parliamentary supremacy Parliament has the right to make any law it wishes and these can include granting arbitrary powers to the state. Also, laws passed by Parliament cannot be challenged through judicial review. This is different from some other countries where the legislative body is subject to the rule of law, so that laws passed by them can be challenged in the courts.

Another problem is that equality before the law in Dicey's theory refers to formal equality. It disregards the differences between people in terms of wealth, power and connections. Real equality can only be achieved if there are mechanisms in place to address these differences. For example, the cost of taking legal cases to court is very high. In order to allow the poorest in society to be able to enforce their rights and so be equal under the law, it is necessary to have some form of state help in financing their case.

Dicey's view of the rule of law is based on abstract ideas. This makes it difficult to apply in real-life situations.

1.5.2 von Hayek

FA von Hayek agreed with Dicey that the key component of the rule of law is the absence of any arbitrary power on the part of the state. Writing in 1971, he put it this way:

'Stripped of all technicalities the Rule of Law means that the government in all its actions is bound by rules fixed and announced in advance.'

He thought that the rule of law had become weaker because, provided actions of the state were authorised by legislation, then any act in accordance with this legislation was lawful. Hayek was an economist and was particularly concerned with the increasing intervention of the state and the replacement of a free-market economy with a planned economy, regulated by an interventionist state.

The modern state no longer just provides a legal framework for the conduct of economic activity but is directly involved in regulating and coordinating such activity. In the 21st century this intervention has increased due to banking problems, with the collapse of some banks and also scandals such as interest-rate fixing that have occurred. In view of these, this intervention seems justified but it conflicts with the concept of the rule of law.

1.5.3 Joseph Raz

Joseph Raz, also writing in the 1970s, recognised that the rule of law was a way of controlling discretion rather than preventing it completely. He saw the rule of law as of negative value, acting to minimise the danger of the use of discretionary power in an arbitrary way. He thought that the key point which emerged from the rule of law was that the law must be capable of guiding the individual's behaviour.

He set out a number of principles which come from this wider idea. Some of these are:

- There should be clear rules and procedures for making laws.
- The independence of the judiciary must be guaranteed.
- The principles of natural justice should be observed; these require an open and fair hearing with all parties being given the opportunity to put their case.
- The courts should have the power to review the way in which the other principles are implemented to ensure that they are being operated as demanded by the rule of law.

Within our legal system there have been changes in the 21st century which support these principles. A major example is the Constitutional Reform Act 2005 which recognised the rule of law and the importance of the independence of the judiciary. Section 1 of that Act states:

'This Act does not adversely affect –

(a) the existing constitutional principle of the rule of law; or

(b) the Lord Chancellor's existing constitutional role in relation to that principle'

While s 3(1) states:

'The Lord Chancellor, other Ministers of the Crown and all with responsibility for matters relating to the judiciary or otherwise to the administration of justice must uphold the continued independence of the judiciary.'

For more on the independence of the judiciary see section 16.10.

In our modern legal system human rights are as important as the rule of law and this is the next topic to be considered.

1.6 Human rights and the English legal system

Under the Human Rights Act 1998, the European Convention on Human Rights was incorporated into our law. This has affected many areas of the English legal system. This section gives a brief summary of some of the key effects. There is fuller detail about the European Convention and the Human Rights Act 1998 in Chapter 20.

Precedent

Section 2(1)(a) of the Human Rights Act states that our courts must take into account any judgment or decision of the European Court of Human Rights. This means that judges when deciding a case must look at human rights cases, as well as our own English law.

Statutory interpretation

Section 3 of the Act states that, so far as it is possible to do so, all legislation (that is Acts of Parliament and other laws made in this country) must be given effect so that it is compatible with the European Convention. For example, if the wording of an Act of Parliament has two possible meanings, then the meaning which fits with the European Convention is the one that must be used.

Trials

Article 6 of the European Convention gives the right to a fair trial. This means that all aspects of the trial must be fair. For example, the way in which juvenile offenders are tried was changed after the case of *T v United Kingdom; V v United Kingdom* (1999). In this case a boy of 10 and a boy of 11 were tried for murder in the Crown Court. The European Court of Human Rights held that the formality of a Crown Court trial would have made it difficult for the boys to understand what was happening. This meant that the trial was not fair and there was a breach of the European Convention. In order to comply with the convention, there are now more flexible procedures for trials of juveniles in the Crown Court. For example, juveniles do not have to sit in the dock but sit alongside their legal advisers. Also, the court sits for shorter hours to allow for the shorter attention span of children.

Sentencing

Where an offender is sentenced to prison for life, it is usual to set a minimum period which must be served before the offender can be considered for parole. This minimum sentence used to be set by the Home Secretary (a government minister). The European Court of Human Rights held that this was a breach of the European Convention. This has been changed so that judges are now responsible for setting any minimum period.

Judicial appointment

Part-time judges in this country used to be appointed for a period of three years. After this time they could then be appointed for further periods of three years. In addition, the appointment was by the Lord Chancellor (a government minister). The length of appointment was changed to five years, as it was thought that

the shorter period meant that there was a risk of the judges not being sufficiently independent from the government. This would have been a breach of the European Convention.

Conclusion

The above points are not the only way in which the English legal system has been affected by the European Convention on Human Rights. However, they are an illustration of how wide-ranging the effect on our legal system has been.

EXAMINATION QUESTIONS

1. **(a)** Explain the importance of the rule of law in England and Wales. [14 marks]
   (b) Discuss the impact of the Human Rights Act 1998 on the legal system of England and Wales. [11 marks]

   LA1, Winter 2011, WJEC

EXTENSION ESSAY

'The rule of law is an ideal, but one which can never be fully achieved.' Discuss.

CHAPTER 2

THE DEVELOPMENT OF LAW

INTRODUCTION

The law of England and Wales has been built up very gradually over the centuries. There is not just one way of creating or developing law; there have been, and still are, a number of different ways. These methods of developing law are usually referred to as sources of law. Historically, the most important ways were custom and decisions of judges. Then, as Parliament became more powerful in the eighteenth and early 19th centuries, Acts of Parliament were the main source of new laws, although judicial decisions were still important as they interpreted the Parliamentary law and filled in gaps where there was no statute law (statute law is explained in Chapter 4). During the 20th century, statute law and judicial decisions continued to be the major sources of law but, in addition, two new sources of law became increasingly important: these were delegated legislation and European law. All these sources of law have combined to make our present-day law as indicated by Figure 2.1.

All these sources of law are examined in turn in this chapter and Chapters 3, 4, 5 and 6.

2.1 Customs

These are rules of behaviour which develop in a community without being deliberately invented. There are two main types of custom: general customs and local customs.

2.1.1 General customs

Historically these are believed to have been very important in that they were, effectively, the basis of our common law (see section 2.2). It is thought that following the Norman conquest (as the country was gradually brought under centralised government) the judges appointed by the kings to travel around the land making decisions in the king's name based at least some of their decisions on the common customs. This idea caused Lord Justice Coke in the 17th century to describe these customs as being 'one of the main triangles of the laws of England'. However, other commentators dispute this theory.

Today, Michael Zander writes that probably a high proportion of the so-called customs were almost certainly invented by the judges. In any event, it is accepted that general customs have long since been absorbed into legislation or case law and are no longer a creative source of law.

2.1.2 Local customs

This is the term used where a person claims that he is entitled to some local right, such as a right of way or a right to use land in a particular way, because

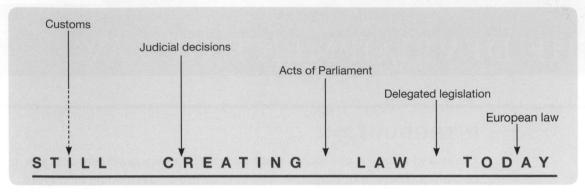

Figure 2.1 *Historical development of sources of law*

this is what has always happened locally. Such customs are an exception to the general law of the land, and will operate only in that particular area.

Since there were (or still are) exceptions to the general common law, the judges, from the earliest times, established a series of rigorous tests or hurdles that had to be passed before they recognised any local custom. These tests still exist today and are used on the rare occasions that a claim to a right comes before the courts because of a local custom. The tests are as follows:

● The custom must have existed since 'time immemorial'.
● The custom must have been exercised peaceably, openly and as of right.
● The custom must be definite as to locality, nature and scope.
● The custom must be reasonable.

It is very unusual for a new custom to be considered by the courts today and even rarer for the courts to decide that it will be recognised as a valid custom, but there have been some such cases. For example in *Egerton v Harding* (1974) the court decided that there was a customary duty to fence land against cattle straying from the common. Another case was *New Windsor Corporation v Mellor* (1974) where a local authority was prevented from building on land because the local people proved there was a custom that they

had the right to use the land for lawful sports. Although customs may develop, they are not part of the law until recognised by the courts; it is the judges who decide which customs will be recognised as enforceable at law.

2.2   Common law

Clearly the legal system in England and Wales could not rely only on customs. Even in Anglo-Saxon times there were local courts which decided disputes, but it was not until after the Norman conquest in 1066 that a more organised system of courts emerged. This was because the Norman kings realised that control of the country would be easier if they controlled, among other things, the legal system. The first Norman king, William the Conqueror, set up the Curia Regis (the King's Court) and appointed his own judges. The nobles who had a dispute were encouraged to apply to have the king (or his judges) decide the matter.

2.2.1 Development of common law

As well as this central court, the judges were sent to major towns to decide any important cases. This meant that judges travelled from London all round the country that was under the control of the king. In the time of Henry II (1154–89) these tours became more regular and Henry divided up the country into 'circuits' or areas for the judges to visit. Initially the judges would use the local customs or the old Anglo-Saxon laws to decide cases, but over a period of time it is believed that the judges on their return to Westminster in London would discuss the laws or customs they had used, and the decisions they had made, with each other. Gradually, the judges selected the best customs and these were then used by all the judges throughout the country. This had the effect that the law became uniform or 'common' through the whole country, and it is from here that the phrase 'common law' seems to have developed.

2.2.2 Definitions of common law

Common law is the basis of our law today: it is unwritten law that developed from customs and judicial decisions. The phrase 'common law' is still used to distinguish laws that have been developed by judicial decisions from laws that have been created by statute or other legislation (see Figure 2.2). For example, murder is a common law crime while theft is a statutory crime. This means that murder has never been defined in any Act of Parliament, but theft is now defined by the Theft Act 1968.

Common law also has another meaning, in that it is used to distinguish between rules that were developed by the common law courts (the King's Courts) and the rules of equity which were developed by the Lord Chancellor and the Chancery courts.

2.3 Equity

Historically this was an important source and it still plays a part today with many of our legal concepts having developed from equitable principles. The word 'equity' has a meaning of 'fairness', and this is the basis on which it operates, when adding to our law.

2.3.1 The development of equity

Equity developed because of problems in the common law. Only certain types of case were recognised. The law was also very technical; if there was an error in the formalities the person making the claim would lose the case.

Another major problem was the fact that the only remedy the common law courts could give was 'damages' – that is an order that the defendant pay a sum of money to the plaintiff (now claimant) by way of compensation. In some cases this would not be the best method of putting matters right between the parties. For example, in a case of trespass to land, where perhaps the defendant had built on his neighbour's land, the building would still be there and the plaintiff would have lost the use of that part of his land. In such a situation

COMMON LAW	
Different meanings	Distinguishes it from:
The law developed by the early judges to form a 'common' law for the country	The local laws used prior to the Norman conquest
The law which has continued to be developed by the judges through the doctrine of judicial precedent	Laws made by a legislative body, such as Acts of Parliament or delegated legislation
Judge-made law	
The law operated in the common law courts before the reorganisation of the courts in 1873–75	Equity – the decisions made in the Chancery courts

Figure 2.2 *Different meanings of the term 'common law'*

the plaintiff would probably prefer to have the building removed, rather than be given money in compensation.

People who could not obtain justice in the common law courts appealed directly to the king. Most of these cases were referred to the King's Chancellor, who was both a lawyer and a priest, and who became known as the keeper of the king's conscience. This was because the Chancellor based his decisions on principles of natural justice and fairness, making a decision on what seemed 'right' in the particular case rather than on the strict following of previous precedents. He was also prepared to look beyond legal documents, which were considered legally binding by the common law courts, and to take account of what the parties had intended to do.

To ensure that the decisions were 'fair' the Chancellor used new procedures such as subpoenas, which ordered a witness to attend court or risk imprisonment for refusing to obey the Chancellor's order. He also developed new remedies which were able to compensate plaintiffs more fully than the common law remedy of damages. The main equitable remedies were: injunctions; specific performance; rescission; and rectification. These are all still used today and are explained more fully in section 2.3.3 of this chapter.

Eventually a Court of Chancery under the control of the Chancellor came into being which operated these rules of fairness or equity. Equity was not a complete system of law; it merely filled the gaps in the common law and softened the strict rules of the common law.

Conflict between equity and common law

The two systems of common law and equity operated quite separately, so it was not surprising that this overlapping of the two systems led to conflict between them. One of the main problems was that the common law courts would make an order in favour of one party and the Court of Chancery an order in favour of the other party. The conflict was finally resolved in the *Earl of Oxford's case* (1615) when the king ruled that equity should prevail; in other words, the decision made in the Chancery court was the one which must be followed by the parties. This ruling made the position of equity stronger and the same rule was subsequently included in s 25 of the Judicature Act 1873.

2.3.2 The operation of equity

Initially, as already stated, there were few guidelines for Chancellors to use. However, as time went on a series of maxims were developed which formed the basis of the rules on which equity operated. As equity became more formal, judges became more likely to follow past decisions. Today the doctrine of judicial precedent (explained in Chapter 3) applies to cases involving equity, just as it applies to cases involving the common law.

Equitable maxims

Many of the rules on which equity is based are expressed in a series of sayings. The most important of these maxims are as follows.

- **Equity looks to the intention and not the form** – this was applied in the case of *Berry v Berry* (1929) where a deed was held to have been altered by a simple contract. Under common law rules a deed could only be altered by another deed, but equity decided that as the parties had intended to alter the deed, it would be fair to look at that intention rather than the fact that they got the formalities wrong.
- **He who comes to equity must come with clean hands** – in other words an equitable principle or remedy will not be granted to a plaintiff who has not acted fairly. This is shown in *D & C Builders Ltd v Rees* (1965) where a small building firm had done work for Mr and Mrs Rees. The total bill was £732 of which Mr and Mrs Rees had paid £250 in advance. When the builders asked for the remaining £482, the Rees, who knew the builders were

in financial difficulties and needed money urgently, claimed that the work had not been done properly and they were only prepared to pay £300. The builders reluctantly agreed to accept the £300 'in completion of the account', but afterwards sued the Rees for the remaining £182. At common law, part payment of a debt is not considered as satisfying the debt and the builders could claim the extra. Equity, however, has a doctrine of equitable estoppel (see section 2.3.4) under which the courts can declare that the plaintiff is prevented (estopped) from asking for the rest. Lord Denning, in the Court of Appeal, refused to apply the doctrine of equitable estoppel because the Reeses had taken unfair advantage of the fact that they knew the builders were in financial difficulties. So far as equity was concerned the Reeses had not come to court with 'clean hands'.

- **Delay defeats equity** – this means that a plaintiff must not wait too long before making a claim as this might lead to unfairness to the other party. In *Leaf v International Galleries* (1950) a plaintiff was sold a painting which both parties mistakenly believed was by Constable. The court did not award the equitable remedy of rescission, since there had been a delay of five years between the contract and the discovery that the painting was not by Constable.

- **Equity will not suffer a wrong to be without a remedy** – this allows equity to create new remedies where otherwise the plaintiff would not have an adequate remedy for the case and would only be able to claim the common law remedy of damages. This maxim allows equity to continue to develop new remedies when they are needed, such as freezing orders and search orders, which are discussed at the end of section 2.3.4.

2.3.3 Equitable remedies

As already stated, one of the important aspects of equity was that it created new remedies to supplement the common law remedy of damages. However, these remedies are discretionary, so that the court does not have to grant them even if the plaintiff wins the case. This is in contrast to the common law remedy of damages which will be awarded to a winning plaintiff as of right. An equitable remedy will only be granted where the court thinks it is fair in all the circumstances. If a party ignores an equitable remedy this is considered contempt of court and the court can fine that party or even send them to prison. The following are the most important equitable remedies.

1 Injunctions

An injunction is an order to one of the people involved in the case to do something or not to do something. Where the court orders one of the parties to do something it is called a mandatory injunction; where the order is to refrain from doing something it is called a prohibitory injunction.

Injunctions are used today in all sorts of situations; for example, in *Kennaway v Thompson* (1980) the court granted an injunction restricting the times when power boats could be raced on a lake. In *Warner Brothers v Nelson* (1937) an injunction was issued ordering the actress Bette Davis not to make a film with another film company as that would have been a breach of her contract with Warner Brothers.

A plaintiff may be awarded both damages and an injunction. The damages will be as compensation for the past problems, for example the noise and nuisance of the racing boats in *Kennaway v Thompson,* and an injunction to prevent (or limit) the event occurring in the future.

An injunction can also be granted to protect one party's rights while waiting for the case to be heard. This is called an interlocutory injunction. Since the case has not been tried the courts have strict guidelines on when an interlocutory injunction should be granted. Basically such an injunction will only be ordered if it is felt that, during the time that the parties have to wait for the case to be heard, one party would suffer irreparable harm which could not be put right by an award of damages at the end of the case.

2 Specific performance

This is an order that a contract should be carried out as agreed. It is granted only in exceptional circumstances where the court feels the common law remedy of damages could not adequately compensate the plaintiff, for example in a contract to purchase land. Specific performance is never granted to order someone to carry out personal services, such as singing at a concert; nor is it granted for a breach of contract where one of the parties is a minor.

3 Rescission

This is another remedy in contract cases and it aims to return the parties as far as possible to their pre-contractual position. So, if a contract involved in buying goods was rescinded, the buyer would have to return the goods to the seller and the seller would have to return the purchase price to the buyer.

4 Rectification

Under this the court will order that, where a mistake has accidentally been made in a document so that it is not a true version of what the parties agreed, that document should be altered to reflect the parties' intention.

Recent remedies

Even in the 20th century the courts were still developing new equitable remedies. These were the freezing order (formerly known as a Mareva injunction) and the search order (formerly known as an Anton Piller Order). The freezing order can be made where there is a risk that one party in a case will move all their assets out of the United Kingdom before the case against them is tried. The effect of the order is that third parties (such as

banks) who have assets owned by the party in their control must freeze those assets so that they cannot be removed from the account.

The search order allows the claimant to search the defendant's premises and remove any documents or other material which could help the claimant to prove his case.

2.3.4 The relevance of equity today

Equitable rights, interests and remedies remain important in the law today. Concepts such as mortgages and trusts are founded on the idea that one person owns the legal interest in property but has to use that property for the benefit of another. This other person is said to have an equitable interest in the property. It is difficult to imagine life today without mortgages – the vast majority of homeowners buy their property with the aid of a mortgage. Trusts are widely used in setting up such matters as pension funds, as well as within families when property is settled on younger members of the family or between husband and wife.

New concepts

Equity can still create new concepts in the law. This happened on a number of occasions in the 20th century. One development was equitable or promissory estoppel. This was first suggested by Lord Denning in *Central London Property Ltd v High Trees House Ltd* (1947) (more usually referred to as the *High Trees* case). In that case a block of flats in South London was leased to a company for a period of 99 years, and the company then sublet individual flats to residents. During the Second World War many people moved out of London because of the bombing, so that it was difficult to let the flats. The main landlord agreed that while the war lasted, the company leasing the block of flats need only pay half the normal rent. After the war the landlord claimed the full rent again. Denning (at that time a High Court judge) decided that they were entitled to it but, in his judgment, he also considered what the legal position would have been if the landlord had tried to claim for the full rent during the war. Strictly speaking the original contract for the 99-year lease would have allowed the landlord to make such a claim. However, Denning said that the landlord would have been estopped from claiming. Since this case the law has recognised that in some situations it would be inequitable (or unfair) to allow one party to rely on the strict terms of the contract when they had led the other party to believe that they would not do so.

Another equitable concept developed in the 20th century was the 'deserted wife's equity'. This was the idea that where a husband deserted his wife and children, the wife had an equitable interest in the matrimonial home, even if it was solely owned by the husband. This allowed the wife to remain in the home while the children were dependent. This right for partners was eventually put into an Act of Parliament in the Matrimonial Homes Act 1967.

Modern use of equitable remedies

Equitable remedies are still important and used in a variety of circumstances. Two examples of the use of injunctions have already been given in 2.3.3. In one an injunction was used to limit the number of times power boats could race in order to prevent the plaintiff from having to suffer too much noise and inconvenience. In the other an injunction was granted to prevent an actress from breaking her contract with a film company.

Injunctions are often used today. They can be ordered in cases of domestic violence as a protection for the abused partner. Such an injunction often forbids the violent partner from entering the premises where the other partner is living or even going within a certain distance of the place. Injunctions are also used to prevent trespass to land or to prevent excessive noise, or smoke or other nuisances. They are used in employment law in various situations. For example, a former employee can be prevented from disclosing trade secrets to anyone, or an injunction may be granted against a trade union to prevent unlawful industrial action.

If you look back to the newspaper article in Source A in Chapter 1 on page 4 there is an example of an injunction being served via the internet, showing that it is a remedy that can adapt to modern life.

Modern equitable remedies

The courts have been prepared to expand equitable remedies, though the principle that they are discretionary still remains. Two 20th-century expansions were Mareva injunctions and Anton Piller orders. The Mareva injunction came from the case of *Mareva Compania Naviera SA v International Bulk Carriers SA* (1975) and is used where there is a risk that the assets of one of the parties will be removed out of the United Kingdom before the case comes to trial. It allows the courts to order that third parties, such as banks, must freeze any assets in their control. This is important as, at the end of the case, it means there will be assets available to pay any damages or costs that the court awards.

The Anton Piller order was first used in *Anton Piller KG v Manufacturing Processes Ltd* (1976) and it ordered the defendant to allow the plaintiff to search his premises and take away any documents or other material that could be relevant to the case. The thought behind it is to prevent the defendant destroying any goods or documents which could be used as evidence in the case.

Both these equitable remedies have been absorbed into the civil court procedure rules. The Mareva injunction is now known as a freezing order and the Anton Piller order as a search order.

From all of this it can be seen that equity still has a role to play in the modern legal system and that it can still create new concepts and remedies to fit the justice of particular cases.

EXAMINATION QUESTIONS

(a) Explain the development of common law and equity. [14 marks]
and

(b) Discuss the impact of modern equity upon the development of the common law. [11 marks]

LA1, Summer 2011, WJEC

EXTENSION ESSAY

Critically discuss the need for equity in the development of our law.

CHAPTER 3

JUDICIAL PRECEDENT

INTRODUCTION

Judicial precedent refers to the source of law where past decisions of the judges create law for future judges to follow. This source of law is also known as case law. It is a major source of law, both historically and today.

3.1 The doctrine of precedent

The English system of precedent is based on the Latin maxim *stare decisis et non quieta movere* (usually shortened to *stare decisis*) which loosely translated means: 'stand by what has been decided and do not unsettle the established'. This supports the idea of fairness and provides certainty in the law.

3.1.1 *Ratio decidendi*

Precedent can only operate if the legal reasons for past decisions are known, therefore at the end of a case there will be a judgment – a speech made by the judge giving the decision and, more importantly, explaining the reasons for that decision. In a judgment the judge is likely to give a summary of the facts of the case, review the arguments put to him by the advocates in the case, and then explain the principles of law he is using to come to the decision. These principles are the important part of the judgment and are known as the *ratio decidendi* which means the reason for deciding (and is pronounced 'ray-she-o des-id-end-i'). This is what creates a precedent for judges to follow in future cases. Sir Rupert Cross defined the *ratio decidendi* as 'any rule expressly or impliedly treated by the judge as a necessary step in reaching his conclusion'.

3.1.2 *Obiter dicta*

The remainder of the judgment is called *obiter dicta* ('other things said') and judges in future cases do not have to follow it. Sometimes a judge will speculate on what his decision would have been if the facts of the case had been different. This hypothetical situation is part of the *obiter dicta* and the legal reasoning put forward may be considered in future cases, although, as with all *obiter* statements, it is not binding precedent.

A major problem when looking at a past judgment is to divide the *ratio decidendi* from the *obiter dicta*, as the judgment is usually in a continuous form, without any headings specifying what is meant to be part of the *ratio decidendi* and what is not.

3.1.3 Judgments

It is also worth realising that there can be more than one speech at the end of a case, depending on the number of judges hearing the case. In courts of first instance there will be only one judge and therefore one judgment. However, in the appeal courts (the Divisional Courts, the Court of Appeal and the Supreme Court) cases are heard by at least two and, usually, three judges. In fact, in the Supreme Court, the panel of judges must consist of an uneven number, so it could be three, five, seven or even nine.

The fact that there are two or more judges does not mean that there will always be several judgments as it is quite common for one judge to give the judgment and the other judge/judges simply to say 'I agree'! However, in cases where there is a particularly important or complicated point of law, more than one judge may want to explain his legal reasoning on the point. This can cause problems in later cases as each judge may have had a different reason for his decision, so there will be more than one *ratio decidendi*. (By the way, the plural of *ratio* is *rationes*.)

As well as learning the Latin phrases *ratio decidendi*, *obiter dicta* and *stare decisis* there are some English phrases which are important for understanding the concept of judicial precedent. These are original or declaratory precedent, binding precedent and persuasive precedent.

3.1.4 Original precedent

If the point of law in a case has never been decided before, then whatever the judge decides will form a new precedent for future cases to follow, i.e. it is an original precedent. As there are no past cases for the judge to base his decision on, he is likely to look at cases which are the closest in principle and he may decide to use similar rules. This way of arriving at a judgment is called reasoning by analogy. Some legal commentators used to hold that the judge is only declaring what the law is (that is, the law has always been there, but it is the first time a judge has had to decide it). This view holds that judges do not create law, they merely declare what it has always been. Nowadays it is accepted that judges do have a law-making role in these situations – when a new point has to be decided, the judge is creating new law.

This idea of creating new law by analogy can be seen in *Hunter and others v Canary Wharf Ltd and London Docklands Development Corporation* (1995). Part of the decision involved whether the interference with television reception by a large building was capable of constituting an actionable private nuisance. The facts of the case were that in 1990 a tower known as the Canary Wharf Tower was built by the first defendant in an enterprise zone in East London. The tower was about 250 metres high and over 50 metres square. The claimant, and hundreds of others suing with her, claimed damages from the first defendant for interference over a number of years with reception of television broadcasts at their homes in East London. The interference was claimed to have been caused by the tower.

ACTIVITY

Read the following extract from the judgment in the case of *Hunter and others v Canary Wharf Ltd and London Docklands Development Corporation*. Then answer the questions below.

When the case was heard on appeal in the Court of Appeal, Lord Justice Pill giving judgment said:

'Lord Irving (counsel for the defendants) submits that interference with television reception by reason of the presence of a building is properly to be regarded as analogous to loss of aspect (view). To obstruct the receipt of television signals by the erection of a building between the point of receipt and the source is not in law a nuisance. In *Aldred's Case* (1610) Wray CJ cited what he had said in *Bland v Moselely*: "for prospect, which is a matter only of delight and not of necessity, no action lies for stopping thereof, and yet it is a great recommendation of a house if it has a long and large prospect ... But the law does not give an action for such things of delight."

'I accept the importance of television in the lives of very many people. However, in my judgment the erection or presence of a building in the line of sight between a television transmitter and other properties is not actionable as an interference with the use and enjoyment of land. The analogy with loss of prospect is compelling. The loss of a view, which may be of the greatest importance to many householders, is not actionable and neither is the mere presence of a building in the sight line to the television transmitter.'

Questions

1. In respect of the interference with television reception, with what did Lord Justice Pill draw an analogy?
2. Do you think that the judge was correct to make an analogy between the two situations? Give reasons for your answer.
3. By drawing this analogy does it mean that the claimant won or lost the case?

3.1.5 Binding precedent

This is a precedent from an earlier case which must be followed even if the judge in the later case does not agree with the legal principle. A binding precedent is only created when the facts of the second case are sufficiently similar to the original case and the decision was made by a court which is senior to (or in some cases the same level as) the court hearing the later case.

3.1.6 Persuasive precedent

This is a precedent that is not binding on the court, but the judge may consider it and decide that it is a correct principle, so he is persuaded that he should follow it. Persuasive precedent comes from a number of sources as explained below:

Courts lower in the hierarchy

Such an example can be seen in *R v R* (1991) where the House of Lords agreed with and followed the same reasoning as the Court of Appeal in deciding that a man could be guilty of raping his wife.

Decisions of the Judicial Committee of the Privy Council

This court is not part of the court hierarchy in England and Wales and so its decisions are not binding, but, since many of its judges are also members of the Supreme Court, their judgments are treated with respect and may often be followed. An example of this can be seen in the law on remoteness of damages in the law of tort and the decision made by the Privy Council in the case of *The Wagon Mound* (No 1) (1961). In later cases courts in England and Wales followed the decision in this case.

This also happened in *A-G for Jersey v Holley* (2005) when the majority of the Privy Council (six out of nine judges) ruled that in the defence of provocation, a defendant is to be judged by the standard of a person having ordinary powers of self-control. This was contrary to an earlier judgment of the House of Lords. As a result, there were conflicting decisions from the House of Lords and the Privy Council. Although a decision by the Privy Council is not binding on English courts, in *R v Mohammed* (2005) the Court of Appeal followed *Holley* rather than the decision of the House of Lords. Then in *R v James; R v Karimi* (2006), a five-member Court of Appeal confirmed that the decision in *Holley* should be followed by courts in England and Wales.

Statements made *obiter dicta* (particularly where the comment was made in a Supreme Court or previously a House of Lords decision)

This is clearly seen in the law on duress as a defence to a criminal charge, where the House of Lords in *R v Howe* (1987) ruled that duress could not be a defence to a charge of murder. In the judgment the Lords also commented, as an *obiter* statement, that duress would not be available as a defence to someone charged with attempted murder. When, later, in *R v Gotts* (1992) a defendant charged with attempted murder tried to argue that he could use the defence of duress, the *obiter* statement from Howe was followed as persuasive precedent by the Court of Appeal.

A dissenting judgment

Where a case has been decided by a majority of judges (for example, 2–1 in the Court of Appeal), the judge who disagreed will have explained his reasons. If that case goes on appeal to the Supreme Court, or if there is a later case on the same point which goes to the Supreme Court, it is possible that the Supreme Court may prefer the dissenting judgment and decide the case in the same way. The dissenting judgment has persuaded them to follow it.

Decisions of courts in other countries

This is especially so where the other country uses the same ideas of common law as in our system.

This applies to Commonwealth countries such as Canada, Australia and New Zealand.

3.2 The hierarchy of the courts

In England and Wales our courts operate a very rigid doctrine of judicial precedent which has the effect that:

- Every court is bound to follow any decision made by a court above it in the hierarchy.
- In general, appellate courts (courts which hear appeals) are bound by their own past decisions.

So the hierarchy of the courts is the next important point to get clear. Which courts come where in

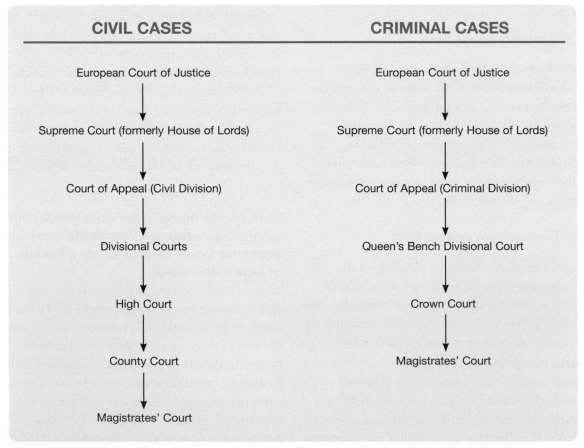

Figure 3.1 *Cascade model of judicial precedent operating in the hierarchy of the courts*

Court	Courts bound by it	Courts it must follow
European Court	All courts	None
Supreme Court	All other courts in the English legal system	European Court
Court of Appeal	Itself (with some exceptions) Divisional Courts All other lower courts	European Court Supreme Court
Divisional Courts	Itself (with some exceptions) High Court All other lower courts	European Court Supreme Court Court of Appeal
High Court	County Court Magistrates' Court	European Court Supreme Court Court of Appeal Divisional Courts
Crown Court	Possibly Magistrates' Court	All higher courts
County Court and Magistrates' Court do not create precedent and are bound by all higher courts		

Figure 3.2 *The courts and precedent*

the hierarchy? Figure 3.1 shows this in the form of a cascade model and Figure 3.2 gives each court and its position in respect of the other courts. The position of each court is also considered in this section and in sections 3.3 and 3.4.

Note that until October 2009 the senior court in the UK legal system was the House of Lords. This court was then abolished and replaced by the Supreme Court. The lower courts have to follow decisions of the Supreme Court and also decisions by the House of Lords which have not been changed by the Supreme Court.

3.2.1 Appellate courts

Appellate courts are those that hear appeals.

The European Court of Justice

Since 1973 the highest court affecting our legal system is the European Court of Justice. For points of European law, a decision made by this court is binding on all other courts in England and Wales. However, there are still laws which are unaffected by European Union law and for these the Supreme Court is the supreme court. An important feature

of the European Court of Justice is that it is prepared to overrule its own past decisions if it feels it is necessary. This flexible approach to past precedents is seen in other legal systems in Europe, and is a contrast to the more rigid approach of our national courts.

Supreme Court

The most senior national court is the Supreme Court and its decisions bind all other courts in the English legal system. The Supreme Court is not bound by its own past decisions, although it will generally follow them. This point is discussed in detail in section 3.3.4.

Court of Appeal

At the next level down in the hierarchy is the Court of Appeal, which has two divisions: Civil and Criminal. Both divisions of the Court of Appeal are bound to follow decisions of the European Court of Justice and the Supreme Court. In addition they must usually follow past decisions of their own; although there are some limited exceptions to this rule, and the Court of Appeal (Criminal Division) is more flexible where the point involves the liberty of the subject. The position of the two divisions is discussed in detail in section 3.4.

Divisional courts

The three Divisional Courts (Queen's Bench, Chancery and Family) are bound by decisions of the European Court of Justice, the Supreme Court and the Court of Appeal. In addition the Divisional Courts are bound by their own past decisions, although they operate similar exceptions to those operated by the Court of Appeal.

3.2.2 Courts of first instance

The term 'court of first instance' means any court where the original trial of a case is held. The appellate courts considered in section 3.2.1 do not hear any original trials. They only deal with appeals from decisions of other courts. Quite often an appeal will be about a point of law. This allows the appellate courts to decide the law and this is why the appellate courts are much more important than courts of first instance when it comes to creating precedent.

Courts of first instance rarely create precedent. They must follow the decisions of the courts above them.

The High Court

This is bound by decisions of all the courts above and in turn it binds the lower courts. High Court judges do not have to follow each other's decisions but will usually do so. In *Colchester Estates (Cardiff) v Carlton Industries plc* (1984) it was held that where there were two earlier decisions which conflicted, then, provided the first decision had been fully considered in the later case, that later decision should be followed.

Inferior courts

These are the Crown Court, the County Court and the Magistrates' Court. They are bound to follow decisions by all higher courts and it is unlikely that a decision by an inferior court can create precedent. The one exception is that a ruling on a point of law by a judge in the Crown Court technically creates precedent for the Magistrates' Court. However, since such rulings are rarely recorded in the law reports, this is of little practical effect.

3.3 The Supreme Court

The main debate about the Supreme Court (and previously the House of Lords) is the extent to which it should follow its own past decisions, and the ideas on this have changed over the years. Originally the view was that the House of Lords had the right to overrule past decisions, but gradually during the 19th century this more flexible approach disappeared. By the end of that century, in *London Street Tramways v London County Council* (1898), the House of Lords held that certainty in the law was more important than the possibility of individual hardship being caused through having to follow a past decision.

So from 1898 to 1966 the House of Lords regarded itself as being completely bound by its own past decisions unless the decision had been made *per incuriam*, that is 'in error'. However, this idea of error referred only to situations where a decision had been made without considering the effect of a relevant statute.

This was not felt to be satisfactory, as the law could not alter to meet changing social conditions and opinions, nor could any possible 'wrong' decisions be changed by the courts. If there was an unsatisfactory decision by the House of Lords, then the only way it could be changed was by Parliament passing a new Act of Parliament. This happened in the law about intention as an element of a criminal offence. The House of Lords in *DPP v Smith* (1961) had ruled that an accused could be guilty of murder if a reasonable person would have foreseen that death or very serious injury might result from the accused's actions. This decision was criticised as it meant that the defendant could be

Key Facts

1898	House of Lords decides in the case of *London Street Tramways* that it is bound to follow its own previous decisions
1966	Issue of the Practice Statement House of Lords will depart from previous decisions when 'it is right to do so'
1968	First use of Practice Statement in *Conway v Rimmer* Only involves technical law on discovery of documents
1972	First major use of Practice Statement in *Herrington v British Railways Board* on the duty of care owed to child trespassers
1980s and 1990s	House of Lords shows an increasing willingness to use Practice Statement to overrule previous decisions, e.g. *R v Shivpuri* (criminal attempts); *Pepper v Hart* (use of *Hansard* in statutory interpretation)
2003	Practice statement used to overrule the decision in *Caldwell* on recklessness in the criminal law

Figure 3.3 *Key facts chart for the operation of judicial precedent in the House of Lords*

guilty even if he had not intended to cause death or serious injury, nor even realised that his actions might have that effect. Eventually Parliament changed the law by passing the Criminal Justice Act 1967.

3.3.1 The Practice Statement

It was realised that the final court of appeal (then the House of Lords) should have more flexibility. For today's system of judicial precedent the critical date is 1966, when the Lord Chancellor issued a Practice Statement announcing a change to the rule in *London Street Tramways v London County Council*. The Practice Statement said:

'Their Lordships regard the use of precedent as an indispensable foundation upon which to decide what is the law and its application to individual cases. It provides at least some degree of certainty upon which individuals can rely in the conduct of their affairs, as well as a basis for orderly development of legal rules.

'Their Lordships nevertheless recognise that the rigid adherence to precedent may lead to

injustice in a particular case and also unduly restrict the proper development of the law. They propose, therefore, to modify their present practice and while treating former decisions of this House as normally binding, to depart from a previous decision when it appears right to do so.

'In this connection they will bear in mind the danger of disturbing retrospectively the basis on which contracts, settlement of property and fiscal arrangements have been entered into and also the especial need for certainty as to the criminal law. This announcement is not intended to affect the use of precedent elsewhere than in this House.'

3.3.2 Use of the Practice Statement

From 1966, this Practice Statement allowed the House of Lords to change the law when it believed that an earlier case was wrongly decided. It had the flexibility to refuse to follow an earlier case when 'it appeared right to do so'. This phrase is, of course, very vague and gave little guidance as to when the House of Lords might overrule a previous decision. In fact, the House of Lords was reluctant to use this power, especially in the first few years after 1966. The first case in which the Practice Statement was used was *Conway v Rimmer* (1968), but this involved only a technical point on discovery of documents.

The first major use did not occur until 1972 in *Herrington v British Railways Board* (1972), which involved the law on the duty of care owed to a child trespasser. The earlier case of *Addie v Dumbreck* (1929) had decided that an occupier of land would only owe a duty of care for injuries to a child trespasser if those injuries had been caused deliberately or recklessly. In *Herrington* the Lords held that social and physical conditions had changed since 1929, and the law should also change.

There continued to be great reluctance in the House of Lords to use the Practice Statement, as can be seen by the case of *Jones v Secretary of State for Social Services* (1972). This case involved the interpretation of the National Insurance (Industrial Injuries) Act 1946 and four out of the seven judges hearing the case regarded the earlier decision in *Re Dowling* (1967) as being wrong. Despite this the Lords refused to overrule that earlier case, preferring to keep to the idea that certainty was the most important feature of precedent. The same attitude was shown in *Knuller v DPP* (1973) when Lord Reid said:

'Our change of practice in no longer regarding previous decisions of this House as absolutely binding does not mean that whenever we think a previous precedent was wrong we should reverse it. In the general interest of certainty in the law we must be sure that there is some very good reason before we so act.'

From the mid-1970s onwards the House of Lords showed a little more willingness to make use of the Practice Statement. For example, in *Miliangos v George Frank (Textiles) Ltd* (1976) the House of Lords used the Practice Statement to overrule a previous judgment that damages could be awarded only in sterling. More recently

in *Murphy v Brentwood District Council* (1990), the House of Lords overruled the decision in *Anns v Merton London Borough* (1977) regarding the test for negligence in the law of tort. Another major case was *Pepper v Hart* (1993) where the previous ban on the use of *Hansard* in statutory interpretation was overruled.

In *Horton v Sadler and another* (2006) the House of Lords used the Practice Statement to depart from a previous decision of its own. The case involved a personal injury claim, but the point of law being decided was about the power to allow service out of time under s 33 of the Limitation Act 1980. The House of Lords departed from their decision in *Walkley v Precision Forgings Ltd* (1979).

The Law Lords departed from *Walkley* for three reasons:

- It unfairly deprived claimants of a right that Parliament had intended them to have.
- It had driven the Court of Appeal to draw distinctions which were correct but were so fine as to reflect no credit on the area of law.
- It went against the clear intention of Parliament.

Lord Bingham in his speech considered the issue of departing from a previous decision. He pointed out that the case was not one in which contracts, settlements of property or fiscal arrangements had been entered into, nor did it involve the criminal law where certainty was particularly important. Also, there would not be any detriment to public administration caused by departing from the previous decision.

3.3.3 The Practice Statement in criminal law

The Practice Statement stressed that criminal law needs to be certain, so it was not surprising that the House of Lords did not rush to overrule any judgments in criminal cases. The first use in a criminal case was in *R v Shivpuri* (1986) which overruled the decision in *Anderton v Ryan* (1985) on attempts to do the impossible. The interesting point was that the decision in *Anderton* had been made less than a year before, but it had been severely criticised by academic lawyers. In *Shivpuri* Lord Bridge said:

'I am undeterred by the consideration that the decision in Anderton v Ryan was so recent. The Practice Statement is an effective abandonment of our pretention to infallibility. If a serious error embodied in a decision of this House has distorted the law, the sooner it is corrected the better.'

In other words, the House of Lords recognised that they might sometimes make errors and the most important thing then was to put the law right. Where the Practice Statement is used to overrule a previous decision, that past case is then effectively ignored. The law is now that which is set out in the new case.

Another important case on the use of the Practice Statement was *R v R and G* (2003). In this case the House of Lords used the Practice Statement to overrule the earlier decision of *Caldwell* (1982) on the law of criminal damage. In *Caldwell* the House of Lords had ruled that recklessness included the situation where the defendant had not realised the risk of his actions causing damage, but an ordinary careful person would have realised there was a risk. In *R v R and G* it was held that this was the wrong test to use. The Law Lords overruled *Caldwell* and held that a defendant is only reckless if he realises that there is a risk of damage and goes ahead and takes that risk.

This case showed the House of Lords as being prepared to use the Practice Statement where they thought it 'right to do so'.

3.3.4 The Supreme Court

With the change over from the House of Lords to the Supreme Court in October 2009, the Practice Statement does not strictly apply to the Supreme Court, so it is not clear whether this court will use the Practice Statement. However, the Practice Rules of the Supreme Court state that 'If an application for permission to appeal asks the Supreme Court to depart from one of its own decisions or from one of the House of Lords' this should be stated clearly in the application and full details must be given.

This suggests that the Supreme Court will operate a similar system to that under the Practice Statement.

ACTIVITY

Read the following passage which comes from an extra explanatory note which was given to the press when the Practice Statement was issued and answer the questions on the next page.

'The statement is one of great importance, although it should not be supposed that there will frequently be cases in which the House thinks it right not to follow their own precedent. An example of a case in which the House might think it right to depart from a precedent is where they consider that the earlier decision was influenced by the existence of conditions which no longer prevail, and that in modern conditions the law ought to be different.

'One consequence of this change is of major importance. The relaxation of the rule of judicial precedent will enable the House of Lords to pay greater attention to judicial decisions reached in the superior courts of the Commonwealth, where they differ from earlier decisions of the House of Lords. That could be of great help in the development of our own law. The superior courts of many other countries are not rigidly bound by their own decisions and the change in the practice of the House of Lords will bring us more into line with them.'

Questions

1. Why was the Practice Statement of great importance?
2. Does the note suggest that the Practice Statement was likely to be used often?
3. Do you agree that 'in modern conditions the law ought to be different'? Give reasons and examples to support your answer.
4. Why would the House of Lords have wanted to consider decisions from Commonwealth countries? What authority do such decisions have in the English legal system?

3.4 The Court of Appeal

As already stated, there are two divisions of this court, the Civil Division and the Criminal Division, and the rules for precedent are not quite the same in these two divisions.

3.4.1 Decisions of courts above it

Both divisions of the Court of Appeal are bound by decisions of the European Court of Justice and the Supreme Court. This is true even though there were attempts in the past, mainly by Lord Denning, to argue that the Court of Appeal should not be bound by the House of Lords (now the Supreme Court). In *Broome v Cassell & Co Ltd* (1971) Lord Denning refused to follow the earlier decision of the House of Lords in *Rookes v Barnard* (1964) on the circumstances in which exemplary damages could be awarded.

Again in the cases of *Schorsch Meier GmbH v Henning* (1975) and *Miliangos v George Frank (Textiles) Ltd* (1976) the Court of Appeal refused to follow a decision of the House of Lords in *Havana Railways* (1961) which said that damages could only be awarded in sterling (English money). Lord Denning's argument for refusing to follow the House of Lords decision was that the economic climate of the world had changed, and sterling

was no longer a stable currency; there were some situations in which justice could be done only by awarding damages in another currency. The case of *Schorsch Meier GmbH v Henning* was not appealed to the House of Lords, but *Miliangos v George Frank (Textiles) Ltd* did go on appeal to the Lords, where it was pointed out that the Court of Appeal had no right to ignore or overrule decisions of the House of Lords. The more unusual feature of *Miliangos* was that the House of Lords then used the Practice Statement to overrule its own decision in *Havana Railways*.

COMMENT

Should the Court of Appeal have to follow Supreme Court/House of Lords decisions?

The main argument in favour of the Court of Appeal being able to ignore Supreme Court/House of Lords decisions is that very few cases reach the Supreme Court, so that if there is an error in the law it may take years before a suitable case is appealed all the way to the Supreme Court. The cases of *Schorsch Meier* and *Miliangos* illustrate the potential for injustice if there is no appeal to the Supreme Court/House of Lords. What would have happened if the Court of Appeal in *Schorsch Meier* had decided that it had to follow the House of Lords decision in *Havana Railways*? It is quite possible that the later case of *Miliangos* would not have even been appealed to the Court of Appeal. After all, why waste money on an appeal when there have been previous cases in both the Court of Appeal and the House of Lords ruling on that point of law? The law would have been regarded as fixed and it might never have been changed.

On the other hand, if the Court of Appeal could overrule the Supreme Court/House of Lords, the system of precedent would break down and the law would become uncertain. There would be two conflicting precedents for lower courts to choose from. This would make it difficult for the judge in the lower court. It would also make the law so uncertain that it would be difficult for lawyers to advise clients on the law. However, since the case of *Miliangos*, there has been no further challenge by the Court of Appeal to this basic idea (in our system of judicial precedent) that lower courts must follow decisions of courts above them in the hierarchy.

3.4.2 Human rights cases

One area of law where the Court of Appeal need not follow the decisions of the House of Lords/ Supreme Court is human rights cases. Section 2(1)(a) of the Human Rights Act 1998 states that courts must take into account any judgment or decision of the European Court of Human Rights. In the case of *Re Medicaments (No 2), Director General of Fair Trading v Proprietary Association of Great Britain* (2001) the Court of Appeal refused to follow the decision of the House of Lords in *R v Gough* (1993) because it was slightly different from decisions of the European Court of Human Rights.

The *Director General* case was about whether a decision should be set aside because of the risk of bias on the part of one of the panel. In *Gough* the test for bias included the appeal court deciding whether there was a real danger that the tribunal was biased. The Court of Appeal said that in the European Court of Human Rights cases the emphasis was on the impression which the facts would give on an objective basis. This they claimed was a 'modest adjustment' of the test in *Gough*. However, this appears to be one situation in which the Court of Appeal need not follow a Supreme Court/House of Lords decision.

3.4.3 The Court of Appeal and its own decisions

The first rule is that decisions by one division of the Court of Appeal will not bind the other division. However, within each division, decisions are normally binding, especially for the Civil Division. This rule comes from the case of *Young v Bristol Aeroplane Co Ltd* (1944) and the only exceptions allowed by that case are:

- Where there are conflicting decisions in past Court of Appeal cases, the court can choose which one it will follow and which it will reject.
- Where there is a decision of the House of Lords (now Supreme Court) which effectively overrules a Court of Appeal decision the Court of Appeal must follow the decision of the House of Lords/ Supreme Court.
- Where the decision was made *per incuriam*, that is, carelessly or by mistake because a relevant Act of Parliament or other regulation has not been considered by the court.

The Civil Division of the Court of Appeal under Lord Denning tried to challenge the rule in *Young's* case, claiming that as it had made the earlier decision it could change it. As Lord Denning said in *Gallie v Lee* (1969): 'It was a self-imposed limitation and we who imposed it can also remove it.' This view was not shared by the other judges in the Court of Appeal, as is shown by the statement of Russell LJ in the same case of *Gallie v Lee* where he said: 'The availability of the House of Lords to correct errors in the Court of Appeal makes it, in my view, unnecessary for the court to depart from its existing discipline.'

However, in *Davis v Johnson* (1979) the Court of Appeal refused to follow a decision made only days earlier regarding the interpretation of the Domestic Violence and Matrimonial Proceedings Act 1976. The case went to the House of Lords on appeal where the Law Lords, despite agreeing with the actual interpretation of the law, ruled that the Court of Appeal had to follow its own previous decisions and said that they 'expressly, unequivocally and unanimously reaffirmed the rule in *Young v Bristol Aeroplane*'.

Since this case and, perhaps more especially since the retirement of Lord Denning, the Court of Appeal has not challenged the rule in *Young*'s case, though it has made some use of the *per incuriam* exception allowed by *Young*'s case.

Per incurlam

In *Williams v Fawcett* (1986) the Court refused to follow previous decisions of their own because these had been based on a misunderstanding of the County Court rules dealing with procedure for committing to prison those who break court undertakings. In *Rickards v Rickards* (1989) the court refused to follow a case it had decided in 1981. This was because of the fact that, in the previous case, it had misunderstood the effect of a House of Lords decision. Even though the court did not follow its own previous decision Lord Donaldson said that it would only be in 'rare and exceptional cases' that the Court of Appeal would be justified in refusing to follow a previous decision. *Rickards v Rickards* was considered a 'rare and exceptional' case because the mistake was over the critical point of whether the court had power to hear that particular type of case. Also it was very unlikely that the case would be appealed to the House of Lords.

In *R v Cooper* (2011) the Court of Appeal appears to have extended the scope of the *per incuriam* exception. The narrow or traditional view of *per incuriam* is that it is used only where the earlier court had failed to take into account

Key Facts

General rules for Court of Appeal	Comment
Bound by European Court of Justice	Since 1972 all courts in England and Wales are bound by the European Court of Justice.
Bound by Supreme Court	This is because the Supreme Court/House of Lords is above the Court of Appeal in the court hierarchy. Also necessary for certainty in the law. Court of Appeal tried to challenge this rule in *Broome v Cassell* (1971) and also in *Miliangos* (1976). The House of Lords rejected this challenge. The Court of Appeal must follow decisions of the House of Lords.
Bound by its own past decisions	Decided by the Court of Appeal in *Young*'s case (1944), though there are minor exceptions (see below). In *Davis v Johnson* (1979) the Court of Appeal tried to challenge this rule but the House of Lords confirmed that the Court of Appeal had to follow its own previous decisions.
Exceptions	**Comment**
Exceptions in *Young*'s case	Court of Appeal need not follow its own previous decisions where: • there are conflicting past decisions • there is a Supreme Court/House of Lords decision which effectively overrules the Court of Appeal decision • the decision was made *per incuriam* (in error).
Limitation of *per incuriam*	Only used in 'rare and exceptional cases' (*Rickards v Rickards* (1989)).
Special exception for the Criminal Division	If the law has been 'misapplied or misunderstood' (*R v Gould* (1968)).

Figure 3.4 *Key facts chart for the Court of Appeal and the doctrine of precedent*

all the relevant legislative provisions and/or case authorities. *R v Cooper* involved the procedure to be followed in the Crown Court when barring an individual convicted of a sexual offence from working with children or vulnerable adults. A new system was being brought in under the Safeguarding Vulnerable Groups Act 2006 and it was not clear what procedure should be followed. The Court of Appeal overruled an earlier decision of its own on the basis that not all the material considerations had been placed before the earlier court. This appears to be wider than failure to take into account all relevant legislation and cases.

3.4.4 The Court of Appeal (Criminal Division)

The Criminal Division, as well as using the exceptions from *Young*'s case, can also refuse to follow a past decision of its own if the law has been 'misapplied or misunderstood'. This extra exception arises because in criminal cases people's liberty is involved. This idea was recognised in *R v Taylor* (1950). The same point was made in *R v Gould* (1968). Also in *R v Spencer* (1985) the judges said that there should not in general be any difference in the way that precedent was followed in the Criminal Division and in the Civil Division, 'save that we must remember that we may be dealing with the liberty of the subject and if a departure from authority is necessary in the interests of justice to an appellant, then this court should not shrink from so acting'.

In *R v Simpson* (2003) the Court of Appeal (Criminal Division), a five-judge panel, overruled an earlier decision made by a three-judge panel on the basis that the law had been misunderstood or misapplied. The case stressed that there was discretion available to a five-judge constitution of the court to decide that a previous decision of the Court of Appeal (Criminal Division) should not be treated as binding. This led to the assumption that a five-judge panel always had the discretion to

depart from earlier decisions of a three-judge panel. However, in *R v Magro* (2010) the Court of Appeal itself pointed out that *Simpson* had not given them the right to overrule a three-judge panel where that decision had been made after full argument and close analysis of the relevant legislative provisions. In particular an earlier case should not be overruled when the consequences of doing so would be to the disadvantage of the defendant.

ACTIVITY

Read the following comments by Lord Scarman in his judgment in *Tiverton Estates Ltd v Wearwell Ltd* (1975) and answer the questions below.

'The Court of Appeal occupies a central but intermediate position in our legal system. To a large extent, the consistency and certainty of the law depend upon it … If, therefore, one division of the court should refuse to follow another because it believed the other's decision to be wrong, there would be a risk of confusion and doubt arising where there should be consistency and certainty.

'The appropriate forum for the correction of the Court of Appeal's errors is the House of Lords, where the decision will at least have the merit of being final and binding, subject only to the House's power to review its own decisions. The House of Lords as the court of last resort needs this power of review; it does not follow that an intermediate court needs it.'

Questions

1. Why did Lord Scarman describe the Court of Appeal as occupying 'a central but intermediate position'?
2. Do you agree with his view that there would be a 'risk of confusion and doubt' if the Court of Appeal was not obliged to follow its own past decisions?

3. Describe the situations in which the Court of Appeal may refuse to follow its own past decisions.
4. Why did the House of Lords (and now the Supreme Court) need the power of review?

3.5 The Judicial Committee of the Privy Council

The Judicial Committee of the Privy Council hears appeals from some Commonwealth countries and from places such as the Channel Islands.

3.5.1 Judges

The judges include the Justices of the Supreme Court and also judges who have held high judicial office in countries which still use it as their final court of appeal. Normally a panel of five judges sits to hear an appeal. There can, however, be more judges on the panel where the case is particularly important.

3.5.2 The Privy Council and precedent

The Judicial Committee of the Privy Council is not part of the English legal system and its decisions are not binding on English courts. However, its decisions are persuasive precedent which courts in England and Wales may decide to follow.

Normally the Judicial Committee of the Privy Council will follow decisions of the Supreme Court (and previously the House of Lords). The exception to this is where the point of law has developed differently in the country from which the appeal has come. In such a situation the court is not bound by Supreme Court decisions and can decide to follow the law of the particular country.

An unusual case was *A-G for Jersey v Holley* (2005), which was an appeal from Jersey on the law of provocation (a special partial defence to murder). An extra-large panel of nine judges, all of whom were also Law Lords, was used to decide the case. They refused, by a majority of six judges to three, to follow a previous decision by the House of Lords in *R v Smith (Morgan James)* (2000), even though the law in Jersey was the same as in England. The judges in the majority actually said that the decision in *Smith* was wrong.

This created problems when the same point of law came before the Court of Appeal (Criminal Division) in a later case. Should the Court of Appeal follow the House of Lords decision in Smith or should it follow the Privy Council decision in *Holley*? Normally the Court of Appeal would be bound by any decision of the House of Lords. However, the Court of Appeal took the unusual decision to follow the ruling by the Privy Council rather than that of the House of Lords. This was mainly because the decision in *Holley* was made by six judges from the House of Lords, even though the case was actually dealt with by the Privy Council.

3.6 Distinguishing, overruling and reversing

3.6.1 Distinguishing

This is a method which can be used by a judge to avoid following a past decision which he would otherwise have to follow. It means that the judge finds that the material facts of the case he is deciding are sufficiently different for him to draw a distinction between the present case and the previous precedent. He is not then bound by the previous case.

Two cases demonstrating this process are *Balfour v Balfour* (1919) and *Merritt v Merritt* (1971). Both cases involved a wife making a claim against her husband for breach of contract. In *Balfour* it was decided that the claim could not succeed because there was no intention to create legal relations; there was merely a domestic arrangement between a husband and wife and so there was no legally binding contract. The second case was successful because the court held that the facts of the two cases were sufficiently different in that, although the parties were husband and wife, the agreement was made after they had separated. Furthermore the agreement was made in writing. This distinguished the case from *Balfour*; the agreement in *Merritt* was not just a domestic arrangement but meant as a legally enforceable contract.

3.6.2 Overruling

This is where a court in a later case states that the legal rule decided in an earlier case is wrong. Overruling may occur when a higher court overrules a decision made in an earlier case by a lower court, for example, the Supreme Court overruling a decision of the Court of Appeal. It can also occur where the European Court of Justice overrules a past decision it has made; or when the House of Lords used its power under the Practice Statement to overrule a past decision of its own.

An example of this was seen in *Pepper v Hart* (1993) when the House of Lords ruled that *Hansard* (the record of what is said in Parliament) could be consulted when trying to decide what certain words in an Act of Parliament meant. This decision overruled the earlier decision in *Davis v Johnson* (1979) when the House of Lords had held that it could not consult *Hansard*.

3.6.3 Reversing

This is where a court higher up in the hierarchy overturns the decision of a lower court on appeal in the same case. For example, the Court of Appeal may disagree with the legal ruling of the High Court and come to a different view of the law; in this situation it reverses the decision made by the High Court.

3.7 Judicial law-making

Although there used to be a school of thought that judges did not actually 'make' new law but merely declared what the law had always been, today it is well recognised that judges do use precedent to create new law and to extend old principles. There are many areas of law which owe their existence to decisions by the judges.

Law of contract

Nearly all the main rules which govern the formation of contracts come from decided cases. Many of the decisions were made in the 19th century, but they still affect the law today.

Tort of negligence

The law of negligence in the law of tort is another major area which has been developed and refined by judicial decisions. An important starting point in this area of law was the case of *Donoghue v Stevenson* (1932) in which the House of Lords, when recognising that a manufacturer owed a duty of care to the 'ultimate consumer', created what is known as the 'neighbour test'. Lord Atkin in his judgment in the case said: 'You must take reasonable care to avoid acts or omissions which you can reasonably foresee would be likely to injure your neighbour.' This concept has been applied by judges in several different situations, so that the tort of negligence has developed into a major tort. An interesting extension was in the case of *Ogwo v Taylor* (1987) where it was held that a man who negligently started a fire in his roof when trying to burn off paint with a blowtorch owed a duty of care to a fireman who was injured trying to put out the fire.

There have also been major developments in case law on liability for nervous shock where there has been negligence. The House of Lords laid down the guidelines for this area of law in the case of *Alcock v Chief Constable of South Yorkshire* (1991) which involved claims made by people who had lost relatives in the Hillsborough tragedy.

Criminal law

In the criminal law the judges have played a major role in developing the law on intention. For

Key Facts

Concept	Definition	Comment
stare decisis	Stand by what has been decided	Follow the law decided in previous cases for certainty and fairness
ratio decidendi	Reason for deciding	The part of the judgment which creates the law
obiter dicta	Others things said	The other parts of the judgment – these do not create law
binding precedent	A previous decision which has to be followed	Decisions of higher courts bind lower courts
persuasive precedent	A previous decision which does not have to be followed	The court may be 'persuaded' that the same legal decision should be made
original precedent	A decision in a case where there is no previous legal decision or law for the judge to use	This leads to judges 'making' law
distinguishing	A method of avoiding a previous decision because facts in the present case are different	e.g. *Balfour v Balfour* not followed in *Merritt v Merritt*
overruling	A decision which states that a legal rule in an earlier case is wrong	e.g. in *Pepper v Hart* the House of Lords overruled *Davis v Johnson* on the use of *Hansard*
reversing	Where a higher court in the same case overturns the decision of the lower court	This can only happen if there is an appeal in the case

Figure 3.5 *Key facts chart for the basic concepts of judicial precedent*

example, it is only because of judicial decisions that the intention for murder covers not only the intention to kill but also the intention to cause grievous bodily harm. Judicial decisions have also effectively created new crimes, as in *Shaw v DPP* (1962) which created the offence of conspiracy to corrupt public morals and *R v R* (1991) when it was decided that rape within marriage could be a crime.

However, there have been cases in which the House of Lords has refused to change the law, saying that such a change should only be made by Parliament. This happened in *C v DPP* (1995) when it refused to abolish the presumption that children between 10 and 14 were incapable of

having the necessary intention to commit a crime. (This presumption meant that there always had to be evidence that the child knew he or she was doing something which was seriously wrong.) In fact the government did change the law later in the Crime and Disorder Act 1998.

COMMENT

Should judges make law?

It is argued that it is wrong for judges to make law. Their job is to apply the law. It is for Parliament to make the law. Parliament is elected to do this but judges are not. This means that law-making by judges is undemocratic.

But in reality judges have to make law in some situations. The first is where a case involves a legal point which has never been decided before. As there is no law on it, the judge in the case has to make a decision. After all, the parties in the case would not want the judge to refuse to deal with the case; they want the matter decided.

The second area is more controversial. This is where judges overrule old cases and in doing so create new law. It is important for the law to be updated in this way. Law for the 21st century needs to be based on today's society and values. Law decided a hundred years or more ago may no longer be suitable. Ideally, Parliament should reform the law, but Parliament is sometimes slow to do this. If judges never overruled old cases, then the law might be 'out of date'.

An example of this is the case of *R v R* (1991). In this case a man was charged with raping his wife. The point the court had to decide was whether, by being married, a woman automatically consented to sex with her husband and could never say 'no'. The old law dated back to 1736 when it was said that 'by their mutual matrimonial consent the wife hath given up herself in this kind to her husband, which she cannot retract'. In other words, once married, a woman was always assumed to consent and could not go back on this. This was still held to be the law in *R v Miller* (1954), even though the wife had already started divorce proceedings. Parliament had not done anything to reform this law.

So, when the case of *R v R* came before the courts, the judges had to decide whether to follow the old law, or whether they should change the law to match the ideas of the late 20th century. In the House of Lords, the judges pointed out that 'the status of women and the status of a married woman in our law

have changed quite dramatically. A husband and wife are now for all practical purposes equal partners in marriage.' As a result it was decided that if a wife did not consent to sex then her husband could be guilty of rape. The House of Lords stated that the common law (judge-made law) 'is capable of evolving in the light of changing social, economic and cultural developments'. This clearly recognised that judges in the House of Lords could change the law if they thought it necessary. The same power now applies to the Supreme Court.

3.8 The effect of an Act of Parliament

Although judges can and do make law, precedent is subordinate to statute law, delegated legislation and European regulations. This means that if (for example) an Act of Parliament is passed and that Act contains a provision which contradicts a previously decided case, that case decision will cease to have effect; the Act of Parliament is now the law on that point. This happened when Parliament passed the Law Reform (Year and a Day Rule) Act in 1996. Up to then judicial decisions meant that a person could only be charged with murder or manslaughter if the victim died within a year and a day of receiving his injuries. The Act enacted that there was no time limit, and a person could be guilty even if the victim died several years later, so cases after 1996 follow the Act and not the old judicial decisions.

3.9 Comparison with other legal systems

3.9.1 Codes of law

Most countries have some system of considering past case decisions, but these are rarely as rigid as the system of judicial precedent followed in

England and Wales. In countries which have a code of law, precedent plays a much less important part. This civil system is operated in many continental countries; the judges are less likely to make law, the code should provide for all situations and so the judge's task is to interpret the code. Since the code is the fountain of the law, judicial decisions are not followed so closely. Even judges in lower courts can refuse to follow a decision by another court if they feel that the code was not correctly interpreted.

3.9.2 Less rigid precedent

Even in other countries which have a common law system similar to England's where case decisions form a major part of the law, the doctrine of precedent is not applied so strictly. For example, in the United States of America a previous precedent is likely to be ignored if it fails to meet with academic approval: if there is considerable criticism of the decision by leading academic lawyers, judges in later cases are likely to take note of that criticism and rule differently. This has happened in England in the case of *R v Shivpuri* (1986), but this is a rare happening, while in America it occurs more frequently.

Also in America, cases where the panel of judges disagreed (so that the decision may have been by three judges to two) are likely to be overruled in the future. In England, the fact that the majority was so slender does not make the precedent less valuable.

3.9.3 Prospective overruling

The other difference is that in America the concept of prospective overruling is used. This means that the law is not changed in the case being decided by the court, but it is changed for the future. In England, the judges cannot do this; if their decision changes the law then it is changed in the actual case. This has been described as 'dog's law'; that is you do not know you have done wrong until the court changes the law in your case, in just the way that a dog does not know it has

done wrong until you punish him. This is what happened in the case of *R v R* (1991) when it was decided that rape within marriage could be a crime. Until that case, previous decisions had held that this was not a crime. This can be viewed as unfair to the parties in a case. The American use of prospective overruling is preferable in such cases.

3.10 Advantages and disadvantages of precedent

As can be seen from the previous sections there are both advantages and disadvantages to the way in which judicial precedent operates in England and Wales. In fact it could be said that every advantage has a corresponding disadvantage.

3.10.1 Advantages

The main advantages are:

1. **Certainty**
   Because the courts follow past decisions, people know what the law is and how it is likely to be applied in their case; it allows lawyers to advise clients on the likely outcome of cases; it also allows people to operate their businesses knowing that financial and other arrangements they make are recognised by law. The House of Lords Practice Statement pointed out how important certainty is.
2. **Consistency and fairness in the law**
   It is seen as just and fair that similar cases should be decided in a similar way, just as in any sport it is seen as fair that the rules of the game apply equally to each side. The law must be consistent if it is to be credible.
3. **Precision**
   As the principles of law are set out in actual cases the law becomes very precise; it is well illustrated and gradually builds up through the different variations of facts in the cases that come before the courts.

4. Flexibility

There is room for the law to change as the Supreme Court can use the Practice Statement to overrule cases. The ability to distinguish cases also gives all courts some freedom to avoid past decisions and develop the law.

5. Time-saving

Precedent can be considered a useful time-saving device. Where a principle has been established, cases with similar facts are unlikely to go through the lengthy process of litigation.

The main advantages have been summed up very neatly as follows:

'The main advantages of the precedent system are said to be certainty, precision and flexibility. Legal certainty is achieved, in theory at least, in that if the legal problem raised has been solved before, the judge is bound to adopt that solution. Precision is achieved by the sheer volume of reported cases containing solutions to innumerable factual situations. No code or statute could ever contain as much.

'Flexibility is achieved by the possibility of decisions being overruled and by the possibility of distinguishing and confining the operation of decisions which appear unsound.'

3.10.2 Disadvantages

However, there are disadvantages as follows:

1. Rigidity

The fact that lower courts have to follow decisions of higher courts, together with the fact that the Court of Appeal has to follow its own past decisions, can make the law too inflexible so that bad decisions made in the past may be perpetuated. There is the added problem that so few cases go to the Supreme Court. Change in the law will only take place if parties have the courage, the persistence and the money to appeal their case.

2. Complexity

Since there are nearly half a million reported cases it is not easy to find all the relevant case law even with computerised databases. Another problem is in the judgments themselves, which are often very long with no clear distinction between comments and the reasons for the decision. This makes it difficult in some cases to extract the *ratio decidendi*; indeed in *Dodd's Case* (1973) the judges in the Court of Appeal said they were unable to find the *ratio* in a decision of the House of Lords.

3. Illogical distinctions

The use of distinguishing to avoid past decisions can lead to 'hair-splitting' so that some areas of the law have become very complex. The differences between some cases may be very small and appear illogical.

4. Slowness of growth

Judges are well aware that some areas of the law are unclear or in need of reform; however, they cannot make a decision unless there is a case before the courts to be decided. This is one of the criticisms of the need for the Court of Appeal to follow its own previous decisions, as only about 50 cases go to the Supreme Court each year. There may be a long wait for a suitable case to be appealed as far as the Supreme Court.

3.11 Law reporting

In order to follow past decisions there must be an accurate record of what those decisions were. Written reports have existed in England and Wales since the 13th century, but many of the early reports were very brief and, it is thought, not always accurate. The earliest reports from about 1275 to 1535 were called Year Books, and contained short reports of cases, usually written in French. From 1535 to 1865 cases were reported by individuals who made a business out of selling the reports to lawyers. The detail and accuracy of these reports varied enormously. However, some are still occasionally used today.

In 1865 the Incorporated Council of Law Reporting was set up – this was controlled by the courts. Reports became accurate, with the judgment usually noted down word for word. This accuracy of reports was one of the factors in the development of the strict doctrine of precedent. These reports still exist and are published according to the court that the case took place in. For example, case references abbreviated to 'Ch' stand for 'Chancery' and the case will have been decided in the Chancery Division; while 'QB' stands for 'Queen's Bench Division'.

There are also other well established reports today, notably the All England series (abbreviated to All ER) and the Weekly Law Reports (WLR). Newspapers and journals also publish law reports, but these are often abbreviated versions in which the law reporter has tried to pick out the essential parts of the judgment.

3.11.1 Internet law reports

All High Court, Court of Appeal and Supreme Court cases are now reported on the Internet. Some websites give the full report free; others give summaries or an index of cases. There are also subscription sites which give a very comprehensive service of law reports.

Internet research   WWW

Search at least one website address and find a recent law report. Some suggestions for websites are given below.

www.lawreports.co.uk gives summaries of important cases in its Daily Law Notes section.

www.supremecourt.gov.uk has reports of Supreme Court judgments.

www.parliament.uk gives reports of House of Lords cases from 1996 to 2009.

www.bailii.org has cases from the Court of Appeal and below.

EXAMINATION QUESTIONS

Study the text below and answer the questions based on it.

'The function of independent judges charged to interpret and apply the law is universally recognised as a cardinal feature of the modern democratic state, a cornerstone of the rule of law itself and it is therefore wrong to stigmatise judicial decision-making as in some way undemocratic.'

Source: Lord Bingham

(a) Explain the doctrine of judicial precedent. [14 marks]

(b) Read the following scenario and consider the application of the doctrine of precedent in this case, with particular reference to whether the High Court has to follow the previous Court of Appeal's decision.

In the case of *Re Worley* (1940), the Court of Appeal held that a trust for the benefit of one's relations could be a charitable trust so long as the relations in question could be considered as 'poor relations'. Charitable status is important because charitable trusts pay less tax. The Inland Revenue wished to claim that such trusts should no longer be regarded as charitable, and in 2010 a case was brought before the High Court concerning a trust established by Lord Arrington. Lord Arrington is a multi-millionaire who had established a trust for a long-lost relative. The relative in questions has assets in excess of £500,000 but in comparison with Lord Arrington is not very well off. [11 marks]

LA2, Summer 2011, WJEC

EXTENSION ESSAY

To what extent, if at all, is it true to say that the doctrine of precedent is applied too rigidly in the English legal system?

CHAPTER 4

ACTS OF PARLIAMENT

INTRODUCTION

In today's world there is often a need for new law to meet new situations. Clearly the method of judicial law-making through precedents is not suitable for major changes to the law, nor is it a sufficiently quick, efficient law-making method for a modern society. The other point to be made is that judges are not elected by the people, and in a democracy, the view is that laws should only be made by the elected representatives of society. So, today, the main legislative body in the United Kingdom is Parliament.

Laws passed by Parliament are known as Acts of Parliament or statutes, and this source of law is usually referred to as statute law. About 60 to 70 Acts are passed each year. In addition to Parliament as a whole enacting law, power is delegated to government ministers and their departments to make detailed rules and regulations, which supplement Acts of Parliament. These regulations are delegated legislation (see Chapter 5) and are called statutory instruments.

4.1 Parliament

Parliament consists of the House of Commons and the House of Lords. Under the normal procedure both Houses must vote in favour of a Bill before it can become a new Act of Parliament.

4.1.1 The House of Commons

The people who sit in the House of Commons are referred to as Members of Parliament (MPs). These members of the House of Commons are elected by the public, with the country being divided into constituencies and each of these returning one Member of Parliament (MP). Under the Fixed-term Parliaments Act 2011 there must be a general election every five years. In addition, there may be individual by-elections in constituencies where the MP has died or retired during the current session of Parliament. The government of the day is formed by the political party which has a majority in the House of Commons.

4.1.2 The House of Lords

At the beginning of 2013 the House of Lords consisted of:

- about 90 hereditary peers;
- about 700 life peers; and
- the most senior bishops in the Church of England.

Note that the 12 most senior judges used to sit in the House of Lords, but they no longer do so. They are now separate from Parliament and sit as the Supreme Court (see Chapter 16).

Originally most of the members of the House of Lords were hereditary peers. During the

The Houses of Parliament

20th century the awarding of a title for life (a life peerage) became more common. The prime minister nominated people who should receive a title for their lifetime, but this title would not pass on to their children. The title was then awarded by the monarch. In this way people who had served the country and were thought to be suitable members of the House of Lords were able to bring their expertise to the House. Most life peerages were given to former politicians who had retired from the House of Commons. For example, Margaret Thatcher, who had been prime minister in the 1980s, was made a life peer.

4.1.3 Reform of the House of Lords

By 1999, there were over 1,100 members of the House of Lords, of whom 750 were hereditary peers. The Labour government decided that in a modern society an inherited title should not automatically allow someone to participate in making law. They felt that some of the members should be elected and some should be nominated. To help decide exactly what reforms should be made, a Royal Commission (known as the Wakeham Commission) was set up to consider how members of the House of Lords should be selected. In the meantime the right of most of the hereditary peers to sit in the House of Lords was abolished in November 1999. Fewer than 100 hereditary peers were allowed to continue to be members of the House of Lords.

The Wakeham Commission reported in 2000 and recommended that one-third of the House should be elected. Also, that there should be a limit on the system of political patronage whereby the prime minister nominates people to the House of Lords. The Commission recommended that an independent House of Lords Appointments Commission should vet all those nominated to the House of Lords. In addition the Commission should be able to appoint 'people's peers'.

The House of Lords Appointments Commission was set up in 2000 and in 2001 recommended the first so-called people's peers for appointment to the House of Lords. These were supposed to be ordinary people who had been recommended by other ordinary people. However, the list was mainly of already famous people, rather than 'Mr Joe Public'.

This was meant to be a temporary solution while the government consulted on the final make-up of the House of Lords. However, there have been major disagreements about how many of the House of Lords should be elected by the general public and how many should be nominated (and by whom). As a result the reform of the House of Lords has not been completed.

4.2 Influences on parliamentary law-making

4.2.1 The government programme

When a government is formed, it will have a programme of reforms it wishes to carry out. These will have been set out in its party manifesto on which it asked people to vote for it in the general election. Also, at the start of each parliamentary session, the government announces (in the Queen's Speech) what particular laws it intends introducing during that session. So most new legislation is likely to arise from government policy.

4.2.2 European Union Law

However, there are other influences on what law is enacted: European Union law can lead to new Acts of Parliament which are passed in order to bring our law in line with the European law. This may be to implement a specific European Regulation or Directive, as in the case of the Consumer Protection Act 1987, or because a decision of the European Court of Justice has shown that our law does not conform with the Treaty of Rome, as with the Sex Discrimination Act 1986. The effect

of European law is considered in more detail in Chapter 7.

4.2.3 Other influences

Other outside influences include proposals for law reform put forward by law reform agencies, commissions or inquiries into the effectiveness of existing law. These law reform agencies are dealt with in detail in Chapter 8. In addition specific events may also play a role in formulating the law. A particularly tragic example was the massacre in March 1996 of 16 young children and their teacher in Dunblane by a lone gunman. After this there was an inquiry into the laws on gun ownership. By March 1997 Parliament passed the Firearms (Amendment) Act 1997 banning private ownership of most handguns.

Another major example of an event leading to new law was the terrorist attack on the Twin Towers in New York in September 2001. (This is often referred to as 9/11.) Following this, Parliament passed the Anti-Terrorism, Crime and Security Act 2001. One of the provisions of this Act was to allow the detention (without charge) of non-UK citizens where the Home Secretary believes that the person's presence in the UK is a risk to national security and suspects that the person is a terrorist. This provision was held to be a breach of human rights in 2005.

Pressure groups may also cause the government to reconsider the law on certain areas. This was seen in 1994 when the government agreed to reduce the age of consent for homosexual acts in private from 21 to 18. Then in 2000 the age of consent was further reduced to 16. Another clear example of the government bowing to public opinion and the efforts of pressure groups was the introduction of the Disability Discrimination Act 1995. This Act gave disabled people certain rights in relation to employment. It also stated that they should have access to shops and hotels and other services.

The Civil Partnership Act 2004 gave the right to same-sex couples to register their partnership and have a civil ceremony. This was the result of changing attitudes to same-sex partnerships.

4.3 The pre-legislative process

On major matters a Green Paper may be issued by the minister with responsibility for that matter. A Green Paper is a consultative document on a topic in which the government's view is put forward with proposals for law reform. Interested parties are then invited to send comments to the relevant government department, so that a full consideration of all sides can be made and necessary changes made to the government's proposals. Following this the government will publish a White Paper with its firm proposals for new law.

Consultation before any new law is framed is valuable as it allows time for mature consideration. Governments have been criticised for sometimes responding in a 'knee-jerk' fashion to incidents and, as a result, rushing law through that has subsequently proved to be unworkable. This occurred with the Dangerous Dogs Act 1991.

ACTIVITY

Read the following article and answer the questions below.

Judge reprieves Dempsey, the harmless pit bull

A High Court judge, who reprieved a pit bull terrier from death row yesterday, savaged the Dangerous Dogs Act (1991) which he said would have sent a 'perfectly inoffensive animal to the gas chamber'.

Dempsey, dubbed Britain's most expensive dog after a long legal battle to save her, will be returned to her overjoyed owner after Lord Justice Staughton and Mr Justice Rougier quashed a destruction order by Ealing Magistrates' Court in 1992.

Dempsey's only crime was being the wrong kind of dog, Judge Rougier said. Magistrates sentenced her to be destroyed after the nephew of her owner, Dianne Fanneran, took her muzzle off in public when she became ill, and she was spotted by a policeman.

Mr Justice Rougier said: 'It seems to me that, while acknowledging the need to protect the public … the Dangerous Dogs Act bears all the hallmarks of an ill-thought-out piece of legislation, no doubt drafted in response to another pressure group … '

The Act was rushed through in 1991 by the then Home Secretary, Kenneth Baker, after pit bull terriers attacked a man in Lincoln and a six-year-old girl in Bradford. It requires them to be put down unless they are neutered, tattooed, microchipped, registered, muzzled and kept on a lead in public.

Taken from an article by Clare Dyer in the *Guardian*, 23 November 1995

Questions
1. Why was the Dangerous Dogs Act 1991 passed?
2. Why was Dempsey in breach of the Act?
3. What did Mr Justice Rougier say about the Act?
4. How might this problem with the Act have been avoided by the government when formulating the legislation?

4.4 Introducing an Act of Parliament

The great majority of Acts of Parliament are introduced by the government – these are initially drafted by lawyers in the civil service who are known as Parliamentary Counsel to the Treasury. Instructions as to what is to be included and the effect the proposed law is intended to have are given by the government department responsible for it.

4.4.1 Bills

When the proposed Act has been drafted it is published, and at this stage is called a Bill. It will only become an Act of Parliament if it successfully completes all the necessary stages in Parliament. Even at this early stage there are difficulties, as the draftsmen face problems in trying to frame the Bill. It has to be drawn up so that it represents the government's wishes, while at the same time using correct legal wording so that there will not be any difficulties in the courts applying it. It must be unambiguous, precise and comprehensive. Achieving all of these is not easy, and there may be unforeseen problems with the language used, as discussed in the chapter on statutory interpretation. On top of this there is usually pressure on time, as the government will have a timetable of when they wish to introduce the draft Bill into Parliament.

4.4.2 Private Members' Bills

Ballot

Bills can also be sponsored by individual MPs. The parliamentary process allows for a ballot each parliamentary session in which 20 private members are selected who can then take their turn in presenting a Bill to Parliament. The time for debate of Private Members' Bills is limited, usually being debated only on Fridays, so that only the first six or seven members in the ballot have a realistic chance of introducing a Bill on their chosen topic. Relatively few Private Members' Bills become law, but there have been some important laws passed as the result of such Bills. A major example was the Abortion Act 1967 which legalised abortion in this country. More recent examples are the Marriage Act 1994, which was introduced by Giles Brandreth, the MP for Chester. This allowed people to marry in any registered place, not only in register offices or religious buildings. Another example is the Household Waste Recycling Act 2003 which places local authorities under a duty to recycle waste.

10-minute rule

Backbenchers can also try to introduce a Bill through the '10-minute' rule, under which any MP can make a speech of up to 10 minutes supporting the introduction of new legislation. This method is rarely successful unless there is no opposition to the Bill, but some Acts of Parliament have been introduced in this way, for example the Bail (Amendment) Act 1993 which gave the prosecution the right to appeal against the granting of bail to a defendant. Members of the House of Lords can also introduce Private Members' Bills.

4.4.3 Public and private Bills

A public Bill involves matters of public policy which will affect either the whole country or a large section of it. Most of the government Bills are in this category, for example, the Criminal Justice Act 2003, the Constitutional Reform Act 2005, the Legal Services Act 2007 and the Legal Aid, Sentencing and Punishment of Offenders Act 2012. However, not all Bills are aimed at changing the law for the entire country; some are designed to pass a law which will affect only individual people or corporations. An example of this was the University College London Act 1996 which was passed in order to combine the Royal Free Hospital School of Medicine, the Institute of Neurology and the Institute of Child Health with University College.

4.5 The process in Parliament

In order to become an Act of Parliament, the Bill will usually have to be passed by both Houses of Parliament, and in each House there is a long and complex process (see Figure 4.1). A Bill may start in either the House of Commons or the House of Lords, with the exception of finance Bills which must start in the House of Commons. All Bills must go through the stages explained below:

First Reading

This is a formal procedure where the name and main aims of the Bill are read out. Usually no

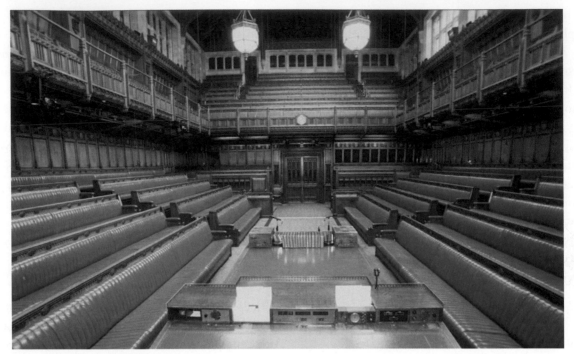

Inside the House of Commons

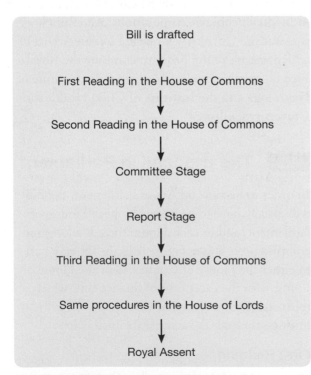

Bill is drafted

↓

First Reading in the House of Commons

↓

Second Reading in the House of Commons

↓

Committee Stage

↓

Report Stage

↓

Third Reading in the House of Commons

↓

Same procedures in the House of Lords

↓

Royal Assent

Figure 4.1 *Flow chart of the passing of an Act of Parliament starting in the House of Commons*

discussion takes place, and usually there will be no vote.

Second Reading

This is the main debate on the whole Bill in which MPs debate the principles behind the Bill. The debate usually focuses on the main principles rather than the smaller details. Those MPs who wish to speak in the debate must catch the Speaker's eye, since the Speaker controls all debates and no one may speak without being called on by the Speaker. At the end of this is a vote. The vote may be verbal: this is when the Speaker of the House asks the members as a whole how they vote and the members shout out 'Aye' or 'No'. If it is clear that nearly all members are in agreement, either for or against, there is no need for a more formal vote. If it is not possible to judge whether more people are shouting 'Aye' or 'No' there will be a formal vote in which the members of the House vote by leaving the

Chamber and then walking back in through one of two special doors on one side or the other of the Chamber. There will be two 'tellers' positioned at each of these two voting doors to make a list of the Members voting on each side. These tellers count up the number of MPs who voted for and against and declare these numbers to the Speaker in front of the members of the House. Obviously there must be a majority in favour for the Bill to progress any further.

Committee Stage

At this stage a detailed examination of each clause of the Bill is undertaken by a committee of between 16 and 50 MPs. This is usually done by what is called a Standing Committee, which, contrary to its name, is a committee chosen specifically for that Bill. The membership of such a committee is decided 'having regard to the qualifications of those members nominated and to the composition of the House'. So, although the government will have a majority, the opposition and minority parties are represented proportionately to the number of seats they have in the House of Commons. The members of Parliament nominated for each Standing Committee will usually be those with a special interest in, or knowledge of, the subject of the Bill which is being considered. For finance Bills the whole House will sit in committee.

Report Stage

At the Committee stage amendments to various clauses in the Bill may have been voted on and passed, so this report stage is where the committee reports back to the House on those amendments. (If there were no amendments at the Committee Stage, there will not be a Report Stage – instead the Bill will go straight on to the Third Reading.) The amendments will be debated in the House and accepted or rejected. Further amendments may also be added. The Report Stage has been

described as 'a useful safeguard against a small Committee amending a Bill against the wishes of the House, and a necessary opportunity for second thoughts'.

Third Reading

This is the final vote on the Bill. It is almost a formality since a Bill which has passed through all the stages above is unlikely to fail at this late stage. In fact in the House of Commons there will only be an actual further debate on the Bill as a whole if at least six MPs request it. However, in the House of Lords there may sometimes be amendments made at this stage.

The House of Lords

If the Bill started life in the House of Commons it is now passed to the House of Lords where it goes through the same five stages outlined above and, if the House of Lords makes amendments to the Bill, then it will go back to the House of Commons for it to consider those amendments. If the Bill started in the House of Lords then it passes to the House of Commons.

Royal Assent

The final stage is where the monarch formally gives approval to the Bill and it then becomes an Act of Parliament. This is now a formality and, under the Royal Assent Act 1967, the monarch will not even have the text of the Bills to which she is assenting; she will only have the short title. The last time that a monarch refused assent was in 1707, when Queen Anne refused to assent to the Scottish Militia Bill.

4.5.1 The Parliament Acts 1911 and 1949

The power of the House of Lords to reject a Bill is limited by the Parliament Acts 1911 and 1949. These allow a Bill to become law even if the

House of Lords rejects it, provided that the Bill is reintroduced into the House of Commons in the next session of Parliament and passes all the stages again there.

The principle behind the Parliament Acts is that the House of Lords is not an elected body, and its function is to refine and add to the law rather than oppose the will of the democratically elected House of Commons. In fact there have only been four occasions when this procedure has been used to by-pass the House of Lords after it had voted against a Bill. Since 1949 the Parliament Acts have been used on only four occasions. These were for the:

- War Crimes Act 1991
- European Parliamentary Elections Act 1999
- Sexual Offences (Amendment) Act 2000
- Hunting Act 2004.

4.5.2 Commencement of an Act

Following the Royal Assent the Act of Parliament will come in force on midnight of that day, unless another date has been set. However, there has been a growing trend for Acts of Parliament not to be implemented immediately. Instead the Act itself states the date when it will commence or passes responsibility on to the appropriate minister to fix the commencement date. In the latter case the minister will bring the Act into force by issuing a commencement order. This can cause problems of uncertainty as it is difficult to discover which sections of an Act have been brought into force. The Criminal Justice Act 2003 is a good example of an Act where the sections have been brought in bit by bit.

The Criminal Justice Act 2003 contained 339 sections as well as several schedules. The commencement section is s 336. It provided that parts of 11 sections (out of the total of 339) would come into effect immediately after the Act received the Royal Assent: this was on 19 November 2003. Most of the sections that came into effect immediately were administrative in nature: for example, allowing the relevant minister to create rules ready for parts of the Act to be implemented.

The commencement section then provided that ss 269–277 would come into effect four weeks after the Royal Assent. These sections are about the effects of life sentences and how long must be served in prison. These came into effect on 18 December 2003. The commencement section provided that all other sections should come into effect when the relevant minister made an order for this. As a result some sections were brought into force in January 2004, others in February 2004, yet others in April 2004, etc. Schedule 3, which concerned how certain cases would be transferred from the Magistrates' Courts to the Crown Court, was only brought into effect in 2012.

It may be that some sections or even a whole Act will never become law. An example of this is the Easter Act 1928, which was intended to fix the date of Easter Day. Although this Act passed all the necessary parliamentary stages, and was given the Royal Assent, it has never come into force.

It can be seen that with all these stages it usually takes several months for a Bill to be passed. However, there have been occasions where all parties have thought a new law is needed urgently and an Act has been passed in less than 24 hours. This happened with the Northern Ireland Bill in 1972.

4.5.3 Example of an Act

Figure 4.3 on pages 53 and 54 is a reproduction of the Law Reform (Year and a Day Rule) Act 1996. This shows what an Act of Parliament looks like. The name of the Act is given immediately under the Royal coat of arms. Underneath the name, '1996 CHAPTER 19' means that it was the nineteenth Act to be passed in 1996. Next follows a short statement or preamble about the purpose of the Act. Then there is a formal statement showing that the Act has been passed by both Houses of Parliament and received the

Royal Assent; this is included in all Acts. After this comes the body of the Act, which is set out in sections; this is an unusually short Act as it has only three sections.

Internet research **WWW**

Look up a recent Act on the Internet. If you do not know of any, try the website **www.legislation.gov.uk**.

Choose an Act and now search for the debates in Parliament on that Act (try **www. parliament.uk**). Don't forget it would be called a Bill before it is passed.

Section 1 abolishes the 'year and a day rule'. Note that the Act actually refers to it in those terms; this is because the rule was a part of the common law and was never written down in any statute. Section 2 sets out when the consent of the Attorney-General is needed before a prosecution can be started. The last section gives the name by which the Act may be cited and it also sets

out that the Act does not apply to cases in which the incident which led to death occurred before the Act was passed. Section 3 is concerned with the commencement of the Act; this sets the commencement date for s 2 at two months after the Act is passed. As s 1 is not specifically mentioned, the normal rule that an Act comes into effect on midnight of the date on which it receives the Royal Assent applies to that section.

4.6 Criticisms of the legislative process

There are many criticisms which can be made about the legislative process. In fact the Renton Committee on the Preparation of Legislation which reported in 1975 pointed out that there had been criticism for centuries, quoting Edward VI as saying more than 400 years ago: 'I would wish that ... the superfluous and tedious statutes were brought into one sum together, and made more plain and short, to the intent that men might better understand them.'

Key Facts

Green Paper	Consultation document on possible new law
White Paper	Government's firm proposals for new law
First Reading	Formal introduction of Bill into the House of Commons
Second Reading	Main debate on Bill's principles
Committee Stage	Clause-by-clause consideration of the Bill by a select committee
Report Stage	Committee reports suggested amendments back to the House of Commons
Third Reading	Final debate on the Bill
Repeat of process in the House of Lords	All stages are repeated BUT if the House of Lords votes against the Bill, it can go back to the House of Commons and, under the Parliament Acts 1911 and 1949, become law if the House of Commons passes it for the second time (rare occurrence)
Royal Assent	A formality – normally Acts of Parliament come into force at midnight after receiving the Royal Assent

Figure 4.2 *Key facts chart for the legislative process*

The Renton Committee said there were four main categories of complaint:

1. The language used in many Acts was obscure and complex.
2. Acts were 'over-elaborate' because draftsmen tried to provide for every contingency.
3. The internal structure of many Acts was illogical with sections appearing to be out of sequence, making it difficult for people to find relevant sections.
4. There was a lack of clear connection between Acts, so that it was not easy to trace all the Acts on a given topic. In addition, the frequent practice of amending small parts of one Act by passing another increased the difficulty of finding out what the law was.

The Committee made 81 recommendations, but only about half of these have been fully implemented.

4.6.1 Lack of accessibility

Ideally, the laws of the land should be easily accessible to citizens but there are some major problems which create difficulties not only for ordinary citizens, but also for lawyers and even in some cases for the Lord Chancellor! As already mentioned, it is difficult to discover which Acts and/ or which sections have been brought into force.

An example of problems with knowing what sections are in force is the Criminal Justice Act 2003 which has 339 sections and several schedules. We have already looked at this in section 4.5.2. Only 11 sections came into force when the Royal Assent was given. Some more came into force four weeks after the Royal Assent. Many of other 300-plus sections have been brought into effect a few at a time over a period of time or not at all. In fact s 43 regarding holding fraud trials without a jury was never brought into effect and was repealed in 2012.

Where sections are brought into effect at different times, it is difficult to know what the law is. This prevents law from being easily accessible.

> **Internet research** **www**
>
> Find the commencement section or schedule in a recent Act of Parliament.
>
> This can be done by looking at a printed copy of an Act in a library or on the Internet at **www.legislation.gov.uk**. There is usually a list of contents at the start of an Act.

4.6.2 Other problems

Many statutes are amended by later statutes so that it is necessary to read two or sometimes more Acts together to make sense of provisions. The law may also be added to by delegated legislation in the form of statutory instruments. All this increases the difficulty of discovering the law that is actually in force.

The language used in Acts is not always easily understood and apart from the obvious difficulties this causes it also results in many cases going to court. In fact about 75 per cent of cases heard by the House of Lords in its judicial capacity each year involve disputes over the interpretation of Acts.

In 1992 the report of a Hansard Society Commission under Lord Rippon underlined five principles for democratic law-making. These were that:

- Laws are made for the benefit of the citizens and all citizens should therefore be involved as fully and openly as possible in the legislative process.
- Statute law has to be rooted in the authority of Parliament and thoroughly exposed to democratic scrutiny.
- Statute law should be as certain and intelligible as possible.
- Statute law has to be as accessible as possible.
- Getting the law right is as important as getting it passed quickly.

If these guidelines were to be followed there would be an improvement to the quality of the

Law Reform (Year and a Day Rule) Act 1996

1996 CHAPTER 19

An Act to abolish the "year and a day rule" and, in consequence of its abolition, to impose a restriction on the institution in certain circumstances of proceedings for a fatal offence. [17th June 1996]

B E IT ENACTED by the Queen's most Excellent Majesty, by and with the advice and consent of the Lords Spiritual and Temporal, and Commons, in this present Parliament assembled, and by the authority of the same, as follows:—

1. The rule known as the "year and a day rule" (that is, the rule that, for the purposes of offences involving death and of suicide, an act or omission is conclusively presumed not to have caused a person's death if more than a year and a day elapsed before he died) is abolished for all purposes.

Abolition of "year and a day rule".

2.—(1) Proceedings to which this section applies may only be instituted by or with the consent of the Attorney General.

Restriction on institution of proceedings for a fatal offence.

(2) This section applies to proceedings against a person for a fatal offence if—

    (a) the injury alleged to have caused the death was sustained more than three years before the death occurred, or

    (b) the person has previously been convicted of an offence committed in circumstances alleged to be connected with the death.

(3) In subsection (2) "fatal offence" means—

    (a) murder, manslaughter, infanticide or any other offence of which one of the elements is causing a person's death, or

    (b) the offence of aiding, abetting, counselling or procuring a person's suicide.

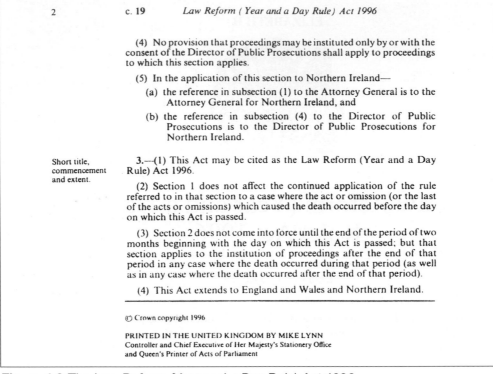

Figure 4.3 *The Law Reform (Year and a Day Rule) Act 1996*

statute book. In addition, codification and/ or consolidation could be used to make the law more accessible. Under this, all the law on one topic could be brought together into one Act of Parliament, making it both more accessible and, hopefully, more comprehensible.

4.7 Parliamentary sovereignty

Parliamentary law is sovereign over other forms of law in England and Wales. This means that an Act of Parliament can completely overrule any custom, judicial precedent, delegated legislation or previous Act of Parliament. This is also referred to as parliamentary supremacy.

The concept of the sovereignty of parliamentary law is based on the idea of democratic law-making. A Member of Parliament is elected by the voters in the constituency, so that in theory that MP is participating in the legislative process on the behalf of those voters. However, this is a very simplistic view since:

- MPs usually vote on party lines rather than how their particular constituents wish.
- Many MPs are elected by only a very small majority and if there were several candidates in the election, it may well be that the MP was only actually voted for by about 30 per cent or even fewer of the voters.
- Parliamentary elections only have to take place once every five years, so that an MP who votes against the wishes of his constituents is not immediately replaced.

In addition, the ideal concept of democracy is lost because much of the drafting of parliamentary law is done by civil servants who are not elected. Finally, there is the point that the House of Lords is not an elected body.

4.7.1 Definition of parliamentary supremacy

The most widely recognised definition of parliamentary supremacy was given by Dicey in the 19th century. He made three main points:

1. Parliament can legislate on any subject matter.
2. No Parliament can be bound by any previous Parliament, nor can a Parliament pass any Act that will bind a later Parliament.
3. No other body has the right to override or set aside an Act of Parliament.

Legislating on any subject matter

There are no limits on what Parliament can make laws about. It can make any law it wants. For example, in the past, Parliament changed the rule on who should succeed to the throne. This was in 1700, when Parliament passed the Act of Settlement which stated that the children of King James II (who were the direct line of the monarchy) could not succeed to the throne.

Parliament can also change its own powers. It did this with the Parliament Acts 1911 and 1949, which placed limits on the right of the House of Lords to block a Bill by voting against it (see section 4.5.1).

Cannot bind successor

Each new Parliament should be free to make or change what laws it wishes. Parliament cannot be bound by a law made by a previous Parliament, and can repeal any previous Act of Parliament.

There are, however, some laws that have become such an important part of the British constitution that they cannot realistically be repealed. For example, the Act of Settlement in 1700 changed the line of succession to the throne. It affected who was entitled to become king or queen. Realistically, after 300 years, this cannot now be repealed.

There are other modern limitations which have been self-imposed by Parliament. These are dealt with in section 4.7.2 below.

Cannot be overruled by others

This rule is kept to even if the Act of Parliament may have been passed because of incorrect information. This was shown by *British Railways Board v Pickin* (1974). A private Act of Parliament, the British Railways Act 1968, was enacted by Parliament. *Pickin* challenged the Act on the basis that that the British Railways Board had fraudulently concealed certain matters from Parliament. This alleged fraud had led to Parliament passing the Act which had the effect of depriving *Pickin* of his land or proprietary rights. The action was struck out because no court is entitled to go behind an Act once it has been passed. A challenge cannot be made to an Act of Parliament even if there was fraud.

4.7.2 Limitations on parliamentary sovereignty

There are now some limitations on Parliament's sovereignty, but all these limits have been self-imposed by previous Parliaments. The main limitations are through:

- membership of the European Union
- the effect of the Human Rights Act 1998.

Membership of the European Union

The United Kingdom joined the European Union in 1973. In order to become a member, Parliament passed the European Communities Act 1972. Although, as Parliament passed that Act, it is theoretically possible for a later Parliament to pass an Act withdrawing from the European Union, political reality means that this is very unlikely. Membership of the EU affects so much of our law and political system.

Membership of the EU means that EU laws take priority over English law even where the English law was passed after the relevant EU law. This was shown by the Merchant Shipping Act 1988, which set down rules for who could own or manage fishing boats registered in Britain. The Act stated that 75 per cent of directors and shareholders had to be British. The European Court of Justice ruled that this was contrary to European Union law, under which citizens of all Member States can work in other Member States. The Merchant Shipping Act 1988 could not be effective so far as other EU citizens were concerned.

Human Rights Act 1998

This states that all Acts of Parliament have to be compatible with the European Convention on Human Rights. It is possible to challenge an Act on the ground that it does not comply with the Convention. Under s 4 of the Human Rights Act, the courts have the power to declare an Act incompatible with the Convention.

The first declaration of incompatibility was in *H v Mental Health Review Tribunal* (2001), where a patient was making an application to be released. The Mental Health Act 1983 placed the burden of proof on the patient to show that he should be released. Human rights meant that it should be up to the state to justify the continuing detention of such a patient. The court made a declaration that the law was not compatible with human rights. Following this declaration of incompatibility, the government changed the law.

However, a declaration of incompatibility does not mean that the government has to change the law. Also, if Parliament wishes it can pass a new Act which contravenes the European Convention on Human Rights.

EXAMINATION QUESTIONS

Read the source material below and answer parts 1(a) to 1(c) which follow.

EXERCISE ON LEGISLATION AND DELEGATED LEGISLATION

Source A

Delegated legislation is made by some persons or body other than Parliament but under the authority of Parliament. This authority is given through an enabling Act. An enabling Act is created by Parliament through its normal processes, an example being the Police and Criminal Evidence Act 1984. This Act will have been accepted by both Houses and received Royal Assent. By conferring powers on others it allows Parliament to utilise expert advice, but Parliament must be careful when it creates an enabling Act because this sets out the limits of power.

Source B

STATUTORY INSTRUMENT (SI)

1991 No. 2687

Police and Criminal Evidence Act 1984

(Tape-recording of interviews) (No. 1) Order 1991

Made	29th November 1991
Laid before Parliament	6th December 1991
Coming into force	1st January 1992

Now, therefore, in pursuance of the said section 60(1)(b), the Secretary of State hereby orders as follows:

2 This Order shall apply to interviews of persons suspected of the commission of indictable offences (serious offences e.g. murder) which are held by police officers at police stations in the police areas specified in the Schedule to this Order and which commence after midnight on 31st December 1991.

3(1) Subject to paragraph (2) below, interviews to which this Order applies shall be tape-recorded in accordance with the requirement of the code of practice on tape-recording which came into operation on 29th July 1988 ...

3(2) The duty to tape-record interviews under paragraph (10) above shall not apply to interviews – (a) where the offence of which a person is suspected is one in respect of which he has been arrested or detained under section 14(1)(a) of the Prevention of Terrorism (Temporary Provisions) Act 1989.

Answer all parts.

1. (a) Describe how an Act of Parliament is made with reference to Source A and your knowledge of legislation. [15 marks]

   (b) Each of the following interviews was conducted by police officers and took place in a police station covered by Statutory Instrument 1991/2687 (Source B), but none of the interviews was tape-recorded. Explain the lawfulness of each of the following interviews:

   (i) On 1 November 1991 Gemma was arrested for a summary offence (not serious) and was interviewed. [5 marks]

   (ii) Carl was suspected of an indictable offence (serious) and was interviewed on 1 November 2000. [5 marks]

   (iii) Hank was detained under section 14(1)(a) of the Prevention of Terrorism (Temporary Provisions) Act 1989 and was interviewed in March 2000. [5 marks]

   (c) With reference to Sources A and B and using your knowledge of delegated legislation:

   (i) Describe the three different types of delegated legislation. [15 marks]

   (ii) Discuss the advantages and disadvantages of delegated legislation. [15 marks]

   G151, June 2011, OCR

NOTE that you will not be able to answer parts (c)(i) and (c)(ii) until you have read Chapter 5.

EXTENSION ESSAY

Analyse the extent to which Parliament is supreme.

DELEGATED LEGISLATION

INTRODUCTION

Delegated legislation is law made by some person or body other than Parliament, but with the authority of Parliament. That authority is usually laid down in a 'parent' Act of Parliament known as an enabling Act which creates the framework of the law and then delegates power to others to make more detailed law in the area. An example of enabling Acts include the Police and Criminal Evidence Act 1984, which gives powers to make Codes of Practice for the use of police powers. Another example is the Criminal Justice Act 2003 which gives the Secretary of State the power to make delegated legislation in several areas. One of these powers enables a code of practice to be created for the use of conditional cautions. A conditional caution is used instead of taking an offender to court.

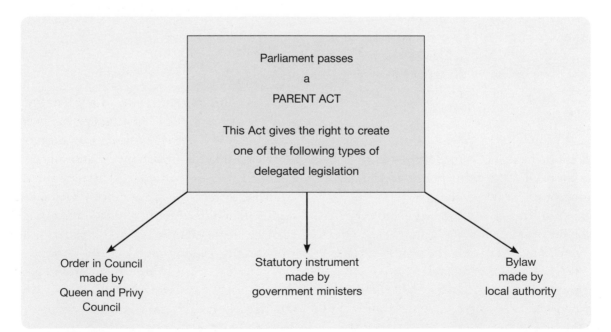

Figure 5.1 *Different types of delegated legislation*

5.1 Types of delegated legislation

There are three different types of delegated legislation. These are:

- Orders in Council
- statutory instruments
- bylaws.

5.1.1 Orders in Council

The Queen and the Privy Council have the authority to make Orders in Council. The Privy Council is made up of the prime minister and other leading members of the government. So this type of delegated legislation effectively allows the government to make legislation without going through Parliament.

Orders in Council can be made on a wide range of matters, especially:

- giving legal effect to European Directives
- transferring responsibility between government departments; e.g. when the Ministry of Justice was created, the powers of the previous Department of Constitutional Affairs and some of the powers of the Home Office were transferred to this new ministry
- bringing Acts (or parts of Acts) of Parliament into force.

In addition, the Privy Council has power to make law in emergency situations under the Civil Contingencies Act 2004.

Orders in Council can also be used to make other types of law. For example, in 2003 an Order in Council was used to alter the Misuse of Drugs Act 1971 so as to make cannabis a Class C drug. Five years later, the government decided that it had been a mistake to downgrade cannabis and another Order in Council was issued changing cannabis back to a Class B drug (see Figure 5.2).

There must be an enabling Act allowing the Privy Council to make Orders in Council on the particular topic. For the change of category of cannabis, the enabling Act was the Misuse of Drugs Act 1971.

Another enabling Act giving the power to make Orders in Council is the Constitutional Reform Act 2005. This allows the Privy Council to alter the number of judges in the Supreme Court.

Internet research   www

Look up recent Orders in Council on the Privy Council website at **www.privy-council. org.uk**.

On the Home page click on Privy Council, then click on Privy Council Meetings. You should now see a series of dates on which meetings took place. Click on any of these dates and you should see a list of Orders made at that meeting.

Look to see which enabling Acts have allowed the orders to be made. The enabling Act is usually given on the left-hand side of the list of orders.

5.1.2 Statutory instruments

The term 'statutory instruments' refers to rules and regulations made by government ministers. Ministers and government departments are given authority to make regulations for areas under their particular responsibility. There are about 15 departments in the government. Each one deals with a different area of policy and can make rules and regulations in respect of matters it deals with. So the Minister for Work and Pensions will be able to make regulations on work-related matters, such as health and safety at work, while the Minister for Transport is able to deal with necessary road traffic regulations.

Statutory instruments can be very short, covering one point, such as making the annual change to the minimum wage. However, other

2008 No. 3130
DANGEROUS DRUGS
The Misuse of Drugs Act 1971 (Amendment) Order 2008

Made	*10th December 2008*
Coming into force	*26th January 2009*

At the Court at Buckingham Palace, the 10th day of December 2008

Present,

The Queen's Most Excellent Majesty in Council

In accordance with section 2(5) of the Misuse of Drugs Act 1971(1) a draft of this Order has been laid before Parliament after consultation with the Advisory Council on the Misuse of Drugs and approved by a resolution of each House of Parliament.

Accordingly, Her Majesty, in exercise of the powers conferred upon Her by sections 2(2) and 2(4) of that Act, is pleased, by and with the advice of Her Privy Council, to order as follows:

Citation, commencement and revocation

1.—(1) This Order may be cited as the Misuse of Drugs Act 1971 (Amendment) Order 2008 and shall come into force on 26th January 2009.

(2) The Misuse of Drugs Act 1971 (Modification) (No. 2) Order 2003(2) is revoked.

Amendments to the Misuse of Drugs Act 1971

2.—(1) Schedule 2 to the Misuse of Drugs Act 1971 (which specifies the drugs which are subject to control under that Act) is amended as follows.

(2) In Part 2 (Class B drugs)—
    (a) in paragraph 1(a), after, Amphetamine' insert—
    'Cannabinol
    Cannabinol derivative
    Cannabis and cannabis resin';
    (b) after paragraph 2 insert—

'2A. Any ester or ether of cannabinol or of a cannabinol derivative.'; and
    (c) in paragraph 3, for 'or 2' substitute ' 2 or 2A'.

(3) In Part 3 (Class C drugs) the following words are repealed —
    (a) in paragraph 1(a), 'Cannabinol', "Cannabinol derivatives' and 'Cannabis and cannabis resin'; and
    (b) in paragraph 1(d), 'or of cannabinol or a cannabinol derivative'.

Judith Simpson
Clerk of the Privy Council

Figure 5.2 *Example of an Order in Council*

statutory instruments may be very long with detailed regulations which were too complex to include in an Act of Parliament.

Examples of statutory instruments which include a lot of detail are:

- Chemicals (Hazard Information and Packaging for Supply) Regulations 2009.
  This statutory instrument was made by the Minister for Work and Pensions under powers given in the European Communities Act 1972 and the Health and Safety at Work etc. Act 1974.
- Police codes of practice in relation to such powers as stop and search, arrest and detention. These were made by the Minister for Justice under powers in the Police and Criminal Evidence Act 1984.

The use of statutory instruments is a major method of law-making as there are over 3,000 statutory instruments brought into force each year.

The Legislative and Regulatory Reform Act 2006

In addition to specific Acts giving ministers powers to make statutory instruments, the Legislative and Regulatory Reform Act 2006 gives ministers power to make *any* provision by order if it will remove or reduce a 'burden' resulting from legislation. For this purpose a burden is defined as:

- a financial cost
- an administrative inconvenience
- an obstacle to efficiency, productivity or profitability
- a sanction which affects the carrying on of any lawful activity.

This means that ministers can change Acts of Parliament, even though the original Act did not give them the power to do this. However, when the Legislative and Regulatory Reform Act was being discussed, the government gave a clear undertaking that orders made under the

Act would 'not be used to implement highly controversial reforms'.

5.1.3 Bylaws

These can be made by local authorities to cover matters within their own area. For example, Norfolk County Council can pass laws affecting the whole county, while a district or town council can only make bylaws for its district or town. Many local bylaws will involve traffic control, such as parking restrictions. Other bylaws may be for such matters as banning drinking in public places or banning people from riding bicycles in local parks.

Bylaws can also be made by public corporations and certain companies for matters within their jurisdiction which involve the public. This means that bodies such as the British Airports Authority and the railways can enforce rules about public behaviour on their premises.

An example of a bylaw is banning drinking in certain areas

5.2 The need for delegated legislation

1. Parliament does not have time to consider and debate every small detail of complex regulations.

2. In addition Parliament may not have the necessary technical expertise or knowledge required; for example, health and safety regulations in different industries need expert knowledge, while local parking regulations need local knowledge. Modern society has become very complicated and technical, so that it is impossible for members of Parliament to have all the knowledge needed to draw up laws on controlling technology, ensuring environmental safety, dealing with a vast array of different industrial problems or operating complex taxation schemes. It is thought that it is better for Parliament to debate the main principles thoroughly, but leave the detail to be filled in by those who have expert knowledge of it.

3. Ministers can have the benefit of further consultation before regulations are drawn up. Consultation is particularly important for rules on technical matters, where it is necessary to make sure that the regulations are technically accurate and workable. In fact, some Acts giving the power to make delegated legislation set out that there must be consultation before the regulations are created. For example, before any new or revised police Code of Practice under the Police and Criminal Evidence Act 1984 is issued, there must be consultation with a wide range of people including:
   - persons representing the interests of police authorities
   - the General Council of the Bar
   - the Law Society.

4. As already seen, the process of passing an Act of Parliament can take a considerable time and in an emergency, Parliament may not be able to pass law quickly enough. This is another reason why delegated legislation is sometimes preferred. It can also be amended or revoked easily when necessary, so that the law can be kept up to date, and ministers can respond to new or unforeseen situations by amending or amplifying statutory instruments.

5.3 Control of delegated legislation

As delegated legislation in many instances is made by non-elected bodies and since there are so many people with the power to make delegated legislation, it is important that there should be some control over this. Control is exercised by Parliament and by the courts. In addition there may sometimes be a public inquiry before a law is passed on an especially sensitive matter, such as planning laws which may affect the environment.

5.3.1 Control by Parliament

This is fairly limited, though obviously Parliament has the initial control with the enabling Act which sets the boundaries within which the delegated legislation is to be made. For example, the Act will state which government minister can make the regulations. It will also state the type of laws to be made and whether they can be made for the whole country or only for certain places. The Act can also set out whether the government department must consult other people before making the regulations.

Parliament also retains control over the delegated legislation as it can repeal the powers in the enabling Act at any time. If it does this then the right to make regulations will cease.

ACTIVITY

Look at the following two sources and answer the questions which follow on the next page.

SOURCE A

2009 No. 606

Health And Safety

The Health and Safety Information for Employees (Amendment) Regulations 2009

Made	*10th March 2009*
Laid before Parliament	*16th March 2009*
Coming into force	*6th April 2009*

The Secretary of State, in exercise of the powers conferred by sections 15(1), (2), (3)(a), (4) and (9) of, and paragraph 15(1) of Schedule 3 to, the Health and Safety at Work etc. Act 1974 ('the 1974 Act'), and for the purpose of giving effect without modifications to proposals submitted to him by the Health and Safety Executive under section 11(3) of the 1974 Act after the carrying out by the said Executive of consultation in accordance with section 50(3) of that Act, hereby makes the following Regulations:

Citation, commencement and interpretation

1. (1) These Regulations may be cited as the Health and Safety Information for Employees (Amendment) Regulations 2009 and shall come into force on 6th April 2009.
   (2) In these Regulations 'the 1989 Regulations' means the Health and Safety Information for Employees Regulations 1989.

Amendment of the 1989 Regulations

2. (1) The 1989 Regulations are amended as follows.
   (2) In regulation 3(3) for 'nine months' substitute 'five years'.
   (3) After regulation 5(1)(b) insert the following—
   '; or (c) information as to how any of his employees may obtain the information referred to in (a) and (b) above.'.

(4) After regulation 5(3)(b) insert the following—
'; or (c) information as to how any of his employees may obtain the information referred to in (a) and (b) above.'.

Extension outside Great Britain

3. These Regulations shall apply to and in relation to premises and activities outside Great Britain to the same extent as provided for in regulation 2(5) of the 1989 Regulations.

Jonathan Shaw

Parliamentary Under Secretary of State

Department for Work and Pensions

10th March 2009

SOURCE B

Alcohol-free zones in Knowsley

Alcohol-free zones are being set up in Knowsley to tackle crime and anti-social behaviour caused by binge drinking. The Safer Knowsley Partnership, which includes Merseyside Police and Knowsley Council, is taking the measure after successfully securing the borough's first Designated Public Place Orders back in 2008.

The orders have been approved in Wignall Park, Court Hey Park, Stadtmoers, Millennium Green and Henley Park, and will come into force on 16th July 2009. The orders will make it an offence for anyone to drink alcohol after being required by a police officer not to do so.

Police have the power to confiscate and dispose of alcohol and it is an arrestable offence to fail to cooperate, without reasonable excuse, with a police officer's request. The ban does not affect drinking in any licensed premises.

Reducing crime and disorder

Knowsley Council's Licensing Committee approved the orders on 25th June 2009. This is part of the Safer Knowsley Partnership's ongoing commitment to reduce alcohol-related crime and disorder and anti-social behaviour.

Taken from Mersey Police website July 2009

Delegated Powers Scrutiny Committee

A Delegated Powers Scrutiny Committee was established in 1993 in the House of Lords to consider whether the provisions of any Bills delegated legislative power inappropriately. It reports its findings to the House of Lords before the Committee stage of the Bill, but has no power to amend Bills. The main problem is that there is no general provision that the regulations made under the enabling Act have to be laid before Parliament for the MPs to consider them. However, a few enabling Acts will say that this has to happen.

Affirmative resolutions

A small number of statutory instruments will be subject to an affirmative resolution. This means that the statutory instrument will not become law unless specifically approved by Parliament. The need for an affirmative resolution will be included in the enabling Act. For example an affirmative resolution is required before new or revised police Codes of Practice under the Police and Criminal Evidence Act 1984 can come into force. One of the disadvantages of this procedure is that Parliament cannot amend the statutory instrument; it can only be approved, annulled or withdrawn.

Negative resolutions

Most other statutory instruments will be subject to a negative resolution, which means that the relevant statutory instrument will be law unless rejected by Parliament within 40 days. Individual ministers may also be questioned by MPs in Parliament on the work of their departments, and this can include questions about proposed regulations.

Scrutiny committee

A more effective check is the existence of a Joint Select Committee on Statutory Instruments (formed in 1973), usually called the Scrutiny Committee. This committee reviews all statutory instruments and, where necessary, will draw the attention of both Houses of Parliament to points that need further consideration. However, the review is a technical one and not based on policy. The main grounds for referring a statutory instrument back to the Houses of Parliament are that:

- It imposes a tax or charge – this is because only an elected body has such a right.
- It appears to have retrospective effect which was not provided for by the enabling Act.
- It appears to have gone beyond the powers given under the enabling legislation or it makes some unusual or unexpected use of those powers.
- It is unclear or defective in some way.

The Scrutiny Committee can only report back its findings; it has no power to alter any statutory instrument.

5.3.2 The Legislative and Regulatory Reform Act 2006

This Act sets out procedure for the making of statutory instruments which are aimed at repealing an existing law in order to remove a 'burden' (see section 5.1.2). Under s 13 of the Act, the minister making the statutory instrument must consult various people and organisations. These include:

- organisations which are representative of interests substantially affected by the proposals
- the Welsh Assembly in relation to matters upon which the Assembly exercises functions
- the Law Commission, where appropriate.

Orders made under this power of this Act must be laid before Parliament. There are three possible procedures:

1. Negative resolution procedure:
   where the minister recommends that this procedure should be used, it will be used unless within 30 days one of the Houses of Parliament objects to this.
2. Affirmative resolution procedure:
   this requires both Houses of Parliament to approve the order: even though the minister has recommended this procedure, Parliament can still require the super-affirmative resolution procedure to be used.
3. Super-affirmative resolution procedure:
   Under this the minister must have regard to:
   - any representations
   - any resolution of either House of Parliament
   - any recommendations by a committee of either House of Parliament who are asked to report on the draft order.

This super-affirmative resolution procedure gives Parliament more control over delegated legislation made under the Legislative and Regulatory Reform Act 2006. It is important that this is the position, as the Act gives ministers very wide powers to amend Acts of Parliament.

5.3.3 Control by the courts

Delegated legislation can be challenged in the courts on the ground that it is *ultra vires*, i.e. it goes beyond the powers that Parliament granted in the enabling Act. This questioning of the validity of delegated legislation may be made through the judicial review procedure (see Chapter 16), or it may arise in a civil claim between two parties, or on appeal (especially case-stated appeals).

Any delegated legislation which is ruled to be *ultra vires* is void and not effective. This was illustrated by *R v Home Secretary, ex parte Fire Brigades Union* (1995) where changes made by the Home Secretary to the Criminal Injuries Compensation scheme were held to have gone beyond the power given to him in the Criminal Justice Act 1988.

The courts will presume that unless an enabling Act expressly allows it, there is no power to do any of the following:

- Make unreasonable regulations – in *Strickland v Hayes Borough Council* (1896) a bylaw prohibiting the singing or reciting of any obscene song or ballad and the use of obscene language generally, was held to be unreasonable and so *ultra vires*, because it was too widely drawn in that it covered acts done in private as well as those in public
- Levy taxes
- Allow sub-delegation.

It is also possible for the courts to hold that delegated legislation is *ultra vires* because the correct procedure has not been followed. For example in the *Aylesbury Mushroom* case (1972) the Minister of Labour had to consult 'any organisation . . . appearing to him to be representative of substantial numbers of employers engaging in the activity concerned'. His failure to consult the Mushroom Growers' Association, which represented about 85 per cent of all mushroom growers, meant that his order establishing a training board was invalid as against mushroom growers, though it was valid in relation to others affected by the order, such as farmers, as the minister had consulted with the National Farmers' Union.

In *R v Secretary of State for Education and Employment, ex parte National Union of Teachers* (2000) a High Court Judge ruled that a statutory instrument setting conditions for appraisal and access to higher rates of pay for teachers was beyond the powers given under the Education Act 1996. In addition, the procedure used was unfair as only four days had been allowed for consultation.

Statutory instruments can also be declared void if they conflict with European Union legislation.

5.4 Criticisms of the use of delegated legislation

1. The main criticism is that it takes law-making away from the democratically elected House of Commons and allows non-elected people to make law. This is acceptable provided there is sufficient control, but, as already seen, Parliament's control is fairly limited. This criticism cannot be made of bylaws made by local authorities since these are elected by local citizens.

2. Another problem is that of sub-delegation, which means that the law-making authority is handed down another level. This causes comments that much of our law is made by civil servants and merely 'rubber-stamped' by the minister of that department.

3. The large volume of delegated legislation also gives rise to criticism since it makes it difficult to discover what the present law is. This problem is aggravated by a lack of publicity, as much delegated legislation is made in private in contrast to the public debates of Parliament.

4. Finally, delegated legislation shares with Acts of Parliament the same problem of obscure wording that can lead to difficulty in understanding the law. This difficulty of how to understand or interpret the law is dealt with in Chapter 7.

Key Facts
Definition
• Law made by bodies other than Parliament, but with the authority of Parliament
Types of delegated legislation

• Orders in Council
  – Made by Crown and Privy Council
• Statutory instruments
  – Made by government ministers
• Bylaws
  – Made by local authorities and public corporations

Reasons for delegated legislation
• Knowledge and expertise • Saving of Parliamentary time • More flexible than Acts of Parliament
Control over delegated legislation

• By Parliament
  – Affirmative/negative resolutions
  – Scrutiny Committee
• By the courts
  – Judicial review
  – Doctrine of *ultra vires*

Disadvantages of delegated legislation
• Undemocratic • Risk of sub-delegation • Large volume • Lack of publicity

Figure 5.3 *Key facts chart for delegated legislation*

EXAMINATION QUESTIONS

Read the source material below and answer parts (a) to (c) which follow.

EXERCISE ON DELEGATED LEGISLATION AND LAW REFORM

Source A

The Legislative and Regulatory Reform Act (2006) sets out the procedure for the making of statutory instruments which are aimed at repealing an existing law. Under s 13 of the Act, the minister making the statutory instrument must consult various people and organisations. These include:

- organisations which are the representative of interests substantially affected by the proposals
- the law commission (a law reform body whose function is to keep the law under review).

Orders made under this power of this Act must be laid before Parliament. There are three possible procedures:

- negative resolution procedure
- affirmative resolution procedure
- super-affirmative resolution procedure.

Source B

Delegated legislation can be challenged through the courts. The questioning of the validity of delegated legislation may be made through the judicial review procedure, or it may arise in a civil claim between two parties, or on appeal.

> Adapted from: J Martin *The English Legal System*,
> 5th edition, 2007, Hodder Education.

(a) Source A refers to the Law Commission. Describe the role of the Law Commission [15 marks]

(b) Explain in the following situations if there would be a successful judicial review.

   (i) A government minister wishes to repeal an old law. He has not consulted relevant bodies, which are affected by the proposals, before introducing new regulations. [5 marks]

   (ii) A government minister is given power to make regulations concerning legal funding. He has now introduced a regulation on immigration. [5 marks]

   (iii) A government minister has made regulations which are argued to be unreasonable. [5 marks]

(c) (i) Source A refers to statutory instruments. Describe statutory instruments and two other types of delegated legislation, using the source and other examples. [15 marks]

   (ii) Source A and Source B refer to a number of controls. Discuss the effectiveness of Parliamentary and judicial controls over delegated legislation. [15 marks]

> G152, January 2009, OCR

NB You will not be able to answer part (a) until you have studied law reform (see Chapter 8).

EXTENSION ESSAY

'Delegated legislation gives too much power to unelected bodies to make law.' Discuss.

CHAPTER 6

EUROPEAN LAW

INTRODUCTION

On 1 January 1973 the United Kingdom joined what was then the European Economic Community, and another source of law came into being: European law. Since then it has had increasing significance as a source of law. The European Economic Community was originally set up by Germany, France, Italy, Belgium, the Netherlands and Luxembourg in 1957 by the Treaty of Rome. The name 'European Union' was introduced by the Treaty of European Union in 1993. Denmark and Ireland joined at the same time as the United Kingdom. In the 1980s and 1990s Greece, Spain, Portugal, Austria, Finland and Sweden joined. Then on 1 May 2004 another ten countries joined the EU. These were Cyprus, Czech Republic, Estonia, Hungary, Latvia, Lithuania, Malta, Poland, Slovak Republic and Slovenia. The most recent members are Bulgaria and Romania who joined on 1 January 2007. There are now 27 Member States (see Figure 6.1).

In 2009 the Treaty of Lisbon restructured the European Union. There are now two treaties setting out its rules. These are the:

● Treaty of European Union (TEU)
● Treaty of the Functioning of the European Union (TFEU).

6.1 The institutions of the European Union

The European Union has a vast and complex organisation with institutions established originally by the Treaty of Rome. The main institutions which exercise the functions of the Union are:

● The Council of the European Union
● The Commission
● The European Parliament
● The European Court of Justice.

In addition there are a number of ancillary bodies, the most important of which is the Economic and Social Committee.

6.1.1 The Council of Ministers

The government of each nation in the Union sends a representative to the Council. The Foreign Minister is usually a country's main representative, but a government is free to send any of its ministers to Council meetings. This means that usually the minister responsible for the topic under consideration will attend the meetings of the Council, so that the precise membership will vary with the subject being discussed. For example, the Minister for Agriculture will attend when the issue to be discussed involves agriculture. Twice a year government heads meet in the European Council or 'Summit' to discuss broad matters of policy.

Date	Countries joining	Comment
1957	Belgium France Germany Italy Luxembourg The Netherlands	These are the founder members Treaty of Rome signed
1973	Denmark Ireland United Kingdom	UK passes the European Communities Act 1972 on joining
1981	Greece	
1986	Portugal Spain	
1995	Austria Finland Sweden	
2004	Cyprus, Czech Republic, Estonia, Hungary, Latvia, Lithuania, Malta, Poland, Slovak Republic and Slovenia	
2007	Bulgaria Romania	

Figure 6.1 *Chart showing the Member States of the European Union*

The Member States take it in turn to provide the President of the Council, each for a six-month period. To assist with the day-to-day work of the Council there is a committee of permanent representatives known as Coreper.

The Council is the principal decision-making body of the Union. Voting in the Council is on a weighted basis with each country having a number of votes roughly in proportion to the size of its population.

6.1.2 The Commission

This consists of 27 Commissioners who are supposed to act independently of their national origin. Each Member State has one Commissioner.

The Commissioners are appointed for a five-year term and can only be removed during this term of office by a vote of censure by the European Parliament. Each Commissioner heads a department with special responsibility for one area of Union policy, such as economic affairs, agriculture or the environment.

The Commission as a whole has several functions as follows:

- It is the motive power behind Union policy as it proposes policies and presents drafts of legislation to the Council for the Council's consideration. In its own booklet on Union law, the European Union says the relationship between the Commission and the Council can be briefly summarised by saying 'the Commission proposes and the Council disposes'
- The Commission is also the 'guardian' of the treaties. It ensures that treaty provisions and other measures adopted by the Union are properly implemented. If a Member State has failed to implement Union law within its own country, or has infringed a Provision in some

Figure 6.2 *Map showing countries of the European Union*

way, the Commission has a duty to intervene and, if necessary, refer the matter to the European Court of Justice. The Commission has performed this duty very effectively, and as a result there have been judgments given by the Court against Britain and other Member States

- It is responsible for the administration of the Union and has executive powers to implement the Union's budget.

Internet research **www**

Use the Internet to find out more about the European Commission. Find out who is the Commissioner for the United Kingdom. Try **http://europa.eu**.

6.1.3 The Assembly

Parliament's main function is to discuss proposals put forward by the Commission, but it has no

direct law-making authority. The members of the European Parliament are directly elected by the people of the Member States in elections which take place once every five years. Within the Parliament the members do not operate in national groups, but form political groups with those of the same political allegiance. The Assembly meets on average about once a month for sessions that can last up to a week. It has standing committees which discuss proposals made by the Commission and then report to the full Parliament for debate. Decisions made by the Parliament are not binding, though they will influence the Council of Ministers.

The main criticism is that the Parliament has no real power. However, the assent of Parliament is required to any international agreements the Union wishes to enter into. This allows it an important role in deciding whether new members should be admitted to the Union. It also has some power over the Union budget, especially in non-compulsory expenditure, where it has the final decision on whether to approve the budget or not.

6.1.4 Economic and Social Committee

This advises the Council and the Commission on economic matters. It is made up of representatives of influential interest groups such as manufacturers, farmers, employees and businesses. It must be consulted on proposed Union measures and although its role is purely consultative, it does exert strong influence on the Union's decision-making process.

6.2 The European Court of Justice

Its function is set out in Article 19 TEU. This states that the Court must 'ensure that in the interpretation and application of the Treaty the law is observed'. The court sits in Luxembourg and has 27 judges, one from each Member State. For a full court 11 judges will sit, but it also sits in

Inside the Assembly of the European Parliament

chambers of five judges or three judges. Judges are appointed under Article 253 (TFEU) from those who are eligible for appointment to the highest judicial posts in their own country or who are leading academic lawyers. Each judge is appointed for a term of six years, and can be reappointed for a further term of six years. The judges select one of themselves to be President of the Court.

The Court is assisted by nine Advocates General who also hold office for six years. Each case is assigned to an Advocate General whose task under Article 253 is to research all the legal points involved and 'to present publicly, with complete impartiality and independence, reasoned conclusions on cases submitted to the Court of Justice with a view to assisting the latter in the performance of its duties'.

6.2.1 Key functions

The court's task is to ensure that the law is applied uniformly in all Member States (see Figure 6.3) and it does this by performing two key functions.

The first is that it hears cases to decide whether Member States have failed to fulfil obligations under the Treaties. Such actions are usually initiated by the European Commission, although they can also be started by another Member State. An early example of such a case was *Re Tachographs: The Commission v United Kingdom* (1979) in which the court held that the United Kingdom had to implement a Council Regulation on the use of mechanical recording equipment (tachographs) in road vehicles used for the carriage of goods (see section 6.3.2 for further information on the effect of Regulations).

6.2.2 Preliminary rulings

The second key function is that it hears references from national courts for preliminary rulings on points of European law. This function is a very important one since rulings made by the European Court of Justice are then binding on courts in all Member States. This ensures that the law is indeed uniform throughout the European Union.

Article 267

A request for a preliminary ruling is made under Article 267 (TFEU). This says that:

'the Court of Justice shall have jurisdiction to give preliminary rulings concerning:

(a) the interpretation of treaties;

(b) the validity and interpretation of acts of the institutions of the Union;

(c) the interpretation of the statutes of bodies established by an act of the Council, where those statutes so provide.'

Article 267 goes on to state that where there is no appeal from the national court within the national system, then such a court *must* refer points of European Law to the European Court of Justice. Other national courts are allowed to make an Article 267 reference, but as there is still an appeal available within their own system, such courts do not have to do so. They have a discretion (i.e. they can choose whether or not to refer the case).

Applied to the court structure in England and Wales, this means that the Supreme Court must refer questions of European law, since it is the highest appeal court in our system. However, the Court of Appeal does not have to refer questions. It has a choice: it may refer if it wishes or it may decide the case without any referral. The same is true of all the lower courts in the English court hierarchy.

However, even courts at the bottom of the hierarchy can refer questions of law under Article 267, if they feel that a preliminary ruling is necessary to enable a judgment to be given. An example of this was in *Torfaen Borough Council v B & Q* (1990) when Cwmbran Magistrates' Court made a reference on whether the restrictions which then existed on Sunday trading were in breach of the Treaty of Rome.

Whenever a reference is made the European Court of Justice only makes a preliminary ruling on the point of law; it does not actually decide the case. The case then returns to the original court for it to apply the ruling to the facts in the case.

6.2.3 Discretionary referrals

In *Bulmer v Bollinger* (1974) the Court of Appeal set out the approach to be used when deciding

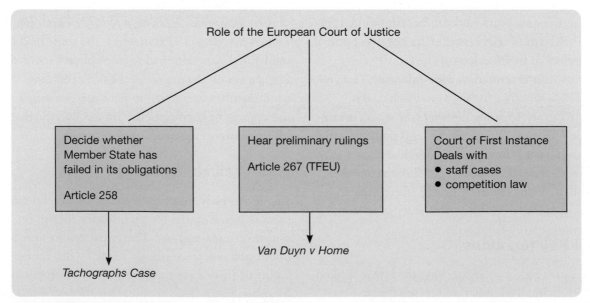

Figure 6.3 *Role of the European Court of Justice*

whether a discretionary referral should be made to the European Court of Justice. The guidelines are as follows:

- Guidance on the point of law must be necessary to come to a decision in the case.
- There is no need to refer a question which has already been decided by the European Court of Justice in a previous case.
- There is no need to refer a point which is reasonably clear and free from doubt; this is known as the '*acte clair*' doctrine.
- The court must consider all the circumstances of the case.
- The English court retains the discretion on whether to refer or not.

The first case to be referred to the European Court of Justice by an English court was *Van Duyn v Home Office* (1974).

6.2.4 Court of First Instance

Since 1988 there has also existed a Court of First Instance which was created to relieve the European Court of Justice of some of its heavy workload. This court hears staff cases, i.e. disputes between the European institutions and their employees. It also hears complex economic cases in the field of competition law, 'anti-dumping' law and under the European Coal and Steel Community Treaty. The Court of First Instance has 12 judges and operates with panels of six, four or three judges.

6.2.5 The operation of the European Court of Justice

When compared with English courts there are several major differences in the way the European Court of Justice operates. First the emphasis is on presenting cases 'on paper'. Lawyers are required to

Key Facts

Council of Ministers
- Consists of ministers from each Member State
- Responsible for broad policy decisions
- Under Article 288 (TFEU) can issue regulations, directives and decisions

Commission
- 27 Commissioners whose duty it is to act in Union's interest
- Proposes legislation
- Tries to ensure the implementation of the Treaties and can bring court action against Member States who do not comply with EU law

Economic and Social Committee
- Non-elected consultative body to represent such groups as employers, employees, consumer associations, etc.

Assembly or European Parliament
- Members voted for by electorate in each of the Member States
- Consultative body, has limited powers

European Court of Justice
- Judges from each Member State, assisted by Advocates-General
- Rules on European law when cases are referred under Article 267 (TFEU)

Figure 6.4 *Key facts chart on the institutions of the European Union*

present their arguments in a written form and there is far less reliance on oral presentation of a case. This requirement is, of course, partly because of the wide range of languages involved, though French is the traditional language of the Court. It also represents the traditional method of case presentation in other European countries. An interesting point to note is that the English system in some areas is now beginning to use this 'paper' submission.

A second major difference is the use of the Advocate General. This independent lawyer is not used in the English system. However in the European Court of Justice the Advocate General who was assigned to the case will present his findings on the law after the parties have made their submissions. The court, therefore, has the advantage of having all aspects of the law presented to them.

The deliberations of the judges are secret and where necessary the decision will be made by a majority vote. However, when the judgment is delivered, again in a written form, it is signed by all the judges who formed part of the panel, so that it is not known if any judges disagreed with the majority. This contrasts strongly with the English system, whereby a dissenting judge not only makes it known that he disagrees with the majority, but also usually delivers a judgment explaining his reasoning.

The other points to be noted are that the European Court of Justice is not bound by its own previous decisions and that it prefers the purposive approach to interpretation (see section 7.9 for an explanation of the purposive approach).

The court has wide rights to study extrinsic material when deciding the meaning of provisions and may study preparatory documents. The European Court of Justice is important, not only because its decisions are binding on English courts, but also because its attitude to interpretation is increasingly being followed by English courts. The European Court of Justice pointed this out in

von Colson v Land Nordrhein-Westfalen (1984) when it said:

'national courts are required to interpret their national law in the light of the wording and the purpose of the directive'.

6.3 European sources of law

These are classed as primary and secondary sources of law. Primary sources are mainly the Treaties, the most important of which was originally the Treaty of Rome itself and now is the Treaty of the European Union. Secondary sources are legislation passed by the institutions of the Union under Article 288 (TFEU). This secondary legislation is of three types: regulations, directives and decisions, all of which are considered below.

6.3.1 Treaties

So far as our law is concerned all treaties signed by our head of government become part of English law automatically. This is as a result of the European Communities Act 1972, s 2(1) which states that:

'All such rights, powers, liabilities, obligations and restrictions from time to time created or arising by or under the Treaties and all such remedies and procedures from time to time provided for by or under the Treaties, as in accordance with the Treaties are without further enactment to be given legal effect or used in the United Kingdom, shall be recognised and available in law and be enforced, allowed and followed accordingly.'

This not only makes Community law part of our law but also allows individuals to rely on it. In the case of *Van Duyn v Home Office* (1974) the European Court of Justice held that an individual was entitled to rely on Article 45 giving the right of freedom of movement. The Article had direct effect and conferred rights on individuals which could be enforced not only in the European Court of Justice, but also in national courts.

This means that citizens of the United Kingdom are entitled to rely on the rights in the Treaty of Rome and other treaties, even though those rights may not have been specifically enacted in English law. This is clearly illustrated by the case of *Macarthys Ltd v Smith* (1980). In this case Wendy Smith's employers paid her less than her male predecessor for exactly the same job. As the two people were not employed at the same time by the employer there was no breach of English domestic law. However, Wendy Smith was able to claim that the company which employed her was in breach of Article 157 (TFEU) over equal pay for men and women and this claim was confirmed by the European Court of Justice.

The growing influence of European law is shown in that British courts are now prepared to apply European Treaty law directly rather than wait for the European Court of Justice to make a ruling on the point. This is illustrated in *Diocese of Hallam Trustee v Connaughton* (1996). In this case the Employment Appeal Tribunal had to consider facts which had some similarity to the Wendy Smith case; Josephine Connaughton was employed as director of music by the Diocese of Hallam from 1990 to September 1994, at which time her salary was £11,138. When she left the position, the post was advertised at a salary of £13,434, but the successful applicant, a man, was actually appointed at a salary of £20,000. In other words, where in Wendy Smith's case she had discovered that her male predecessor was paid more than she was, in the *Connaughton* case it was the immediate successor who was receiving considerably higher pay.

The Employment Appeal Tribunal considered Article 157 (TFEU) of the Treaty of Rome and decided as a preliminary point that its provisions were wide enough to allow Miss Connaughton to make a claim, saying;

'We are sufficiently satisfied as to the scope of Article 141 so as to decide this appeal without further reference to the European Court of Justice.'

Similarly the House of Lords in *R v Secretary of State ex parte EOC* (1994) decided, without referring the case to the European Court of Justice, that the longer period of qualification for redundancy for those working less than 16 hours a week discriminated against women and was contrary to Article 157.

Key Facts		
Type of law	**Effect**	**Source**
Treaties	Directly applicable	Section 2(1) of the European Communities Act 1972
	Have direct effect (both vertically and horizontally) if give individual rights and are clear	*Macarthys v Smith* (1979)
Regulations	Directly applicable	Article 288 (TFEU)
	Have direct effect (both vertically and horizontally) if give individual rights and are clear	
Directives	NOT directly applicable	Article 288 (TFEU)
	Have vertical direct effect if give individual rights and are clear	*Marshall case*
	NO horizontal direct effect	*Duke v GEC Reliance*
	But individual can claim against state for loss caused by failure to implement	*Francovich v Italian Republic*

Figure 6.5 *Key facts chart showing effect of EU laws*

6.3.2 Regulations

Under Article 288 (TFEU) the European Union has the power to issue regulations which are

'binding in every respect and directly applicable in each Member State'.

Such regulations do not have to be adopted in any way by the individual states as Article 288 makes it clear that they automatically become law in each member country.

This 'direct applicability' point was tested in *Re Tachographs: Commission v United Kingdom* (1979), where a regulation requiring mechanical recording equipment to be installed in lorries was issued. The United Kingdom government of the day decided not to implement the regulation, but to leave it to lorry owners to decide whether or not to put in such equipment. When the matter was referred to the European Court of Justice it was held that Member States had no discretion in the case of regulations. The wording of Article 288 was explicit and meant that regulations were automatically law in all Member States. States could not pick and choose which ones they would implement. In this way regulations make sure that laws are uniform across all the Member States.

6.3.3 Directives

Directives are the main way in which harmonisation of laws within Member States is reached. There have been directives covering many topics including company laws, banking, insurance, health and safety of workers, equal rights, consumer law and social security.

As with regulations, it is Article 288 (TFEU) that gives the power to the Union to issue directives. There is, however, a difference from regulations in that Article 288 says such directives

'bind any Member State to which they are addressed as to the result to be achieved, while leaving to domestic agencies a competence as to form and means'.

This means that Member States will pass their own laws to bring directives into effect (or implement them) and such laws have to be brought in within a time limit set by the European Commission.

The usual method of implementing directives in the United Kingdom is by statutory instrument. An example is the Unfair Terms in Consumer Contracts Regulations 1994, which implemented a directive aimed at giving consumers protection from unfair terms in contracts. Directives can, however, be implemented by other law-making methods. An example is the Consumer Protection Act 1987. A directive on liability for defective products was issued in July 1985. (By the way, this was some nine years after the proposal had first been put forward by the Commission!) The directive had to be implemented by 30 July 1988. This was done in this country by Parliament passing the Consumer Protection Act 1987, which came into force on 1 March 1988. Directives can also be implemented by an order in Council made by the Privy Council.

Working time directive

Another example of a directive is the Working Time Directive which was issued in 1993. This directive gave detailed instructions of the maximum number of hours that should be worked, the rest periods and the amount of paid holiday to which workers were entitled. It should have been implemented by November 1996 but the United Kingdom government did not implement it until October 1998 with the Working Time Regulations 1998.

Direct effect

Where Member States have not implemented a directive within the time laid down, the European Court of Justice has developed the concept of 'direct effect'.

If the purpose of a directive is to grant rights to individuals and that directive is sufficiently clear, it may be directly enforceable by an individual against the Member State. This will be so even though that state has not implemented the directive, or has implemented it in a defective way. The important point is that an individual who is adversely affected by the failure to implement only has rights against the state. This is because of the concepts of vertical effect and horizontal effect (see Figure 6.6).

Vertical direct effect

In *Marshall v Southampton and South West Hampshire Area Health Authority* (1986) the facts were that Miss Marshall was required to retire at the age of 62 when men doing the same work did not have to retire until age 65. Under the Sex Discrimination Act 1975 in English law this was not discriminatory. However, she was able to succeed in an action for unfair dismissal by relying on the Equal Treatment Directive 76/207. This directive had not been fully implemented in the United Kingdom but the European Court of Justice held that it was sufficiently clear and imposed obligations on the Member State. This ruling allowed Miss Marshall to succeed in her claim against her employers because her employers were 'an arm of the state'; i.e. they were considered as being part of the state. The

directive had vertical effect allowing her to rely on it and take action against them. This idea of vertical effect is shown in diagram form in Figure 6.6.

The concept of the state for these purposes is quite wide, as it was ruled by the European Court of Justice in *Foster v British Gas plc* (1990) that the state was:

'a body, whatever its legal form, which has been made responsible, pursuant to a measure adopted by the State, for providing a public service under the control of the State and has for that purpose special powers beyond those which result from the normal rules applicable in relations between individuals'.

In view of this wide definition the House of Lords decided that British Gas, which at the time was a nationalised industry, was part of the state, and Foster could rely on the Equal Treatment Directive.

The concept of vertical effect means that a Member State cannot take advantage of its own failure to comply with European law and implement a directive. Individuals can rely on the directive when bringing a claim against the state.

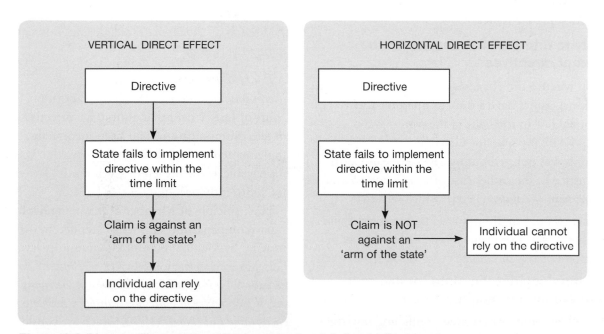

Figure 6.6 *Diagram illustrating vertical and horizontal direct effect*

This concept of vertical effect was used in the case of *Gibson v East Riding of Yorkshire Council* (1999). In this case Mrs Gibson was employed as a part-time swimming instructor. She did not get paid holidays. The Employment Appeal Tribunal held that under the Working Time Directive she was entitled to four weeks' paid holiday from November 1996, the date that the directive should have been implemented. Her employers were an 'emanation of the state' and could not rely on the lack of domestic legislation to defeat her claim.

Horizontal direct effect

Directives which have not been implemented do not, however, give an individual any rights against other people. So in *Duke v GEC Reliance Ltd* (1988), Mrs Duke was unable to rely on the Equal Treatment Directive as her employer was a private company. This illustrates that directives do not have horizontal effect and this has been confirmed by an Italian case, *Paola Faccini Dori v Recreb Srl* (1994), in which the Italian government failed to implement directive 85/447 in respect of consumer rights to cancel certain contracts. Dori could not rely on the directive in order to claim a right of cancellation against a private trader.

Duty to interpret national law in the light of directives

Even where a directive has not been implemented, national courts have a duty to interpret their national law in the light of the wording and purpose of any relevant directive.

This was pointed out by the European Court of Justice in the earlier case of *von Colson v Land Nordrhein-Westfalen* (1984), which said that

'national courts are required to interpret their national law in the light of the wording and the purpose of the directive'.

Actions against the state for failure to implement a directive

Clearly it is unfair that these conflicting doctrines of vertical and horizontal effect should give rights to individuals in some cases and not in others. The European Court of Justice has developed another strategy under which it may be possible to take an action to claim damages against the Member State which has failed to implement the European directive. This was decided in *Francovich v Italian Republic* (1991) where the Italian government failed to implement a directive aimed at protecting wages of employees whose employer became insolvent. As a result when the firm for which Francovich worked went into liquidation owing him wages, he sued the state for his financial loss. The European Court of Justice held that he was entitled to compensation. The court said that:

'Community law required the Member States to make good damage caused by a failure to transpose a directive, provided three conditions were fulfilled;

'First, the purpose of the directive had to be to grant rights to individuals.

'Second, it had to be possible to identify the content of those rights on the basis of the provisions of the directive.

'Finally, there had to be a causal link between the breach of the State's obligations and the damage suffered.'

In *R v HM Treasury, ex parte British Telecommunications plc* (1996) the European Court of Justice held that although a directive on telecommunications had been incorrectly implemented in English law, compensation was not payable as the breach of Community law was not sufficiently serious.

The principle of Member States being liable to pay compensation has been extended to other breaches by Member States of Community law. This was seen in the joined cases of *Brasserie du Pêcheur SA v Federation of Republic of Germany* and *R v Secretary of State for Transport, ex parte Factortame Ltd (No 4)* (1996) which are considered in section 6.4.

COMMENT

The importance of rulings of the European Court of Justice

The development of the concept of direct effect has been a very important one for the effectiveness of EU law. If the European Court of Justice had not developed this concept citizens of Member States would not have been able to enforce the rights given to them.

In particular where the government has not implemented a directive, the rights of individuals in many important areas, especially employment law and discrimination, would have been lost. The rulings of the European Court of Justice have allowed individuals to rely on EU law in claims against the state or an arm of the state, and also forced the government to implement EU law more fully.

The development of the *Francovich* principle has provided citizens with a remedy against the state, when otherwise they would not have had one. However, this brings its own problems as the European Court of Justice has no mechanism for enforcing its judgments.

ACTIVITY

Below in Source A are set out extracts from Articles 1 and 2 of the Equal Treatment Directive 76/207. Read these and then apply them, giving reasons for your decision, to the facts set out in Source B.

SOURCE A

Council Directive No. 76/207

Article 1

1. The purpose of this Directive is to put into effect in the Member States the principle of equal treatment as regards access to employment, including pro-motion, and to vocational training and as regards working conditions . . . This principle is hereinafter referred to as the 'principle of equal treatment'.

Article 2

1. For the purposes of the following provisions, the principle of equal treatment shall mean that there shall be no discrimination whatsoever on the grounds of sex either directly or indirectly by reference in particular to marital or family status.
2. This Directive shall be without prejudice to the right of Member States to exclude from its field of application those occupational activities and, where-appropriate, the training leading thereto, for which, by reason of their nature or the context in which they are carried out, the sex of the worker constitutes a determining factor.
3. This Directive shall be without prejudice to provisions concerning the protection of women, particularly as regards pregnancy and maternity.
4. This Directive shall be without prejudice to measures to promote equal opportunity for men and women, in particular by removing existing inequalities which affect women's opportunities in the areas referred to in Article 1(1).

SOURCE B

Case facts: Amy Austin and Ben Bowen are employed by Green Gardens Ltd. There is a vacancy for a pro-motion to section manager, and both have applied for the post. Green Gardens have interviewed Amy and Ben and decided that both are equally qualified for the position. In this situation, if there are fewer women employed at the relevant level, Green Gardens have a policy of appointing the female applicant.

Ben complains that this is discriminatory and contrary to the Equal Treatment Directive.

Key Facts

1963	*Van Gend en Loos*	European Court of Justice has right to decide whether Community law or national law prevails
1964	*Costa v ENEL*	European law takes precedence over national law
1974	*Van Duyn v Home Office*	Principle of direct applicability Citizens can rely directly on an article of the Treaty of Rome which confers rights on individuals
1986	*Marshall v Southampton etc. Health Authority*	Vertical direct effect of directives In an action against the state, individuals can rely on a directive which has not been implemented
1991	*Francovich v Italy*	Individual can claim compensation from state for its failure to implement directive
1996	*Brasserie du Pêcheur Factortame No 4*	State liable to compensate for breaches of Community law

Figure 6.7 *Key facts chart of some important decisions of the European Court of Justice*

6.3.4 Decisions

This does not refer to decisions made by the European Court of Justice, but to decisions issued under the power of Article 288 (TFEU). Such decisions may be addressed either to a Member State or an individual (person or company). Article 288 says that they are 'binding in every respect for the addressees named therein'. They are generally administrative in nature.

Article 288 also allows for recommendations and opinions to be issued, but these have no binding force.

6.4 Conflict between European law and national law

European law takes precedence over national law. This was first established in *Van Gend en Loos* (1963) which involved a conflict of Dutch law and European law on customs duty. The Dutch government argued that the European Court of Justice had no jurisdiction to decide whether European law should prevail over Dutch law; that was a matter for the

Dutch courts to decide. However, the European Court rejected this argument. In *Costa v ENEL* (1964) the European Court of Justice held that even if there was a later national law it did not take precedence over the European law. In this case the European Court of Justice said:

'the Member States have limited their sovereign rights, albeit within limited fields, and have thus created a body of law which binds both their nationals and themselves'.

This conflict was seen clearly in the *Factortame* case (1990) when the European Court of Justice decided that Britain could not enforce the Merchant Shipping Act 1988. This Act had been passed to protect British fishermen by allowing vessels to register only if 75 per cent of directors and shareholders were British nationals. It was held that this contravened the Treaty of Rome.

This breach of Community law has had another effect in that the European Court of Justice held in a later action in the joined cases of *Brasserie du Pêcheur SA v Federation of Republic of Germany* and *R v Secretary of State for Transport, ex parte*

Factortame Ltd (No 4) (1996) that governments were liable for financial loss suffered as a result of their breach of European law. In *Brasserie du Pêcheur* a French company claimed that it was forced to discontinue exports of beer to Germany, because the German authorities considered that the beer did not comply with the purity requirements laid down in German law. In *Factortame* European fishermen claimed that they had been deprived of the right to fish as result of the Merchant Shipping Act 1988. In both cases there was a claim for compensation from the State concerned.

The European Court of Justice held that Community law did give the right to compensation provided that three conditions were met. These were:

- The rule of Community law infringed must be intended to confer rights on individuals.
- The breach must be sufficiently serious.
- There must be a direct causal link between the breach of the obligation resting on the state and the damage sustained by the injured parties.

6.4.1 The effect of European law on the sovereignty of Parliament

From the cases given above it can be seen that Member States, including Britain, have definitely transferred sovereign rights to a Community created by them. None of the Member States can rely on their own law when it is in conflict with European Union Law.

It is also a principle of the Treaty of Rome that no Member State may call into question the status of Community law as a system of uniformly and generally applicable law throughout the Community. It therefore follows from this that Community law has priority over any conflicting law of Member States. This is true both of national laws which were enacted before the Community law and also of national laws which were enacted after the relevant Community law.

While Britain is member of the European Union it is therefore true to say that the sovereignty of Parliament has been affected and that, in the areas it operates, European law has supremacy over national law.

EXAMINATION QUESTIONS

1 (a) Explain the roles of the institutions of the European Union. [14 marks]
   (b) Consider whether the European Parliament's powers are sufficient to allow it to act as an effective legislator. [11 marks]
   LA1, January 2009, WJEC

EXTENSION ESSAY

Critically analyse what effect the decisions of the European Court of Justice has had on the vertical effect of directives.

CHAPTER 7

STATUTORY INTERPRETATION

INTRODUCTION

As seen at the beginning of this chapter, many statutes are passed by Parliament each year. The meaning of the law in these statutes should be clear and explicit but this is not always achieved. In order to help with the understanding of a statutes, Parliament sometimes includes sections defining certain words used in that statute: such sections are called interpretation sections. In the Theft Act 1968, for example, the definition of 'theft' is given in section one, and then sections two to six define the key words in that definition. To help the judges with general words, Parliament has also passed the Interpretation Act 1978 which makes it clear that, unless the contrary appears, 'he' includes 'she', and singular includes plural.

7.1 The need for statutory interpretation

Despite the aids mentioned above, many cases come before the courts because there is a dispute over the meaning of an Act of Parliament. In such cases the court's task is to decide the exact meaning of a particular word or phrase. There are many reasons why the meaning may be unclear:

- **A broad term**
  There may be words designed to cover several possibilities; this can lead to problems as to how wide this should go. In the Dangerous Dogs Act 1991 there is a phrase: 'any dog of the type known as the pit bull terrier' which seems simple but has led to problems. What is meant by 'type'? Does it mean the same as 'breed'? In *Brock v DPP* (1993) this was the key point in dispute and the Queen's Bench Divisional Court decided that 'type' had a wider meaning than 'breed'. It could cover dogs that were not pedigree pit bull terriers, but had a substantial number of the characteristics of such a dog.

- **Ambiguity**
  This is where a word has two or more meanings; it may not be clear which meaning should be used.

- **A drafting error**
  The Parliamentary Counsel who drafted the original Bill may have made an error which has not been noticed by Parliament; this is particularly likely to occur where the Bill is amended several times while going through Parliament.

- **New developments**
  New technology may mean that an old Act of Parliament does not apparently cover present-day situations. This is seen in the case of *Royal College of Nursing v DHSS* (1981) where medical science and methods had changed since the passing of the Abortion Act in 1967. This case is discussed more fully in section 7.5.1.

- **Changes in the use of language**
  The meaning of words can change over the years. This was one of the problems in the case of *Cheeseman v DPP* (1990). *The Times* law report of this case is set out below in the activity section.

ACTIVITY

Read the following law report and answer the questions below.

Lurking policemen not 'passengers'

Cheeseman v Director of Public Prosecutions

Before Lord Justice Bingham and

Mr Justice Waterhouse

[Judgment October 19]

Police officers who witnessed a man masturbating in a public lavatory were not 'passengers' within the meaning of section 28 of the Town Police Clauses Act 1847 when they had been stationed in the lavatory following complaints.

The Queen's Bench Divisional Court so held in allowing an appeal by way of case stated by Ashley Frederick Cheeseman against his conviction by Leicester City Justices of an offence of wilfully and indecently exposing his person in a street to the annoyance of passengers.

Section 81 of the Public Health Amendment Act 1902 extended the meaning of the word 'street' in section 28 to include, inter alia, any place of public resort under the control of the local authority.

Mr Stuart Rafferty for the appellant: Mr David Bartlett for the prosecution.

LORD JUSTICE BINGHAM, concurring with Mr Justice Waterhouse, said that the *Oxford English Dictionary* showed that in 1847 when the Act was passed 'passenger' had a meaning, now unusual except in the expression 'foot-passenger' of 'a passer-by or -through: a traveller (usually on foot); a wayfarer'.

Before the meaning of 'street' was enlarged in 1907 that dictionary definition of passenger was not hard to apply: it clearly covered anyone using the street for ordinary purposes of passage or travel.

The dictionary definition could not be so aptly applied to a place of public resort such as a public lavatory, but on a common-sense reading when applied in context 'passenger' had to mean anyone resorting in the ordinary way to a place for one of the purposes for which people would normally resort to it.

If that was the correct approach, the two police officers were not 'passengers'. They were stationed in the public lavatory in order to apprehend persons committing acts which had given rise to earlier complaints. They were not resorting to that place of public resort in the ordinary way but for a special purpose and thus were not passengers.

Solicitors: Bray & Bray, Leicester: CPS Leicester.

The Times Law Report, 2 November 1990 © The Times 1990/nisyndication.com

Questions

1. In this case the meaning of the word 'street' was important. How did the court discover the meaning of the word in this case?

2. The meaning of the word 'passenger' was also important. How did the court discover what this word meant in 1847?

3. The court decided that 'passenger' meant 'a passer-by or -through; a traveller (usually on foot); a wayfarer'. Why did that definition not apply to the police officers who arrested the defendant?

4. The defendant was found not guilty because of the way the court interpreted 'passenger'. Do you think this was a correct decision? Give reasons for your answer.

7.2 Literal approach versus purposive approach

The case of *Cheeseman* illustrates several of the problems of statutory interpretation. It is an example of the courts taking the words literally. However, it can be argued that the defendant was 'wilfully and indecently exposing his person in a street' and that he was caught doing that. Is it important whether the police officers were 'passengers'? After all, they were there because of previous complaints about this type of behaviour and presumably the defendant thought they were ordinary members of the public. Some people would argue that the whole purpose of the Act was to prevent this type of behaviour; this is the purposive approach to statutory interpretation – instead of looking at the precise meaning of each word, a broader approach is taken.

This conflict between the literal approach and the purposive approach is one of the major issues in statutory interpretation. Should judges examine each word and take the words literally or should it be accepted that an Act of Parliament cannot cover every situation and that the meanings of words cannot always be exact? In European law the purposive approach is taken. The Treaty of Rome sets out general principles but without explicit details. As Lord Denning said of the Treaty in *Bulmer Ltd v Bollinger SA* (1974):

'It lays down general principles. It expresses its aims and purposes. All in sentences of moderate length and commendable style. But it lacks precision. It uses words and phrases without defining what they mean. An English lawyer would look for an interpretation clause, but he would look in vain. There is none. All the way through the Treaty there are gaps and lacunas. These have to be filled in by the judges.'

In fact, since European treaties, regulations and directives are issued in several languages it would be difficult, if not impossible, to take the meanings of words literally. It is not always possible to have an exact translation from one language to another.

In English law the judges have not been able to agree on which approach should be used, but instead, over the years they have developed three different rules of interpretation. These are:

- The literal rule
- The golden rule
- The mischief rule.

These rules take different approaches to interpretation and some judges prefer to use one rule, while other judges prefer another rule. This means that in English law the interpretation of a statute may differ according to which judge is hearing the case. However, once an interpretation has been laid down, it may then form a precedent for future cases under the normal rules of judicial precedent. Since the three rules can result in very different decisions, it is important to understand them.

7.3 The literal rule

Under this rule courts will give words their plain, ordinary or literal meaning, even if the result is not very sensible. This idea was expressed by Lord Esher in *R v Judge of the City of London Court* (1892) when he said:

'If the words of an act are clear then you must follow them even though they lead to a manifest absurdity. The court has nothing to do with the question whether the legislature has committed an absurdity.'

The rule developed in the early 19th century and has been the main rule applied ever since then. It has been used in many cases, even though the result has made a nonsense of the law. This is illustrated in *Whiteley v Chappell* (1868) where the defendant was charged under a section which made it an offence to impersonate 'any person entitled to vote'. The defendant had pretended to be a person whose name was on the voters' list, but who had died. The court held that the defendant was not guilty since a dead person is not, in the literal meaning of the words, 'entitled to vote'.

The rule is also criticised because it can lead to what are considered harsh decisions, as in *London & North Eastern Railway Co v Berriman* (1946) where a railway worker was killed while doing maintenance work, oiling points along a railway line. His widow tried to claim compensation because there had not been a look-out man provided by the railway company in accordance with a regulation under the Fatal Accidents Act. This stated that a look-out should be provided for men working on or near the railway line 'for the purposes of relaying or repairing' it. The court took the words 'relaying' and 'repairing' in their literal meaning and said that oiling points was maintaining the line and not relaying or repairing, so that Mrs Berriman's claim failed.

With decisions such as the two above it is not surprising that Professor Michael Zander has denounced the literal rule as being mechanical and divorced from the realities of the use of language.

Another problem of using the literal rule occurs when a word has more than one meaning. It may be difficult to decide which meaning should be used.

7.4 The golden rule

This rule is a modification of the literal rule. The golden rule starts by looking at the literal meaning but the court is then allowed to avoid an interpretation which would lead to an absurd result. There are two views on how far the golden rule should be used. The first is very narrow and is shown by Lord Reid's comments in *Jones v DPP* (1962) when he said:

'It is a cardinal principle applicable to all kinds of statutes that you may not for any reason attach to a statutory provision a meaning which the words of that provision cannot reasonably bear. If they are capable of more than one meaning, then you can choose between those meanings, but beyond this you cannot go.'

So under the narrow application of the golden rule the court may only choose between the possible meanings of a word or phrase. If there is only one meaning then that must be taken. This narrow view of the golden rule can be seen in practice in *Adler v George* (1964). In this case, the Official Secrets Act 1920 made it an offence to obstruct Her Majesty's Forces 'in the vicinity' of a prohibited place. The defendants had obstructed HM Forces actually *in* the prohibited place. They argued they were not guilty as the literal wording of the Act did not apply to anyone in the prohibited place. It only applied to those 'in the vicinity', i.e. outside but close to it. The Divisional Court found the defendants guilty as it would be absurd if those causing an obstruction outside the prohibited place were guilty, but anyone inside was not. The words should be read as being 'in or in the vicinity of' the prohibited place.

The second and wider application of the golden rule is where the words have only one clear meaning, but that meaning would lead to a repugnant situation. In such a case the court will invoke the golden rule to modify the words of the statute in order to avoid this problem. A very clear example of this was the case of *Re Sigsworth* (1935), where a son had murdered his mother. The mother had not made a will, so normally her estate would have been inherited by her next of kin according to the rules set out in the Administration of Estates Act 1925. This meant that the murderer son would have inherited as her 'issue'. There was no ambiguity in the words of the Act, but the court was not prepared to let a murderer benefit from his crime, so it was held that the literal rule should not apply, and the golden rule would be used to prevent the repugnant situation of the son inheriting. Effectively the court was writing into the Act that the 'issue' would not be entitled to inherit where they had killed the deceased.

The golden rule respects the exact words of Parliament except in limited situations. Where there is a problem with using the literal rule, the golden rule provides an 'escape route'.

It allows the judge to choose the most sensible meaning where there is more than one meaning to the words in the Act. It can also provide sensible decisions in cases where the literal rule would lead to a repugnant situation. It would clearly have been unjust to allow the son in *Re Sigsworth* to benefit from his crime. This shows how it can avoid the worst problems of the literal rule.

It is very limited in its use, so it is only used on rare occasions. Another problem is that it is not always possible to predict when courts will use the golden rule.

Michael Zander has described it as a 'feeble parachute'. In other words, it is an escape route but it cannot do very much.

7.5 The mischief rule

This rule gives a judge more discretion than the other two rules. The definition of the rule comes from *Heydon's case* (1584), where it was said that there were four points the court should consider. These, in the original language of that old case, were:

1. 'What was the common law before the making of the Act?
2. What was the mischief and defect for which the common law did not provide?
3. What was the remedy the Parliament hath resolved and appointed to cure the disease of the commonwealth?
4. The true reason of the remedy.

'Then the office of all the judges is always to make such construction as shall suppress the mischief and advance the remedy.'

Under this rule, therefore, the court should look to see what the law was before the Act was passed in order to discover what gap or 'mischief' the Act was intended to cover. The court should then interpret the Act in such a way that the gap is covered. This is clearly a quite different approach from the literal rule.

7.5.1 Cases using the mischief rule

The mischief rule was used in *Smith v Hughes* (1960) to interpret s 1(1) of the Street Offences Act 1959 which said 'it shall be an offence for a common prostitute to loiter or solicit in a street or public place for the purpose of prostitution'. The court considered appeals against conviction under this section by six different women. In each case the women had not been 'in a street'; one had been on a balcony and the others had been at the windows of ground-floor rooms, with the window either half open or closed. In each case the women were attracting the attention of men by calling to them or tapping on the window, but they argued that they were not guilty under this section since they were not literally 'in a street or public place'. The court decided that they were guilty, with Lord Parker saying:

'For my part I approach the matter by considering what is the mischief aimed at by this Act. Everybody knows that this was an Act to clean up the streets, to enable people to walk along the streets without being molested or solicited by common prostitutes. Viewed in this way it can matter little whether the prostitute is soliciting while in the street or is standing in the doorway or on a balcony, or at a window, or whether the window is shut or open or half open.'

A similar point arose in *Eastbourne Borough Council v Stirling* (2000) where a taxi driver was charged with 'plying for hire in any street' without a licence to do so. His vehicle was parked on a taxi rank on the station forecourt. He was found guilty as, although he was on private land, he was likely to get customers from the street. The court referred to *Smith v Hughes* and said that it was the same point. A driver would be plying for hire in the street when his vehicle was positioned so that the offer of services was aimed at people in the street.

Another case in which the House of Lords used the mischief rule was *Royal College of Nursing v DHSS* (1981). In this case the wording of the Abortion Act 1967 which provided that a pregnancy should be 'terminated by a registered medical practitioner' was in issue. When the Act was passed in 1967 the procedure to carry out an abortion was such that only a doctor (a registered medical practitioner) could do it. From 1972 onwards improvements in medical technique meant that the normal method of terminating a pregnancy was to induce premature labour with drugs. The first part of the procedure was carried out by a doctor, but the second part was performed by nurses without a doctor present. The court had to decide if this procedure was lawful under the Abortion Act. The case went to the House of Lords where the majority (three) of the judges held that it was lawful, whilst the other two said that it was not lawful.

The three judges in the majority based their decision on the mischief rule, pointing out that the mischief Parliament was trying to remedy was the unsatisfactory state of the law before 1967 and the number of illegal abortions. They also said that the policy of the Act was to broaden the grounds for abortion and ensure that they were carried out with proper skill in hospital. The other two judges took the literal view and said that the words of the Act were clear and that terminations could only be carried out by a registered medical practitioner. They said that the other judges were not interpreting the Act but 'redrafting it with a vengeance'.

COMMENT

The mischief rule

The mischief rule promotes the purpose of the law as it allows judges to look back at the gap in the law which the Act was designed to cover. The emphasis is on making sure that the gap in the law is filled. This is more likely to produce a 'just' result.

The Law Commission prefers the mischief rule and, as long ago as 1969, recommended that it should be the only rule used in statutory interpretation.

However, there are problems with using the mischief rule. First, there is the risk of judicial law-making. Judges are trying to fill the gaps in the law with their own views on how the law should remedy the gap. Also, the case of *Royal College of Nursing v DHSS* (see section 7.5.1) shows that judges do not always agree on the use of the mischief rule.

The use of the mischief rule may lead to uncertainty in the law. It is impossible to know when judges will use the rule or what result it might lead to. This makes it difficult for lawyers to advise clients on the law. Finally, the mischief rule is not as wide as the purposive approach (see section 7.9) as it is limited to looking back at the gap in the old law. It cannot be used for a more general consideration of the purpose of the law.

It is clear that the three rules can lead to different decisions on the meanings of words and phrases. Opposite is an activity based on a real case in which the different rules could result in different decisions.

7.6 Rules of language

Even the literal rule does not take words in complete isolation. It is common sense that the other words in the Act must be looked at to see if they affect the word or phrase which is in dispute. In looking at the other words in the Act the courts have developed a number of minor rules which can help to make the meaning of words and phrases clear where a particular sentence construction has been used. These rules, which also have Latin names, are:

- the *ejusdem generis* rule
- the express mention of one thing excludes others
- a word is known by the company it keeps.

ACTIVITY

Read the facts of the case set out below then apply the different rules of interpretation.

CASE: *FISHER V BELL* [1960] 1 QB 394
The Restriction of Offensive Weapons Act 1959 s 1(1)

'Any person who manufactures, sells or hires or offers for sale or hire or lends or gives to any other person – (a) any knife which has a blade which opens automatically by hand pressure applied to a button, spring or other device in or attached to the handle of the knife, sometimes known as a "flick knife" … shall be guilty of an offence.'

Facts: The defendant was a shopkeeper, who had displayed a flick knife marked with a price in his shop window; he had not actually sold any. He was charged under s 1(1) and the court had to decide whether he was guilty of offering the knife for sale. There is a technical legal meaning of 'offers for sale', under which putting an article in a shop window is not an offer to sell. (Students of contract law should know this rule!)

Questions
Consider the phrase 'offers for sale' and explain how you think the case would have been decided using:

(a) The literal rule
(b) The golden rule
(c) The mischief rule.

Note: The court's decision on the case is given in Appendix 1.

7.6.1 The *ejusdem generis* rule

This states that where there is a list of words followed by general words, then the general words are limited to the same kind of items as the specific words. This is easier to understand by looking at cases. In *Hobbs v CG Robertson Ltd* (1970) a workman had injured his eye when brickwork which he was removing splintered. He claimed compensation under the Construction (General Provision) Regulation 1961. These regulations made it a duty for employers to provide goggles for workmen when 'breaking, cutting, dressing or carving of stone, concrete, slag or similar material. The court held that brick did not come within the term 'a similar material'. Brick was not *ejusdem generis* with stone, concrete, slag. The reason was that all the other materials were hard, so that bits would fly off them when struck with a tool, whereas brick was a soft material. This ruling meant that the workman's claim for compensation failed.

There must be at least two specific words in a list before the general word or phrase for this rule to operate. In *Allen v Emmerson* (1944) the court had to interpret the phrase 'theatres and other places of amusement' and decide if it applied to a funfair. As there was only one specific word, 'theatres', it was decided that a funfair did come under the general term 'other places of amusement' even though it was not of the same kind as theatres.

7.6.2 *Expressio unius exclusio alterius* (the mention of one thing excludes others)

Where there is a list of words which is not followed by general words, then the Act applies only to the items in the list. In *Tempest v Kilner* (1846) the court had to consider whether the Statute of Frauds 1677 (which required a contract for the sale of 'goods, wares and merchandise' of more than £10 to be evidenced in writing) applied to a contract for the sale of stocks and shares. The list 'goods, wares and merchandise' was not followed by any general words, so the court held that only contracts for those three types of things were affected by the statute; because stocks and shares were not mentioned they were not caught by the statute.

7.6.3 *Noscitur a sociis* (a word is known by the company it keeps)

This means that the words must be looked at in context and interpreted accordingly; it involves looking at other words in the same section or at other sections in the Act. Words in the same section were important in *Inland Revenue Commissioners v Frere* (1965), where the section set out rules for 'interest, annuities or other annual interest'. The first use of the word 'interest' on its own could have meant any interest paid, whether daily, monthly or annually. Because of the words 'other annual interest' in the section, the court decided that 'interest' only meant annual interest.

Other sections of the Act were considered by the House of Lords in *Bromley London Borough Council v Greater London Council* (1982). The issue in this case was whether the GLC could operate a cheap fare scheme on their transport systems, where the amounts being charged meant that the transport system would run at a loss. The decision in the case revolved around the meaning of the word 'economic'. The House of Lords looked at the whole Act and, in particular, at another section which imposed a duty to make up any deficit as far as possible. As a result they decided that 'economic' meant being run on business lines and ruled that the cheap fares policy was not legal since it involved deliberately running the transport system at a loss and this was not running it on business lines.

7.7 Presumptions

The courts will also make certain presumptions or assumptions about the law, but these are only a starting point. If the statute clearly states the opposite, then the presumption will not apply and it is said that the presumption is rebutted. The most important presumptions are:

1. **A presumption against a change in the common law**

   In other words it is assumed that the common law will apply unless Parliament has made it plain in the Act that the common law has been altered. An example of this occurred in Leach v R (1912), where the question was whether a wife could be made to give evidence against her husband under the Criminal Evidence Act 1898. Since the Act did not expressly say that this should happen, it was held that the common law rule that a wife could not be compelled to give evidence still applied. If there had been explicit words saying that a wife was compellable then the old common law would not apply. This is now the position under s 80 of the Police and Criminal Evidence Act 1984, which expressly states that in a crime of violence one spouse can be made to give evidence against the other spouse.

2. **A presumption that *mens rea* is required in criminal cases**

   The basic common law rule is that no one can be convicted of a crime unless it is shown that they had the required intention to commit it. In *Sweet v Parsley* (1970) the defendant was charged with being concerned with the management of premises which were used for the purposes of smoking cannabis. The facts were that the defendant was the owner of premises which she had leased out and the tenants had smoked cannabis there without her knowledge. She was clearly 'concerned in the management' of the premises and cannabis had been smoked there, but because she had no knowledge of the events she had no *mens rea*. The key issue was whether *mens rea* was required; the Act did not say there was any need for knowledge of the events. The House of Lords held that she was not guilty as the presumption that *mens rea* was required had not been rebutted.

3. **A presumption that the Crown is not bound by any statute** unless the statute expressly says so
4. **A presumption that legislation does not apply retrospectively**
   This means that no Act of Parliament will apply to past happenings; each Act will normally only apply from the date it comes into effect.

7.8 Unified approach

So how do all these rules fit together? Sir Rupert Cross wrote that there was a unified approach to interpretation, so that:

1. A judge should start by using the grammatical and ordinary or, where appropriate, technical meaning of the words in the general context of the statute.
2. If the judge considers that this would produce an absurd result, then he may apply any secondary meaning which the words are capable of bearing.
3. The judge may read in words which he considers to be necessarily implied by the words which are in the statute, and he has a limited power to add to, alter or ignore words in order to prevent a provision from being unintelligible, unworkable or absurd.
4. In applying these rules the judge may resort to the various aids and presumptions (see sections 7.7 and 7.10).

However, this unified approach is based on the literal approach and does not allow for the purposive approach. Today there is a move towards the purposive approach, although not all judges agree that it should be used.

COMMENT

Should there be one preferred rule?
It would be helpful if there was one specific method of statutory interpretation which was always used in cases. At the moment it is entirely up to the individual judge who

is hearing the case to use whichever rule or approach he wants. Some judges may use the literal rule; other judges may use the mischief rule or the modern purposive approach. This makes it difficult for lawyers to advise on what meaning a court may put on a disputed phrase in an Act of Parliament.

In some instances, a judge may decide to use the literal rule in one case and the mischief rule in another case. This happened with Lord Parker, who used the mischief rule in *Smith v Hughes* (see section 3.3.4) but in the case of *Fisher v Bell* he used the literal rule. It could be said that this means that a judge decides what result he wants in the case and then finds the rule which brings about that result.

In 1969 the Law Commission proposed that Parliament should pass an Act of Parliament which would mean that the mischief rule was to be used in order 'to promote the general legislative purpose'. However, this proposal has been ignored, although Lord Scarman in both 1980 and 1981 introduced a Bill on the matter into the House of Lords. The first time he was forced to drop the proposal; the second time the House of Lords voted for it, but the matter was never taken to the House of Commons.

There is an argument that, even if there were an Act of Parliament, there would still be variations in which rule judges would use. This has been shown in New Zealand, which has a law that encourages interpretation 'as will best ensure the attainment of the object of the Act'. Even though this should mean that this is done in every case, one writer points out that it is sometimes difficult to discover which approach has been used and 'the most that can be said is that some judges at some periods have been fairly consistent in using the approach that they prefer'.

7.9   The purposive approach

This goes beyond the mischief rule in that the court is not just looking to see what the gap was in the old law; the judges are deciding what they believe Parliament meant to achieve. The champion of this approach in English law was Lord Denning. His attitude towards statutory interpretation is shown when he said in the case of *Magor and St Mellons v Newport Corporation* (1950):

'We sit here to find out the intention of Parliament and carry it out, and we do this better by filling in the gaps and making sense of the enactment than by opening it up to destructive analysis.'

However, his attitude was criticised by judges in the House of Lords when they heard the appeal in the case. Lord Simonds called Lord Denning's approach 'a naked usurpation of the legislative function under the thin disguise of interpretation' and pointed out that 'if a gap is disclosed the remedy lies in an amending Act'.

Another judge, Lord Scarman, said:

'If Parliament says one thing but means another, it is not, under the historic principles of the common law, for the courts to correct it. The general principle must surely be acceptable in our society. We are to be governed not by Parliament's intentions but by Parliament's enactments.'

This speech shows the problem with the purposive approach. Should the judges refuse to follow the clear words of Parliament? How do they know what Parliament's intentions were? Opponents of the purposive approach say that it is impossible to discover Parliament's intentions; only the words of the statute can show what Parliament wanted.

CASE EXAMPLE

An example of the use of the purposive approach is the case of *R (Quintavalle) v Secretary of State for Health* (2003). The House of Lords used the purposive approach in deciding that organisms created by cell nuclear replacement (CNR) came within the definition of 'embryo' in the Human Embryology and Fertilisation Act 1990. Section 1(1)(a) of this Act states that 'embryo means a live human embryo where fertilisation is complete'. CNR was not possible in 1990 when the Act was passed and the problem is that fertilisation is not used in CNR. Lord Bingham said:

'[T]he court's task, within permissible bounds of interpretation, is to give effect to Parliament's purpose … Parliament could not have intended to distinguish between embryos produced by, or without, fertilisation since it was unaware of the latter possibility.'

You can see how this goes beyond the mischief rule. At the time of the Act, Parliament was considering the mischief (or gap in the law) of the risk of wrong use of embryos created through fertilisation. The Act was aimed at that. Parliament did not know of any gap in relation to CNR embryos: they hadn't been invented.

So the purposive approach is trying to make sure the purpose of the Act is given effect. The mischief rule only looks at what the gap was in the law at the time Parliament passed the Act.

7.9.1 The European approach

The purposive approach is the one preferred by most European countries when interpreting their own legislation. It is also the approach

Literal approach	Purposive approach
Words taken in their ordinary grammatical meaning	Looks for the purpose of Parliament and interprets the law to ensure that purpose
Case: *LNER v Berriman* Not 'relaying or repairing' track, but was oiling points (maintenance) Literal approach – held maintenance was not within the literal meaning of the words 'relaying or repairing' Could not claim compensation	**Case: *R (Quintavalle) v Secretary of State for Health*** Act stated embryo meant 'a live human embryo where fertilisation is complete' Embryos were created by cell nuclear replacement, so there was no fertilisation Purposive approach – Parliament could not have intended to distinguish between embryos The Act applied
Advantages of literal approach • leaves law-making to Parliament • makes law more certain	**Advantages of purposive approach** • leads to justice in individual cases • broad approach covering more situations • fills in the gaps in the law • allows for new technology
Disadvantages of literal approach • assumes that every Act is perfectly drafted • words have more than one meaning • can lead to absurd results • can lead to unjust decisions	**Disadvantages of purposive approach** • leads to judicial law-making • can make law uncertain • difficult to discover the intention of Parliament

Figure 7.1 *Comparing the literal approach and the purposive approach*

which has been adopted by the European Court of Justice (see Chapter 6) in interpreting European law. This influence of the European preference for the purposive approach has affected the English courts in two ways. First they have had to accept that the purposive approach is the correct one to use when dealing with European law. Second, using the purposive approach for European law is making judges more accustomed to it, and therefore more likely to apply it to English law.

7.9.2 Interpreting European Union law

Where the law to be interpreted is based on European law, the courts must interpret it in the light of the wording and purpose of the European law. This is because the Treaty of Rome, which sets out the duties of European Member States, says that all Member States are required to 'take all appropriate measures . . . to ensure fulfilment of the obligations'. The European Court of Justice in the *Marleasing* case (1992) ruled that this includes interpreting national law in every way possible in the light of the text and aim of the European law.

An example of the English courts interpreting law by looking at the purpose of the relevant European Union law is *Diocese of Hallam Trustee v Connaughton* (1996). This case is discussed in full in the chapter on European law, section 6.3.1.

7.10 Finding Parliament's intention

There are certain ways in which the courts can try to discover the intention of Parliament and certain matters which they can look at in order to help with the interpretation of a statute.

7.10.1 Intrinsic aids

These are matters within the statute itself that may help to make its meaning clearer. The court can consider the long title, the short title and the preamble (if any). Older statutes usually have a preamble which sets out Parliament's purpose in enacting that statute. Modern statutes either do not have a preamble or contain a very brief one: for example, the Theft Act 1968 states that it is an Act to modernise the law of theft. The long title may also explain briefly Parliament's intentions. An unusual approach was taken in the Arbitration Act 1996 where a statement of the principles of the Act is set out in s 2. This is a new development in statutory drafting and one that could both encourage and help the use of the purposive approach.

The other useful internal aids are any headings before a group of sections, and any schedules attached to the Act. There are often also marginal notes explaining different sections, but these are not generally regarded as giving Parliament's intention as they will have been inserted after the Parliamentary debates and are only helpful comments put in by the printer.

7.10.2 Extrinsic aids

These are matters which are outside the Act – it has always been accepted that some external sources can help explain the meaning of an Act. These undisputed sources are:

- Previous Acts of Parliament on the same topic
- The historical setting
- Earlier case law
- Dictionaries of the time.

As far as other extrinsic aids are concerned, attitudes have changed. Originally the courts had very strict rules that other extrinsic aids should not be considered. However, for the following three aids the courts' attitude has changed. These three main extrinsic aids are:

- *Hansard*: the official report of what was said in Parliament when the Act was debated.
- Reports of law reform bodies, such as the Law Commission, which led to the passing of the Act.
- International conventions, regulations or directives which have been implemented by English legislation.

The use of *Hansard*

Until 1992 there was a firm rule that the courts could not look at what was said in the debates in Parliament. Some years earlier Lord Denning had tried to attack this ban on *Hansard* in *Davis v Johnson* (1979), which involved the interpretation of the Domestic Violence and Matrimonial Proceedings Act 1976. He admitted that he had indeed read *Hansard* before making his decision, saying:

'Some may say . . . that judges should not pay any attention to what is said in Parliament. They should grope about in the dark for the meaning of an Act without switching on the light. I do not accede to this view.'

In the same case the House of Lords disapproved of this, and Lord Scarman explained their reasons by saying:

'Such material is an unreliable guide to the meaning of what is enacted. It promotes confusion, not clarity. The cut and thrust of debate and the pressures of executive responsibility . . . are not always conducive to a clear and unbiased explanation of the meaning of statutory language.'

However, in *Pepper v Hart* (1993) the House of Lords relaxed the rule and accepted that *Hansard* could be used in a limited way. This case was unusual in that seven judges heard the appeal, rather than the normal panel of five. These seven judges included the Lord Chancellor, who was the only judge to disagree with the use of *Hansard*. The majority ruled that *Hansard* could be consulted. Lord Browne-Wilkinson said in his judgment that:

'the exclusionary rule should be relaxed so as to permit reference to parliamentary materials where: (a) legislation is ambiguous or obscure, or leads to an absurdity; (b) the material relied on consists of one or more statements by a minister or other promoter of the Bill together if necessary with such other parliamentary material as is necessary to understand such statements and their effect; (c) the statements relied on are clear. Further than this I would not at present go.'

So *Hansard* may be considered but only where the words of the Act are ambiguous or obscure or lead to an absurdity. Even then *Hansard* should only be used if there was a clear statement by the minister introducing the legislation, which would resolve the ambiguity or absurdity. The Lord Chancellor opposed the use of *Hansard* on practical grounds, pointing out the time and cost it would take to research *Hansard* in every case.

The only time that a wider use of Hansard is permitted is where the court is considering an Act that introduced an international convention or European Directive into English law. This was pointed out by the Queen's Bench Divisional Court in *Three Rivers District Council and others v Bank of England* (*No 2*) (1996). In such a situation it is important to interpret the statute purposively and consistently with any European materials and the court can look at ministerial statements, even if the statute does not appear to be ambiguous or obscure.

Since 1992 *Hansard* has been referred to in a number of cases, even sometimes when there did not appear to be any ambiguity or absurdity. The Lord Chancellor's predictions on cost have been confirmed by some solicitors, with one estimating that it had added 25 per cent to the bill. On other occasions it is clear that *Hansard* has not been helpful or that the court would have reached the same conclusion in any event.

In *Jackson and others v Her Majesty's Attorney General* (2005) the Law Lords approved the use of *Hansard* as an aid to statutory interpretation. They said:

'In some quarters the *Pepper v Hart* principle is currently under something of a judicial cloud. In part this is due to judicial experience that references to Hansard seldom assist. In part this seems also to be due to continuing misunderstanding of the limited role ministerial statements have in this field . . . It would be unfortunate if *Pepper v Hart* were now to be sidelined. The *Pepper v Hart* ruling is sound in principle, removing as it did a self-created judicial anomaly. There are occasions when ministerial statements are useful in practice as an interpretive aid, perhaps especially as a confirmatory aid.'

Law reform reports

As with *Hansard*, the courts used to hold that reports by law reform agencies should not be considered by the courts. However, this rule was relaxed in the *Black Clawson* case in 1975, when it was accepted that such a report should be looked at to discover the mischief or gap in the law which the legislation based on the report was designed to deal with.

International conventions

In *Fothergill v Monarch Airlines Ltd* (1980) the House of Lords decided that the original convention should be considered as it was possible that in translating and adapting the convention to our legislative process, the true meaning of the original might have been lost. The House of Lords in that same case also held that an English court could consider any preparatory materials or explanatory notes published with an international convention. The reasoning behind this was that other countries allowed the use of such material, known as *travaux préparatoires*, and it should therefore be allowed in this country in order to get uniformity in the interpretation of international rules.

Key Facts

	Brief definition	Case examples
Literal approach	• Approaching problems of statutory interpretation by taking the words at their face value	*Fisher v Bell*
Purposive approach	• Looking at the reasons why a law was passed and interpreting the words accordingly	*R v Registrar-General, ex parte Smith*
The 'three rules' Literal rule	• Words given ordinary, plain, grammatical meaning	*Whiteley v Chappell*
Golden rule	• Avoids absurd or repugnant situations	*R v Allen*
Mischief rule	• Looks at the gap in the previous law and interprets the words 'to advance the remedy'	*Smith v Hughes*
Rules of language *Ejusdem generis*	• General words which follow a list are limited to the same kind	*Powell v Kempton Park*
Expressio unius	• The express mention of one thing excludes others	*Tempest v Kilner*
Noscitur a sociis	• A word is known by the company it keeps	*IRC v Frere*
Presumptions	• No change to common law • Crown not bound • *Mens rea* required • No retrospective effect	*Leach v R* *Sweet v Parsley*
Aids to finding Parliament's intention	• Intrinsic – within the Act, e.g. interpretation section • Extrinsic – outside the Act, e.g. *Hansard*, Law Commission Reports	*Pepper v Hart* *Black Clawson Case*

Figure 7.2 *Key facts chart for statutory interpretation*

Explanatory notes

Since 1998 explanatory notes have been produced alongside new Bills. (Remember that before a law becomes an Act of Parliament, it is referred to as a Bill.) These notes are much fuller than any previous explanatory memorandum. They are produced by the government department responsible for the Bill. The notes usually explain the background to any proposed law, summarise its main provisions and, where a point is complicated, give worked examples.

These notes are a potential new extrinsic aid to statutory interpretation. They could be helpful to courts when they have to interpret a law. However, the notes are not part of the law. This is likely to cause conflict on whether they should be used for statutory interpretation. Judges who use the purposive approach are likely to support their use, but judges who use the literal approach will not use them. This is because explanatory notes are not intended to have legal effect; they are not part of the Act itself.

Example of the use of extrinsic aids

Several extrinsic aids were considered in *Laroche v Spirit of Adventure (UK) Ltd* (2009). The claimant had been injured as the result of a sudden landing of a hot-air balloon in which he was travelling. The meaning of the word 'aircraft' was important. Was a hot-air balloon within the definition of 'aircraft'? If so, then the claim would fail as it had not been made within two years of the accident.

In deciding the case, the Court of Appeal first looked at the definition of 'aircraft' in the *Pocket Oxford Dictionary*. This defined 'aircraft' as 'aeroplane(s), airship(s) and balloon(s). The court also looked at the Air Navigation Order 2000 (a statutory instrument). This supported the view that a hot-air balloon should be regarded as an 'aircraft'.

In addition, the court pointed out that the English law had to be interpreted in a similar way to international carriage by air, which is ruled by an international convention, the Warsaw Convention.

As a result of considering these three extrinsic aids, the court ruled that a hot-air balloon was regarded as an 'aircraft'. This meant that the claim failed as it had not been brought within the two-year time limit.

7.11 The Human Rights Act 1998

Section 3 of the Human Rights Act says that, so far as it is possible to do so, legislation must be read and given effect in a way which is compatible with the rights in the European Convention on Human Rights. This applies to any case where one of the rights is concerned, but it does not apply where there is no involvement of human rights.

A good example of the difference the Human Rights Act has made to interpretation is *R v Offen* (2001). This case considered the meaning of the word 'exceptional' in the Crime (Sentences) Act 1997 where any offender committing a second serious offence must be given a life sentence unless there are 'exceptional circumstances'. Before the Human Rights Act came into force the courts in *R v Kelly* (2000) had said that 'exceptional' was an ordinary English adjective, saying:

'To be exceptional a circumstance need not be unique or unprecedented or very rare; but it cannot be one that is regularly or routinely or normally encountered.'

This led to a strict approach where offenders were given life sentences even when the earlier crime had been committed a long time ago and the second offence was not that serious of its type.

In *Offen* the Court of Appeal said that this restricted approach could lead to the sentence being arbitrary and disproportionate and a breach of Articles 3 and 5 of the European Convention on Human Rights. In order to interpret the Crime (Sentences) Act in a way which was compatible with the Convention, it was necessary to consider whether the offender was a danger to the public. If he was not then he was an exception to the normal rule in the Act and this could be considered exceptional circumstances so that a life sentence need not be given.

7.12 Conclusion

The attitude of English courts to interpretation has changed over recent years with a move towards the purposive approach and the increasing use of extrinsic aids. However, the method used in interpreting a statute is still left to the individual judge and it is quite possible that one judge will prefer the literal view, while another judge could form the opposite conclusion by applying the mischief rule or the purposive approach.

A final case illustrates this dilemma. In *R v Registrar-General, ex parte Smith* (1990), the court had to consider s 51 of the Adoption Act 1976 which stated:

'(1) Subject to subsections (4) and (6), the Registrar-General shall on an application made in the prescribed manner by an adopted person a record of whose birth is kept by the Registrar-General and who has attained the age of 18 years supply to that person ... such information as is necessary to enable that person to obtain a certified copy of the record of his birth.'

Subsection (4) said that before supplying that information the Registrar-General had to inform the applicant about counselling services available. Subsection (6) stated that if the adoption was before 1975 the Registrar-General could not give the information unless the applicant had attended an interview with a counsellor.

The case involved the application by Charles Smith for information to enable him to obtain his birth certificate. Mr Smith had made his application in the correct manner and was prepared to see a counsellor. On a literal view of the Act the Registrar-General had to supply him with the information, since the Act uses the phrase 'shall ... supply'. The problem was that Mr Smith had been convicted of two murders and was detained in Broadmoor as he suffered from recurring bouts of psychotic illness. A psychiatrist thought that it was possible he might be hostile towards his natural mother. This posed a difficulty for the court: should they apply the clear meaning of the words in this situation? The judges in the Court of Appeal decided that the case called for the purposive approach, saying that, despite the plain language of the Act, Parliament could not have intended to promote serious crime. So, in view of the risk to the applicant's natural mother if he discovered her identity, they ruled that the Registrar-General did not have to supply any information.

EXAMINATION QUESTIONS

1. Study the text and answer the questions based on it.

'... reference to Parliamentary material should be permitted as an aid to the construction of legislation which is ambiguous or obscure or the literal meaning of which leads to an absurdity'

(Lord Browne-Wilkinson in *Pepper v Hart* (1992))

(a) Explain the role of Hansard in the interpretation of statutes. [14 marks]

(b) Using your knowledge of statutory interpretation, consider whether an offence has been committed in the situation set out below.

Great concern was expressed in 2008 about the depletion of fish stocks particularly by ocean-going trawlers. As a result, Parliament passed the Coastal Waters (Prevention of Fishing) Fictitious Act 2009

Coastal Waters (Prevention of Fishing) Fictitious Act 2009

Section 1: Any fishing boat under 100 tons which fishes within 5 miles of the coast will require a licence.

Section 2: Any fishing in coastal waters undertaken in the course of a business and conducted without a licence constitutes a criminal offence.

Walter, who operates a 1,000-ton ocean-going trawler and is therefore ineligible to hold a licence, pays Alison, who holds a licence in respect of a small fishing boat, £10,000, on the understanding that Alison would give him first refusal on all her catches. Alison has returned from a fishing trip with a full catch and offered them to Walter, whereupon he was arrested and charged under the Act. Advise Walter.

WJEC LA2 Summer 2010

EXTENSION ESSAY

'The rules of statutory interpretation allow judges to decide case as they wish.' Discuss.

CHAPTER 8

LAW REFORM

8.1 The need for an independent law reform body

In Chapters 3, 4, 5 and 6 we examined the different sources of law, and saw that the law of England and Wales comes from a variety of sources. This fact makes it important to keep the law under review, to ensure that it is reformed when necessary, and to try to keep it in an accessible and manageable state. There are many influences on the way our law is formed and the impetus for reform can come from a number of sources. Some of these will have more effect than others, while in some situations there may be competing interests in the way that the law should be reformed.

The government of the day effectively has the major say in what laws will be enacted, and the government will set out its agenda for law reform in each session of Parliament. However, much of this will be concerned with more politically motivated areas, rather than 'pure law' reform. In addition, we have already seen with the Dangerous Dogs Act 1991 in Chapter 4 that Acts of Parliament can actually lead to more confusion and complication of the law. This is especially true where one Act is used to amend another so that the law is contained in a series of Acts, all of which must be consulted before the law can be discovered.

Pressure groups can provide the impetus for law reform. Where a subject has a particularly high profile, Parliament may bow to public opinion and alter the law. The Law Commission (see section 8.4) in its consultation process will also receive the views of pressure groups with a special interest in the area of law under review.

As seen in Chapter 3, judges play a role in law reform by means of judicial precedent. In some instances they may actually create new law, as occurred in *R v R* (1991), when the courts ruled that a man could be guilty of raping his wife. In some cases the courts may feel unhappy with the decision they have to come to because of the clear wording of an existing Act of Parliament or because they are bound by a previous precedent. In this situation the judges may when giving judgment draw attention to the need for reform.

However, these influences do not lead to our law developing in an organised and controlled way. The law needs to be reformed so that it adapts to the changing needs of society. This may require new laws to be passed or, in some cases, old laws to be cancelled. Confused law also creates expense. Simpler law would save legal fees.

8.1.1 History of law reform bodies

The need to have a body supervising systematic reform has been recognised for centuries, with various Lord Chancellors (as far back as 1616) calling for the appointment of 'law commissioners' to revise the laws and keep them up to date. Prior to the 19th century, there were no organised efforts at law reform. In the 19th century there were piecemeal reforms, with some statutes which codified parts of the criminal law and others codifying the common law on specialised areas of contract law.

In the 20th century calls for an institution to be set up with responsibility for law reform led to the creation in 1934 of the Law Revision Committee. This has been described as the 'source of the modern machinery of law reform', but it operated only until the outbreak of World War II in 1939. After the war, from 1945 to 1952, there was no permanent law reform body. It was not until 1965 that a full-time body with wide responsibility came into existence in the shape of the Law Commission (see section 8.4).

8.2 Law Reform Committee

This was created in 1952 and was in effect a revival of the pre-war Law Revision Committee. It is part-time and considers only small areas of the civil law, often rather narrow and technical points, which are referred to it by the government. Its proposals have led to Parliament passing such Acts as the Occupiers' Liability Act 1957, the Civil Evidence Act 1968 and the Latent Damage Act 1986. The Law Commission has consulted this committee on areas of civil law such as trust law.

8.3 Criminal Law Revision Committee

This was set up in 1957 and was another part-time body which recommended changes to the criminal law. This Committee sat monthly until 1986 and produced 18 reports. Many of its smaller, specific recommendations became law, though its recommendations for broad changes to the law were often not taken up due to lack of parliamentary time. One of its main achievements was the virtual codification of theft and related offences in the Theft Act 1968.

8.4 The Law Commission

This is the main law reform body. It was set up in 1965 by the Law Commissions Act. It is a full-time body and consists of a chairman, who is a High Court Judge, and four other Law Commissioners. There are also support staff to assist with research and four Parliamentary Draftsmen who help with the drafting of proposed Bills. The Commission considers areas of law which are believed to be in need of reform. The role of the Law Commission is set out in s 3 of the Law Commissions Act which states:

'It shall be the duty of each of the Commissions to take and keep under review all the law with which they are respectively concerned with a view to its systematic development and reform, including in particular the codification of such law, the elimination of anomalies, the repeal of obsolete and unnecessary enactments, the reduction of the number of separate enactments and generally the simplification and modernisation of the law.'

8.4.1 The way in which the Law Commission works

Topics may be referred to it by the Lord Chancellor on behalf of the government, or it may itself select areas in need of reform and seek governmental approval to draft a report on them.

The Law Commission works by researching the area of law that is thought to be in need of reform. It then publishes a consultation paper seeking views on possible reform. The consultation paper will describe the current law, set out the problems and look at options for reform (often including explanations of the law in other countries).

Following the response to the consultation paper, the Commission will then draw up positive proposals for reform. These will be presented in a report which will also set out the research that led to the conclusions. There will often be a draft Bill attached to the report with the intention that this is the exact way in which the new law should be formed. Such a draft Bill must, of course, go before Parliament and go through the necessary Parliamentary stages if it is to become law.

8.4.2 Repeal and consolidation

Repeal

There are many very old and sometimes ridiculous statutes which are still on the statute book, but which have long since ceased to have any relevance. In order to get rid of this problem, the Law Commission prepares a Statute Law (Repeals) Bill for Parliament to pass. By 2011 there had been 18 Statute Law (Repeals) Acts. Over 2,500 out-of-date Acts of Parliament have been completely repealed. In addition, parts of thousands of other Acts have also been repealed. In 2012 the nineteenth Statute Law (Repeals) Bill was published. This will result in the repeal of 817 Acts in their entirety and the removal of redundant provisions from 50 other Acts. The fact of how out of date the laws are is illustrated by the fact that the Acts listed for repeal include a 1696 Act to raise money to rebuild St Paul's Cathedral after the Great Fire of 1666, and four 19th century Acts to promote the illumination of homes and streets by the use of gaslight. This 'tidying-up' of the statute book helps to make the law more accessible.

Consolidation

This is needed because in some areas of law there are a number of statutes, each of which sets out a small part of the total law. The aim of consolidation is to draw all the existing provisions together in one Act. This is another way in which the law is being made more accessible. The Law Commission produces about five Consolidation Bills each year, though it is perhaps true to say that as fast as one area is consolidated, another

area is being fragmented by further Acts of Parliament!

This happened with the law on sentencing. The law was consolidated in the Powers of Criminal Courts (Sentencing) Act 2000. However, within a few months the law was changed again by the Criminal Justice and Courts Services Act 2000, which renamed some of the community penalties and also created new powers of sentencing. Then in 2003 the Criminal Justice Act 2003 changed much of the sentencing law again. Other reforms have since been put in place for young offenders and, in 2012, the Legal Aid, Sentencing and Punishment of Offenders Act made further changes in the law on sentencing.

8.4.3 Codification

Codification involves bringing together all the law on one topic into one source of law. It was specially referred to by s 3 of the Law Commissions Act 1965 as part of the Law Commission's role. Indeed when the Law Commission was first formed in 1965 an ambitious programme of codification was announced, aimed at codifying family law, contract law, landlord and tenant laws and the law of evidence. However, the Law Commission has gradually abandoned these massive schemes of codification in favour of what might be termed the 'building-block' approach. Under this it has concentrated on codifying small sections of the law that can be added to later.

In fact the whole concept of codification is the subject of debate. Those in favour of it say that it makes the law both accessible and understandable. In addition it gives consistency and certainty: the law is contained in one place and both lawyers and the people can easily discover what the law is. The opposite viewpoint is that a very detailed code makes the law too rigid; while if a code is drafted in broad terms without detail, it will need to be interpreted by the courts and in this way would be just as uncertain as the existing common law.

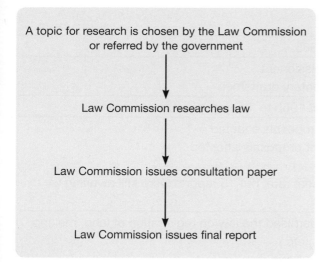

A topic for research is chosen by the Law Commission or referred by the government

↓

Law Commission researches law

↓

Law Commission issues consultation paper

↓

Law Commission issues final report

Figure 8.1 *The way the Law Commission works*

8.4.4 Success of the Law Commission

Although the Law Commission has not achieved its original ideas of codification, it has been successful in dealing with smaller areas of law. The success rate of the Law Commission's proposals was initially high, and its first 20 law reform programmes were enacted within an average of two years. These included the Unfair Contract Terms Act 1977, the Criminal Attempts Act 1981, the Supply of Goods and Services Act 1982 and the Occupiers' Liability Act 1984.

In fact, in the first ten years of its existence it had a high success rate with 85 per cent of its proposals being enacted by Parliament. During the next ten years, however, only 50 per cent of its suggested reforms became law. This lack of success was due to lack of parliamentary time, and an apparent disinterest by Parliament in technical law reform. The rate hit an all-time low in 1990 when not one of its reforms was enacted by Parliament and, by 1992, there was a backlog of 36 Bills which Parliament had failed to consider.

Since then the implementation rate has improved, although there are still reports waiting to be made law. The Law Commission's Annual Report of 2011–12 showed that there were 15 reports awaiting implementation. In addition, the government has completely rejected about 1 in 6 of the Law Commission's reports.

However, some important reforms have been passed in recent years. These include:

- The Land Registration Act 2002 – this reformed and modernised the method of registering land. This is important as it affects everyone who buys and sells a house, flat or any other land or building.
- The Fraud Act 2006, which simplified the law on fraud.
- The Corporate Manslaughter and Corporate Homicide Act 2007, which made corporations and organisations criminally liable for deaths caused by their working practices.

Criminal Code

The reform of the criminal law is the biggest unresolved problem. The Law Commission worked with three leading academics to produce a draft Criminal Code which was published in 1985. Part one covered general principles of criminal liability, while part two dealt with specific offences which were grouped into five chapters containing linked offences (for example, offences against the person). The offences covered by the Code were said to cover between 90 and 95 per cent of the work of the criminal courts.

This Code was laid before Parliament but not considered. In view of the amount of law covered in it, the Law Commission decided to split it into manageable sections and produce draft Bills on each of these. The first such draft Bill was on offences against the person and was published in 1993. This aimed at simplifying some of the areas of law which have become very complex and which create difficulties for the courts and defendants. For example, in 1994 the House of Lords spent two days considering what the words 'inflict' and 'cause' meant in the Offences Against the Person Act 1861. This sort of dispute would be avoided by the implementation of the draft Bill.

Key Facts

Originated	By the Law Commissions Act 1965
Personnel	Chairman and four other Commissioners Support staff including Parliamentary draftsmen
Function	Under s 3 Law Commissions Act 1965 to 'keep the law under review'
Success rate	First 10 years – 85 per cent of proposals enacted Second 10 years – 50 per cent of proposals enacted 1990 – no enactments Gradual improvement in implement rate, but 15 reports were still awaiting implementation in 2012
Recent reforms	Land Registration Act 2002 modernised the law on registration of land, making it easier to transfer land (houses, etc.) Fraud Act 2006 simplifying law in fraud Corporate Manslaughter and Corporate Homicide Act 2007 creating criminal liability of corporations and organisations for manslaughter

Figure 8.2 *Key facts chart on the Law Commission*

However, Parliament failed to find the necessary time to debate the proposal. Eventually, in 2008 the Law Commission announced that it would no longer seek to codify the criminal law but would instead concentrate on reform of specific areas of the law. Even when the Law Commission has produced reports on smaller areas of law, the government has been slow to implement them. In the Lord Chancellor's report in 2012 on implementation, he stated that the Report on Participating in Crime (2007) (Law Com 305) and the Report on Conspiracy and Attempts (2009) (Law Com 318) were not priority areas and would not be implemented during the lifetime of the current Parliament which will last until 2015.

COMMENT

The Law Commission was set up by Parliament; many of its law reform projects have been referred to it by the government. Yet, despite this, Parliament is slow to implement the reforms recommended by the Law Commission and make them into law.

It is true that the Law Commission has had a major impact, with more than 80 per cent of its reports becoming law, but a number of reports still await government action. This is partly due to limited parliamentary time, but also partly due to lack of commitment to reform of 'lawyers' law'. The Lord Chancellor's statement that the reports on Participating in Crime and Conspiracy and Attempts would not be implemented in the lifetime of the 2010–15 Parliament reinforces the view that Parliament cannot give sufficient time to law reform.

Perhaps delegated legislation could be used in some areas of technical law. But this raises the problem that law should only be made by our democratically elected Parliament. Using delegated legislation is undesirable in politically sensitive areas of law-making.

Although not all its reports are implemented, the Law Commission has effects in other ways. In its report for 2011 it was pointed out that the Law Commission's work had been cited in 310 cases in the United Kingdom and in 38 cases in other common law jurisdictions such as Canada.

8.5 Royal Commissions

Apart from the full-time bodies there are also temporary committees or Royal Commissions set up to investigate and report on one specific area of law. These are dissolved after they have completed their task. Such Royal Commissions were used frequently from 1945 to 1979, but from 1979 to 1990 when Margaret Thatcher was Prime Minister, none was set up. In the 1990s there was a return to the use of such commissions.

Some Royal Commissions have led to important changes in the law; the Royal Commission on Police Procedure (the Phillips Commission) reported in 1981 and many of its recommendations were given effect by the Police and Criminal Evidence Act 1984. However, the government does not always act on recommendations, as was seen with the Pearson Commission on Personal Injury cases which reported in 1978.

With the Runciman Commission (the Royal Commission on Criminal Justice) which reported in 1993, the government implemented many of the proposals but not all.

In 1999 a Royal Commission (the Wakeham Commission) considered how the House of Lords could be reformed. This has been partly implemented by the government, but full reform of the House of Lords is still awaited.

8.5.1 Reviews by judges

Apart from actual Royal Commissions, judges may be asked to lead an investigation into technical areas of law. Recent examples of this have been the Woolf Committee on civil justice which led to major reforms of the civil court system in 1999

(see Chapter 9) and the review of the criminal justice system carried out by Sir Robin Auld in 2001 (see Chapters 12 and 13).

EXAMINATION QUESTIONS

Study the text below and answer the questions based on it.

'Pressure groups are an important element in promoting the reform of English and Welsh law. They are organisations of people who all believe in the same cause. Whether it is a sectional group, campaigning for personal gain, or a cause group, working towards a specific cause, they all possess strongly held views and wish to influence some aspect of society. They use many methods to influence including the use of traditional media such as newspapers but more commonly nowadays through the use of electronic media such as the Internet. Other than these, the most common methods they tend to use involve carrying out petitions, distributing leaflets whilst come pressure groups employ professional lobbyists to speak to MPs on the group's behalf.'

Source: unattributed

1. (a) Explain, with examples, the role of pressure groups in promoting law reform. [14 marks]
   (b) Evaluate the role of the Law Commission in the law reform process in England and Wales. [11 marks]

LA2, Winter 2011, WJEC

EXTENSION ESSAY

Critically analyse the role of the Law Commission.

CHAPTER 9

CIVIL CASES

INTRODUCTION

As already stressed in Chapter 1, it is important to understand the differences between civil cases and criminal cases. Civil cases cover a wide range of matters, so there cannot be a very specific definition which will cover all of them. However, a basic definition for civil claims is to say that these arise when an individual or a business believes that their rights have been infringed in some way. Some of the main areas of civil law are contract law, the law of tort, family law, employment law and company law.

As well as dealing with different areas of law, the types of dispute that can arise within the field of civil law are equally varied. A company may be claiming that money is owed to it (contract law); this type of claim may be for a few pounds or for several million. An individual may be claiming compensation for injuries suffered in an accident (the tort of negligence), while in another tort case the claim might not be for money but for another remedy: such as an injunction to prevent someone from building on disputed land. Other types of court orders include the winding up of a company which cannot pay its debts or a decree of divorce for a marriage that has failed. The list is almost endless.

9.1 Negotiation

In most civil matters people regard a court case as a last resort and will try to resolve the problem without going to court, so that when a dispute arises it is likely that some form of negotiation will take place. The most usual situation is that the person making the complaint will either go to see the other side and explain the problem (this is common where shoppers take back substandard goods) or they will write to the other side, setting out the complaint. Many cases will be resolved at this stage by the other party agreeing to refund money, change goods, pay the debt or take some other desired action.

The need to try to settle any dispute is stressed in the leaflets issued by the Court Service on taking action in court. Their leaflet, *I'm in a dispute – what can I do?*, includes the following information:

Do all disputes have to be settled in court?

No. Going to court should always be a last resort. It can be expensive, stressful and time consuming.

Before going to court you should always try to reach an agreement. For example, if you are in dispute with an organisation, you should use the organisation's complaints procedure before thinking of making a claim through the court.

If you make a claim through the court without making any effort to reach an agreement first, you may find that the judge will hold this against you when considering payment of costs in the case. You may not get your costs back, or the court may order you to pay the other party's costs, even if you win the case.

Other ways you might try to reach an agreement include processes like negotiation, mediation and arbitration. They are often more informal than the court process.

Legal advice

If the other party will not settle the claim, then the aggrieved person must decide whether they are prepared to take the matter further. The most common next stage is to get legal advice and perhaps get a solicitor to write to the other person. This may lead to a 'bargaining' situation where a series of letters is written between the parties and eventually a compromise is reached. However, if, after all this, the other side refuses to pay the debt or compensation or whatever else is claimed, then the aggrieved person must decide if the matter is worth pursuing any further. This may involve starting a court case, or an alternative form of dispute resolution may be used (these alternatives to going to court are considered in the next chapter).

Going to court

Taking a case to court can be an expensive exercise, even if you decide to 'do-it-yourself' and not use a lawyer. There will be a court fee based on the type and size of the claim, which can be claimed back from the other party if you win the case, but there is always the risk that you will lose the case and have to pay the other side's costs. Even if you win, your problems may not be over as the other person may not have enough money to pay the claim and refund your costs. If the case is complicated

it could take years to complete and may cost hundreds or thousands of pounds.

Given these problems, it is not surprising that many people who believe they have a good claim decide not to take court action.

However, starting a court case does not mean that it will actually go to court. The vast majority of cases are settled out of court so that fewer than 1 per cent of all cases started in the civil courts get as far as a court hearing. This is because the dispute is a private one between the parties involved and they can settle their own dispute at any time, even after court proceedings have been started.

9.2 Starting a court case

The civil justice system was reformed in 1999 following the Woolf Report (see section 9.6).

Parties are encouraged to give information to each other, in an attempt to prevent the need for so many court cases to be started. So before a claim is issued, especially in personal injury cases, a pre-action 'protocol' should be followed. This is a list of things to be done and if the parties do not follow the procedure and give the required information to the other party, they may be liable for certain costs if they then make a court claim.

The information is usually in a letter explaining brief details of how the claim arises; why it is claimed that the other party is at fault; details of injury or other damage; and any other relevant matters. The defendant is then given three months to investigate the claim and must then reply, setting out if liability is admitted or if it is denied, with the reasons for the denial. If expert evidence is going to be needed, then the parties should try to agree to use one expert. This should lead to many claims being settled, but there will still be some which need to go to court.

9.2.1 Which court to use?

Where the decision is made to go to court, then the first problem is which court to use. The two courts which hear civil cases are:

- The County Court
- The High Court.

For cases where the claim is for £25,000 or less, the case must be started in the County Court. For larger claims you can usually choose to start a case in either the County Court or the High Court. This is still the position after the Woolf Reforms. However, there are some restrictions laid down in the High Court and County Courts Jurisdiction Order 1991. These are that:

- Personal injury cases for less than £50,000 must be started in the County Court.
- Defamation actions must be started in the High Court.

So for most cases over £25,000 a claimant will be able to choose the most convenient court for starting the case. The main points to consider in making the decision are the amount that is being claimed and whether the case is likely to raise a complex issue of law. The fact that a case is started in one court does not necessarily mean that the trial will be there; cases may be transferred from one court to the other for the actual trial, if this is thought necessary. Once a case is defended the case is then allocated to the appropriate track and at the same time it is possible for it to be transferred to another court.

Internet research   www

Look up court forms such as N1 (see Figure 9.1) on the website **www.courtservice.gov.uk**.

Also use that website to find guidance on starting cases in the County Court.

9.2.2 Issuing a claim

If you are using the County Court, then you can choose to issue the claim in any of the 230 or so County Courts in the country. If you are using the High Court, then you can go to one of the 20 District Registries or the main court in London. You need a claim form called 'N1' (see Figure 9.1). The court office will give you notes explaining how to fill in the form.

Court staff can help to make sure that you have filled in the claim form properly, or you may get help from advice centres or a Citizens Advice Bureau. Once the form is filled in you should photocopy it so that you have a copy for the court, a copy for yourself and a copy for each defendant. Then take the form to the court office. A court fee for issuing the claim has to be paid. This fee varies according to how much the claim is for.

At the beginning of 2013 the fee for a claim of up to £300 was £35 with the maximum fee for a small claim (under £5,000) being £120. Claims of £5,000 to £15,000 had a fee of £245, while at the top end of the scale claims of over £300,000 had a fee of £1,670.

9.2.3 Defending a claim

When the defendant receives the claim form there are several routes which can be taken. They may admit the claim and pay the full amount. Where this happens the case ends. The claimant has achieved what was wanted. In other cases the defendant may dispute the claim. If the defendant wishes to defend the claim, he or she must send either an acknowledgement of service (Form N9) or a defence to the court within 14 days of receiving the claim. If only an acknowledgement of service is sent, then the defendant has an extra 14 days in which to serve the defence.

If the defendant does not do either of these things, then the claimant can ask the court to make an order that the defendant pays the money

Claim Form

In the

for court use only

Claim No.

Issue date

Claimant

SEAL

Defendant(s)

Brief details of claim

Value

£

	Amount claimed	
Defendant's name and address	Court fee	
	Solicitor's costs	
	Total amount	

The court office at

is open between 10am and 4pm Monday to Friday. When corresponding with the court, please address forms or letters to the Court Manager and quote the claim number.

NI Claim form (CPR Part 7) (01.02)

Printed on behalf of The Court Service

Figure 9.1 *Form N1*

Claim No.	

Does, or will, your claim include any issues under the Human Rights Act 1998?   Yes ☐   No ☐

Particulars of Claim (attached)(to follow)

Statement of Truth
*(I believe)(The Claimant believes) that the facts stated in these particulars of claim are true.
*I am duly authorised by the claimant to sign this statement

Full name

Name of claimant's solicitor's firm

signed_____   position or office held _____
*(Claimant)(Litigation friend)(Claimant's solicitor)   (if signing on behalf of firm or company)

*delete as appropriate

Claimant's or claimant's solicitor's address to which documents or payments should be sent if different from overleaf including (if appropriate) details of DX, fax or e-mail.

Figure 9.1 *(Continued)*

and costs claimed. This is called an order in default. Once a claim is defended the court will allocate the case to the most suitable 'track' or way of dealing with the case.

9.2.4 Allocation of cases

The decision on which track should be used is made by the District Judge in the County Court or the Master (a procedural judge) in the High Court. The tracks are:

1. **The small claims track**
   This is normally used for disputes under £5,000, except for personal injury cases and housing cases where the limit is usually £1,000.
2. **The fast track**
   This is used for straightforward disputes of £5,000 to £25,000.
3. **The multi-track**
   This is for cases over £25,000 or for complex cases under this amount.

Note that in 2011 the government consulted on possible reforms to the civil court system. In that consultation it was suggested that the limit for small track cases could be raised to at least £10,000 to keep in line with inflation.

To help the judge consider to which track a claim should be allocated, both parties are sent an allocation questionnaire. If it is thought necessary, the judge can allocate a case to a track that normally deals with claims of a higher value. Alternatively, if the parties agree, the judge can allocate a case to a lower-value track.

For claims over £25,000 there may also be a decision to transfer the case from the County Court to the High Court or vice versa. Claims for between £25,000 and £50,000 are generally tried in the court in which the proceedings were started. Claims for over £50,000 are usually tried in the High Court, though they can be tried in the County Court. This is shown in Figure 9.2.

Value of claim	Court in which case will usually be tried
Under £5,000	County Court small claims procedure
£5,000 to £25,000	County Court fast-track procedure
£25,000 to £50,000	Either High Court or County Court multi-track procedure
Over £50,000	High Court multi-track procedure (though can be heard in County Court)

Figure 9.2 *Summary of where cases are likely to be tried*

We will now go on to consider the different courts and tracks.

9.3 Small claims

Clearly, it is important to have a relatively cheap and simple way of making a claim for a small amount of money, otherwise the costs of the action will be far more than the amount in dispute. For that reason the small claims procedure was started in 1973, and originally only claims of up to £75 could be made there. The limit has since been raised several times, especially in 1991 when the limit was increased to £1,000; in 1996 after the Woolf Report the limit was increased to £3,000; and in 1999 it became £5,000. The limit is likely to be raised again in the near future to at least £10,000.

9.3.1 Small claims procedure

People are encouraged to take their own case so that costs are kept low. However, under the new rules small claims cases are started in the same way as all other cases. This makes it more difficult for the ordinary person. The use of lawyers is discouraged, as, though it is possible to have a lawyer to represent you at a small claims hearing, the winner cannot claim the costs of using a lawyer from the losing party. An alternative to using a lawyer is to have a 'lay representative', that is a non-legally qualified person, to help put your case.

Small claims cases used to be heard in private, but under the Woolf reforms they are now heard in public. The procedure still allows the District Judge to be flexible in the way he hears the case but the process is no longer as informal as under the previous system. District Judges are encouraged to be more inquisitorial and are given training in how to handle small claims cases, so that they will take an active part in the proceedings, asking questions and making sure that both parties explain all their important points.

9.3.2 Advantages of small claims

1. The cost of taking proceedings is low.
2. If you lose you will not have to pay the other person's lawyers' costs.
3. People do not have to use lawyers, but can take the case themselves.
4. The procedure is quicker than for other cases. In 2011 it took 30 weeks from the issue of a claim to the hearing, compared to 56 weeks for other cases.
5. The District Judge should help the parties to explain their case.

9.3.3 Disadvantages of small claims

1. For cases over £1,500, a small allocation fee has to be paid.
2. Legal funding for paying for a lawyer is not available, though it may be possible to fund the case through a 'no win, no fee' (see Chapter 19).
3. Where the other side is a business they are more likely to use a lawyer. This can put an unrepresented claimant at a disadvantage.
4. Research by John Baldwin has shown that District Judges are not always very helpful to unrepresented claimants.

5. Even when you win your case it does not mean that you will get your money from the defendant. Only about 60 per cent of successful claimants actually received all the money awarded by the court.

9.4 County Court

There are about 230 County Courts, so that most major towns will have a court. The courts can try nearly all civil cases. The main types of cases are:

- All contract and tort claims
- All cases for the recovery of land
- Disputes over partnerships, trusts and inheritance up to a value of £30,000.

In addition some County Courts have the jurisdiction to hear divorce cases, bankruptcy cases, low-level claims in admiralty cases and matters under the Race Relations Act 1976. Note that the Crime and Courts Bill 2012 has provision to create a new separate Family Court. All family matters currently dealt with in the County Court will be eventually transferred to this new court.

The County Court can try small claims, fast-track and multi-track cases and its workload is much greater than the High Court. In 2011 just over 1.5 million cases were started in the County Courts, including small claims.

Despite the large total of claims issued, only a very small number of cases actually proceed to a trial. In 2011 only 15,941 fast-track or multi-track cases were tried in County Courts. In addition, there were 36,719 cases dealt with by the small claims track.

Cases will nearly always be heard in open court and members of the public are entitled to attend. The whole hearing is more formal and many claimants and defendants will be represented, usually by a solicitor but sometimes by a barrister. The winner of a case may claim costs, including the cost of legal representation. All this makes a case in the County Court much more expensive than in the small claims track. John Baldwin's research found that 40 per cent of those taking cases in the main County Court viewed it as 'an inappropriate and disproportionately expensive way of resolving' their dispute.

The government's consultation paper, *Solving Disputes in the County Court* (2011), pointed out that for lower-level claims, the cost of a case was often greater than the amount claimed.

Cases are heard by Circuit Judges, though in rare cases it is possible for a jury of eight to sit with the judge. (For further information on the use of juries in civil cases see Chapter 18.)

9.4.1 Fast-track cases

Claims between £5,000 and £25,000 needed a faster and cheaper method of dealing with them. In 1998, before the Woolf reforms, the statistics for the year show that the average wait for cases in the County Court was 85 weeks from the issue of the claim to the actual hearing in court. As well as delay, cases were too expensive. Indeed, the Woolf Report found that the costs of cases were often higher than the amount claimed.

As a result of this the new fast-track idea was brought in. Once a case is defended, the District Judge at the County Court will send out the allocation questionnaire and then make the decision of whether the case is suitable for the fast track. Personal injury cases and housing cases over £1,000 and up to £25,000 are also dealt with as fast-track cases.

Fast track means that the court will set down a very strict timetable for the pre-trial matters. This is aimed at preventing one or both sides from wasting time and running up unnecessary costs. Once a case is set down for hearing, the aim is to have the case heard within 30 weeks. The new timetables have lessened the delays considerably. In 2011 the wait from issue of claim to hearing was 56 weeks. This is a seven-month improvement

on the pre-Woolf era. However, the total time of 56 weeks is still quite a long time to wait for a trial of what is meant to be a fast-track case. The actual trial will usually be heard by a Circuit Judge and take place in open court with a more formal procedure than for small claims. In order to speed up the trial itself, the hearing will be limited to a maximum of one day and the number of expert witnesses restricted, with usually only one expert being allowed.

9.4.2 Multi-track cases

Claims for more than £25,000 are usually allocated to the multi-track. If the case was started in a County Court then it is likely to be tried there, though it can be sent to the High Court, especially for claims of over £50,000. The case will be heard by a Circuit Judge who will also be expected to 'manage' the case from the moment it is allocated to the multi-track route. The judge can set timetables. It is even possible to ask the parties to try an alternative method of dispute resolution in an effort to prevent waste of costs.

9.5 High Court

The High Court is based in London but also has judges sitting at 26 towns and cities throughout England and Wales. It has the power to hear any civil case and has three divisions each of which specialises in hearing certain types of case. These divisions are the Queen's Bench Division, the Chancery Division and the Family Division.

9.5.1 Queen's Bench Division

The President of the Queen's Bench Division is the Lord Chief Justice and there are over 70 judges sitting in the division. It deals with contract and tort cases where the amount claimed is over £50,000, though, as seen earlier in this chapter, a claimant can start an action for any amount of

The Royal Courts of Justice

£25,000 and above. Only multi-track cases should be dealt with in the High Court. Also, certain types of action are thought to be more suitable for the High Court than the County Court.

Usually cases are tried by a single judge but there is a right to jury trial for fraud, libel, slander, malicious prosecution and false imprisonment cases. When a jury is used there will be 12 members.

Cases in the High Court are expensive and can take a long time. The average time between issuing a claim and the trial is about three years. Cases are expensive because of the need to use lawyers and also because of court fees. As well as fees for issuing the claim and other preliminary stages, there is a trial fee of £1,090.

Commercial Court

This is a special court which is part of the Queen's Bench Division. This court has specialist judges to deal with insurance, banking and other commercial matters, for example the problems of the Lloyd's 'names' for the losses caused by large insurance claims. In this court a simplified speedier procedure is used and the case may be decided on documentary evidence.

Admiralty Court

There is also an Admiralty Court dealing with shipping and deciding such matters as claims for damage caused by collision at sea. It also decides disputes over salvage rights when a ship has sunk or been stranded. The judge in the Admiralty Court sits with two lay assessors, who are chosen from Masters of Trinity House, and who are there to advise the judge on questions of seamanship and navigation.

Also, in 1998 the Technology and Construction Court was set up to take over from what had been called the Official Referee's Court. This court deals with any cases in the Chancery or the Queen's Bench Division which involve technically complex issues, such as building and engineering disputes or litigation over computers.

Judicial review

The Queen's Bench Division also has important supervisory functions over inferior courts and other bodies with decision-making powers, such as government ministers or local councils. Judicial review is concerned with whether a decision-making process has been carried out legally, as distinct from the merits of the decision in question.

9.5.2 Chancery Division

The Chancellor of the High Court is the head of the division. There are about 17 High Court Judges assisting in the division. The main business of this division involves disputes concerned with such matters as insolvency, for both companies and individuals, the enforcement of mortgages, disputes relating to trust property, copyright and patents, intellectual property matters and contested probate actions. There is also a special Companies Court in the division which deals mainly with winding up companies.

Juries are never used in the Chancery Division and cases are heard by a single judge. The criticisms of cost and delay which apply to the Queen's Bench Division apply equally to the Chancery Division.

9.5.3 Family Division

The head of this division is the President, and 19 High Court Judges are assigned to the division. It has jurisdiction to hear wardship cases and all cases relating to children under the Children Act 1989. It also deals with other matters regarding the family, such as declarations of nullity of marriage, and grants probate in non-contentious probate cases.

Cases are heard by a single judge and, although juries were once used to decide defended divorce cases, juries are not now used in this division.

Note that the Crime and Courts Bill 2012 has provision to create a new separate Family Court. All family matters currently dealt with in the Family Division will be eventually transferred to this new court.

ACTIVITY

Advise the people in the following situations:

1. Sarah has bought a television set with a built-in DVD player costing £370 from a local electrical superstore. The DVD player has never worked properly, but the store has refused to replace it or to refund the purchase price to Sarah. She wishes to claim against the store. Advise her as to which court to start the case in and how she should go about this. Also explain to her the way in which the case will be dealt with if the store defends it and there is a court hearing.

2. Thomas has been badly injured at work and alleges that the injuries were the result of his employer's failure to take proper safety precautions. He has been advised that his claim is likely to be worth £200,000. Advise him as to which court or courts could hear his case.

3. Imran wishes to start an action for defamation against a national newspaper. Advise him as to which court he should use and explain to him who tries defamation cases.

9.6 The Woolf reforms

The present system of civil justice is based on the reforms recommended by Lord Woolf in his report *Access to Justice* (1996).

In 1995 Lord Woolf stated that a civil justice system should:

- Be just in the results it delivers.
- Be fair in the way it treats litigants.

- Offer appropriate procedures at a reasonable cost.
- Deal with cases at a reasonable speed.
- Be understandable to those who use it.
- Provide as much certainty as the nature of particular cases allows.
- Be effective, adequately resourced and organised.

The Report found that virtually none of these points was being achieved in the civil courts, and criticised the system for being unequal, expensive, slow, uncertain and complicated. The report contained 303 recommendations. The most important ones proposed:

- Extending small claims up to £3,000 (from the then limit of £1,000).
- A fast track for straightforward cases up to £10,000.
- A multi-track for cases over £10,000, with capping of costs.
- Encouraging the use of alternative dispute resolution.
- Giving judges more responsibility for managing cases.
- More use of information technology.
- Simplifying documents and procedures and having a single set of rules governing proceedings in both the High Court and the County Court.
- Shorter timetables for cases to reach court and for lengths of trials.

The proposal to increase the small claims limit to £3,000 was implemented before the full report was issued. Before committing itself to the remainder of the reforms, the Labour government, which came to power in 1997, commissioned the Middleton Report as a 'second opinion'. This supported most of the Woolf proposals, but suggested that the small claims limit should be raised to £5,000 and the fast-track route to £15,000 (which has since been increased to £25,000). As a result of the Woolf and Middleton

Reports, the civil justice system was radically reformed in April 1999.

9.6.1 The Civil Procedure Rules

From 26 April 1999, new Civil Procedure Rules were brought into effect. These use much simpler language than previous rules. They also changed the vocabulary used in court cases. For example, anyone starting a civil case is now called 'the claimant'; previously the term used in most cases was 'the plaintiff'. The document used to start cases is a claim form, rather than a writ or a summons. The new terms are used in this book, but the old terms still appear in reports of cases decided before April 1999.

Overriding objective

Rule 1.1 of the Civil Procedure Rules states that the overriding objective is to enable the court to deal with cases justly. This means that courts should try to:

- Ensure that the parties in any case are on an equal footing.
- Save expense.
- Deal with cases in a way which is proportionate to:
  - the amount involved (that is avoid the costs of the case being more than the amount claimed)
  - the importance of the case (for example, is there a major point of law involved?)
  - the complexity of the issues in the case.
- Ensure that the case is dealt with quickly and fairly.
- Allocate an appropriate share of the court's resources (so smaller claims do not take up more time than they justify).

Judges have more control over proceedings than previously. They can set timetables and make sure that the parties do not drag out a case unnecessarily. Rule 1.4 of the Civil Procedure

Rules explains that as well as fixing timetables, 'active case management' by judges includes:

- Identifying the issues at an early stage.
- Deciding which issues need investigation and trial.
- Encouraging the parties to use alternative dispute resolution if this is appropriate.
- Dealing with any procedural steps without the need for the parties to attend court.
- Giving directions to ensure that the trial of a case proceeds quickly and efficiently.

9.6.2 Applying the rules in court

Case management has led to the issues in cases being identified more quickly, so that more cases are settling without the need for a trial. In some cases judges have stayed cases for mediation to be tried. Use of alternative dispute resolution (ADR) has been encouraged by the courts making cost orders against those who unreasonably refuse to attempt ADR.

The judges also apply the timetables strictly. This was illustrated by *Vinos v Marks and Spencer plc* (2000). In this case the claimant's solicitors had issued the claim just within the time limit and had told the defendant's insurers that they had done so. However, they were then nine days late in serving that claim on the defendant. The claim was struck out by the court because of this.

9.6.3 Effect of the Woolf reforms

In 2005, *The Management of Civil Cases: The Courts and the post-Woolf Landscape*, by Professors Peysner and Seneviratne of Nottingham Law School, Nottingham Trent was published by the then Lord Chancellor's Department. This considered the effect of the Woolf reforms.

The findings were that:

- The culture of litigation had changed for the better, with cooperation between the parties improving.

- There were mixed views over whether delay had been reduced.
- Case management conferences were felt to be one of the major successes of the Civil Procedure Rules (CPR).
- There was a more uniform procedure across the country.
- There was a very high rate of settlement, often more than 60 per cent, and in some courts over 80 per cent.
- Part 36 process and sanctions attached to it were found to be effective, although it was felt to be too complicated and difficult to explain to the client.
- There was little or no increase in ADR and out-of-court mediation: in practice judges rarely stay cases for mediation, and ADR had not become incorporated into the court process.
- Costs increased overall as a result of the CPR and the front-loading of costs, with costs in fast-track cases being disproportionate.
- the courts were still under-resourced and the IT systems 'primitive' compared with those used by practitioners.

In 2011 the government in their consultation paper, *Solving Disputes in the County Court*, pointed out that it was 15 years since the Woolf Report and the system has not kept pace with the 'major economic and social shifts that have taken place since'. They believe that the system needs to focus more on dispute resolution and debt recovery, rather than the ideals of 'justice'. In particular, they pointed out that the costs of taking a case to court are often more than the amount claimed. The ideal is that disputes:

'should be resolved in the most appropriate forum, so that processes and costs are commensurate with the complexity of the issues involved'.

They proposed a range of options to achieve this, including:

- Fixed costs (already used for traffic accidents under £10,000) to be extended to other personal injury claims for up to £25,000 or even £50,000.

- Requiring all cases below the small claims limit to have attempted settlement by mediation, before being considered for a hearing.
- Introducing mediation information/assessment sessions for claims above the small claims limit to try to divert more cases into alternative dispute resolution.
- Increasing the upper level for small claims to at least £10,000.

9.7 Appellate courts

These are courts which hear appeals from lower courts. The main appellate courts are the Divisional Courts, the Court of Appeal and the House of Lords.

9.7.1 Divisional Courts

Each division of the High Court has what is called a Divisional Court which has the power to hear appeals from inferior courts and tribunals. For most appeals two or three of the judges from the particular division will sit together to hear the case.

Queen's Bench Divisional Court

The most important of the Divisional Courts is the Queen's Bench Divisional Court. This has two main functions:

1. It hears appeals by way of case stated from criminal cases decided in the Magistrates' Court. This is dealt with more fully in Chapter 13.
2. It has supervisory powers over inferior courts and tribunals and also over the actions and

Key Facts

Courts dealing with civil cases	• County Court • High Court
Different tracks for claims	• Small claims • Fast track • Multi-track
Problems of civil cases	• Cost • Delay • Complexity
1999 reforms	• Encourage use of ADR • Simpler forms and language • Increase small claims limit to £5,000 • Fast track for claims between £5,000 and £25,000 • Judges responsible for case management • Strict timetables
Effect of 1999 reforms	• Cases settle earlier • Initial costs are high • Delays are getting shorter • Courts strict on timetables

Figure 9.3 *Key facts chart on civil justice*

decisions of public bodies and government ministers. This process is known as 'judicial review' and for this purpose the court has the power to make what are called 'prerogative orders'. These orders are a mandatory order, which is an order to perform a duty; a prohibitory order, which is an order to prevent an inferior court from hearing a case which it has no power to deal with; and a quashing order, which removes the decision to the Queen's Bench Division so that its legality can be enquired into and the decision quashed if it is found to be invalid.

The Queen's Bench Divisional Court also hears applications for *habeas corpus* from those who allege that they are being unlawfully detained. This is an important way of protecting the right to liberty.

Chancery Divisional Court

This deals with only a small number of appeals, mainly from decisions made by Tax Commissioners on the payment of tax and appeals from decisions of the County Court in bankruptcy cases.

Family Divisional Court

The main function of this court is to hear appeals from the decisions of the magistrates regarding family matters and orders affecting children.

9.7.2 Court of Appeal (Civil Division)

The Court of Appeal was set up by the Judicature Act 1873 and was initially intended to be the final court of appeal. However, the position of the House of Lords as the final appellate court was reinstated by the Appellate Jurisdiction Act 1876. Today the Court of Appeal has two divisions,

Civil and Criminal. There are 38 Lords Justices of Appeal and each division is presided over by its own head. The Civil Division is the main appellate court for civil cases and it is headed by the Master of the Rolls.

The Court of Appeal (Civil Division) mainly hears appeals from the following courts:

- all three divisions of the High Court
- the County Court for multi-track cases
- the Upper Tier tribunal.

Permission to appeal

Permission to appeal is required in most cases. It can be granted by the lower court where the decision was made or by the Court of Appeal. Permission to appeal will only be granted where the court considers that an appeal would have a real prospect of success or that there was some other compelling reason why the appeal should be heard.

Permission to appeal is not required in cases where the liberty of the individual is in issue: for example in an appeal against a committal to prison for breaking an injunction.

9.7.3 Supreme Court

This is the final court of appeal in the English legal system. It hears appeals from the Court of Appeal, the Divisional Courts and, on rare occasions, direct from the High Court under what are called the 'leapfrog' provisions. Appeals are heard by the Justices of the Supreme Court. They have to sit as an uneven-number panel, so there can be three, five, seven or even nine judges sitting to hear an appeal.

Permission to appeal

On an appeal from the Court of Appeal or the Divisional Courts it is necessary to be given permission to appeal to the Supreme Court.

This permission can be given by either the Supreme Court or the lower court. It is difficult to get leave to appeal; for example, the statistics for 2011 show that out of 171 cases, leave to appeal to the Supreme Court was given in only 48.

In leapfrog cases from the High Court under the Administration of Justice Act 1969, not only must the Supreme Court give permission to appeal, but the trial judge must also grant a certificate of satisfaction. This will be done only if the case involves a point of law of general public importance which *either* involves the interpretation of a statute *or* is one where the trial judge is bound by a previous decision of the Court of Appeal or House of Lords/Supreme Court. This would mean that an appeal to the Court of Appeal would be of no effect as it would also be bound by that previous decision. Leapfrog appeals are rare, with permission to appeal being asked for in only two or three cases each year.

However, once over the hurdle of getting leave to appeal, there is quite a high chance in civil cases that the appeal will be allowed. In 2011 more than half of the appeals actually heard by the Supreme Court were successful. The number of appeals heard by the Supreme Court is small, usually about 60 cases per year involving civil law, with about three-quarters of these involving a question of statutory interpretation.

Internet research   www

Use the Internet to look up cases:

1. in which there has been an appeal to the Supreme Court; and
2. which are waiting for an appeal to be heard. This can be found on **www.supremecourt. gov.uk**.

9.8 Appeal routes in civil cases

Although the detail on the appellate courts is given in section 9.7, it is probably helpful to have a list of the normal appeal routes from both the County Court and the High Court.

9.8.1 Appeals from the County Court

Since May 2000, the appeal routes from the County Court are as set out in Part 52 of the Civil Procedure Rules. This means that generally:

- for fast-track cases dealt with by a District Judge the appeal is heard by a Circuit Judge
- for fast-track cases dealt with by a Circuit Judge the appeal is heard by a High Court Judge
- for final decisions in multi-track cases heard in the County Court (whether by a Circuit Judge or by a District Judge) the right of appeal is to the Court of Appeal.

Appeals from small claims

In October 2000 appeals against decisions in small claims cases became possible. This right of appeal was introduced in order to comply with Article 6 (the right to a fair trial) of the European Convention on Human Rights. The appeal routes are the same as for fast-track cases. This means that the appeal is to the next judge up in the hierarchy, so if the case was tried by a District Judge the appeal is to a Circuit Judge; if the case was dealt with by a Circuit Judge then the appeal is to a High Court Judge.

Second appeals

Where the first appeal is heard by a Circuit Judge or a High Court Judge, then there is a possible further appeal to the Court of Appeal. However, this will only happen in exceptional cases as s 55 of the Access to Justice Act 1999 states that:

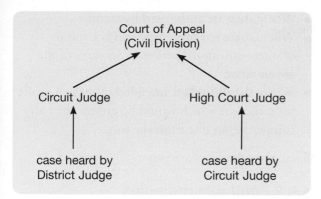

Figure 9.4 *Appeal routes from the County Court*

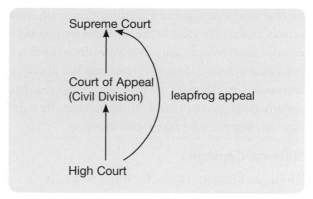

Figure 9.5 *Appeal routes from the High Court*

'no appeal may be made to the Court of Appeal . . . unless the Court of Appeal considers that

(a) the appeal would raise an important point of principle or practice, or

(b) there is some other compelling reason for the Court of Appeal to hear it'.

These appeal routes are shown in Figure 9.4.

9.8.2 Appeals from the High Court

1. From a decision in the High Court the appeal usually goes to the Court of Appeal (Civil Division).
2. In rare cases there may be a 'leapfrog' appeal direct to the Supreme Court under the Administration of Justice Act 1969. Such an appeal must involve a point of law of general public importance which is either concerned with the interpretation of a statute or which involves a binding precedent of the Court of Appeal or the Supreme Court/House of Lords which the trial judge must follow. In addition the Supreme Court has to give permission to appeal.

These appeal routes are shown in Figure 9.5.

9.8.3 Further appeals

From a decision of the Court of Appeal there is a further appeal to the Supreme Court but only if the Supreme Court or Court of Appeal gives permission to appeal. Also note that if a point of European law is involved the case may be referred to the European Court of Justice under Article 267 of the Treaty of the Functioning of the European Union. Such a referral can be made by any English court.

9.9 Remedies in civil cases

9.9.1 Damages

The main remedy awarded by the courts is an order that an amount of money be paid to the claimant. This is called an award of damages. The object of an award of damages in cases of breach of contract is to put the claimant in the same position, as far as money can do it, as he would have been had the contract not been broken. There is a similar aim in tort cases of awarding damages to place the claimant in the same position as if the tort had not been committed. Obviously there are many situations where monetary compensation does not really compensate for the loss caused by the breach of contract or the tort. This is particularly true of tort cases where the claimant has suffered serious personal injury and may be left with a permanent disability.

Special damages

This is the term for damages which can be calculated specifically. For example, in an action for the tort of negligence following a car crash, it is possible to set out exactly the cost of repairing the car, hiring a replacement while your car is off the road and replacing damaged clothing. It will also be possible to calculate the loss of earnings that has already taken place because of the injuries, though any sick pay must be taken into account.

General damages

These are for matters which cannot be neatly itemised. In personal injury cases this will include an amount for pain and suffering and also for future loss of earnings. It will also include an amount for the cost of nursing or other necessary assistance, or for adapting a home to accommodate a disabled person.

Nominal damages

Where the claimant wins the case but cannot show that there has been actual loss, it is open to the court to award a small amount of money in recognition that the claimant's rights were infringed. This usually happens in actions for torts which are 'actionable *per se*', that is 'of themselves' or just because they happened. An example is the tort of trespass to land, where the claimant may establish that the defendant has walked across the claimant's field without permission or lawful excuse. This is enough for the court to award nominal damages to the claimant. Of course, if in the process of crossing the field the defendant had damaged a gate then the claimant would also be entitled to specific damages to cover the cost of repairing the gate.

Exemplary damages

These are also called 'punitive damages', and this is exactly what they are – damages which are intended to punish the defendant, not merely compensate the claimant. Exemplary damages are not available for breach of contract and are only awarded in tort cases in the following situations:

- Where they are authorised by statute.
- Where there has been oppressive, arbitrary or unconstitutional action by servants of the government.
- Where the defendant intended to make a profit from the tort which would be greater than any compensation due from the tort.

Exemplary damages are very rarely awarded.

9.9.2 Equitable remedies

As already seen in Chapter 2, these are remedies which have been developed by equity and the key factor of such remedies is that they are not given automatically. The court has a discretion in deciding whether or not an equitable remedy should be granted. The major equitable remedies are injunctions, specific performance, rescission and rectification.

Injunctions

Temporary injunctions called interlocutory injunctions can be granted during the course of a case. An interlocutory injunction is usually granted in order to try to preserve the *status quo* between the parties while the case is awaiting a full trial. A final injunction may be granted at the end of a case where the judge is satisfied that damages would not be an adequate remedy.

Injunctions are used in many areas of law. For example, they may be used in contract law to stop a threatened breach of contract, in the law of tort to prevent the continuation of a nuisance or restrain an ongoing trespass to land, in family law to control domestic violence, or in administrative law to prevent public authorities from acting unlawfully. Breach of an injunction is a contempt of court and, in extreme cases, a person breaking an injunction can be sent to prison.

Specific performance

This is a remedy that is used only in contract law and it is an order that a contract should be carried out as

Key Facts

Remedy	Effect	Comment
Damages	The defendant is ordered to pay the claimant an amount of money	There are different types of damages: • Special – for specific amounts • General – for pain and suffering • Nominal – small amount where no actual loss has been caused • Exemplary – to punish the defendant
Injunctions	Orders defendant to do or not to do something	Discretionary remedy – court may decide that damages will be sufficient
Specific performance	Orders defendant to complete contract	Discretionary remedy – used only in rare cases
Rescission	Puts parties back in their pre-contractual position	Discretionary remedy
Rectification	Alters document to show parties' real intention	Discretionary remedy

Figure 9.6 *Key facts chart on remedies*

agreed. It is granted only in exceptional circumstances where the court feels the common law remedy of damages could not adequately compensate the claimant, for example in a contract to purchase land. Specific performance is not ever granted to order someone to carry out personal services such as singing at a concert. Nor is it granted for a breach of contract where one of the parties is a minor.

Rescission

Again this remedy is available only in contract cases. The aim of the courts in awarding rescission is to return the parties as far as possible to their pre-contractual position. The main grounds for rescission are a misrepresentation which has induced one party to enter into a contract or a mistake which has a fundamental effect on a contract.

Rectification

This is a court order that a document should be altered to reflect the parties' intention. The court will grant such an order only where it is satisfied that a mistake was made in drawing up the

document so that it is not a true version of what the parties agreed.

EXAMINATION QUESTIONS

1. (a) Explain the civil procedure rules. [14 marks]
   (b) Discuss the impact of the Woolf Reforms on civil cases in England and Wales. [11 marks]

   LA1, Summer 2011, WJEC

2. (a) Describe the jurisdiction of the civil courts and the three-track system at first instance. [18 marks]
   (b) Discuss whether the track system and other recent reforms have improved the running of the civil courts. [12 marks]

   G151, June 2011, OCR

EXTENSION ESSAY

Critically analyse the effect of the Woolf reforms on the civil justice system.

CHAPTER 10

ALTERNATIVE METHODS OF DISPUTE RESOLUTION

INTRODUCTION

In Chapter 9 we saw that using the courts to resolve disputes can be costly, in terms of both money and time. It can also be traumatic for the individuals involved and may not lead to the most satisfactory outcome for the case. An additional problem is that court proceedings are usually open to the public and the press, so there is nothing to stop the details of the case being published in local or national newspapers. It is not surprising, therefore, that more and more people and businesses are seeking other methods of resolving their disputes. Alternative methods are referred to as 'ADR', which stands for 'Alternative Dispute Resolution', and include any method of resolving a dispute without resorting to using the courts. There are many different methods which can be used, ranging from very informal negotiations between the parties, to a comparatively formal commercial arbitration hearing.

Encouraging ADR

In the 1990s there were many moves to encourage the use of ADR: for example, the Woolf Report included more use of ADR as one of its recommendations. As a result the 1999 Civil Procedure Rules allow judges to 'stay' court proceedings, that is stop the proceedings temporarily, so that the parties can try mediation or other ADR methods.

Employment cases

This is an area of law where alternative dispute resolution has long been used in the shape of ACAS (Advisory Conciliation and Arbitration Service). When any claim is filed at an employment tribunal, a copy of that claim is sent to ACAS who will then contact the two parties involved and offer to attempt to resolve the dispute without the need for the matter to

go to a tribunal. ACAS has specially trained conciliation officers who have a great deal of experience of employment disputes. The success of this service can be seen from the fact that over half of all claims filed are settled in this way. However, there is criticism that the amount paid in such settlements is less than would have been awarded by a tribunal. This suggests that employees are at a disadvantage and feel under pressure to settle.

Funding of cases

Under the legal aid rules, funding is not available for a court case if it could be dealt with by an alternative method of resolution.

So it can be seen that there is an increased awareness of the use of alternative dispute resolution in all sorts of disputes. However, as pointed out in the opening paragraph of this

Negotiation	Parties themselves
Mediation	Parties with help of neutral third party
Conciliation	Parties with help of neutral third party who plays an active role in suggesting a solution
Arbitration	Parties agree to let third party make a binding decision
Litigation	Parties go to court and a judge decides the case

Figure 10.1 *Methods of dispute resolution*

chapter, ADR includes any method of resolving a dispute, other than 'going to court' and it is important to realise that there is a wide variety of methods available. The main ones are negotiation, mediation, conciliation and arbitration, and a brief summary of these is given in Figure 10.1.

10.1 Negotiation

Anyone who has a dispute with another person can always try to resolve it by negotiating directly with them. This has the advantage of being completely private, and is also the quickest and cheapest method of settling a dispute. If the parties cannot come to an agreement, they may decide to take the step of instructing solicitors, and those solicitors will usually try to negotiate a settlement. In fact, even when court proceedings have been commenced, the lawyers for the parties will often continue to negotiate on behalf of their clients, and this is reflected in the high number of cases which are settled out of court. Once lawyers are involved, there will be a cost element – clearly, the longer negotiations go on, the higher the costs will be. One of the worrying aspects is the number of cases that drag on for years, only to end in an agreed settlement literally 'at the door of the court' on the morning that the trial is due to start. It is this situation that other alternative dispute resolution methods and, in particular,

the 1999 Civil Procedure Rules are aimed at avoiding.

10.2 Mediation

This is where a neutral mediator helps the parties to reach a compromise solution. The role of a mediator is to consult with each party and see how much common ground there is between them. He/she will explore the position with each party, looking at their needs and carrying offers to and fro, while keeping confidentiality. A mediator will not usually tell the parties his/her own views of the merits of the dispute; it is part of the job to act as a 'facilitator', so that an agreement is reached by the parties. However, a mediator can be asked for an opinion of the merits, and in this case the mediation becomes more of an evaluation exercise, which again aims at ending the dispute.

Mediation is only suitable if there is some hope that the parties can cooperate. Companies who are used to negotiating contracts with each other are most likely to benefit from this approach. Mediation can also take different forms, and the parties will choose the exact method they want. The important point in mediation is that the parties are in control: they make the decisions.

10.2.1 Formalised settlement conference

This is a more formal method of approaching mediation. It involves a 'mini-trial' where each side presents its case to a panel composed of a decision-making executive from each party, and a neutral party. Once all the submissions have been made, the executives, with the help of the neutral advisor, will evaluate the two sides' positions and try to come to an agreement. If the executives cannot agree, the neutral adviser will act as a mediator between them. Even if the whole matter is not resolved, this type of procedure may be able to narrow down the issues so that if the case does go to court, it will not take so long.

An advantage of mediation and mini-trials is that the decision need not be a strictly legal one sticking to the letter of the law. It is more likely to be based on commercial common sense and compromise. The method will also make it easier for companies to continue to do business with each other in the future, and it may include agreements about the conduct of future business between the parties. This is something that cannot happen if the court gives judgment, as the court is only concerned with the present dispute. It avoids the adversarial conflict of the courtroom and the winner/loser result of court proceedings – it has been said that with mediation, everyone wins.

10.2.2 Mediation services

There are a growing number of commercial mediation services. One of the main ones is the Centre for Dispute Resolution which was set up in London in 1991. It has many important companies as members including almost all of the big London law firms. Businesses say that using the Centre to resolve disputes has saved several thousands of pounds in court costs. The typical cost of a mediator is about £2,000. This compares with potential litigation costs which are frequently over £100,000 and sometimes may even come to more than one million pounds, especially in major commercial cases.

The main disadvantage of using mediation services is that there is no guarantee the matter will be resolved, and it will then be necessary to go to court after the failed attempt at mediation. In such situations there is additional cost and delay through trying mediation. However, the evidence is that a high number of cases will be resolved; the Centre for Dispute Resolution claims that over 80 per cent of cases in which it is asked to act are settled. There is also the possibility that the issues

may at least have been clarified, and so any court hearing will be shorter than if mediation had not been attempted.

There are also mediation services aimed at resolving smaller disputes, for example those between neighbours. An example of such a service is the West Kent Mediation Service. This offers a free service that will try to help resolve disagreements between neighbours arising from such matters as noise, car parking, dogs or boundary fence disputes. The Service is run by trained volunteers who will not take sides or make judgements on the rights and wrongs of an issue. They will usually visit the party who has made the complaint to hear their side of the matter, then, if that party agrees, ask to visit the other person and get their point of view. Finally, if both parties are willing, the mediator arranges a meeting between them in a neutral place. The parties are in control and can withdraw from the mediation process at any time.

The latest idea is Online Dispute Resolution. There are an increasing number of websites offering this, e.g. *www.disputemediationservices.co.uk* and *www.themediationroom.com*.

> ### COMMENT
>
> Research into mediation has found some interesting facts showing that it has advantages and disadvantages. On the positive side it has been noted that, even if the actual mediation session did not resolve the dispute, the parties were more likely to settle the case without going to court than in non-mediated cases. However, there are also disadvantages. Amounts paid in mediated settlements are often lower than the amounts agreed in other settlements and considerably lower than amounts awarded by the courts.
>
> Another problem is that successful mediation requires a skilled mediator with 'natural talent, honed skills and accumulated experience'. If

these qualities are not present mediation can become a bullying exercise in which the weaker party may be forced into a settlement. This was recognised by one person who said:

'Leaning on people is the only way that you will get a settlement. If you lean on two halves of a see-saw it is usually the weaker half that will break and that is where you should apply your effort.'

However, overall it appears that voluntary mediation can promote early settlement and can lead to a situation in which the sense of grievance is reduced and an acceptable settlement reached.

10.3 Conciliation

This has similarities to mediation in that a neutral third party helps to resolve the dispute, but the main difference is that the conciliator will usually play a more active role. He will be expected to suggest grounds for compromise, and the possible basis for a settlement. In industrial disputes ACAS can give an impartial opinion on the legal position. As with mediation, conciliation does not necessarily lead to a resolution and it may be necessary to continue with a court action.

10.4 Advantages of using ADR

There are many advantages to using ADR instead of going to court. The main ones are that it is:

● faster
● cheaper
● more flexible
● less stressful
● possible to agree resolutions that are not available in court.

With regard to this last point, the courts can only award damages or one of the equitable remedies. With ADR the parties may ask for a variety of

resolutions. For example, repayments of a debt may be restructured over a long period of time. Or where faulty goods are an issue, the item may be repaired or replaced. Where the parties are likely to continue to do business in the future, they may agree terms for the future.

10.5 Arbitration

The word 'arbitration' is used to cover two quite different processes. The first is where the courts use a more informal procedure to hear cases; this is the way proceedings in the Commercial Court of the Queen's Bench Division are described. The second meaning of the word 'arbitration' is where the parties agree to submit their claims to private arbitration; this is the type of arbitration that is relevant to alternative dispute resolution, as it is another way of resolving a dispute without the need for a court case.

Private arbitration is now governed by the Arbitration Act 1996 and s 1 of that Act sets out the principles behind it. This says that:

'(a) the object of arbitration is to obtain the fair resolution of disputes by an impartial tribunal without unnecessary delay or expense;

(b) the parties should be free to agree how their disputes are resolved, subject only to such safeguards as are necessary in the public interest.'

So arbitration is the voluntary submission by the parties, of their dispute, to the judgment of some person other than a judge. Such an agreement will usually be in writing, and indeed the Arbitration Act 1996 applies only to written arbitration agreements. The precise way in which the arbitration is carried out is left almost entirely to the parties' agreement.

10.5.1 The agreement to arbitrate

The agreement to go to arbitration can be made by the parties at any time. It can be before a dispute arises or when the dispute becomes apparent. Many commercial contracts include what is called a *Scott v Avery* clause, which is a clause where the parties in their original contract agree that in the event of a dispute arising between them, they will have that dispute settled by arbitration. Figure 10.2 shows a *Scott v Avery* clause in the author's contract for writing this book.

Where there is an arbitration agreement in a contract, the Arbitration Act 1996 states that the court will normally refuse to deal with any dispute; the matter must go to arbitration as agreed by the parties. The rules, however, are different for consumer claims where the dispute is for an amount which can be dealt with in the small claims track. In such circumstances the consumer may choose whether to abide by the agreement to go to private arbitration, or whether to insist that the case be heard in the small claims track.

An agreement to go to arbitration can also be made after the dispute arises. Arbitration is becoming increasingly popular in commercial cases.

Arbitration

24. If any difference shall arise between the PROPRIETOR and the PUBLISHERS touching the meaning of this Agreement or the rights and liabilities of the parties hereto, the same shall in the first instance be referred to the informal Disputes Settlement Scheme of the Publishers' Association, and failing agreed submission by both parties to such Scheme shall be referred to the arbitration of two persons (one to be named by each party) or their mutually agreed umpire in accordance with the provisions of the Arbitration Act 1996, or any amending or substituted statute for the time being in force.

Figure 10.2 *Arbitration clause from author's contract*

10.5.2 The arbitrator

Section 15 of the Arbitration Act 1996 states that the parties are free to agree on the number of arbitrators, so that a panel of two or three may be used or there may be a sole arbitrator. If the parties cannot agree on a number then the Act provides that only one arbitrator should be appointed. The Act also says that the parties are free to agree on the procedure for appointing an arbitrator. In fact most agreements to go to arbitration will either name an arbitrator or provide a method of choosing one, and in commercial contracts it is often provided that the president of the appropriate trade organisation will appoint the arbitrator.

There is also the Institute of Arbitrators which provides trained arbitrators for major disputes. In many cases the arbitrator will be someone who has expertise in the particular field involved in the dispute, but if the dispute involves a point of law the parties may decide to appoint a lawyer. If there is no agreement on who or how to appoint, then, as a last resort, the court can be asked to appoint an appropriate arbitrator.

10.5.3 The arbitration hearing

The actual procedure is left to the agreement of the parties in each case, so that there are many forms of hearing. In some cases the parties may opt for a 'paper' arbitration, where the two sides put all the points they wish to raise into writing and submit this, together with any relevant documents, to the arbitrator. He will then read all the documents, and make his decision. Alternatively the parties may send all these documents to the arbitrator, but before he makes his decision both parties will attend a hearing at which they make oral submissions to the arbitrator to support their case. Where necessary, witnesses can be called to give evidence. If witnesses are asked to give evidence orally then this will not normally be given on oath, i.e. the person will not have to swear to tell the truth. However, if the parties wish, then the witness can be asked to give evidence on oath and the whole procedure will be very formal. If witnesses are called to give evidence, the Arbitration Act 1996 allows for the use of court procedures to ensure the attendance of those witnesses.

The date, time and place of the arbitration hearing are all matters for the parties to decide in consultation with the arbitrator. This gives a great degree of flexibility to the proceedings; the parties can choose what is most convenient for all the people concerned.

10.5.4 The award

The decision made by the arbitrator is called an award and is binding on the parties. It can even be enforced through the courts if necessary. The decision is usually final, though it can be challenged in the courts on the grounds of serious irregularity in the proceedings or on a point of law (s 68 Arbitration Act 1996).

10.5.5 Advantages of arbitration

There are several advantages which largely arise from the fact that the parties have the freedom to make their own arbitration agreement, and decide exactly how formal or informal they wish it to be. The main advantages are:

- The parties may choose their own arbitrator, and can therefore decide whether the matter is best dealt with by a technical expert or by a lawyer or by a professional arbitrator.
- If there is a question of quality this can be decided by an expert in the particular field, saving the expense of calling expert witnesses and the time that would be used in explaining all the technicalities to a judge.
- The hearing time and place can be arranged to suit parties.
- The actual procedure used is flexible and the parties can choose that which is most suited to the situation; this will usually result in a more informal and relaxed hearing than in court.
- The matter is dealt with in private and there will be no publicity.

- The dispute will be resolved more quickly than through a court hearing.
- Arbitration proceedings are usually much cheaper than going to court.
- The award is normally final and can be enforced through the courts.

10.5.6 Disadvantages of arbitration

However, there are some disadvantages of arbitration, especially where the parties are not on an equal footing as regards their ability to present their case. This is because legal aid is not available for arbitration and this may disadvantage an individual in a case against a business; if the case had gone to court, a person on a low income would have qualified for legal aid and so had the benefit of a lawyer to present their case. The other main disadvantages are that:

- An unexpected legal point may arise in the case which is not suitable for decision by a non-lawyer arbitrator.
- If a professional arbitrator is used, his fees may be expensive.
- It will also be expensive if the parties opt for a formal hearing, with witnesses giving evidence and lawyers representing both sides.
- The rights of appeal are limited.
- The delays for commercial and international arbitration may be nearly as great as those in the courts if a professional arbitrator and lawyers are used.

This problem of delay and expense has meant that arbitration has, to some extent, lost its popularity with companies as a method of dispute resolution. More and more businesses are turning to the alternatives offered by centres such as the Centre for Dispute Resolution or, in the case of international disputes, are choosing to have the matter resolved in another country. One of the problems was that the law on arbitration had become complex and the Arbitration Act 1996 is an attempt to improve the process. In general it can be said that certain types of dispute are suitable for arbitration. This especially includes commercial disagreements between two businesses where the parties have little hope of finding sufficient common ground to make mediation a realistic prospect, and provided there is no major point of law involved.

D Complaints

3. Disputes arising out of, or in connection with, this contract which cannot be amicably settled may (if you so wish) be referred to arbitration under a special scheme devised by arrangement with the Association of British Travel Agents (ABTA) but administered independently by the Chartered Institute of Arbitrators. The scheme provides for a simple and inexpensive method of Arbitration on documents alone, with restricted liability on you in respect of costs. The scheme does not apply to claims greater than £1,500 per person or £7,500 per booking form or to claims which are solely or mainly in respect of physical injury or illness or the consequences of such injury or illness. If you elect to use the scheme, written notice requesting arbitration must be made within 9 months after the scheduled date of return from holiday.

Figure 10.3 *Optional arbitration clause in a consumer contract*

ACTIVITY

Find an arbitration clause in a consumer contract, for example for a package holiday or insurance or for a mobile phone.

10.6 Tribunals

Tribunals operate alongside the court system and have become an important part of the legal system. Many tribunals were created in the second half of the 20th century, with the development of the welfare state. They were created in order to give people a method of enforcing their entitlement to certain social rights. However, unlike alternative dispute resolution, where the parties decide not to use the courts, the parties in tribunal cases cannot go to court to resolve their dispute. The tribunal must be used instead of court proceedings.

10.6.1 Role of tribunals

Tribunals enforce rights which have been granted through social and welfare legislation. There are many different rights, such as:

- the right to a mobility allowance for those who are too disabled to walk more than a very short distance
- the right to a payment if one is made redundant from work
- the right not to be discriminated against because of one's sex, race, age or disability
- the right of immigrants to have a claim for political asylum heard.

These are just a few of the types of rights that tribunals deal with.

10.6.2 Tribunals, Courts and Enforcement Act 2007

Tribunals were set up as the welfare state developed, so new developments resulted in the creation of a new tribunal. This led to more than 70 different types of tribunal. Each tribunal was separate and the various tribunals used different procedures. This made the system confused and complicated.

The whole system was reformed by the Tribunals, Courts and Enforcement Act 2007. This created a unified structure for tribunals, with a First-tier Tribunal to hear cases at first instance and an Upper Tribunal to hear appeals.

First-tier Tribunal

Since the First-tier Tribunal deals with about 300,000 cases each year and has nearly 200 judges and 3,600 lay members, it operates in seven Chambers (divisions). These are:

- the Social Entitlement Chamber – this covers a wide range of matters such as child support, criminal injuries compensation and gender recognition.
- the Health, Education and Social Care Chamber – this includes the former Mental

Health Review Tribunal which dealt with appeals against the continued detention of those in mental hospitals. This Chamber also deals with special educational needs issues.

- the War Pensions and Armed Forces Compensation Chamber.
- the General Regulatory Chamber.
- the Taxation Chamber.
- the Land, Property and Housing Chamber.
- the Asylum and Immigration Chamber.

As well as these, there is one tribunal which still operates separately from the First-tier Tribunal. This is the Employment Tribunal. However, it is likely that this will eventually become part of the First-tier Tribunal.

Upper Tribunal

The Upper Tribunal is divided into four Chambers (divisions). These are:

- the Administrative Appeals Chamber, which hears appeals from the Social Entitlement Chamber, the Health, Education and Social Care Chamber and the War Pensions and Armed Forces Compensation Chamber
- the Tax and Chancery Chamber
- the Lands Chamber
- the Asylum and Immigration Chamber.

From the Upper Tribunal there is a further possible appeal route to the Court of Appeal and from here a final appeal to the Supreme Court.

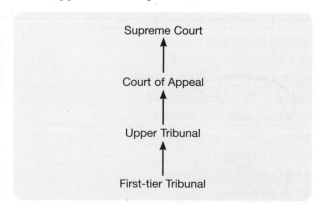

Figure 10.4 *Appeal route in tribunal cases*

10.6.3 Composition

Cases in the First-tier Tribunal are heard by a Tribunal Judge. Also, for some types of case, two lay members will sit with the judge to make the decision. These lay members will have expertise in the particular field of the tribunal. For example, the lay members in a hearing about a claim to mobility allowance would be medically qualified, while there would be surveyors sitting on the Lands Tribunal. In employment tribunals there are also two lay members. These will usually be one person from an employers' organisation and one from an employees' organisation. This gives them a very clear understanding of employment issues.

10.6.4 Procedure

Both sides must be given an opportunity to put their case. In some tribunals, especially employment and asylum tribunals, this will be done in a formal way with the witness giving evidence on oath and being cross-examined. Other tribunals will operate in a less formal way.

Funding for representation is available in only a few tribunals, so most applicants will not have a lawyer, but will present their own case. Where an applicant is putting his own case, then the Tribunal Judge must try to make sure that the applicant puts the case fully.

The decision of the tribunal is binding.

10.6.5 The Administrative Justice and Tribunals Council

This was set up under the Tribunals, Courts and Enforcement Act 2007. It replaced the previous Council on Tribunals which had operated since 1957. Its duties include:

- keeping the working of tribunals under review
- reporting on the constitution and working of tribunals
- considering and reporting on any other matter relating to tribunals.

A member of the Council may attend (as observer) any proceedings of a tribunal.

10.6.6 Advantages of tribunals

Tribunals were set up to prevent the overloading of the courts with the extra cases that social and welfare rights claims generate.

For the applicant in tribunal cases, the advantages are that such cases are dealt with:

- more cheaply
- more quickly
- more informally
- by experts in the area.

Cheapness

As applicants are encouraged to represent themselves and not use lawyers, tribunal hearings do not normally involve the costs associated with court hearings. It is also rare for an order for costs to be made by a tribunal, so that an applicant need not fear a large bill if they lose the case.

Quick hearings

Most tribunal hearings are very short and can be dealt with in one day.

Informality

The hearing is more informal than in court. Parties are encouraged to present their own case. In addition, most cases are heard in private.

Expertise

In some tribunals two lay members sit to hear the case with the Tribunal Judge. These lay members are experts in the type of case being heard. This gives them good knowledge and understanding of the issue in dispute.

10.6.7 Disadvantages of tribunals

Lack of funding

Public funding is not available for most tribunals, which may put an applicant at a disadvantage if the other side (often an employer or government department) uses a lawyer. Legal aid is available for cases where fundamental human rights are involved, such as in cases about whether an asylum seeker has the right to remain in the United Kingdom or whether a patient should remain in a secure mental hospital.

Key Facts	
First-tier Tribunal	• operates in 7 Chambers (divisions) • deals with about 300,000 cases a year NB Employment Tribunal operates separately
Upper Tribunal	• operates in 4 Chambers (divisions) • hears appeals from the First-tier Tribunal • there is a further appeal to the Court of Appeal
Panel	• cases may be heard by a Tribunal Judge OR • by a Tribunal Judge sitting with two experts
Legal aid availability	• only for certain types of case, e.g. asylum rights or the right of a mental patient not to be detained
Administrative Justice and Tribunals Council	• keeps the work of tribunals under review • reports on the work of tribunals

Figure 10.5 *Key facts chart on tribunals*

More formal than ADR

A tribunal hearing is more formal than using ADR. The place is unfamiliar and the procedure can be confusing for individuals presenting their own cases. Where applicants are not represented the judge is expected to take an inquisitorial role and help to establish the points that the applicant wishes to make. But this ideal is not always achieved.

Delay

Although the intention is that cases are dealt with quickly, the number of cases dealt with by tribunals means that there can be delays in getting a hearing. The use of lay members can add to this problem as they sit part-time, usually one day a fortnight. If a case is complex, lasting several days, this can lead to proceedings being spread over a number of weeks or even months.

10.6.8 Domestic tribunals

These are effectively 'in-house' tribunals set up by private bodies, usually for their own internal disciplinary control. They must keep to the rules of natural justice and their decisions are subject to judicial review. In addition, for many professional disciplinary tribunals there is an appeal route to the Judicial Committee of the Privy Council, in cases where the tribunal has decided to strike off a member from the professional register. For example, this applies to decisions of the disciplinary committee of the General Medical Council, and also to other medical disciplinary tribunals.

EXAMINATION QUESTIONS

1. (a) Explain the alternative methods of dispute resolution available in England and Wales. [14 marks]
   (b) Evaluate arbitration as a mechanism for resolving disputes in England and Wales. [11 marks]

   LA1, Summer 2011, WJEC

EXTENSION ESSAY

Critically discuss the need for alternative forms of dispute resolution.

CHAPTER 11

CRIME AND POLICE INVESTIGATIONS

11.1 Crime statistics

Criminal cases are frequently headline news in the papers; society as a whole is concerned about the crime rate. The statistics for recorded crime show that there was a massive increase in the last half of the 20th century. In 1950 there were only half a million recorded crimes, but by the 1990s the figure had reached five million. By 1998–99 there were 5.4 million recorded crimes.

In 2002 the National Crime Recording Standard was introduced to try to make sure that all police forces kept to the same guidelines for recording crime. Following this, and partly because of the new way of recording figures, the recorded crime rate increased for two years, before decreasing again. For 2011–12 there were 3.9 million recorded crimes.

Even these crime figures are not believed to give a true picture of the amount of criminal activity in England and Wales. It is thought that a large amount of crime is not recorded. This is shown by the British Crime Survey.

11.1.1 The British Crime Survey

The BCS is a face-to-face survey in which a sample of people resident in households in England and Wales are asked about their experiences of crime in the 12 months prior to interview. For 2011–12 the British Crime Survey interviewed just over 46,000 people. The Survey then used the figures from these interviews to estimate the full extent of crime. The fact that the Survey relies on people's experience of crime means that crimes where there was no victim will not be reported in this survey. This is particularly true of drug offending. In 2011–12 the British Crime Survey estimated that there were 9.1 million crimes.

11.1.2 Annual variations

Within the figures for any one year, there will be a variation in different crimes, with some showing large increases, others small increases or even a decrease. These variations can be caused by police policy in targeting certain types of crime. Full statistics for recorded crime are published by the Home Office each year. Figure 11.1 shows the change in recorded crime between 2009–10 and 2010–2011.

Figure 11.2 shows the change in different offences for the same period according to the British Crime Survey.

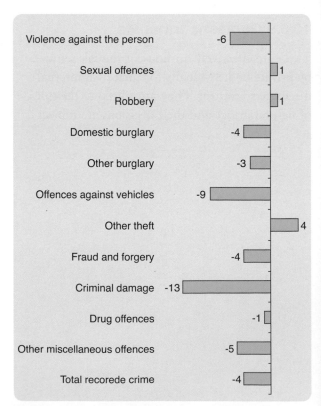

Figure 11.1 *Percentage changes in the main types of police recorded crime, 2009–10 to 2010–11*

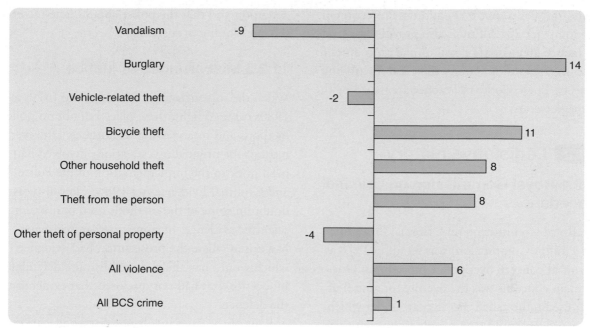

Figure 11.2 *Percentage changes in the main crime types: 2010/11 British Crime Survey compared to 2009/10*

11.1.3 Investigating crime

It is still clear that the crime rates are worryingly high. It is obviously necessary to have an authority which has sufficient power to investigate possible crimes by being able to stop suspects, search them, arrest people and interview them about suspected criminal activity. In this country the police are given this authority. However, only about one in four recorded crimes is detected.

It is clearly necessary that the police should have appropriate power to investigate crimes, but it is also necessary to keep a balance between protecting individual liberty by preventing people from being unnecessarily harassed and/or detained, and giving the police adequate powers to prevent or detect crime.

During the 1970s and 1980s there were several serious miscarriages of justice in individual cases. Many of these miscarriages stemmed from questionable police procedures and as a result Parliament has tried to regulate this area of the law. The main police powers are set out in the Police

and Criminal Evidence Act 1984 (PACE), with some additions and amendments made by the Criminal Justice and Public Order Act 1994, the Criminal Justice Act 2003, the Serious Organised

ACTIVITY

Look at Figures 11.1 and 11.2.

Questions

1. Which offence do the recorded crime figures show as having the biggest increase for 2009–10 to 2010–11?
2. Which offence do the BCS figures show as having the biggest increase for the same period?
3. What factors might explain why the two charts show that different offences had the biggest increase?
4. What overall difference is there between the two sets of percentages?
5. What factors might explain the difference in the figures?

Crime and Police Act 2005 and the Protection of Freedoms Act 2012. PACE also provides for Codes of Practice giving extra detail on the procedures for searching, detaining, questioning and identifying suspects. These Codes of Practice are issued by the Home Secretary.

11.2 Legislative history

11.2.1 Royal Commission on Criminal Procedure

The Royal Commission on Criminal Procedure (the Phillips Commission) was set up in 1978 as a result of concern over police procedures. One of the main concerns was the overuse (or abuse) of what used to be called the 'sus' law under which police officers could stop people if they felt there was anything suspicious. This usually meant young men, and particularly members of ethnic minorities, were likely to be stopped, often for no real cause.

The Royal Commission found that the law on police powers that existed before 1984 was piecemeal and haphazard. There were provisions in the common law, local bylaws and over 70 different Acts of Parliament giving the right to stop, search or arrest in a variety of different circumstances. This obviously made the law confusing, for both suspects and the police. The Commission also stressed the need to find a balance between 'the interests of the community in bringing offenders to justice and the rights and liberties of persons suspected or accused of crime'.

The findings of this Commission led to Parliament enacting the Police and Criminal Evidence Act 1984. This Act tried to both rationalise and modernise the law on many aspects of police procedure. Some of the most significant changes were in the requirement that police should keep records of such matters as stops and searches, and custody records relating to those in police

detention and that the police should tape-record the questioning of suspects.

11.2.2 Miscarriages of justice

When the miscarriages of justice of the 1970s and 1980s came to light, these placed doubt on police methods and interviewing techniques. However, most of the original investigations involved had been prior to the implementation of the Police and Criminal Evidence Act 1984. They also cast doubt on some of the methods used in obtaining scientific evidence. In some cases, miscarriages had arisen where the prosecution had evidence which would have helped establish the defendant's innocence, but had not disclosed that evidence to the defence.

Four of the cases involved separate allegations of terrorist activities on behalf of the IRA. These were the Guildford Four, the Birmingham Six, the Maguires and Judith Ward. The Guildford Four were convicted in 1975 of bombing a pub in Guildford and the evidence against them consisted almost entirely of confessions which were supposed to have been made to police during interviews. The original police evidence claimed that police officers had made a contemporaneous handwritten note of what was said during the interview with Armstrong, one of the four accused. Eventually a set of typed police notes with amendments, both typed and written, and rearrangement of material was discovered. This cast considerable doubt on the police version of the interview and, when the case was finally referred back to the Criminal Division of the Court of Appeal in 1989, the Court quashed the convictions.

In the Birmingham Six case, the accused claimed that they had been beaten up by the police and forced into making untrue confessions and, as with the Guildford Four case, later evidence cast doubt on police notes and the credibility of the police evidence. Later evidence also supported the men's claim that they had been beaten up by the police while in custody, being questioned about the bomb attack. There was also a problem with scientific evidence as to whether the men had handled nitroglycerine (an explosive substance). Scientific knowledge showed that such tests could be faulty and give a positive reading from quite innocent substances such as paint, or even from the washing-up liquid used to clean the dishes in which the samples were then tested. When it was first discovered that the men had tested 'positive' this had been put down to them touching adhesive tape. However, Dr Skuse, a forensic scientist, said 'categorically' in evidence that the only possible explanation of the 'positive' tests was that they had been handling explosives. Their convictions were finally quashed by the Court of Appeal.

The case of Stefan Kiszko was different in that scientific evidence which supported his innocence had been available to the prosecution defence (see article below).

These various cases also cast doubts on the appeal system as the defendants had appealed against conviction in all the cases, but the original appeal had not been allowed. At the same time, there was concern over the number of acquittals in criminal trials and a belief that the rules of PACE under which the police worked were too restrictive and led to many guilty people going free. It was clear that a full review of the criminal justice system was necessary.

11.2.3 The Runciman Commission

The terms of reference of this Commission on Criminal Justice were to:

'examine the effectiveness of the criminal justice system in England and Wales in securing the

---

EXAMPLE

Evidence could have prevented prosecution: Court's quashing of murder conviction reopens questions over judicial system

The latest in the litany of miscarriages of justice is arguably the most shocking.

For even before Stefan Kiszko stood trial, there was unequivocal evidence of his innocence.

Scientists had shown that Mr Kiszko was infertile and that Lesley Molseed's attacker was not. Mr Kiszko has a condition known as hypogonadism, making it impossible for him to secrete sperm. Spermheads were found on the dead girl's clothing.

The evidence lay buried for 16 years, until yesterday when it was used to prove his innocence.

The Lancashire police investigation into the affair will seek to discover who was involved in that suppression and whether it was deliberate, negligent or accidental.

Certainly Dr Edward Tierney, the police surgeon who ordered the tests, said he knew of the evidence's potential to clear Mr Kiszko. He said he had informed senior investigating officers in the West Yorkshire murder squad, headed by Detective Chief Supt Jack Dibb, who has since died, of its importance.

It is not known whether this information was passed to the prosecution authorities and lawyers. However, its suppression meant that Mr Kiszko served those years at first in prison and then, when his mental health deteriorated in jail, in a secure psychiatric hospital, and that the real attacker escaped justice.

An extract from an article by Heather Mills in the *Independent*, 19 February 1992 © The Independent, 1992, www.independent.co.uk

conviction of those guilty of criminal offences and the acquittal of those who are innocent, having regard to the efficient use of resources'.

This was neatly put by Michael Zander, one of the Commission, as a remit with three distinct component elements:

- the need to convict the guilty
- the need not to convict the innocent, and
- due economy.

The Commission had 22 research studies carried out into how the criminal justice system worked in practice; it also heard evidence from over 600 organisations and its report was published in 1993, containing 352 recommendations.

These recommendations ranged from police investigations, for example, suggesting continuous videoing of police custody suites to pre-trial procedures such as the suggestion for abolishing the defendant's right to choose trial by jury. Other recommendations were concerned with the disclosure of evidence, and the setting up of an independent body to investigate possible miscarriages of justice.

Many of the recommendations were implemented by the Criminal Justice and Public Order Act 1994. The recommendation for an independent body to investigate possible miscarriages of justice led to the setting up of the Criminal Cases Review Commission in 1997 (see Chapter 13 for detail on its work).

11.2.4 The Labour government's policies

In May 1997 a Labour government was elected for the first time in 18 years. In its election manifesto the party had promised to be 'tough on crime and tough on the causes of crime'. The first major piece of legislation aimed at this promise was the Crime and Disorder Act 1998. This Act added new powers to deal with persistent petty criminals

and also those on the borders of committing crime. In particular it allows local authorities to seek anti-social behaviour orders against those who are sometimes called 'the neighbours from hell'. This idea was extended by the Anti-Social Behaviour Act 2003.

Other changes to the criminal justice system in the Crime and Disorder Act 1998 included alterations to court procedure to speed up the process; more cooperation between police and local authorities and other organisations such as the newly created Youth Offending Teams; and restrictions on the number of warnings an offender can be given before being taken to court.

The Criminal Justice Act 2003 extended the time the police could detain suspects. The same Act also changed sentencing powers, including creating extended sentences for violent or sex offenders (see Chapter 14).

The Serious Organised Crime and Police Act 2005 changed the police powers of arrest, so that police could arrest those suspected of any level of offence, including offences which do not carry a prison sentence. Prior to 2005, in general the police could arrest only for offences which carried a substantial prison sentence (see section 11.3.4).

11.2.5 The MacPherson Report

In 1993 a black teenager, Stephen Lawrence, was stabbed to death in a racist attack. The police handled the investigation into the murder in a very incompetent way. Some of their failings included not searching properly for evidence and suspects and not investigating tip-offs about the identity of the killers. In addition, Stephen Lawrence's parents were not treated with proper respect and sensitivity.

In 1997 the government set up a judicial inquiry into the handling of the police investigation. This inquiry was chaired by Sir William MacPherson, a former High Court

Judge. A report was published in 1999. This report accused the Metropolitan Police of 'institutional racism'. It contained many recommendations about the way police and also the Crown Prosecution Service should deal with cases.

As a result of the report, the Race Relations Act 1976 was amended to make it unlawful for any public authority when carrying out its public functions, including the police, to discriminate against a person on racial grounds. This covers activities by the police such as stop and search, arrests and investigating offences.

The interests of victims and victims' families were given a higher profile, especially in a new Code for Crown Prosecutors first issued in 2000. It stressed that victims (or their families) should be told about decisions which make a significant difference to the case.

11.3 Police powers

The police, like everyone else, must respect the individual's civil rights. People are entitled to be allowed to move freely and to have their person and their property respected. However, as already stated, there must be sufficient powers for the police to investigate crime – Parliament has therefore given them special powers which can be used in certain circumstances. These powers include the right to stop suspects, to search them, to arrest and interview people when necessary and to take fingerprints and samples (such as blood) for scientific analysis. Without powers such as these, it would be impossible to investigate crimes. However, it is important that, at the same time, ordinary people are not unnecessarily harassed by the police and that suspects are protected from overzealous police methods.

The law on police powers is mainly contained in the Police and Criminal Evidence Act 1984 and the Codes of Practice made under s 66 of that Act. There are eight codes as follows:

1. Code A to deal with the powers to stop and search.
2. Code B for the powers to search premises and seize property.
3. Code C to deal with the detention, treatment and questioning of suspects.
4. Code D on the rules for identification procedures.
5. Code E on the tape-recording of interviews with suspects.
6. Code F on visual recording with sound of interviews (i.e. videoing interviews).
7. Code G on powers of arrest.
8. Code H on detention, treatment and questioning of those arrested under s 41 of the Terrorism Act 2000.

11.3.1 Powers to stop and search

Police powers to stop and search people and vehicles are set out in ss 1–7 of PACE. Section 1 gives the police the right to stop and search people and vehicles in a public place. 'Public place' not only means in the street, but also extends to areas such as pub car parks, and even private gardens, if the police officer has good reasons for believing that the suspect does not live at that address. To use this power under PACE a police officer must have reasonable grounds for suspecting that the person is in possession of (or the vehicle contains) stolen goods or prohibited articles. Prohibited articles include such items as offensive weapons and articles for use in connection with burglary or theft.

Safeguards

As these powers are very wide there are safeguards in that the police officer must give his name and station and the reason for the search. This was shown in *Osman v DPP* (1999) where the officers did not give their names and station. The Queen's Bench Divisional Court held this made a search of Mr Osman unlawful and so he could not be guilty of assaulting the police in the execution of their duty. The court stressed that the formality of providing the suspect with the officer's name and station was 'of great importance in relation to civil liberties'.

This view was confirmed in *Michaels v Highbury Corner Magistrates' Court* (2009) where Michaels was seen by police apparently trying to hide from them. He then walked towards them and was seen to place something in his mouth. He was questioned and then told that he was going to be searched. He was asked to open his mouth and did so. A wrap of drugs was in his mouth. The police told him not to swallow it and took hold of him. However, he did swallow it. He was charged with obstructing the police during their search. His conviction was quashed by the Queen's Bench Divisional Court

as the officers had not given their names or station before asking him to open his mouth as part of their search. This made the search unlawful.

Also, if the officer fails to give a reason for the search, then that search is unlawful. If the search is in public, the police can only request that the suspect removes outer coat, jacket and gloves (s 2(9)). A written report must be made as soon as possible after the search.

Statistics

Home Office statistics show that the police made increasing use of the power to stop and search. The number of stops and searches rose from just over 100,000 in 1986 to well over a million by 1998. However, after the MacPherson Report in 1999 (see section 11.2.5), the number of stops and searches in 1999–2000 was well under a million at about 850,000. This was a decrease of 21 per cent on the previous 12 months. In the Metropolitan police force area (the police force criticised in the MacPherson Report), the decrease was 41 per cent.

Between 2000 and 2005 the number of stops and searches each year remained around 850,000. From 2005 there was a steady increase in the number of stops and searches reaching a peak in 2008–09 of 1.5 million. Much of the increase was due to extra stops and searches under section 60 of the Criminal Justice and Public Order Act 1994 and searches under terrorism laws. Although the overall number of stops and searches has decreased in the last few years, the number under PACE has increased. In 2010–11 there were over 1.2 million such stops and searches recorded (see Figure 11.3).

Code of Practice

Code of Practice A contains details and guidance on when these powers should be used. In particular it stresses that police officers must not act just because of a person's characteristics. Paragraph 2.2 of Code A says:

Police carrying out a stop and search

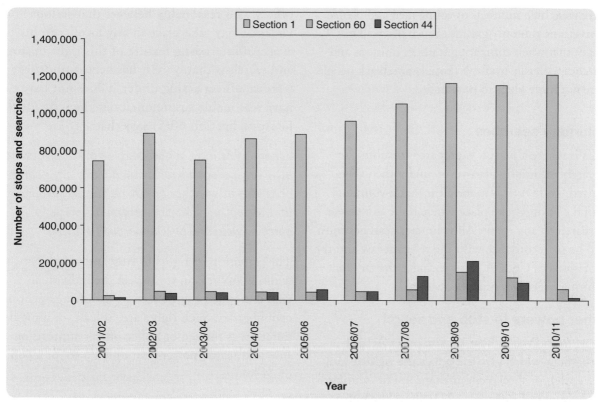

Figure 11.3 *Number of stops and searches by reason for search*

'Reasonable suspicion can never be supported on the basis of personal nature. It must rely on intelligence or information about, or some specific behaviour by, the person concerned.'

For example, unless the police have a description of a suspect, a person's physical appearance (including any of the 'protected characteristics' set out in the Equality Act 2010), or the fact that a person is known to have a previous conviction, cannot be used alone or in combination with each other, or in combination with any other factor, as the reason for searching that person.

Reasonable suspicion cannot be based on generalisations or stereotypical images of certain groups or categories of people as more likely to be involved in criminality.

The protected characteristics set out in the Equality Act are age, disability, gender reassignment, race, religion or belief, sex and sexual orientation, marriage and civil partnership, pregnancy and maternity.

Despite this guidance in the Code of Practice, there is still evidence that certain types of people, especially black youths, are more likely to be stopped than other groups.

A Home Office publication, *Statistics on Race and the Criminal Justice System, 2009–10*, showed that black people were seven times more likely than white people to be stopped and searched. This figure is based on the resident population in each police area.

However, research by Miller, Quinton and Bland in 2000 looked at the population actually 'available' at a number of sites and compared this with stops and searches in these areas. 'Available' meant actually out in public places at times when stops and searches were most likely to happen. This research showed that there were high numbers of young men and people from ethnic minority groups in such places. This meant that when comparing statistics on stops and searches with this 'available' population, black people were not more likely to be searched.

Voluntary searches

This is where a person is prepared to submit to a search voluntarily. However, under the 2004 revised Code A, it is made clear that a voluntary search can only take place where there is a power to search in any event. All voluntary searches must also be in accordance with the relevant law and the provisions of Code A. This includes the fact that voluntary searches must be recorded.

Other powers to stop and search

Apart from PACE there are also other Acts of Parliament which give the police the right to stop and search in special circumstances. For example, the Misuse of Drugs Act 1971 allows the police to search for controlled drugs. The Terrorism Act 2000 used to allow searches of people where it was thought 'expedient' as an anti-terrorist measure. There did not have to be reasonable suspicion, nor did the search have to be considered necessary. However, in *Gillan v United Kingdom: Quinton v United Kingdom* (2010) the European Court of Human Rights ruled that the wording of 'expedient' breached Article 8 (right to respect for private life) as the discretion conferred on individual police officers was too broad.

The powers in the Act were amended by the Protection of Freedoms Act 2012 so that now a search of the basis of terrorism can take place only if the police officer reasonably suspects the person to be a terrorist.

Section 60 of the Criminal Justice and Public Order Act 1994 gives the police an additional power of the right to stop and search in anticipation of violence. This can occur only where it has been authorised by a senior police officer who reasonably believes that serious violence may take place in any locality in his area. An interesting feature of this right to stop and search is that once it has been authorised, a police officer acting under it does not have to have reasonable suspicion about the individual he stops. Section 60(5) says that:

'A constable may, in the exercise of those powers, stop any person or vehicle and make any search he thinks fit whether or not he has any grounds for suspecting that the person or vehicle is carrying weapons or (dangerous) articles.'

The extension of rights to stop and search without any reason to suspect the individual who is stopped can be seen as an infringement of civil liberties. Such rights are, at least, of limited duration as the senior police officer authorising stop and search powers can only do so for a period of 24 hours.

> **COMMENT**
>
> ### Abuse of stop and search powers?
> Although there are well over a million people stopped and searched each year, only about 11 per cent of these are then arrested. This suggests that the police are overusing their powers to stop and search. When the figures for stop and search went down in 2000, a slightly higher percentage (13 per cent) of people were arrested. This appears to show that a more targeted approach to stop and search is more successful in identifying offenders.
>
> One main problem with stop-and-search procedure is that having reasonable grounds for suspecting the person is in possession of stolen goods or prohibited articles gives a wide discretion to individual police officers. The police are now keeping a database on stop/search powers which may identify officers who overuse this power.

In 1996, when the police in the Tottenham area of London were required to hand out a leaflet explaining stop-and-search rights, the number of stop-and-search incidents dropped by over 50 per cent. At the same time the proportion of arrests from stops and searches went up from 10 to 12 per cent. However, there was also an increase of 17 per cent in crimes such as burglary and street robbery in the area. So fewer stops and searches may well lead to more crimes.

11.3.2 Road checks

Where there is a reasonable suspicion that a person who has committed an indictable offence is at large in a particular area, s 4 of PACE gives permission for road checks to be made in that area. Such a check can normally only be authorised by a high-ranking police officer, that is a superintendent or higher rank, but an officer of a lower rank can authorise a road check if it is urgent. A road check allows all vehicles in the particular locality to be stopped.

11.3.3 The power to search premises

In certain circumstances the police have the power to enter and search premises. PACE sets out most of these powers, though there are other Acts which allow the police to obtain search warrants (see Figure 11.4 for powers under PACE).

Search warrants

The police can enter premises without the occupier's permission to make a search, if a warrant authorising that search has been issued by a magistrate. Such a warrant will normally be issued under s 8 of PACE. It will be granted if the magistrate is satisfied that the police have reasonable grounds for believing that an indictable offence has been committed, and that there is material on the premises which is likely to be of substantial value in the investigation of the offence and relevant evidence. In addition, the magistrate should be satisfied that it is not practicable to communicate with any person entitled to grant entry or access, or that entry will be refused unless a search warrant is produced, or that the purpose of the search may be frustrated unless police arriving at the premises can gain immediate entry. Search warrants are designed to prevent evidence being removed or destroyed through the need to give warning of an intended search.

Requirements of a warrant

A warrant must specify the premises to be searched and, as far as possible, the articles or persons to be sought. The warrant usually only authorises one entry on one occasion and must be executed within one month from the date of issue. The Serious Organised Crime and Police Act 2005 introduced an 'all premises' warrant to allow all premises occupied or controlled by the defendant to be searched. Search warrants can now allow access on more than one occasion.

The police are required to enter and search at a reasonable hour, unless it appears that the purpose of the search would be frustrated by an entry at a reasonable hour. They are also required to identify themselves as police officers, to show the warrant to any person at the premises and give that person a copy of the warrant.

However, the courts have held that the police need not comply precisely with these requirements if the circumstances of the case make it wholly inappropriate. In particular that the identification of the searcher as a police officer and the production of the warrant need not be carried out on entry, but only before the actual search begins. This was the position in *R v Longman* (1988) where the police, who had a warrant to search premises for drugs, knew that it would be difficult to gain entry. They therefore arranged for a plain-clothes policewoman to pose as a delivery girl from Interflora and get the occupants of the premises

Type of power	Law giving power	Comment
With a warrant	s 8 PACE gives power to magistrates to issue warrants	• Warrant must specify premises • *R v Longman* – need not show warrant before entry, only before search
Without a warrant: (a) to arrest person (b) to search premises controlled by an arrested person (c) to search premises which a person was in at or immediately before arrest	s 17 PACE s 18 PACE s 32 PACE	• *O'Loughlin v Chief Constable of Essex* – police must state reason for entry whenever possible • *R v Badham* – must make search immediately after arrest
To prevent a breach of the peace	Common law	• Applies to private homes as well as public places • *McLeod v Commissioner of Police for the Metropolis*

Figure 11.4 *Summary of police powers to enter and search premises*

to open the door. Once the door was opened, the police burst into the premises without identifying themselves as police officers or showing the search warrant. The Court of Appeal held that force or subterfuge could be lawfully used in order to gain entry with a search warrant.

Section 16 of PACE and Code of Practice B set out full guidelines for executing search warrants.

Powers to enter premises without a search warrant

Police officers may enter and search premises if it is in order to arrest a person named in an arrest warrant, or to arrest someone for an offence, or to recapture an escaped prisoner. This power is set out in s 17 of PACE. The police must give anybody present in the premises the reason for the entry. In *O'Loughlin v Chief Constable of Essex* (1998) police forced their way in without explaining that it was in order to arrest O'Loughlin's wife for criminal damage. This made the entry unlawful and O'Loughlin was able to sue the police for damages.

Police can only enter without giving a reason if the circumstances make it impossible, impracticable or undesirable to give the reason. Section 17 also gives the police the right to enter premises for the purpose of 'saving life or limb or preventing serious damage to property'.

In *Syed v DPP* (2010) the police attended at the Syeds' property because of a phone call from a neighbour reporting a disturbance. Syed told them he had had a verbal argument with his brother. There was no sign of any damage or injury. When the police questioned Syed further he became evasive. They told him they had a right to enter, but he prevented them from doing so, head-butting one of the police officers. He was arrested for assaulting an officer in the execution of his duty.

The Queen's Bench Divisional Court quashed his conviction as the police had no right to enter in the circumstances. Section 17 only gave the right to enter where there was risk of serious injury or serious damage to property. The fact that the police stated they were concerned for the welfare of others within the property was not sufficient to give them a right to enter.

PACE also gives the police the right to enter premises without a search warrant after making an arrest, if an officer has reasonable grounds for suspecting that there is evidence on premises relating to the offence for which the person has just been arrested, or to a possible connected or similar offence. The police can enter premises which are occupied or controlled by the person under arrest (s 18), or premises in which that person was at the time of arrest, or immediately before he was arrested (s 32). It was held in *R v Badham* (1987) that this power under s 32 only allows a search to be made immediately after the arrest; it does not allow the police to return to the premises several hours later to make a search.

To prevent a breach of the peace

There is still a right under the common law for police to enter premises if there is need for them to deal with, or prevent, a breach of the peace. This right applies even to private homes, as was shown by the case of *McLeod v Commissioner of Police for the Metropolis* (1994) in which the police had entered domestic premises when there was a violent quarrel taking place, fearing a breach of the peace.

Searching with the consent of the occupier of the premises

The police may, of course, enter and search premises without a warrant if the occupier of those premises gives them permission to do so. However, that consent must be given in writing and, if, at any time, the occupier indicates that he has withdrawn his consent, the police must stop the search and leave the premises. Figure 11.4 summarises these powers to search premises.

Unlawful entry and searches

Where the police exceed their powers, the occupier of the premises or any other person affected can make a civil claim for damages against the police under the tort of trespass. However, if the police obtain any evidence in an unlawful search, it is possible that that evidence may be used as the basis of a prosecution. The defence can try to have such evidence excluded under s 78 of PACE which says that a court may refuse to allow evidence to be given if it appears that, having regard to all the circumstances, the admission of the evidence would have such an adverse effect on the fairness of the proceedings that the court ought not to admit it. This means that it may be possible to persuade the judge at the trial to refuse to allow the prosecution to put forward any evidence obtained as a result of an unlawful search.

11.3.4 Powers of arrest

Section 24 of PACE sets out the powers the police have to arrest suspects. These powers were completely changed at the beginning of 2006 by the Serious Organised Crime and Police Act 2005 (SOCPA). Section 110 of SOCPA substituted a new s 24 into PACE.

Previously, there had to be an arrestable offence, but now an arrest can be made for any offence. The new s 24 of PACE reads:

'24(1)   A constable may arrest without a warrant:
(a) anyone who is about to commit an offence;
(b) anyone who is in the act of committing an offence;
(c) anyone whom he has reasonable grounds for suspecting to be about to commit an offence;
(d) anyone whom he has reasonable grounds for suspecting to be committing an offence.

(2)   If a constable has reasonable grounds for suspecting that an offence has been committed, he may arrest anyone without a warrant whom he has reasonable grounds to suspect of being guilty of it.

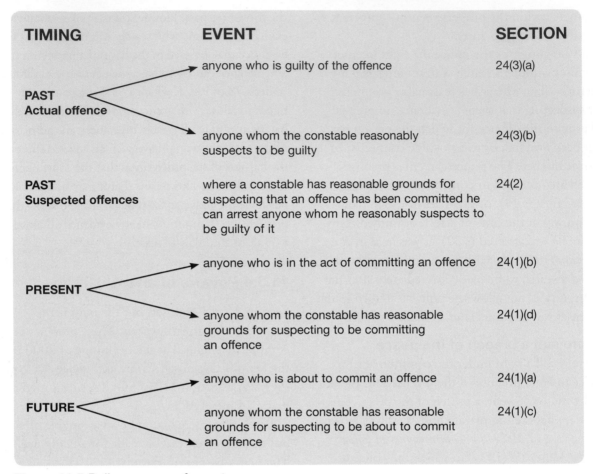

TIMING	EVENT	SECTION
PAST **Actual offence**	anyone who is guilty of the offence	24(3)(a)
	anyone whom the constable reasonably suspects to be guilty	24(3)(b)
PAST **Suspected offences**	where a constable has reasonable grounds for suspecting that an offence has been committed he can arrest anyone whom he reasonably suspects to be guilty of it	24(2)
PRESENT	anyone who is in the act of committing an offence	24(1)(b)
	anyone whom the constable has reasonable grounds for suspecting to be committing an offence	24(1)(d)
FUTURE	anyone who is about to commit an offence	24(1)(a)
	anyone whom the constable has reasonable grounds for suspecting to be about to commit an offence	24(1)(c)

Figure 11.5 *Police powers of arrest*

(3) If an offence has been committed, a constable may arrest without a warrant:
  (a) anyone who is guilty of the offence;
  (b) anyone whom he has reasonable grounds for suspecting to be guilty of it.'

Figure 11.5 gives a summary of these powers of arrest.

Limitations on arrest

An arresting officer can arrest only if he has reasonable grounds for believing that it is necessary to make the arrest for one of the following reasons:

- to enable the person's name or address to be ascertained
- to prevent the person:
  - causing physical injury to himself or any other person
  - suffering physical injury
  - causing loss of or damage to property
  - committing an offence against public decency
  - causing an unlawful obstruction of the highway
- to protect a child or other vulnerable person
- to allow the prompt and effective investigation of the offence or of the conduct of the person

- to prevent any prosecution for the offence from being hindered by the disappearance of the person in question.

PACE Code of Practice G

Code of Practice G gives guidelines for arrest under these powers. It says:

'2.1 A lawful arrest requires two elements:
- A person's involvement or suspected involvement or attempted involvement AND
- Reasonable grounds for believing that the person's arrest is necessary.
2.2 Arresting officers are required to inform the person arrested that they have been arrested, even if this fact is obvious, and of the relevant circumstances in respect to both elements.'

The Code points out that the power to arrest is exercisable only if the constable has reasonable grounds for believing that it is necessary to arrest the person. It remains an operational decision at the discretion of the arresting officer as to:

- what action he or she may take at the point of contact with the individual
- the necessary criteria, if any, which apply
- whether to arrest, report for summons, grant street bail, issue a fixed penalty notice or take any other action open to the officer.

The test for 'necessary' was considered in *Richardson v Chief Constable of West Midlands* (2011). Richardson, a teacher of good character, had attended voluntarily by appointment at a police station to be interviewed about a possible common assault on a pupil. Because the full facilities at the police station were not open, he was asked to travel to another police station and meet the police officer there. When he arrived at the second police station he was arrested. After hearing his explanation of the incident, the police decided to take no further action. Richardson then sued the police for false imprisonment.

The judge at the High Court hearing found that the arrest had not been necessary. Richardson had attended voluntarily to be interviewed and had even gone to another police station because it was more convenient for the police. The reason the police put forward for the arrest was that it was necessary 'to allow the prompt and effective investigation of the offence'. The judge held that there was no reason to think that Richardson would not stay to be questioned, so the arrest was not justified. Richardson was awarded £1,000 damages.

Other statutory rights of arrest

The Criminal Justice and Public Order Act 1994 added an extra power of arrest to PACE. This is now in s 46A of PACE and gives the police the right to arrest without a warrant anyone who, having been released on police bail, fails to attend at the police station at the set time. The Criminal Justice and Public Order Act 1994 also gives police the right to arrest for a variety of new offences including collective and aggravated trespass, in connection with offences committed in preparing for or attending a 'rave', or intentional harassment.

Arrest for breach of the peace

As well as rights given to them by Acts of Parliament, the police still retain a common law right to arrest where there has been, or is likely to be, a breach of the peace. This applies even if the behaviour complained of was on private premises as demonstrated by the case of *McConnell v Chief Constable of the Greater Manchester Police* (1990). In this case the manager of a carpet store had asked McConnell to leave, but he had refused to do so. A police officer had then taken McConnell outside, but McConnell attempted to re-enter, so the officer arrested him for conduct whereby a breach of the peace might be occasioned. McConnell later sued the police for false imprisonment arguing that the arrest was unlawful, as a breach of the peace could not occur on private premises, but the Court of Appeal held that it could do so and that the arrest was lawful.

In *Bibby v Chief Constable of Essex Police* (2000), the Court of Appeal summarised the conditions that must apply for this common law power of arrest to be used. These were:

- there must be a sufficiently real and present threat to the peace
- the threat must come from the person to be arrested
- the conduct of that person must clearly interfere with the rights of others and its natural consequence must be 'not wholly unreasonable' violence from a third party
- the conduct of the person to be arrested must be unreasonable.

Arrest with a warrant

The police may make an application to a magistrate for a warrant to arrest a named person. Such a warrant is issued under s 1 of the Magistrates' Court Act 1980 which requires written information, supported by evidence on oath showing that a person has committed (or is suspected of committing) an offence. A warrant for arrest will only be granted if the offence involved is punishable by imprisonment, so a warrant can never be granted for offences for which are only punishable by, for example, a fine.

Manner of arrest

Whenever the police make an arrest they should at the time of, or as soon as practicable after, tell the person arrested that they are under arrest and the reason for it, even if it is perfectly obvious why they are being arrested. There is no set form of words to be used and, as is often portrayed in television dramas, it is sufficient if the arresting officer says something like 'you're nicked for theft'.

Lawful arrest

In *Taylor v Chief Constable of Thames Valley Police* (2004) the Court of Appeal held that the test of whether the words of arrest were sufficient is:

'was the person arrested told, in simple non-technical language that he could understand, the essential legal and factual grounds for his arrest?'

Taylor was a 10-year-old boy who had been throwing stones during an anti-vivisection demo. When he was present at a later protest he was identified by a police officer who said: 'I am arresting you on suspicion of violent disorder on April 18, 1998 at Hillgrove Farm.'

The Court of Appeal held that this was understandable and so there was a lawful arrest.

Where necessary the police may use reasonable force to make an arrest.

The right to search an arrested person

Where a person has been arrested the police have a right to search that person for anything which might be used to help an escape, or anything which might be evidence relating to an offence. If such a search takes place in public the police can only require the suspect to remove outer coat, jacket and gloves.

Arrest by private citizens

The Serious Organised Crime and Police Act 2005 also created a new s 24A in PACE. This sets out the rights of private citizens to make an arrest. The first point is that private citizens can only make an arrest in respect of indictable offences.

The arrest can be made if someone is in the act of committing an indictable offence or where the citizen has reasonable grounds for suspecting the person to be committing an indictable offence. A private citizen can also arrest where there has been an indictable offence and there are reasonable grounds for suspecting the person to be guilty of it.

However, there are also limitations. It must appear that it is not reasonably practicable for a constable to make the arrest and it must be necessary because the citizen has reasonable grounds to believe the arrest is necessary to prevent the person:

- causing physical injury to himself or any other person
- suffering physical injury
- causing loss of or damage to property
- making off before a constable can assume responsibility for him.

ACTIVITY

State whether there has been a lawful arrest in the following situations. Give reasons for your answers.

Questions

1. After an incident in which a man was stabbed and seriously hurt, a police officer grabs hold of Damon. When Damon protests and asks why, the police officer says 'You know what it's for.' The police officer did not see the incident but was told by someone else at the scene that Damon was responsible.

2. Tony, a taxi driver, sees Gary climbing out of the window of a house. Tony catches hold of Gary and takes him to a nearby police station.

3. Amanda is stopped by the police for speeding. When one of the police officers asks her name, she replies 'Superwoman'. She is then asked for her address and refuses to give it. The police officer arrests her and takes her to the police station.

11.3.5 Powers of detention

Once a person has been arrested and taken to a police station there are rules setting out very strict time limits on how long they may be held there. These limits are longer if the offence being investigated is an indictable offence. There are also rules about the treatment of people in detention; these are contained in PACE as amended by the Criminal Justice and Public Order Act 1994, together with Code of Practice C.

Time limits on detention

The general rules on detention are that the police may detain a person for 24 hours. After this the police must charge or release any person who has been arrested on suspicion of a summary offence. Where the person has been arrested on suspicion of an indictable offence the police can detain the suspect for another 12 hours (making a total of 36 hours), but only with the permission of a senior officer (superintendent or above). To detain a person beyond 36 hours, the police must apply to the Magistrates' Court. The magistrates can order detention for up to a maximum total of 96 hours. The detainee has the right to be represented and oppose such an application. The time limits on detention are set out in Figure 11.6.

The detention must also be reviewed by the custody officer. Initially this must be not later than six hours after the detention, and then at

Time factor	Event(s)
Start of detention	Arrested person arrives at police station and the custody officer decides there is reason to detain him/her
Six hours	First review by custody officer
15 hours and every nine hours thereafter	Second and subsequent reviews by custody officer
24 hours	Summary offence – must charge or release For indictable offences – after 24 hours the permission of a superintendent or above is needed to extend the detention to 36 hours
36 hours	Police may apply to magistrates to extend the period of detention for an indictable offence
96 hours	Maximum time for detaining an arrested person (except under Terrorism Act 2006). Police must charge or release suspect

Figure 11.6 *Time limits on detention of a suspect*

intervals of not less than nine hours. If at any time the custody officer becomes aware that there are no grounds for continuing the detention, then he is under a duty to order an immediate release from custody. Also, while a person remains in custody under powers of detention, the custody officer must keep a record of all events that occur (such as interviews or visits to the cell by police officers).

Terrorism cases

Longer periods of detention are allowed where the suspect has been arrested for terrorism offences.

The Terrorism Act 2000 allows terrorist suspects to be detained for up to 14 days before charge. If the police wish to hold a suspect beyond the normal detention limits they have to apply to a District Judge in the Magistrates' Court. The suspect has the right to represented at the hearing.

Rights of a detained person

Detainees must be told their rights by the custody officer. These rights include:

- having someone informed of the arrest
- being told that independent legal advice is available free and being allowed to consult privately with a solicitor
- being allowed to consult the Code of Practice.

The right to have someone informed of the arrest

The right to have someone informed of the arrest is given by s 56 of PACE. The arrested person can nominate any friend, relative or any other person who they think is likely to take an interest in their welfare. The person nominated by the detainee must be told of the arrest and where the person is being held. This should normally be done as soon as practicable, but, in the case of

Key Facts		
Right	**Source**	**Comment**
To have someone informed of detention	s 56 PACE	Can be delayed for up to 36 hours for an indictable offence
To speak to someone on the telephone	Code of Practice C	Not compulsory – police can refuse
To be told of their right to legal advice	Code of Practice C	Notices displayed in police stations. Duty of custody officer to bring this to the suspect's attention
To legal advice	s 58 PACE	Can be delayed for up to 36 hours for an indictable offence BUT only in exceptional circumstances: *R v Samuel*
To have appropriate adult present at interview	Code of Practice C	Applies to those under 17 and also to mentally ill or handicapped: *R v Aspinall*
To consult the Codes of Practice	The Codes of Practice	

Figure 11.7 *Key facts chart on rights of suspects in police detention*

an indictable offence a senior police officer may authorise that there be a delay of up to 36 hours. This can only be done if there are reasonable grounds for believing that telling the named person will lead to: interference; harm to evidence or to other persons; the alerting of others involved in the offence or hinder the recovery of property obtained through the offence. Code C states that, in addition to the right to have someone informed of the arrest, a detained person should be allowed to speak on the telephone 'for a reasonable time to one person'. If the suspect is under the age of 17 the police must also contact a person 'responsible for his welfare' and inform them of the arrest.

The right to legal advice

A detained person may either contact their own solicitor, or they can use the system of duty solicitors which is provided free for anyone under arrest. In fact the Code of Practice tries to make sure that detained people are aware of their right to legal advice. Under the Code the custody officer, when authorising the detention of someone at the police station, must get the suspect to sign the custody record at that time saying whether he/she wishes to have legal advice. Police stations must have posters 'prominently displayed' advertising the right to free legal advice, and an arrested suspect must not only be told orally of this right, but also given a written notice of it.

It is possible for a senior police officer to authorise a delay to a suspect's right to see a solicitor in the case of an indictable offence for up to 36 hours. However, this can only occur if there are reasonable grounds for believing that giving access to a solicitor will lead to: interference with, or harm to, evidence or to other persons; the alerting of others involved in the offence, or hinder the recovery of property obtained through the offence. The case of *R v Samuel* (1988) stressed that it would only be on rare occasions that such a delay was justified, and that it must be based on specific aspects of the case, not a

general assumption that access to a solicitor might lead to the alerting of accomplices. In *Samuel*'s case, the defendant was a 24-year-old man, whose mother had already been informed of her son's arrest some hours before he was refused access to a solicitor. The Court of Appeal felt that if anyone was likely to be alerted then it would already have happened, and that there was no reason to deny Samuel his 'fundamental freedom' of consulting a solicitor. As his final interview with the police had taken place after his solicitor had been refused access, the evidence of what was said at that interview was inadmissible in court and so Samuel's conviction for robbery was quashed.

In *R v Grant* (2005) the Court of Appeal held that the court would not tolerate illegal conduct by the police. In this case there had been deliberate interference by the police with the detained suspect's right to the confidence of privileged communication with his solicitor. This was such a serious abuse of process that it justified his conviction for murder being quashed.

11.3.6 Police interviews of suspects

Any detained person may be questioned by the police. All interviews at a police station must be tape-recorded and trials are being conducted on the feasibility of videoing rather than just audio-taping. A problem in many cases is that questioning of the suspect starts before they arrive at the police station (possibly in the police car on the way to the station) and these informal interviews are not recorded. In many cases, the defendant challenges the truth of police evidence about an alleged informal interview. In order to protect suspects from the possibility of police fabricating evidence of a confession made outside the police station, the Runciman Commission recommended that if a confession was allegedly made outside the police station, then that confession should be put to the suspect at the beginning of any tape-recorded interview that subsequently takes place. This allows a suspect a chance to make comments about it in the taped interview.

Suspects have the right to have a solicitor present at any interview, unless it is one of the rare occasions referred to in *Samuel* above. However, if the suspect does not ask for a solicitor, the police may conduct the interview without one being present. In addition, if the matter is urgent or the solicitor likely to be delayed for some time, the police have the right to start questioning a suspect before a solicitor arrives.

In *R v Halliwell* (2012) at Bristol Crown Court on 9 May 2012 a judge ruled that, under s 78, a confession made by D about a murder of a young woman and the location of her body should not be admissible as evidence.

The circumstances of the interview were that D had been arrested on suspicion of the abduction of a woman. The arresting police officers tried to interview him as a matter of urgency before taking him to a police station. They did this because they hoped the woman might still be alive and any information the defendant could give about her was important. D refused to speak to them and asked to be taken to a police station and to see a solicitor. The arresting officers contacted the senior investigation office (SIO) and told him this.

The SIO told them not to take D to the police station. Instead he arranged to meet them and D at an outdoors location away from the police station. At this location the SIO interviewed D about the whereabouts of the woman. The SIO did not caution D before starting the interview. During this interview D asked the SIO if he wanted 'another one'. The SIO took this to be a reference to a second murder but he still did not caution D about this second possible offence and continued to question him. D then admitted murdering a woman some seven or eight years earlier. During the interview D made repeated requests to be taken to a police station and to be allowed to speak to a solicitor.

D was eventually taken to a police station four hours after his arrest. At the police station he was allowed a solicitor. He was also properly cautioned and interviewed. During this interview he refused to say anything except 'no comment'.

A pre-trial hearing was held to decide if the information given in the interview away from the police station should be given in evidence at the trial. It was ruled that the interview was not admissible as the rules under PACE had been completely disregarded.

Appropriate adult

If the suspect is under the age of 17 or is mentally handicapped then there must be an 'appropriate adult' present during all interviews. This right is in addition to the right to legal advice. Research suggests that many mentally vulnerable individuals are not being given this protection; the Runciman Commission recommended that the police should be given clearer guidelines on identifying suspects who need an appropriate adult. The Commission also suggested there should be trials of the use of 'duty psychiatrist schemes' to see whether a permanent scheme would be appropriate in busy city centre police stations.

In *R v Aspinall* (1999) the Court of Appeal ruled that a defendant who suffered from schizophrenia should have had an appropriate adult present when interviewed by police. This was so even though the defendant appeared able to understand the police questions. The interview was, therefore, not admissible as evidence.

Treatment of suspects and exclusion of evidence

The law gives some protection to suspects as to the way they should be treated whilst being detained and questioned. Section 76 of PACE states that the court shall not allow statements which have been obtained through oppression to be used as evidence. Oppression is defined as including torture, inhuman or degrading treatment and the use or threat of violence. Code C also gives protection to suspects who are being questioned in regard to the physical conditions of the interview. For example, the code states that interview rooms must be adequately lit, heated and ventilated and that suspects must be given adequate breaks for meals, refreshments and sleep.

In theory the treatment of a suspect is monitored by the custody officer who is supposed to keep accurate records of all happenings during the detention period. This should include the length and timing of interviews and other matters, such as visits of police officers to the defendant's cell, so that any breaches of the rules will be obvious. However, research by Sanders and Bridge suggests that a substantial minority of custody records (about 10 per cent) are falsified.

Evidence can also be excluded under s 78 of PACE. Under this section, the trial judge has discretion to refuse to admit evidence. The judge considers whether the breaches of PACE and the evidence obtained through them would have an adverse effect on the fairness of the trial. The judge in *R v Halliwell* (2012) (see above) exercised his discretion under this section in refusing to admit evidence of the defendant's confession to murder.

The right to silence

Until the Criminal Justice and Public Order Act 1994 was enacted, defendants could refuse to answer any questions without any adverse conclusion being drawn on their silence if the case came to trial. In fact, the previously used caution given before a police interview commenced contained the phrase 'you do not have to say anything'. This right to remain silent was considered by the Runciman Commission, which recommended that it should be retained in essence. However, the government decided that this rule was allowing guilty people to go free and that the right to silence should be curbed. This was done by ss 34–39 of the Criminal Justice and Public Order Act 1994.

These sections allow inferences to be made from the fact that a defendant has refused to answer questions. As a result the wording of the caution given to a suspect before interviewing commences now states:

'You do not have to say anything. But it may harm your defence if you do not mention when questioned something which you later rely on in court. Anything you do say may be given in evidence.'

This change in the law does not mean that the defendant can be forced to speak; he can still remain silent. At any trial which follows, however, the judge may comment on the defendant's failure to mention a crucial matter, and this failure can form part of the evidence against him. It is argued that this alters the basic premise of criminal trials that the prosecution must prove the defendant's guilt. However, a defendant's silence is not enough for a conviction on its own; there must be prosecution evidence as well.

Under the Criminal Justice and Public Order Act 1994 an adverse inference could only be drawn if the defendant was aged 14 or over. The Crime and Disorder Act 1998 allowed an adverse inference to be drawn from the defendant's failure to answer questions or give evidence regardless of the defendant's age, so that the rule applies to 10- to 13-year-olds as well as older defendants.

One interesting point to note is that other enactments have already removed the right to silence in certain cases. In particular, under the Criminal Justice Act 1987, s 2, the Director of the Serious Fraud Office can require anyone whom he thinks has relevant information to attend to answer questions. Failure to comply with such a requirement is a criminal offence.

Interview after charge

Once a person has been charged with an offence or been told that he will be prosecuted, the police should interview him further only if it is necessary. The suspect should also be informed what offence the police are interviewing him about. In *Charles v Crown Prosecution Service* (2009) the suspect was found asleep in his car slumped over the steering wheel. The police arrested him for being in charge of a motor vehicle whilst under the influence of drink or drugs. A breath test showed that he was over the limit and he was informed he would be charged.

After this the police then interviewed him. They did not tell him that they were considering any other offence. During the interview he admitted he had driven the car. At the end of the interview he was charged with driving whilst under the influence of alcohol. This was not the offence they had told him he would be charged with but a more serious offence. Also, they had not they told him they were investigating a driving offence.

The Queen's Bench Divisional Court quashed his conviction as there had been two breaches of the Code on interviewing suspects. The court held that what he said in the interview was not admissible in evidence because of these breaches.

Key Facts

Power	Sections in PACE or other Act	Code of Practice	Comments
Stop and search	ss 1–7 of PACE, also other Acts, e.g. Misuse of Drugs Act 1971	A	• Must be in a public place and must have reasonable grounds for suspecting person
Enter premises	With search warrant (s 8 PACE) OR to arrest person (s 17 PACE) OR to prevent breach of the peace	B	• Magistrates issue warrant • Even applies to private homes
Arrest	With a warrant OR under sections 24 or 25 of PACE		• Magistrates issue warrant • Must have reasonable grounds

Detention	ss 34–46 PACE Limits 24 hours (summary offence) OR 36 (extendable to 96) for an indictable offence	C	• Detainee has rights to:
			  • have someone told
			  • to be told of availability of legal advice
			  • to see Code of Practice

Searches	ss 54, 55 PACE	C	• Intimate search must be by person of same sex
Fingerprinting	ss 61 PACE		
Samples	ss 62, 63 PACE		• Intimate samples must be taken by qualified person
Police interviews	s 53 PACE Also ss 34–39 Criminal Justice and Public Order Act 1994 re 'silence'	E	• Police must caution • Should tape-record • Appropriate adult present for those under 17

Figure 11.8 *Key facts chart on police powers*

11.3.7 Searches, fingerprints and body samples

When a person is being held at a police station the police have no automatic right to search them. However, the custody officer has a duty to record everything a person has with them when they are brought to the police station, and if the custody officer thinks a search is necessary to carry out this duty, then a non-intimate search may be made.

Strip searches

These are defined in code C as searches 'involving the removal of more than outer clothing'. The code stresses that a strip search may only take place if it is necessary to remove an article which a person in detention should not be allowed to keep, and there is reasonable suspicion that the person might have concealed such an article.

Such searches should not take place in an area where the search can be seen by any person who does not need to be present, nor by a member of the opposite sex. Suspects should not normally be required to remove all their clothing at the same time. A man should be allowed to put his shirt back on before he removes his trousers and a woman should be given a robe or similar garment to wear once she has removed her top garment.

Intimate searches

In addition a high-ranking police officer can authorise an intimate search, if there is reason to believe that the person has with them an item which could be used to cause physical injury to themselves or others or that he/she is in possession of a Class A drug. An intimate search is defined as 'a search which consists of the physical examination of a person's body orifices other than the mouth'. If it is a drugs-related search then it may only be carried out by a suitably qualified person, for example, a doctor or nurse. If it is a search for other items then, if practicable, it should be carried out by a suitably qualified person, but can be by another person if a high-ranking police officer authorises it.

Fingerprints and body samples

While a person is detained the police may take fingerprints and non-intimate body samples such as hair and saliva without the person's consent. If necessary the police may use reasonable force to obtain these. There are different rules for intimate samples. Intimate samples are defined as:

(a) 'a sample of blood, semen or any other tissue fluid, urine or pubic hair;
(b) a dental impression;
(c) a swab taken from any part of a person's genitals or from a person's body orifice other than the mouth.'

These can only be taken by a registered medical practitioner or a nurse. Although a sample will only be taken where there is reasonable ground for suspecting involvement in a particular recordable offence, the sample may then be checked against information held on other crimes.

ACTIVITY

Advise whether or not in the following situations there have been breaches of the rules in PACE and the Codes of Practice.

Questions

1. Leroy, aged 23, has been arrested on suspicion of murder. He is taken to the police station at 7 am. The custody officer tells him that he will not be allowed to see a lawyer. Leroy is interviewed for eight hours that day about the alleged murder. He continually denies any involvement and demands to see a lawyer. The police take his fingerprints and a sample of saliva for DNA testing. Leroy spends the night in the police station cells. The following morning the police finally allow him to make a telephone call to his brother at 11 am.

2. Martin, aged 16, has been arrested for breaking into an office and stealing money. The police believe he may have been responsible for several other burglaries and that he has an accomplice. On the way to the police station they question him about this. At the police station he is taken into an interview room and told that the police have enough evidence 'to lock him up for years' but that if he tells them who was with him, the police will only caution him. Martin asks if he can see his father but the police refuse to call his father until Martin signs an admission.

Retention of samples

Until 2001, fingerprints and samples were only kept where the suspect was found guilty of an offence. In 2001 the law was changed so that, even where a person was not charged, DNA profiles and fingerprints could be kept indefinitely on the national database.

This was challenged in two cases which eventually went to the European Court of Human Rights. These cases were *S* where the defendant, aged 11 at the time of his arrest, had been found not guilty of attempted robbery and *Marper* where the defendant was charged with harassment of his partner but the case was later discontinued. The defendants argued that the retention was contrary to their right to respect for private and family life under Article 8(1) of the European Convention on Human Rights.

The European Court of Human Rights held that the indefinite detention of DNA samples of people who had not been convicted was a breach of Article 8. Following this decision the law was changed. Initially the time limit for keeping records where a person was either not charged or not convicted was six years. Now under the Protection of Freedoms Act 2012, the time limit

for retention of fingerprints and DNA profiles is three years. In addition, where the person has not even been charged, there is an extra safeguard that the permission of the Commissioner for the Retention and Use of Biometric Material must be obtained.

An exception to the three-year rule is where the person, although either not charged or not convicted of the offence for which the samples were taken, has a previous conviction for a recordable offence. In this instance the records may be kept indefinitely.

Taking of fingerprints prior to arrest

Fingerprints can be taken prior to arrest away from the police station as it is now possible to check against the National Automated Fingerprint Identification System in a matter of minutes. This power can only be used where:

- the officer reasonably suspects that the person is committing or attempting to commit an offence, or has committed or attempted to commit an offence; and
- either the name of the person is unknown to, and cannot be readily ascertained by, the officer, or the officer has reasonable grounds for doubting whether the name given by the person is his real name.

11.4 Complaints against the police

Citizens who believe that the police have exceeded their powers can complain to the police authorities. Any complaint about police behaviour must be recorded. The type of complaint then determines how it is dealt with, although in all instances, the police are under a duty to take steps to obtain and/or preserve evidence which is relevant to the complaint. Minor complaints will be dealt with informally, and if the complaint is proved, the individual will receive an apology and that will probably be an end of the matter. If disciplinary action is thought to be necessary, then the complaint should be investigated by the police force concerned; if it involves a high-ranking officer, the investigation is carried out by another police force.

11.4.1 The Independent Police Complaints Commission

The Independent Police Complaints Commission (IPCC) was set up in April 2004 to supervise the handling of complaints against the police and police staff such as Community Support Officers. The IPCC sets down standards for the police to follow when dealing with complaints. They also monitor the way that complaints are dealt with by local police forces.

In addition, the IPCC itself investigates serious issues. These include:

- any incident involving death or serious injury
- allegations of serious or organised corruption
- allegations against senior officers
- allegations involving racism
- allegations of perverting the course of justice.

The fact that the IPCC can carry out its own investigations into such matters is an improvement on the previous system where police from one area would be asked to investigate complaints about police in another area. This was felt to be insufficiently independent. The IPCC is totally independent of the police.

Who can make a complaint?

Any member of the public who:

- has been a victim of misconduct by a person serving with the police
- was present when the alleged misconduct took place and suffered loss, damage, distress or inconvenience, or was put in danger or at risk
- is a friend or relative of the victim of the alleged misconduct, or
- has witnessed the alleged misconduct.

A complaint can be made directly to the police force concerned or through the IPCC or any advice organisation such as the Citizens Advice Bureau or a Youth Offending Team. Instead of making the complaint direct, an individual can ask a solicitor or their MP to make the complaint for them.

11.4.2 Court actions

Where the police have committed a crime in the unlawful execution of their duties, criminal proceedings may be brought against them. Such proceedings are usually for assault and may be commenced by a private prosecution or, as seen above, by the state.

If there is a breach of civil rights, citizens may also be able to take proceedings in the civil courts against the police. This can be done under a claim in tort for trespass to property, as would be the case if the police entered premises without a search warrant or other permission, or for trespass to the person where any arrest is unlawful. There can also be civil proceedings for false arrest or malicious prosecution.

EXAMINATION QUESTIONS

1. (a) Describe the powers of the police to stop and search a person on the street. [18 marks]
   (b) Malcolm is running down a busy street with a large bag. He is trying to catch a train in order to get to a concert on time. He is stopped by a police officer who identifies himself as PC Newman. He is asked to remove his shoes and his bag is searched. As nothing is found, Malcolm is told he can go.

   Advise Malcolm on whether the police acted lawfully with regards to the stop and search. [12 marks]

   G151, January 2011, OCR

2. (a) Describe the powers of the police at the police station to detain and interview a person suspected of a serious offence, and any limitation on these powers. [18 marks]

   (b) Barry is arrested on suspicion of the serious offence of robbery. He is taken to the police station and detained for 36 hours without anyone being notified of his whereabouts. He is given a strip search by a male officer to search for stolen property. A female officer is also present. He is made to remove all of his clothes. Hair from his head and a sample of blood are taken from Barry by force.

   Explain to Barry whether his treatment at the police station was lawful. [12 marks]

   G151, June 2011, OCR

EXTENSION ESSAY

Critically discuss the extent to which the rights of those detained at a police station are protected.

CHAPTER 12

PRE-TRIAL PROCEDURE IN CRIMINAL CASES

INTRODUCTION

The criminal law is set down by the state. A breach of the criminal law can lead to a penalty, such as imprisonment or a fine, being imposed on the defendant in the name of the state. Therefore, bringing a prosecution for a criminal offence is usually seen as part of the role of the state. Indeed, the majority of criminal prosecutions are conducted by the Crown Prosecution Service which is the state agency for criminal prosecutions (the role of the Crown Prosecution Service is dealt with in section 12.3).

It is also possible for a private individual or business to start a prosecution. Bodies like the RSPCA regularly bring prosecutions. However, it is unusual for an individual to bring a prosecution. This will probably only happen where the police have refused to act to investigate a complaint, or where the Crown Prosecution Service has decided to drop a case after the police had brought charges.

In order to start a prosecution, the individual must present a written account of the alleged offence to a magistrate and, if the magistrate is persuaded that there is sufficient reason, he or she will issue a summons to be served on the defendant. The summons sets out a date on which the case will be heard at the Magistrates' Court. The Attorney-General does have the right, on behalf of the state, to take over any private criminal prosecution and to then decide whether the prosecution should continue or not.

However, regardless of whether the prosecution has been brought by the state or by a private individual, the same matters have to be dealt with and the defendant will probably have to attend court more than once before the trial takes place.

12.1 Pre-trial hearings

All criminal cases will first go to the Magistrates' Court but it is unusual for a case to be completed at this first hearing, although it is possible for minor offences to be dealt with at this point. This would only be where the defendant pleads guilty and is either already legally represented or does not want legal representation. For most driving offences there is a special procedure which allows the defendant to plead guilty by post, so that no attendance at court is necessary. Even in these cases the magistrates may need to adjourn the case to get further information about the defendant.

Category of offence	Place of trial	Examples of offences
Summary	Magistrates' Court	Driving without insurance Taking a vehicle without consent Common assault
Triable either way	Magistrates' Court OR Crown Court	Theft Assault causing actual bodily harm
Indictable	Crown Court	Murder Manslaughter Rape Robbery

Figure 12.1 *The three categories of offence*

12.1.1 Categories of offences

The type of offence that is being dealt with affects the number and type of pre-trial hearings, and where the final trial will take place. Criminal offences are divided into three main categories. These are:

1. **Summary offences**
   These are the least serious offences and are always tried in the Magistrates' Court. They include nearly all driving offences, common assault and criminal damage which have caused less than £5,000 worth of damage.
2. **Triable-either-way offences**
   These can be regarded as the middle range of crimes and they include a wide variety of offences, such as theft and assault causing actual bodily harm. As the name implies, these cases can be tried in either the Magistrates' Court or the Crown Court.
3. **Indictable offences**
   These are the more serious crimes and include murder, manslaughter and rape. All indictable offences must be tried at the Crown Court, but the first hearing is dealt with at the Magistrates' Court. After this the case is transferred to the Crown Court.

12.1.2 Pre-trial procedure for summary offences

It is possible for cases to be dealt with on a first appearance in court but often an adjournment may be needed. This could be because the Crown Prosecution Service has not got all the information required to complete the case, or because the defendant wants to get legal advice. Another reason for adjourning a case is where the magistrates want pre-sentence reports on a defendant who pleads guilty, before they decide what sentence to impose. When a defendant wishes to plead not guilty, there will almost always have to be an adjournment, as witnesses will have to be brought to court. One of the main points to be decided on an adjournment is whether the defendant should be remanded on bail or in custody (see section 12.2).

Early administrative hearings

In order to prevent unnecessary delays, the first hearing is now an early administrative hearing (EAH). The hearing can be dealt with by a single lay magistrate, or even by the clerk of the court. The hearing is aimed at discovering if the defendant wants to apply for legal aid and, if so, enquiring into whether he is eligible for it;

requesting pre-sentence or medical reports if these are appropriate; and deciding if the defendant should be remanded in custody or on bail. There is a limit on the clerk's powers in this last respect as the clerk cannot change any conditions where bail has previously been granted.

12.1.3 Cases going for trial at the Crown Court

Triable-either-way offences

For these there will be further hearings at the Magistrates' Court. The defendant will be asked whether he pleads guilty or not guilty. If he pleads not guilty then a decision has to be made as to whether the case will be tried in the Magistrates' Court or the Crown Court (see section 13.1.3 for more information).

Indictable offences

All indictable offences are sent to the Crown Court immediately after the early administrative hearing in the Magistrates' Court. All other pre-trial matters are dealt with by a judge at the Crown Court.

12.2 Bail

An important pre-trial matter to be decided is whether the defendant should stay in custody while awaiting the trial or whether bail should be granted. A person can be released on bail at any point after being arrested by the police. Being given bail means that the person is allowed to be at liberty until the next stage in the case.

12.2.1 Police powers to grant bail

The police may release a suspect on bail while they make further inquiries. This means that the suspect is released from police custody on the condition that they return to the police station on a specific date in the future.

The police can also give bail to a defendant who has been charged with an offence. In this case the defendant is bailed to appear at the local Magistrates' Court on a set date. The decision on whether to grant bail or not is made by the custody officer under s 38 of PACE as amended by the Criminal Justice and Public Order Act 1994. The custody officer can refuse bail if the suspect's name and address cannot be discovered, or if there is a doubt as to whether the name and address given are genuine. Apart from this, the normal principles as to when bail should be granted apply. These are set out in the Bail Act 1976 and are given in section 12.2.2. If any person granted bail by the police fails to surrender to that bail (i.e. attend at the next stage of the case), then the police are given the right to arrest them.

Conditional bail

The Criminal Justice and Public Order Act 1994 gave the police the power to impose conditions on a grant of bail. The types of conditions include asking the suspect to surrender his passport, report at regular intervals to the police station or get another person to stand surety for him. These conditions can be only imposed in order to make sure that the suspect surrenders to bail, does not commit an offence while on bail and does not interfere with witnesses or interfere in any other way with the course of justice.

No police bail

Where, having charged a defendant with a crime, the police are not prepared to allow bail, they must bring the defendant in front of the Magistrates' Court at the first possible opportunity. If (as usually happens) the magistrates cannot deal with the whole case at that first hearing, the magistrates must then make the decision as to whether the defendant should be given bail or remanded in custody. The question as to whether bail should be given can also be considered by a court at any later stage of the criminal proceedings.

Statistics published by the Home Office show that the majority of those prosecuted are summonsed to court, rather than charged. This means that the question of bail or custody is not relevant; they are automatically at liberty. Of those who are charged, about five out of every six are released on bail by the police pending the court proceedings, so in fact only a small number of defendants are refused bail by the police. In these cases the courts must then decide whether to grant bail.

Key Facts

Bail can be granted by:	• police • magistrates • Crown Court
Bail Act 1976	There is a presumption in favour of bail BUT • for an offence while already on bail, bail can only be given if the court is satisfied there is no significant risk of further offending • there must be exceptional circumstances for bail to be granted for murder, attempted murder, manslaughter, rape or attempted rape where the defendant has already served a custodial sentence for such an offence
In all cases bail can be refused if there are reasonable grounds for believing the defendant:	• would fail to surrender • would commit further offences • would interfere with witnesses
Conditions can be imposed	• sureties • residence in bail hostel • curfew • hand in passport, etc.
Comment	Some of those in prison are awaiting trial and could have been given bail Problem of balancing this against need to protect public

Figure 12.2 *Key facts chart on bail*

12.2.2 The Bail Act 1976

This is the key Act, starting with the assumption that an accused person should be granted bail, though this right is limited for certain cases (see section 12.2.3). Section 4 of the Bail Act 1976 gives a general right to bail, but the court need not grant a defendant bail if it is satisfied that there are substantial grounds for believing that the defendant, if released on bail, would:

1. Fail to surrender to custody.

2. Commit an offence while on bail.
3. Interfere with witnesses or otherwise obstruct the course of justice.

The court can also refuse bail if it is satisfied that the defendant should be kept in custody for his own protection.

In deciding whether to grant bail, the court will consider various factors including:

● The nature and seriousness of the offence (and the probable method of dealing with it).

- The character, antecedents (that is, past record), associations and community ties of the defendant.
- The defendant's record as respects the fulfilment of his obligations under previous grants of bail in criminal proceedings; in other words whether he has turned up (surrendered to his bail) on previous occasions.
- The strength of the evidence against him.

If a defendant is charged with an offence which is not punishable by imprisonment, bail can only be refused if the defendant has previously failed to surrender to bail and there are grounds for believing that he will not surrender on this occasion. Where there is no real prospect that a defendant will be given a custodial sentence if convicted, then that defendant must be granted bail.

A court can make conditions for the granting of bail. These are similar to conditions which can be set by the police and may include the surrender of passport and/or reporting to a police station. The court can also make a condition as to where the accused must reside while on bail; this could be at a home address or at a bail hostel.

Sureties

The court (and the police) can require a surety for bail. A surety is another person who is prepared to promise to pay the court a certain sum of money if the defendant fails to attend court. This promise is called a recognisance and no money is paid unless the defendant fails to answer to his bail. This system is different from that of other countries, especially the USA, where the surety must pay the money into court before the defendant is released on bail, but gets the money back when the defendant attends court as required.

Renewed applications and appeals

Normally only one further application can be made to the magistrates, unless there is a change of circumstance. The defendant can appeal against a refusal to grant bail. Such an appeal is made to a judge at the Crown Court. A defendant who has been sent for trial to the Crown Court can also apply there for bail.

12.2.3 Restrictions on bail

The right to liberty is a human right and the right to bail is therefore part of that right. This means that even for serious offences, bail must be available in suitable cases. However, in some situations the public need to be protected from a potentially dangerous person. In such circumstances the right to bail is restricted.

Repeat serious offences

Where a person is charged with murder, attempted murder, manslaughter, rape or attempted rape and they have already served a custodial sentence for a similar offence, they only have the right to bail if the court thinks that there are exceptional circumstances.

Offence committed while on bail

Where a defendant, aged 18 or over, was on bail when the present alleged offence was committed, s 14 of the Criminal Justice Act 2003 amends the Bail Act 1976 to read:

'he may not be granted bail unless the court is satisfied that there is no significant risk of his committing an offence on bail (whether subject to conditions or not)'.

Restrictions on bail for adult drug users

Section 19 of the Criminal Justice Act 2003 amended the Bail Act 1976 to place restrictions on bail for adult offenders who have tested positive for specified Class A drugs where:

- the offender is charged with either possession or possession with intent to supply a Class A drug, or

- the court is satisfied that there are substantial grounds for believing that the misuse of a Class A drug caused or contributed to the offence or that the offence was motivated wholly or partly by his intended misuse of such a drug, and
- the defendant has refused to agree to participate in an assessment or follow-up in relation to his dependency upon or propensity to misuse specified Class A drugs.

Such a defendant may not be granted bail unless the court is satisfied that there is no significant risk of his committing an offence on bail (whether subject to conditions or not).

12.2.4 Prosecution appeals

When a defendant is granted bail, the prosecution has the right to appeal to a judge in the Crown Court against the decision.

12.2.5 Balancing conflicting interests

The problem is that the criminal justice system has to balance the conflicting interests of the defendant (who is presumed innocent at this stage and entitled to his liberty) against the needs of the public to be protected from potentially dangerous criminals. For this reason there are the restrictions on bail which are set out in the section above. There are also methods of trying to ensure that an offender who is given bail will not reoffend. The first is the provision of bail hostels where offenders can live while they are on bail. The second is the use of electronic tagging of those who are on bail. This allows the police to know if any conditions attached to bail, such as not going to a certain area, are broken.

It is argued that too many people are refused bail, as about 9 per cent of those in our prisons are defendants who have not yet been tried but are remanded in custody. Some of these will be found not guilty, but will not be entitled to any compensation for the time they spent in custody. Even where the defendant is later found guilty,

statistics show that 20 per cent are given non-custodial sentences.

> **ACTIVITY**
>
> Consider each of the following situations and explain with reasons whether you think bail would be granted or not.
>
> 1. Alex, aged 19, is charged with a robbery in which he threatened a shopkeeper with a gun and stole £2,000. He has no previous convictions and lives at home with his mother.
> 2. Homer, aged 43, is charged with three offences of burglary. He has been convicted of burglary on two occasions in the past.
> 3. Melanie, aged 21, is charged with theft of items from a sportswear shop. She is currently unemployed and living rough. She has no previous convictions.

12.3   Crown Prosecution Service (CPS)

Before 1986 prosecutions brought by the state were normally conducted by the police. This led to criticism as it was thought that the investigation of crime should be separate from the prosecution of cases. The Royal Commission on Criminal Procedure (the Phillips Commission), whose report led to the enactment of PACE, had also pointed out that there was no uniform system of prosecution in England and Wales. The Commission thought it was desirable to have an independent agency to review and conduct prosecutions. Eventually the Crown Prosecution Service (CPS) was established by the Prosecution of Offences Act 1985 and began operating in 1986.

12.3.1 Organisation of the CPS

The head of the CPS is the Director of Public Prosecutions (DPP), who must have been qualified as a lawyer for at least ten years. The DPP is appointed by, and is subject to supervision by, the Attorney-General. Below the DPP are Chief Crown Prosecutors who each head one of the 13 areas into which the country is divided. Each area is subdivided into branches, each of which is headed by a Senior District Crown Prosecutor. Within the branches there are several lawyers and support staff, who are organised into teams and given responsibility for cases.

12.3.2 The functions of the CPS

These involve all aspects of prosecution and can be summarised as:

- Deciding on what offence(s) should be charged. This used to be done in all cases by the police, but sometimes inappropriate charges were brought which meant that the case had to be discontinued. Now all serious charges are decided by the CPS.
- Reviewing all cases passed to them by the police to see if there is sufficient evidence for a case to proceed, and whether it is in the public interest to do so; this is to avoid weak cases being brought to court.
- Being responsible for the case after it has been passed to them by the police.
- Conducting the prosecution of cases in the Magistrates' Court; this is usually done by lawyers working in the Crown Prosecution Service as Crown Prosecutors or Associate Prosecutors who are specially trained lay people working in the CPS.
- Conducting cases in the Crown Court. This can be by instructing either an independent lawyer to act as prosecuting counsel at court or a Crown Prosecutor with the appropriate advocacy qualification.

On a practical level, once a defendant has been charged or summonsed with an offence the police role is at an end. They must send the papers for each case to the CPS – each case is then assigned to a team in the local branch of the CPS, and that team will be responsible for the case throughout the prosecution process. This is aimed at ensuring continuity and better communication in each case.

12.3.3 Discontinuation of cases

Once papers are received, the CPS is under a duty to review the case to see if the prosecution should continue. There were criticisms over the number of cases in which the CPS decides that the prosecution should be discontinued. In order to overcome some of this criticism the DPP, in 1994, issued a revised code of practice for the CPS and the code was amended again in 2000, 2004 and 2011. This code shows the factors taken into account when deciding whether to go ahead with a prosecution.

Evidential test

The two main factors are the 'evidential test' and the 'public interest test'. The first is concerned with whether there is sufficient evidence to provide a 'realistic prospect of conviction' in the case. Under this the CPS has to consider what the strength of the evidence is, and whether magistrates or a jury are more likely than not to convict. It will ask itself whether the evidence is admissible or whether it has been obtained by breaching the rules of PACE; whether a witness's background may weaken the case (for example, the witness has a dubious motive so that the evidence is unreliable); and how strong the evidence of identification of the defendant is.

Public interest test

The second test, whether it is in the public interest to continue with the case, is more controversial as it involves very wide-ranging considerations. The code of practice gives lists of some 'common public interest factors' both for and against prosecution. It stresses that the lists are not exhaustive and that the factors that will apply depend on the facts in each case. These factors are reproduced in the activity on pages 164–5.

In its annual reports the CPS shows that the number of discontinued cases in the Magistrates' Courts has decreased so that it is now under 10 per cent:

- 2001–02: 16.2 per cent of cases discontinued
- 2003–04: 13.9 per cent
- 2005–06: 11.6 per cent
- 2007–08: 9.9 per cent
- 2009–10: 9.0 per cent
- 2011–12: 9.6 per cent.

In 2011–12 the CPS prosecuted nearly 800,000 people in the Magistrates' Courts. The conviction rate has steadily increased over the past few years, so that in 2011–12, 86.7 per cent of all cases in the Magistrates' Courts resulted in a conviction. In the same period in the Crown Court the CPS prosecuted just over 100,000 defendants. Of these, 80.8 per cent of cases resulted in a conviction.

Victims

In 2005 a Code of Practice for Victims was issued. This Code sets out the services that victims can expect to receive from the criminal justice system. This includes notifying vulnerable victims within one working day, and all other victims within five working days, if there is insufficient evidence to charge a suspect.

ACTIVITY

Read these two extracts and then answer the questions which follow each.

1. SOME COMMON PUBLIC INTEREST FACTORS IN THE FAVOUR OF PROSECUTION

4.16 A prosecution is more likely to be required if:

a) a conviction is likely to result in a significant sentence;

b) a conviction is likely to result in an order of the court in excess of that which a prosecutor is able to secure through a conditional caution;

c) the offence involved the use of a weapon or the threat of violence;

d) the offence was committed against a person serving the public (for example, a member of the emergency services; a police or prison officer; a health or social welfare professional; or a provider of public transport);

e) the offence was premeditated;

f) the offence was carried out by a group;

g) the offence was committed in the presence of, or in close proximity to, a child;

h) the offence was motivated by any form of discrimination against the victim's ethnic or national origin, gender, disability, age, religion or belief, political views, sexual orientation or gender identity; or the suspect demonstrated hostility towards the victim based on any of those characteristics;

i) the offence was committed in order to facilitate more serious offending;

j) the victim of the offence was in a vulnerable situation and the suspect took advantage of this;

k) there was an element of corruption of the victim in the way the offence was committed;

l) there was a marked difference in the ages of the suspect and the victim and the suspect took advantage of this;

m) there was a marked difference in the levels of understanding of the suspect and the victim and the suspect took advantage of this;

n) the suspect was in a position of authority or trust and he or she took advantage of this;

o) the suspect was a ringleader or an organiser of the offence;

p) the suspect's previous convictions or the previous out-of-court disposals which he or she has received are relevant to the present offence;

q) the suspect is alleged to have committed the offence in breach of an order of the court;

r) a prosecution would have a significant positive impact on maintaining community confidence;

s) there are grounds for believing that the offence is likely to be continued or repeated.

Questions

1. Look at the list of factors in favour of prosecution and decide if you think any of the factors should be more important than others.
2. Are there any factors in this list which you do not think should be considered when deciding whether to prosecute a defendant?
3. What, if any, other factors would you like to see considered?

2. SOME COMMON PUBLIC INTEREST FACTORS AGAINST PROSECUTION

4.17 A prosecution is less likely to be required if:

a) the court is likely to impose a nominal penalty;

b) the seriousness and the consequences of the offending can be appropriately dealt with by an out-of-court disposal which the suspect accepts and with which he or she complies …;

c) the suspect has been subject to any appropriate regulatory proceedings, or any punitive or relevant civil penalty … which adequately addresses the seriousness of the offending and any breach of trust involved;

d) the offence was committed as a result of a genuine mistake or misunderstanding;

e) the loss or harm can be described as minor and was the result of a single incident, particularly if it was caused by a misjudgement;

f) there has been a long delay between the offence taking place and the date of the trial, unless:
   - the offence is serious;
   - the delay has been caused wholly or in part by the suspect;

   - the offence has only recently come to light;
   - the complexity of the offence has meant that there has been a long investigation; or
   - new investigative techniques have been used to re-examine previously unsolved crimes and, as a result, a suspect has been identified.

g) a prosecution is likely to have an adverse effect on the victim's physical or mental health, always bearing in mind the seriousness of the offence and the views of the victim about the effect of a prosecution on his or her physical or mental health;

h) the suspect played a minor role in the commission of the offence;

i) the suspect has put right the loss or harm that was caused (but a suspect must not avoid prosecution or an out-of-court disposal solely because he or she pays compensation or repays the sum of money he or she unlawfully obtained);

j) the suspect is, or was at the time of the offence, suffering from significant mental or physical ill health, unless the offence is serious or there is a real possibility that it may be repeated …

k) a prosecution may require details to be made public that could harm sources of information, international relations or national security.

Questions

1. Do you think any of the factors in this list are more important than others? Give reasons for your answer.
2. Which, if any, of the above factors do you think should not be considered when deciding whether or not to prosecute a defendant?
3. Compare the two lists. Are they well balanced? Do they provide a good framework for deciding when it is in the public interest to prosecute? Give reasons for your answer.

Civil actions

There have also been cases in which a civil case has been taken because the Crown Prosecution Service refuses to prosecute. The standard of proof in civil cases is not as high as in criminal cases, but even so some of these cases have then spurred the Crown Prosecution Service to prosecute. In particular in 1998 the family of a murdered black woman doctor, Joan Francisco, took a civil case for trespass to the person against her ex-boyfriend. The family alleged that the man had murdered her. They were successful in this civil case: the police and the Crown Prosecution Service then reviewed the evidence and discovered that there was a test for discovering very small amounts of blood which they had not used in the first investigation. When this test was used, it revealed that there were spots of the man's blood on the woman's T-shirt. The CPS then prosecuted the man for murder and in 1999, six years after the murder, he was convicted.

Criticism of the CPS

There has been criticism that the CPS is not always ready to proceed with cases at court. This criticism was supported by the findings of the Public Accounts Committee. This reported on the CPS in October 2006 in *Crown Prosecution Service: Effective Use of Magistrates' Courts Hearings* for 2004–05. It pointed out that there was a large number of cases, both trial and pre-trial, which did not proceed on the day.

Where the trial did not go ahead, the defence was most often to blame. However, the CPS was responsible in 38 per cent of cases. It was either not ready to proceed or dropped charges on the day of the trial. The Committee identified that delays cost the taxpayer over £173 million. Of this it identified £24 million as being attributable to the CPS.

The CPS's response was to point out that the ineffective trial rate had dropped sharply from 31 per cent in July to September 2002 to 23 per cent in January to March 2005. It also pointed out that more progress had been made since the period considered by the Committee.

Since then the CPS has improved its performance. In particular, the discontinuance rate of cases has fallen substantially.

However, there were still problems in some areas. In March 2010 a report, *Review of the Performance of the CPS London 2009–10*, by the Crown Prosecution Service Inspectorate showed that the CPS in London did not always perform well. The report highlighted that Crown Court work was too often poorly prepared and that this had adverse effects on readiness and presentation at court. By 2011–12 the Inspectorate in their annual report found that substantial progress had been made in most areas.

EXAMINATION QUESTIONS

1. (a) Explain the powers available to grant bail. [14 marks]
   (b) Discuss the role of the Crown Prosecution Service within the English and Welsh legal system. [11 marks]

   LA1, Winter 2011, WJEC

EXTENSION ESSAY

Critically consider the rules relating to bail in the legal system in England and Wales.

CHAPTER 13

CRIMINAL COURTS

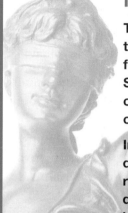

INTRODUCTION

The two courts which hear criminal trials are the Magistrates' Court and the Crown Court. As already explained in Chapter 12, the actual court for the trial is decided by the category of crime involved in the charge. Summary offences can only be tried at the Magistrates' Court, indictable offences can only be tried at the Crown Court, while triable-either-way offences may be tried at either court.

In both the Magistrates' Court and the Crown Court the majority of defendants plead guilty to the charge against them. In these cases the role of the court is to decide what sentence should be imposed on the defendant. Where the accused pleads not guilty, the role of the court is to try the case and decide if the accused is guilty or not guilty; the burden of proof is on the prosecution who must prove the case beyond reasonable doubt. The form of the trial is an adversarial one, with prosecution and defence presenting their cases and cross-examining each other's witnesses, while the role of the judge is effectively that of referee, overseeing the trial and making sure that legal rules are followed correctly. The judge cannot investigate the case, nor ask to see additional witnesses.

13.1 Magistrates' Courts

There are about 400 Magistrates' Courts in England and Wales. They are local courts so there will be a Magistrates' Court in many towns, while big cities will have several courts. Each court deals with cases that have a connection with its geographical area and they have jurisdiction over a variety of matters involving criminal cases. Cases are heard by magistrates, who may be either qualified District Judges or unqualified lay justices (see Chapter 17 for further details on magistrates). There is also a legally qualified clerk attached to each court to give advice on the law to the magistrates.

13.1.1 Jurisdiction of the Magistrates' Courts

So far as criminal cases are concerned the courts have jurisdiction in a variety of matters. They have a very large workload and they do the following:

1. Try all summary cases.
2. Try any triable-either-way offences which it is decided should be dealt with in the Magistrates' Court (see section 13.1.3).
3. These first two categories account for about 97 per cent of all criminal cases.
4. Deal with the first hearing of all indictable offences. These cases are then sent to the Crown Court.

5. Deal with all the side matters connected to criminal cases, such as issuing warrants for arrest and deciding bail applications.

6. Try cases in the Youth Court where the defendants are aged 10–17 inclusive.

Civil jurisdiction

The Magistrates' Courts also have some civil jurisdiction. Strictly speaking, this side of their work belongs in Chapter 9 – however, for completeness, and to illustrate the wide variety of work carried out by Magistrates' Court, this side of their work is listed below. It includes:

- Enforcing council tax demands and issuing warrants of entry and investigation to gas and electricity authorities.
- Family cases including orders for protection against violence and maintenance orders (NB Magistrates' Courts cannot grant divorces).
- Proceedings concerning the welfare of children under the Children Act 1989.
- Hearing appeals against the refusal of a licence to sell alcohol.

13.1.2 Summary trials

These are the least serious criminal offences and are subdivided into offences of different 'levels' – level one being the lowest level and level five the highest. The use of levels allows a maximum fine to be set for each level which is increased in line with inflation from time to time. The current maximum fines date from the Criminal Justice Act 1991 and are: level one: maximum £200, level two: £500, level three: £1,000, level four: £2,500 and level five: £5,000. However, for certain breaches of environmental law and health and safety legislation, a business can be fined up to £20,000 by the magistrates. The maximum prison sentence that can be given on summary trial is six months, although the Criminal Justice Act 2003 gives power for this to be increased to 15 months in future.

At the start of any case, the clerk of the court will check the defendant's name and address and then ask whether he pleads guilty or not guilty. Over 90 per cent of defendants in the Magistrates' Court plead guilty and the process is then concerned with establishing an appropriate penalty for the case.

Guilty plea

The usual sequence of events where the defendant pleads guilty to a summary offence is as follows:

1. The Crown Prosecutor or Associate Prosecutor from the CPS will give the court a résumé of the facts of the case.

2. The defendant is asked if he agrees with those facts (if he does not, the magistrates may have to hold an inquiry, called a Newton hearing, to establish the facts).

3. The defendant's past record of convictions, if any, is given to the court.

4. Other information about the defendant's background, especially his financial position, is given to the court.

5. Any relevant reports are considered by the magistrates; these may include a pre-sentence report prepared by a probation officer and/or a medical report on the defendant's mental health.

6. The defendant or his lawyer can then explain any matter which might persuade the magistrates to give a lenient sentence. This is called making a speech in mitigation.

7. The magistrates decide the sentence.

This is shown in a flow chart form in Figure 13.1.

Not guilty plea

When a defendant pleads not guilty the procedure is longer and more complicated, as both sides produce evidence to the court. Since the burden of proof is on the prosecution, it will begin the case – usually by making a short speech outlining what the case is about and what they hope to prove. The prosecution witnesses will then be called one

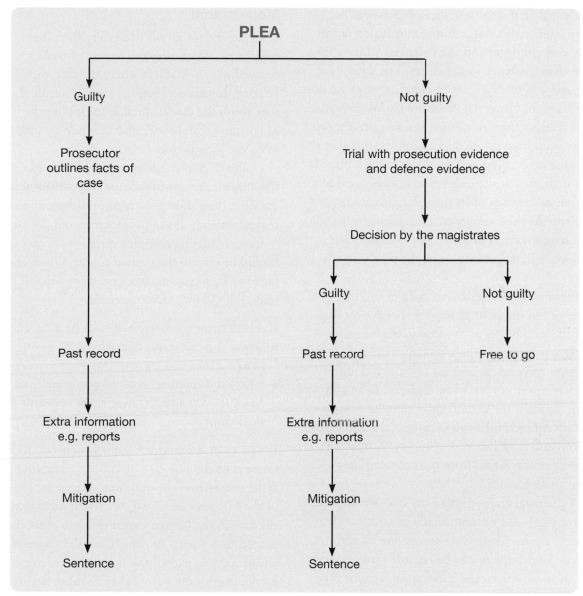

PLEA

- Guilty
  - Prosecutor outlines facts of case
  - Past record
  - Extra information e.g. reports
  - Mitigation
  - Sentence

- Not guilty
  - Trial with prosecution evidence and defence evidence
  - Decision by the magistrates
    - Guilty
      - Past record
      - Extra information e.g. reports
      - Mitigation
      - Sentence
    - Not guilty
      - Free to go

Figure 13.1 *Flow chart of proceedings for a summary offence in the Magistrates' Court*

at a time to give evidence, and the prosecutor will question each to establish what he or she saw and heard. This is called the examination in chief. After the prosecution finishes the examination in chief of a witness, the defence will then cross-examine that witness to test their evidence and try to show that it is not reliable. The prosecution may also produce relevant exhibits, such as property found in the possession of the defendant or documents which help establish the case.

At the end of the prosecution case the defence can submit to the magistrates that there is no case to answer and that the case should be dismissed at this point. This is because the prosecution has to prove the case and if its evidence does not establish a case, then it must be dismissed.

Only a very small number of cases will be dismissed at this stage. In the vast majority the case will continue and the defence will have to give their evidence to the court. The defendant himself will usually give evidence, though he does not have to. However, since the Criminal Justice and Public Order Act 1994, the magistrates can draw their own conclusions from the fact that the accused stays silent and does not explain his side of the matter. If the defendant does give evidence, he can be cross-examined by the prosecutor, as can any defence witnesses. The defence can call any witnesses and produce any evidence that it believes will help to disprove the prosecution's case.

Once all the evidence has been given, the defence has the right to make a speech pointing out the weaknesses of the case to the magistrates and try to persuade them to acquit the defendant. Further speeches are not usually allowed unless there is a point of law to be argued. The magistrates then decide if the defendant is guilty or not guilty. If they convict, they will then hear about his past record and may also look at reports and hear a speech in mitigation from the defence. They will then pass sentence.

If the magistrates dismiss the case, the defendant is free to go and cannot usually be tried for that offence again. There is, however, one exception when the defendant can be retried. This is where the prosecution successfully appeals against the acquittal in a 'case stated' appeal (see section 13.3.2 for the rules on these).

13.1.3 Triable-either-way offences

Plea before venue

Under the plea before venue procedure the defendant is first asked whether he pleads guilty or not guilty. If he pleads guilty, then he has no right to ask to go to the Crown Court although the magistrates may still decide to send him there for sentence.

Mode of trial

If the defendant pleads not guilty then the magistrates must carry out 'mode of trial' proceedings to establish where the case will be tried. In this the magistrates first decide if they think the case is suitable for trial in the Magistrates' Court and whether they are prepared to accept jurisdiction.

Under s 19 of the Magistrates' Court Act 1980 they must consider the nature and seriousness of the case, their own powers of punishment and any representations of the prosecution and defence.

Cases involving complex questions of fact or law should be sent to the Crown Court. Other relevant factors which may make a case more suitable for trial at the Crown Court include:

- where there was breach of trust by a person
- where the crime was committed by an organised gang
- where the amount involved was more than twice the amount the magistrates can fine the defendant.

In rare cases where the Attorney-General, Solicitor-General or the Director of Public Prosecutions is the prosecutor, the magistrates, under s 19(4) of the Magistrates' Court Act 1980, must send the case to the Crown Court if that is what the prosecution wants. In other cases the prosecution's wishes are just part of the matters to be considered by the magistrates before they decide whether they are prepared to hear the case or whether it should be tried at the Crown Court.

Defendant's election

If the magistrates are prepared to accept jurisdiction, the defendant is then told he has the right to choose trial by jury, but may be tried by the magistrates if he agrees to this course. However, he is also warned that if the case is tried by the magistrates and at the end of the case he is found guilty, the magistrates can send him to the

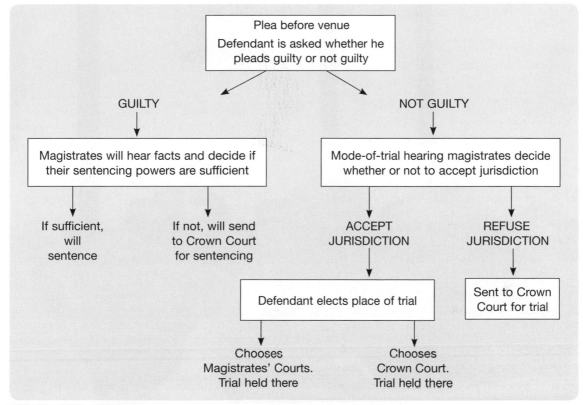

Figure 13.2 *Flow chart of procedure for triable either-way offences*

Crown Court for sentence if they feel their powers of punishment are insufficient.

The procedure for triable-either-way offences is shown in flow chart form in Figure 13.2.

13.1.4 Choosing trial by jury

Since 1997 defendants pleading guilty to a triable-either-way offence at the Magistrates' Court in the plea-before-venue procedure have not been able to choose to go to the Crown Court. This is sensible since there will be no trial of the case, so the defendants are not losing a right to trial by jury. Defendants who are pleading not guilty have had the right to choose where they want the case to be dealt with. This has been seen as an important part of civil liberties, as trial by jury is viewed as a protection of individual rights.

However, not many defendants elect to go to the Crown Court. It was noticeable that when all defendants could choose to go to the Crown Court less than one out of 20 elected to do so.

Implications of choosing jury trial

There are several factors involved in a defendant's choice of the Crown Court as the venue for his trial. The main reason for choosing the Crown Court is that the decision on guilt or innocence is made by a jury and this gives a better chance of an acquittal. Only 20 per cent of defendants who plead not guilty at the Magistrates' Court will be found not guilty by the magistrates, whereas 60 per cent of those who plead not guilty at the Crown Court are acquitted. This does not mean the jury acquits a large number as this figure

Inside a Magistrates' Court

includes cases where the case is discharged by the judge without a trial. This is when the prosecution at the Crown Court does not offer evidence against the defendant. This may be because by the time the case reaches the Crown Court, the prosecution accepts that the defendant is not guilty, or it may be because witnesses have failed or refused to come to court and the prosecution is left with insufficient evidence for the case to proceed.

Other points to be considered are that:

- There will be a longer wait before the trial and there will also be committal proceedings in the Magistrates' Court before the case goes to the Crown Court.

- Cases at the Crown Court are more expensive, but the defendant is also more likely to get legal representation through the Criminal Defence Service.
- If the defendant is represented this must be by a barrister or solicitor with a certificate of advocacy giving rights of audience at the Crown Court.
- There is a risk of a higher sentence if the defendant is found guilty in the Crown Court.

A study by Hedderman and Moxon showed that most defendants who chose the Crown Court did so on the advice of their lawyers and the main factor was the higher chance of an acquittal. There were many factors, however, which influenced the choice, including (where defendants were in custody) a wish to serve part of the sentence in a remand prison!

Should the right to choose trial by jury be kept?

It is very much more expensive to hold trials at the Crown Court than at the Magistrates' Court. In addition, statistics show that many of the defendants who choose jury trial then go on to plead guilty at the Crown Court. This has led to the questioning of whether defendants should have the right to elect trial by jury in cases where they are charged with a triable-either-way offence. In fact this right to jury trial has already been cut down by the fact that many offences which used to be triable either way have been reclassified as summary offences. These include the offences of assaulting a police officer in the execution of his duty, and driving whilst disqualified and drink driving.

In the past the government has attempted to limit the defendant's right to jury trial. In 1999 and 2000 the Labour government tried to pass laws abolishing the defendant's right to elect trial by jury in triable-either-way cases. On both occasions the House of Lords voted against the change in the law.

Then, in 2003, the Criminal Justice Bill contained two measures aimed at limiting jury trials. One proposal was for situations where there had already been an attempt to tamper with a jury so that the jury had to be discharged. Where this happened the prosecution could apply for the trial to be by judge alone. This was enacted in s 44 of the Criminal Justice Act 2003. The other proposal allowed the prosecution to apply for trial without a jury in lengthy or complex cases or where there was danger of the jury being interfered with.

In 2012 this clause of the Criminal Justice Act 2003 was abolished by the Protection of Freedoms Act without ever having come into effect.

The strong opposition to abolishing the right to trial by jury is because this right is seen as a safeguard of people's liberty.

13.1.5 Sending cases to the Crown Court

Where the trial is going to be held at the Crown Court, the magistrates must officially send the case to the Crown Court.

For indictable offences the case is transferred to the Crown Court immediately from the first hearing at the Magistrates' Court. This is under s 51 of the Crime and Disorder Act 1998. For triable-either-way offences, magistrates will hold a plea before venue and, if the defendant pleads not guilty, a mode-of-trial hearing. If at this hearing it is decided that the case is to be tried in the Crown Court, the magistrates will then transfer the case to the Crown Court.

13.1.6 Committal for sentence

Magistrates can commit a defendant charged with a triable-either-way offence for sentence to the Crown Court. However, this will only happen when, at the end of a case, having heard the defendant's past record, they feel that their powers of punishment are insufficient.

The magistrates must be of the opinion that the offence, or the combination of offences, is so serious that a greater punishment than they have power to inflict should be imposed. In cases of violent or sexual offences, the magistrates may commit for sentence if they think that a long sentence of imprisonment is necessary to protect the public from serious harm.

After the introduction of plea before venue (see section 13.1.3), the number of committals for sentence more than doubled. About 28,000 defendants each year are sent by the magistrates to the Crown Court for sentencing. There are criticisms that magistrates commit too many defendants for sentence, since a significant percentage of those committed for sentence do not receive more than the magistrate could have imposed on them.

13.1.7 The role of the clerk

Every bench of magistrates is assisted by a clerk who is also known as legal adviser. The senior clerk in each court has to be a barrister or solicitor of at least five years' standing. The role of the clerk is to guide the magistrates on questions of law, practice and procedure. The clerk makes sure that the correct procedure is followed in court. For example, at the start of a case it is the clerk who will ask the defendant if he pleads guilty or not guilty. The clerk is not meant to take part in the decision-making process; that is the magistrates' role. This means that the clerk should not retire with the justices when they leave the court at the end of a case to consider their verdict.

The senior clerk has been granted greater powers to deal with routine matters which previously had to be done by magistrates. For example, clerks can now issue warrants for arrest, extend police bail, adjourn criminal proceedings (where the defendant is on bail and the terms on the bail are not being changed), and conduct early administrative hearings.

13.2 Youth Courts

Young offenders aged from 10 to 17 are dealt with in the Youth Court which is a branch of the Magistrates' Court. Children under the age of 10 cannot be charged with a criminal offence.

There are some exceptional cases in which young offenders can be tried in the Crown Court. These are cases where the defendant is charged with murder or manslaughter, rape, and causing death by dangerous driving. In addition it is possible for those aged 14 and over to be sent to the Crown Court for trial in any case where they are charged with a serious offence (usually one which for an adult carries a maximum prison sentence of at least 14 years).

The Youth Court sits in private, with only those who are involved in the case allowed into the courtroom. Members of the press may be present, but they cannot publish the name of any young offender or other information which could identify him, such as address or school.

The magistrates who sit on the bench in these courts must have had special training to deal with young offenders. There must be at least one female magistrate and one male magistrate on the bench. The procedure in the court is less formal than in the adult courts and the parents or guardians of any child under 16 are required to be present for the proceedings. The court can also ask parents of those aged 16 or 17 to attend.

13.3 Appeals from the Magistrates' Court

There is a system of appeal routes available from a decision by the Magistrates' Court. The route used will depend on whether the appeal is only on a point of law, or whether it is for other reasons. The two appeal routes are to the Crown Court, or to the Queen's Bench Divisional Court.

13.3.1 Appeals to the Crown Court

This is the normal route of appeal and is only available to the defence. If the defendant pleaded guilty at the Magistrates' Court, then he can only appeal against sentence. If the defendant pleaded not guilty and was convicted, then the appeal can be against conviction and/or sentence. In both cases the defendant has an automatic right to appeal and does not need to get leave (permission) to appeal.

At the Crown Court the case is completely re-heard by a judge and two magistrates. They can come to the same decision as the magistrates and confirm the conviction, or they can decide that the case is not proved and reverse the decision. In some cases it is possible for them to vary the decision and find the defendant guilty of a lesser offence.

Where the appeal is against sentence, the Crown Court can confirm the sentence or they can increase or decrease it. However, any increase can only be up to the magistrates' maximum powers for the case.

Over the last few years there have been about 13,500 appeals to the Crown Court each year, and judicial statistics published by the Ministry of Justice show that the appeal is allowed in approximately less than half of cases.

If it becomes apparent that there is a point of law to be decided, then the Crown Court can decide that point of law, but there is the possibility of a further appeal by way of a case-stated appeal being made to the Queen's Bench Divisional Court (see section 13.3.2). A diagram setting out the appeal routes from the Magistrates' Court is shown in Figure 13.3.

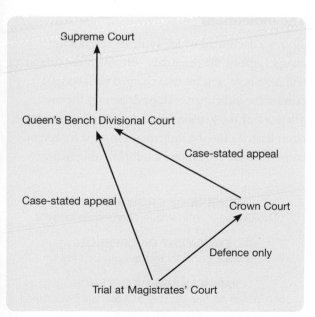

Figure 13.3 *Appeal routes from the Magistrates' Court*

13.3.2 Case-stated appeals

These are appeals on a point of law which go to the Queen's Bench Divisional Court. Both the prosecution and the defence can use this appeal route and it can be direct from the Magistrates' Court, or following an appeal to the Crown Court. The magistrates (or the Crown Court) are asked to state the case by setting out their findings of fact and their decision. The appeal is then argued on the basis of what the law is on those facts; no witnesses are called. The appeal is heard by a panel of two or three High Court Judges from the Queen's Bench Division, though in some cases a judge from the Court of Appeal may form part of the panel.

This route is only used by the defendant against a conviction, or by the prosecution against an acquittal. It cannot be used to challenge the sentence. The appeal is because they claim the magistrates came to the wrong decision because they made a mistake about the law. The Divisional Court may confirm, vary or reverse the decision or remit (send back) the case to the Magistrates' Court for the magistrates to implement the decision on the law.

There are usually less than 100 appeals by way of case stated made each year.

Further appeal to the Supreme Court

From the decision of the Queen's Bench Divisional Court there is a possibility of a further appeal to the Supreme Court (formerly the House of Lords). Such an appeal can only be made if:

1. The Divisional Court certifies that a point of law of general public importance is involved.
2. The Divisional Court or the Supreme Court gives leave (permission) to appeal because the point is one which ought to be considered by the Supreme Court.

An example of a case which followed this appeal route was *C v DPP* (1994). This case concerned the legal point about the presumption of criminal responsibility of children from the age of 10 up to their 14th birthday. Until this case, it had been accepted that a child of this age could only be convicted if the prosecution proved that the child knew he was doing wrong. The Divisional Court held that times had changed and that children were more mature and the rule was not needed. They decided that children of this age were presumed to know the difference between right and wrong, and that the prosecution did not need to prove 'mischievous discretion'.

The case was then appealed to the House of Lords who overruled the Divisional Court, holding that the law was still that a child of this age was presumed not to know he or she was doing wrong, and therefore not to have the necessary intention for any criminal offence. A child of this age could only be convicted if the prosecution disproved this presumption by bringing evidence to show that the child was aware that what he or she was doing was seriously wrong. This ruling was on the basis that it was for Parliament to make such a major change to the law, not the courts. The courts were bound by precedent.

13.4 The Crown Court

Until 1971 very serious criminal cases were dealt with by High Court Judges when they toured the country holding Assize Courts. Other indictable offences were heard at Quarter Sessions, which were intended to sit four times a year. This system was out of date and unable to cope with the growing number of criminal cases – following the Beeching Commission Report 1969, both Assizes and Quarter Sessions were abolished. In their place, the Courts Act 1971 set up the Crown Court to deal with all cases which were not tried at the Magistrates' Court.

The Crown Court currently sits in 77 different centres throughout England and Wales. There are three kinds of centre:

1. **First tier**
   These exist in main centres throughout the country. For example, there are first tier Crown Courts in Bristol, Birmingham, Leeds and Manchester. At each court there is a High Court and a Crown Court with separate judges for civil and criminal work. The Crown Court is permanently staffed by High Court Judges as well as Circuit Judges and Recorders, and the court can deal with all categories of crime triable on indictment.

2. **Second tier**
   This is a Crown Court only, but High Court Judges sit there on a regular basis to hear criminal cases, as well as Circuit Judges and Recorders. All categories of crime triable on indictment can be tried here.

3. **Third tier**
   This is staffed only by Circuit Judges and Recorders. The most serious cases, such as murder, manslaughter and rape are not usually tried here as there is no High Court Judge to deal with them.

13.4.1 Preliminary matters

The indictment

This is a document which formally sets out the charges against the defendant. Although the defendant will have been sent for trial charged with specific crimes, the indictment can be drawn up for any offence that the witness statements reveal. In more complicated cases the indictment may be for several counts. Figure 13.4 shows a sample indictment.

DONBRIDGE CROWN COURT
The Queen v John Wilkie charged as follows:

STATEMENT OF OFFENCE
Murder contrary to the common law

PARTICULARS OF OFFENCE
John Wilkie on the 4th day of April 1997 murdered Abraham Lincoln

---

Figure 13.4 *Sample indictment*

Criminal Procedure Rules

Criminal Procedure Rules to deal with all aspects of criminal cases came into force in April 2005. The overriding objective of the Rules is that 'criminal cases be dealt with justly'.

Disclosure by prosecution and defence

The Criminal Procedure and Investigations Act 1996 places a duty on both sides to make certain points known to the other. The prosecution, who have already given the defence statements of all the evidence they propose to use at the trial, must also disclose previously undisclosed material 'which in the prosecutor's opinion might reasonably be considered capable of undermining the case for the prosecution against the accused'. This is designed to prevent the sort of miscarriage of justice which occurred in Stefan Kiszko's case (see Chapter 8) through the prosecution 'hiding' something which could help prove the innocence of the defendant.

The 1996 Act also imposes a duty on the defence in cases which are to be tried on indictment. In these, after the prosecution's primary disclosure, the defence must give a written statement to the prosecution setting out:

- the nature of the accused's defence, including any particular defences on which he intends to rely
- the matters of fact on which he takes issue with the prosecution and why he takes issue
- any point of law which he wishes to take, and the case authority on which he will be relying.

The defendant also has to give details about any alibi and the witnesses he intends calling to support that alibi. This information allows the prosecution to run police checks on the alibi witnesses.

Plea and case management hearing

Under the Criminal Procedure Rules, most cases sent to the Crown Court are dealt with first at a plea and case management hearing (PCMH). The first purpose of a PCMH is to find out whether the defendant is pleading guilty or not guilty. All the charges on the indictment are read out to the defendant in open court, and he is asked how he pleads to each charge. This process is called the 'arraignment'.

If the defendant pleads guilty, the judge will, if possible, sentence the defendant immediately. This means that defendants who plead guilty will not have an unnecessarily long wait for their case to come to court.

Where a defendant pleads not guilty the judge will require the prosecution and defence to identify the key issues, both of fact and law, which are involved in the case. He will then give any directions that are necessary to organise the actual trial; for instance, the prosecution and defence may agree that certain witnesses need not attend court as their evidence is not in dispute. Other points such as whether it will be necessary to use a video link for any witnesses are also agreed on. The aim of the PCMH is to speed up the actual trial process and to ensure that time will not be wasted on unnecessary points. It also allows the court to plan its lists.

The Criminal Procedure Rules encourage active case management. Case management in the Crown Court includes:

- the early identification of the real issues
- the early identification of the needs of witnesses
- achieving a certainty as to what must be done, by whom, and when, in particular by the early setting of a timetable for the progress of a case
- monitoring the progress of the case and compliance with directions
- ensuring that the evidence, whether disputed or not, is presented in the shortest and clearest way.

The full Criminal Procedure Rules are available online on the Ministry of Justice website, www.justice.gov.uk.

13.4.2 The trial

It is normal for a defendant appearing at the Crown Court to be represented, usually by a barrister, although solicitors who have a certificate of advocacy can also appear at the Crown Court. Defendants can represent themselves, but there was concern over the effect this could have on witnesses who were cross-examined at length by a defendant in person. As a result the Youth Justice and Criminal Evidence Act 1999 forbids cross-examination in person by defendants who are charged with sexual offences, or where there is a child witness.

At the trial where the defendant pleads not guilty, the order of events will normally be:

1. The jury is sworn in to try the case (for further information on juries see Chapter 18).
2. The prosecution will make an opening speech to the jury explaining what the case is about and what they intend to prove.
3. The prosecution witnesses give evidence and can be cross-examined by the defence; the prosecution will also produce any other evidence such as documents or video recordings.
4. At the end of the prosecution case the defence may submit that there is no case to go to the jury; if the judge decides there is no case he will direct the jury to acquit the defendant.
5. The defence may make an opening speech provided they intend calling evidence other than the defendant.
6. The defence witnesses give evidence and are cross-examined by the prosecution; the defendant does not have to give evidence personally but the judge may comment on the failure to do in his summing-up to the jury.
7. The prosecutor makes a closing speech to the jury pointing out the strengths of the prosecution case.
8. The defence makes a closing speech to the jury pointing out the weaknesses of the prosecution.
9. The judge sums up the case to the jury and directs them on any relevant law.
10. The jury retires to consider their verdict in private.
11. The jury's verdict is given in open court.
12. If the verdict is guilty the judge then sentences the accused; if the verdict is not guilty the accused is discharged. Normally, once a defendant is found not guilty he can never be tried for that offence again. However, the Criminal Justice Act 2003 removes this 'double jeopardy' rule for serious cases if 'new and compelling evidence' comes to light, so that a defendant can be tried a second time. The DPP has to consent to the reopening of investigations in the case. Once the evidence has been found, then the prosecution has to apply to the Court of Appeal for the original acquittal to be quashed. This power has been used in cases where new techniques of DNA testing now show that a defendant who is acquitted is in fact the offender. The first case in which this power was used is shown in the example. In 2011 two defendants who had been previous acquitted of the murder of black teenager, Stephen Lawrence, were retried and convicted some 19 years after the murder. Part of the new evidence was a DNA match with Stephen's blood found on the clothing of one of them. This evidence became available due to improved DNA testing techniques.

13.5 Appeals from the Crown Court

It is important that there should be adequate routes of appeal. The functions of an appeal process serve not only to protect the defendant

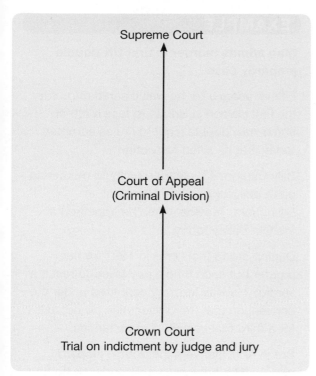

Figure 13.5 *Appeal routes from the Crown Court*

from a miscarriage of justice, but also to allow uniform development of the law. Figure 13.5 shows appeal routes from the Crown Court.

13.5.1 Appeals by the defendant

The defendant has the possibility of appealing against conviction and/or sentence to the Court of Appeal (Criminal Division). So, at the end of any trial in which a defendant has been found guilty, his lawyer should advise him on the possibility of an appeal.

Leave to appeal

The rules on appeals are set out in the Criminal Appeal Act 1995 and in all cases the defendant must get leave to appeal from the Court of Appeal, or a certificate that the case is fit for appeal from the trial judge. The idea of having to

get leave is that cases which are without merit are filtered out and the court's time saved.

The application for leave to appeal is considered by a single judge of the Court of Appeal in private, although if he refuses it is possible to apply to a full Court of Appeal for leave. It is difficult to get leave to appeal – in 2011, 4,606 applications were considered by a single judge, but leave to appeal was granted in only 1,284 cases (fewer than 30 per cent). Even when a defendant gets leave to appeal that does not mean that the actual appeal will be successful. On appeal against conviction only one-third of defendants are successful in their appeals.

The Criminal Appeal Act 1995

The Criminal Appeal Act 1995 simplified the grounds under which the court can allow an appeal. The Act states that the Court of Appeal:

(a) 'shall allow an appeal against conviction if they think that the conviction is unsafe; and
(b) shall dismiss such an appeal in any other case'.

Since the European Convention on Human Rights has been incorporated into our law by the Human Rights Act 1998, the Court of Appeal has taken a broad approach to the meaning of 'unsafe'. In particular, a conviction has been held to be 'unsafe' where the defendant has been denied a fair trial.

New evidence

Any new evidence must appear to be capable of belief and would afford a ground for an appeal. This has to be considered together with whether it would have been admissible at the trial and why it was not produced at that trial.

Court of Appeal's powers

The Court of Appeal can allow a defendant's appeal and quash the conviction. Alternatively it can vary the conviction to that of a lesser offence of which the jury could have convicted the defendant. As far as sentencing is concerned the court can decrease but not increase it on the defendant's appeal. Where the appeal is not successful, the court can decide to dismiss the appeal.

The Court of Appeal also has the power to order that there should be a retrial of the case in front of a new jury. The power was given to it in 1988, but initially was not often used; for example, in 1989 only one retrial was ordered. However, its use has increased, with between 50 and 70 retrials being ordered each year.

13.5.2 Appeals by the prosecution

Originally the prosecution had no right to appeal against either the verdict or sentence passed in the Crown Court. Gradually, however, some limited rights of appeal have been given to it by Parliament.

Against an acquittal

With two small exceptions, the prosecution cannot appeal against a finding of not guilty by a jury. One exception is for cases where the acquittal was the result of the jury or witnesses being 'nobbled', i.e. where some jurors are bribed or threatened by associates of the defendant. In these circumstances, provided there has been an actual conviction for jury nobbling, the Criminal Procedure and Investigations Act 1996 allows an application to be made to the High Court for an order quashing the acquittal. Once the acquittal is quashed, the prosecution could then start new proceedings for the same offence. As yet this power has never been used.

The other exception is where the prosecution can apply for an acquittal to be quashed because there is 'new and compelling evidence' against the defendant (see 13.4.2 and the example opposite for examples of this).

EXAMPLE

Man admits murder in first UK double jeopardy case

Fifteen years after he was cleared of murder, the first person in Britain to face a retrial under new double jeopardy rules admitted today that he killed his victim.

Billy Dunlop, 43, pleaded guilty to murdering pizza delivery girl Julie Hogg, 22, in Billingham, Teeside, when he appeared at the Old Bailey today.

Dunlop stood trial twice in 1991 for her murder but each time a jury failed to reach a verdict. He was formally acquitted under the convention that the prosecution do not ask for a third trial in such circumstances.

But in April last year the double jeopardy rule – which prevented a defendant who had been acquitted from being tried again for the same offence – was changed under the Criminal Justice Act 2003.

The following November the Director of Public Prosecutions announced the legal process to retry Dunlop had begun. The case was sent to the Court of Appeal where his acquittal was quashed.

Taken from an article in the Daily Mail, *11 September 2006*

Referring a point of law

However, the prosecution has a special referral right in cases where the defendant is acquitted. This is under s 36 of the Criminal Justice Act 1972 which allows the Attorney-General to refer a point of law to the Court of Appeal, in order to get a ruling on the law. The decision by the Court of Appeal on that point of law does not affect the acquittal but it creates a precedent for any future case involving the same point of law.

Key Facts

Party	Court which hears appeal	Reason for appealing	Relevant Act of Parliament
Defence	Court of Appeal	against sentence and/or conviction need leave to appeal	Criminal Appeal Act 1995 conviction 'unsafe'
Defence	Further appeal to Supreme Court	on point of law of general public importance need leave to appeal	
Prosecution	High Court	asking for order to quash acquittal because of interference with witness or jury	Criminal Procedure and Investigations Act 1996
Prosecution	Court of Appeal	Attorney-General's reference on a point of law: does not affect acquittal	Criminal Justice Act 1972
Prosecution	Court of Appeal	Attorney-General against lenient sentence	Criminal Justice Act 1988
Prosecution	Further appeal to Supreme Court	on point of law of general public importance need leave to appeal	

Figure 13.6 *Key facts chart on appeal rights from the Crown Court*

Against sentence

Under s 36 of the Criminal Justice Act 1988 the Attorney-General can apply for leave to refer an unduly lenient sentence to the Court of Appeal for re-sentencing. This power was initially available for indictable cases only, but was extended in 1994 to many triable-either-way offences, provided that the trial of the case took place at a Crown Court. This power is used successfully in a number of cases each year. There has recently been an increase in the number of such referrals.

The main difficulty is: how does the Attorney-General learn of cases which ought to be referred to the Court of Appeal? In fact, about 300 cases are brought to the Attorney-General's attention each year, with most of these being sent to him by the Crown Prosecution Service. It is also possible for the public to contact the Attorney-General's office and a small number of cases a year are reported in this way, usually by distressed relatives of the victim of the crime, who feel that the original sentence was inadequate. Members of Parliament will also sometimes refer cases to the Attorney-General on behalf of aggrieved constituents.

Whenever a case is sent to the Attorney-General he will look through the papers on the trial and decide whether to refer the case to the Court of Appeal.

In 2011, 118 cases referred by the Attorney-General were heard by the Court of Appeal. The sentences in 98 of these cases were increased. The case included one defendant whose sentence for two offences of rape was increased from 3.5 years' imprisonment to 11 years' imprisonment.

13.5.3 Appeals to the Supreme Court

Both the prosecution and the defence may appeal from the Court of Appeal to the Supreme Court, but it is necessary to have the case certified as involving a point of law of general public importance, and to get leave to appeal, either from the Supreme Court or from the Court of Appeal. There are very few criminal appeals heard by the Supreme Court. In 2011 there were 12 petitions for leave to appeal considered, but leave was granted in only seven of these.

References to the European Court of Justice

Where a point of European law is involved in a case it is possible for any court to make a reference to the European Court of Justice under Article 267 of the Treaty of the Functioning of the European Union (see Chapter 6). However, this is a fairly rare occurrence in criminal cases, as most of the criminal law is purely 'domestic' and not affected by European Union law.

13.6 The Criminal Cases Review Commission

The large number of miscarriages of justice (see section 11.1.2) which had not been corrected through the normal appeal system led to demands for a review body. It was true that the Home Secretary had power to review cases and refer them to the Court of Appeal, but cases such as the Birmingham Six and Judith Ward left people feeling that the Home Secretary was not sufficiently independent of the government. The Runciman Commission, when considering the question, recommended that an independent review body should be set up to consider possible miscarriages of justice. This recommendation was implemented by the Criminal Appeal Act 1995 which set up the Criminal Cases Review Commission.

Powers

The Commission has the power to investigate possible miscarriages of justice (including summary offences) and to refer cases back to the courts. In order for the Commission to be able to refer a case there must normally have already been an appeal to the Court of Appeal, although the Commission has a discretion to refer a case where 'there are exceptional circumstances'.

In addition the Court of Appeal may direct the Commission to investigate and report to the court on any matter which comes before it in an appeal if it feels an investigation is likely to help the court resolve the appeal.

The members of the Commission are appointed by the Queen – at least one-third are legally qualified and at least two-thirds have relevant experience of the criminal justice system. They have about 60 support staff, treble the number previously used in the Home Office for such work. However, most of the reinvestigation work is done by the police. This is felt to be unsatisfactory as it does not really make such a reinvestigation independent, although it is true to say that many of the past miscarriages of justice have come to light as the result of investigation by other police forces.

Work

The Criminal Cases Review Commission took over the investigation of miscarriages of justice at the beginning of April 1997.

The main bulk of cases it investigates are brought to its attention by defendants themselves or by defendants' families, though some cases have been referred by the Court of Appeal and others have been identified by the Commission itself. Some of the first cases it investigated were alleged miscarriages of justice from over 40 years ago, such as the case of Derek Bentley. Bentley was hanged for murder in 1953, while his co-defendant, Craig, who actually fired the fatal shot, was not hanged due to his youth. Over the years there have been many attempts to have the case reopened but it was not until the

Criminal Cases Review Commission took over the investigation that the case was referred back to the Court of Appeal. In July 1998 the Court of Appeal held that the summing-up of the judge at the trial had not been fair and it quashed the conviction.

Referrals to the Court of Appeal

By 2012 the Criminal Cases Review Commission had received over 15,000 applications. The Commission had referred 504 cases to the Court of Appeal – 461 of these had been heard and the convictions quashed in 325 cases.

Cases which attracted a lot of publicity have included that of Sally Clark who, in 2003, had her conviction for murdering her two babies quashed after the scientific evidence was shown to be flawed. In 2004, Sion Jenkins's conviction for the murder of his foster daughter was quashed, also because of flawed scientific evidence.

In 2012 the conviction of Sam Hallam for murder was quashed. Sam, who was only 17 when convicted, had always insisted that he was not at the scene of the murder. The Commission's review of the evidence revealed that Sam's mobile phone pictures showed he was not present at the attack. The police had failed to examine his mobile phone during their investigation into the murder.

Appeal. The system now allows justice to be done in many more cases.

However, there are still problems in the system. In order to refer a case the Commission must consider that there is 'a real possibility' that the conviction would not be upheld by the Court of Appeal were a reference to be made. This means that the Commission has to 'second-guess' what the Court of Appeal will do.

It is noticeable that the Scottish Commission set up after the Commission for England and Wales was given wider powers. The Scottish Commission may refer a case if it believes '(a) that a miscarriage of justice may have occurred and (b) that it is in the interests of justice that a reference should be made'. There is major argument for giving the Commission for England and Wales the same power as the Scottish Commission.

There are also criticisms of what the Criminal Cases Review Commission is allowed to consider in making its decision whether to refer or not. There must be evidence or an argument which was not raised at the trial or on appeal. This means that a reference cannot be made if the point was raised at the trial or on appeal but not adequately considered.

COMMENT

The creation of the Criminal Cases Review Commission is a great improvement on the previous system under which only the Home Secretary had the power to refer cases to the Court of Appeal. The Home Secretary made very few referrals whereas the Criminal Cases Review Commission had referred over 500 by 2012. Of these, about three-quarters of the convictions were quashed by the Court of

Internet research   WWW

Check the website for the Criminal Cases Review Commission (**www.ccrc.gov.uk**) and find out:

1. How many cases has the Commission now dealt with?
2. How many cases has it referred to the Court of Appeal?
3. In how many cases has the defendant had his or her conviction quashed?

EXAMINATION QUESTIONS

1. (a) Describe how It is decided in which court a criminal trial will be heard. Include all categories of offence. [18 marks]

   (b) Discuss the advantages and disadvantages of choosing to be tried in the Crown Court when charged with a triable-either-way offence. [12 marks]

   G151, June 2011, OCR

2. (a) Explain the role of the Criminal Cases Review Commission in the appeal process. [14 marks]

   (b) Discuss the impact of the Criminal Cases Review Commission. [11 marks]

   LA1, Summer 2010, WJEC

EXTENSION ESSAY

'The appeal system in the criminal justice system does not always allow justice to be done. This problem is remedied by the role of the Criminal Cases Review Commission'. Discuss.

CHAPTER 14

SENTENCING

14.1 The role of the courts

Whenever a person pleads guilty, or is found guilty of an offence, the role of the court is to decide what sentence should be imposed on the offender. Judges and magistrates have a fairly wide discretion as to the sentence they select in each case, although they are subject to certain restrictions. Magistrates can only impose a maximum of six months' imprisonment for one offence (12 months' for two) and a maximum fine of £5,000. Judges in the Crown Court have no such limits; they can impose up to life imprisonment for some crimes and there is no maximum figure for fines. Figure 14.1 shows the percentages of different sentences imposed in Magistrates' Courts and at the Crown Court in 2011–12. The differing percentages of offenders given an immediate custodial sentence stress that the Crown Court is dealing with more serious offences.

14.1.1 Restrictions on the courts' powers

However, there are other restrictions, in both the Magistrates' Court and the Crown Court. Each crime has a maximum penalty for that type of offence set by Parliament – for example, the crime of theft has a fixed maximum of seven years' imprisonment, so that no matter how much has been stolen, the judge can never send an offender to prison for longer than this. Some offences have a maximum sentence of life imprisonment: these include manslaughter and rape. In such cases the judge has complete discretion when sentencing; the offender may be sent to prison for life or given a shorter prison sentence, or a non-custodial sentence may even be thought appropriate. Murder is the exception as it carries a mandatory life sentence; in other words, the judge has to pass life imprisonment: there is no other sentence available.

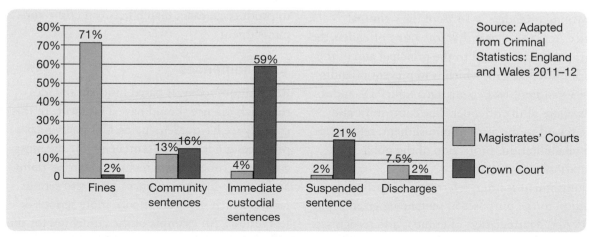

Figure 14.1 *Sentencing in the Magistrates' Courts and Crown Court*

14.1.2 Minimum sentences

Although Parliament has set down various maximum sentences for offences, there are no minimum sentences for first-time offenders. However, Parliament in the Crime (Sentences) Act 1997 set down minimum sentences for some persistent offenders. This idea followed American laws which impose minimum sentences for those who offend repeatedly. There are minimum sentences for drug dealers and burglars.

14.2 Aims of sentencing

When judges or magistrates have to pass a sentence they will not only look at the sentences available, they will also have to decide what they are trying to achieve by the punishment they give. Section 142 of the Criminal Justice Act 2003 sets out the purposes of sentencing for those aged 18 and over, saying that a court must have regard to:

- the punishment of offenders
- the reduction of crime (including its reduction by deterrence)
- the reform and rehabilitation of offenders
- the protection of the public, and
- the making of reparation by offenders to persons affected by their offences.

For young offenders, s 142A of the Criminal Justice Act 2003 states that for young offenders the court must have regard to the principal aim of the youth justice system, which is to prevent offending (or reoffending) by persons aged under 18, and to the welfare of the offender. The court must also have regard to the aims of punishment, reform and rehabilitation, protection of the public and reparation.

Punishment is often referred to as retribution. In addition to the purposes of sentencing given in the 2003 Act, denunciation of crime is also recognised as an aim of sentencing. Each of the aims will now be examined in turn.

14.2.1 Retribution

This is based on the idea of punishment because the offender deserves punishment for his or her acts. It does not seek to reduce crime or alter the offender's future behaviour. This idea was expressed in the 19th century by Kant in *The Metaphysical Elements of Justice* when he wrote:

'Judicial punishment can never be used merely as a means to promote some other good for the criminal himself or for civil society, but instead it must in all cases be imposed on him only on the ground that he has committed a crime.'

Retribution is therefore concerned only with the offence that was committed and making sure that the punishment inflicted is in proportion to that offence.

The crudest form of retribution can be seen in the old saying 'an eye for an eye and a tooth for a tooth and a life for a life'. This was one of the factors used to justify the death penalty for the offence of murder. In America, at least one judge has been known to put this theory into practice in other offences, by giving victims of burglary the right to go, with a law officer, to the home of the burglar and take items up to the approximate value of those stolen from them. In other crimes it is not so easy to see how this principle can operate to produce an exact match between crime and punishment.

Tariff sentences

Retribution, today, is based more on the idea that each offence should have a set tariff. In this country we have a Sentencing Council which produces guidelines on sentencing for the most common crimes. These include a starting point and a range for the sentence. They also set out factors which make an offence more serious or less serious. An example of the guidelines for the offence of assault causing actual bodily harm is shown in Figure 14.2.

STEP ONE Determining the offence category	
The court should determine the offence category using the table below.	
Category 1	Greater harm (serious injury must normally be present) **and** higher culpability
Category 2	Greater harm (serious injury must normally be present) **and** lower culpability; **or** lesser harm **and** higher culpability
Category 3	Lesser harm **and** lower culpability

The guidelines then give factors which indicate higher or lower culpability. They also give factors to help decide the level of harm.

STEP TWO Starting point and category range		
Having determined the category, the court should use the corresponding starting points to reach a sentence within the category range below. The starting point applies to all offenders irrespective of plea or previous convictions. A case of particular gravity, reflected by multiple features of culpability in step one, could merit upward adjustment from the starting point before further adjustment for aggravating or mitigating features, set out below.		
Offence Category	Starting point (applicable to all offenders)	Category range (applicable to all offenders)
Category 1	1 year 6 months' custody	1–3 years' custody
Category 2	26 weeks' custody	Low-level community order – 51 weeks' custody
Category 3	Medium-level community order	Band A fine – high-level community order

Figure 14.2 *Sentencing guidelines for assault causing actual bodily harm*

All guidelines produced must include a starting point for sentencing and a range for the offence. When producing guidelines, the Council also has to produce a resource assessment of the effect of the guidelines. This means that they have to identify whether the guidelines are likely to increase the numbers being sent to prison or if there will be an effect on the probation service. The intention behind this is to allow the government to forecast more accurately the requirements of the prison and probation services.

This system upholds the aim of punishing offenders and leads to consistency in sentencing. However, it is sometimes difficult for courts to impose sentences aimed at reforming offenders. The guidelines leave very little discretion in sentencing with the judges.

Some states in the USA operate a very rigid system in which each crime has a set tariff with the judge being allowed only to impose a penalty within a very narrow tariff range. This removes almost all the element of discretion in sentencing from the judges and ensures that sentences for offences are uniform. The objections to this are that it does not allow sufficient consideration of mitigating factors, and may produce a sentence which is unjust in the particular circumstances. The concept of retribution and giving the offender his 'just deserts' should not be so rigid as to ignore special needs of the offender.

There is also a problem in applying this principle to fines. A tariff system of fines involves having a fixed sum as the correct fine for particular offences; however, this takes no account of the financial situation of the offender. So a fine of £500 might be a very severe penalty for an offender who is unemployed, while the same amount would be negligible to a millionaire.

Revenge

Retribution contains an element of revenge: society and the victim are being avenged for the wrong done. It is on the basis of revenge that long prison sentences for causing death by dangerous or drink driving can be justified. In 1993 the government, in response to public opinion, increased the maximum penalties available for these offences from five years' to ten years' imprisonment.

14.2.2 Denunciation

This is society expressing its disapproval of criminal activity. A sentence should indicate both to the offender and to other people that society condemns certain types of behaviour. It shows people that justice is being done. Lord Denning when giving written evidence to the Royal Commission on Capital Punishment put it in this way:

'Punishment is the way in which society expresses its denunciation of wrongdoing: and in order to maintain respect for the law it is essential that the punishment inflicted for grave crimes should adequately reflect the revulsion felt by the great majority of citizens for them.'

Denunciation also reinforces the moral boundaries of acceptable conduct and can mould society's views on the criminality of particular conduct – for example, drink driving is now viewed by the majority of people as unacceptable behaviour. This is largely because of the changes in the law and the increasingly severe sentences that are imposed. By sending offenders to prison, banning them from driving and imposing heavy fines, society's opinion of drink driving has been changed.

The ideas of retribution and denunciation were foremost in the concepts behind the Criminal Justice Act 1991. That Act was based on the government White Paper on Crime and Punishment (1990) which stated that: 'The first objective for all sentences is the denunciation of and retribution for crime.'

However, as already seen, this aim of sentencing is not included in the purposes of sentencing set out in the Criminal Justice Act 2003. This demonstrates how different purposes may be considered more at one time than at another.

14.2.3 Incapacitation or protection of the public

The concept behind this and the next three principles of sentencing is that the punishment must serve a useful purpose. Useful in this context can mean that it serves a purpose for society as a whole, or that it will help the offender in some way. Incapacitation means that in some way the offender is made incapable of reoffending. Of course, the ultimate method of incapacitation is the death penalty, and in some countries the hands of thieves are cut off to prevent them reoffending. Another controversial method of incapacitation is the use in some American states of medical means to incapacitate sex offenders, and thus ensure that they cannot reoffend.

The use of minimum sentences for persistent offenders is aimed at protecting the public from their repeated criminal activities. Electronic tagging of offenders is a method of protecting the public from the offender without having to send the offender to prison.

There are other penalties that can be viewed as incapacitating the offender – for example, in driving offences, the offender can be banned from driving. There is also a move to using community-based sentences that will incapacitate the offender in the short term and protect the public. These include exclusion orders under which an offender is banned from going to the place where he offends (usually a pub or a football ground), and curfew orders which order an offender to remain at a given address for certain times of the day or night.

14.2.4 Deterrence

This can be individual deterrence or general deterrence. Individual deterrence is intended to ensure that the offender does not reoffend, through fear of future punishment. General deterrence is aimed at preventing other potential offenders from committing crimes. Both are aimed at reducing future levels of crime.

Individual deterrence

There are several penalties that can be imposed with the aim of deterring the individual offender from committing similar crimes in the future. These include a prison sentence, a suspended sentence or a heavy fine. However, prison does not appear to deter as about 55 per cent of adult prisoners reoffend within two years of release. With young offenders, custodial sentences have even less of a deterrent effect. Over 70 per cent of young offenders given a custodial sentence reoffend within two years.

Critics of the theory of deterrence point out that it assumes that an offender will stop to consider what the consequences of his action will be. In fact most crimes are committed on the spur of the moment, and many are committed by offenders who are under the influence of drugs or alcohol. These offenders are unlikely to stop and consider the possible consequences of their actions.

It is also pointed out that fear of being caught is more of a deterrent and that while crime detection rates are low, the threat of an unpleasant penalty, if caught, seems too remote. Fear of detection has been shown to be a powerful deterrent by the success rate of closed-circuit television used for surveying areas. In one scheme on London's District Line of the Underground system there was an 83 per cent reduction in crime in the first full year that surveillance cameras were used.

General deterrence

The value of this is even more doubtful as potential offenders are rarely deterred by severe sentences passed on others. However, the courts do occasionally resort to making an example of an offender in order to warn other potential offenders of the type of punishment they face.

General deterrence also relies on publicity so that potential offenders are aware of the level of punishment they can expect. Deterrent sentences will, therefore, be even less effective in cases of drug smuggling by foreign nationals, yet this is one of the crimes in which the courts seem tempted to resort to the hope that a severe sentence passed on one or more offenders will somehow deter other potential offenders.

General deterrence is in direct conflict with the principle of retribution, since it involves sentencing an offender to a longer term than is deserved for the specific offence. It is probably the least effective and least fair principle of sentencing.

14.2.5 Rehabilitation

Under this the main aim of the penalty is to reform the offender and rehabilitate him or her into society. It is a forward-looking aim, with the hope that the offender's behaviour will be altered by the penalty imposed, so that he or she will not offend in the future (it aims to reduce crime in this way). This principle of sentence came to the fore in the second half of the 20th century with the development of community sentences.

Key Facts

Theory	Aim of theory	Suitable punishment
Retribution	Punishment imposed only on ground that an offence has been committed	• Tariff sentences • Sentence must be proportionate to the crime
Denunciation	Society expressing its disapproval Reinforces moral boundaries	• Reflects blameworthiness of the offence
Incapacitation	Offender is made incapable of committing further crime Society is protected from crime	• Death penalty for murder • Long prison sentences • Tagging
Deterrence	Individual – the offender is deterred through fear of further punishment General – potential offenders warned as to likely punishment	• Prison sentence • Heavy fine • Long sentence as an example to others
Rehabilitation	Reform offender's behaviour	• Individualised sentence • Community sentence
Reparation	Repayment/reparation to victim or to community	• Compensation order • Unpaid work • Reparation schemes

Figure 14.3 *Key facts chart on aims of sentencing*

As the abuse of drugs is the cause of many offences, there are also community sentences – drug testing and treatment orders and drug abstention orders – aimed at trying to rehabilitate drug abusers.

Reformation is a very important element in the sentencing philosophy for young offenders, but it is also used for some adult offenders. The court will be given information about the defendant's background, usually through a pre-sentence report prepared by the probation service. Where relevant, the court will consider other factors, such as school reports, job prospects, or medical problems.

Individualised sentences

Where the court considers rehabilitation, the sentence used is an individualised one aimed at the needs of the offender. This is in direct contrast to the concept of tariff sentences seen in the aim of retribution. One of the criticisms of this approach

is, therefore, that it leads to inconsistency in sentencing. Offenders who have committed exactly the same type of offence may be given different sentences because the emphasis is on the individual offender. Another criticism is that is tends to discriminate against the underprivileged. Offenders from poor home backgrounds are less likely to be seen as possible candidates for reform.

Persistent offenders are usually thought less likely to respond to a reformative sentence. The Powers of Criminal Courts (Sentencing) Act 2000 states that, in considering the seriousness of an offence, the court may take into consideration any previous failures to respond to previous sentences.

14.2.6 Reparation

This is aimed at compensating the victim of the crime usually by ordering the offender to pay a sum of money to the victim or to make restitution, for example by returning stolen property to its rightful owner. The idea that criminals should pay compensation to the victims of their crimes is one that goes back to before the Norman Conquest to the Anglo-Saxon courts. In England today, the courts are required to consider ordering compensation to the victim of a crime, in addition to any other penalty they may think appropriate. Under s 130 of the Powers of Criminal Courts (Sentencing) Act 2000, courts are under a duty to give reasons if they do not make a compensation order. There are also projects to bring offenders and victims together, so that the offenders may make direct reparation.

The concept of restitution also includes making reparation to society as a whole. This can be seen mainly in the use of an unpaid work requirement where offenders are required to do so many hours' work on a community project under the supervision of the probation service.

14.3 Sentencing practice in the courts

The court will usually consider both the offence and the background of the offender, as well as the aims of sentencing. In order to do this, the court must know details of the offence, so where the defendant pleads guilty the prosecution will outline the facts of the case. As seen in Chapter 13, the defendant is asked if he agrees with those facts and, if not, a Newton hearing will be held for the facts to be established. This is important as the details of the offence can affect the sentence. Where the defendant has pleaded not guilty and been convicted after a trial, the court will have heard full information about the case during the trial.

14.3.1 Factors surrounding the offence

In looking at the offence, the most important point to establish is how serious it was, of its type.

This is now set out in s 143(1) of the Criminal Justice Act 2003 which states that:

'In considering the seriousness of the offence, the court must consider the offender's culpability in committing the offence and any harm which the offence caused, or was intended to cause or might reasonably foreseeably have caused.'

The Act goes on to give certain factors which are considered as aggravating factors making an offence more serious. These are:

- previous convictions for offences of a similar nature or relevant to the present offence
- the fact that the defendant was on bail when he committed the offence
- racial or religious hostility being involved in the offence
- hostility to disability or sexual orientation being involved in the offence.

Other points the courts will want to know may include, for example in a case of theft, how much was stolen, and whether the defendant was in a position of trust. In a case of assault the court will need to know what injuries were inflicted and whether the assault was premeditated; was the victim particularly vulnerable (perhaps elderly)?

Where the offender was in a position of trust and abused that trust, then the offence will be considered as being more serious and meriting a longer than usual sentence.

Where several defendants are convicted of committing a crime jointly, the court will want to know if any of them played a greater part than the others, and who was involved in planning it. The sentences that each receives will reflect the part they played in the offence.

14.3.2 Reduction in sentence for a guilty plea

There can be a reduction in sentence for a guilty plea, particularly where made early in the

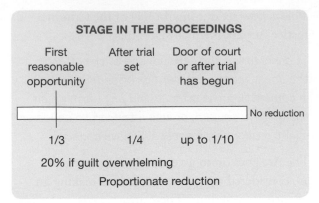

Figure 14.4 *Reduction in sentence for a guilty plea*

proceedings. A guilty plea at the first reasonable opportunity should attract a reduction of up to one-third, but where the prosecution case is overwhelming, only 20 per cent; whereas a plea of guilty after the trial has started would only be given a one-tenth reduction. The amount of reduction is on a sliding scale as shown in Figure 14.4.

The concept of reducing the level of sentence imposed on a defendant just because he has pleads guilty has caused controversy. Many people believe that if someone has 'done the crime, they should do the time'. However, in its draft guidelines, the Sentencing Guidelines Council gave its reasons for allowing discounts in sentences for guilty pleas by stating:

'A reduction in sentence is appropriate because a guilty plea avoids the need for a trial, shortens the gap between charge and sentence, saves considerable cost, and, in the case of an early plea, saves victims and witnesses from the concern about having to give evidence.'

14.3.3 The offender's background

Previous convictions

As far as the offender is concerned, the court will want to know whether he has any previous convictions. The court may also take into account the failure of an offender to respond to previous sentences, in deciding the seriousness of the current offence. The past record of the offender will also determine whether he has to receive a minimum sentence or an automatic life sentence for certain offences.

Another important factor is whether the offender was on bail when he committed the offence. If this is the case, the court must treat that fact as an aggravating factor.

Pre-sentence reports

These are prepared by the probation service. The court does not have to (but usually will) consider such a report before deciding to impose a custodial sentence, though for very serious offences such a report may not be relevant. Where the court is considering a community sentence, it is likely to have a report before it decides on the sentence. The report will give information about the defendant's background and suitability, or otherwise, for a community-based sentence. The defendant's background may be important in showing both why the offender committed a crime, and indicating if he is likely to respond to a community-based penalty.

Medical reports

Where the offender has medical or psychiatric problems, the court will usually ask for a report to be prepared by an appropriate doctor. Medical conditions may be important factors in deciding the appropriate way of dealing with the offender; the courts have special powers where the defendant is suffering from mental illness. The treatment of mentally ill defendants is considered further in section 14.6.

The financial situation of the offender

Where the court considers that a fine is a suitable penalty, it must inquire into the financial circumstances of the offender, and take this into account when setting the level of the fine.

14.3.4 Sentencing guidelines

Originally the Court of Appeal used to issue sentencing guidelines on the correct level of sentencing for certain types of offence. However, it could only do this when a suitable case came before it. For example, in *R v Billam* (1986) the court laid down tariffs for rape cases. In 1998 the Sentencing Advisory Panel was formed to give advice to the Court of Appeal on guidelines. But this was only an advisory body and had no power to issue its own guidelines.

Sentencing Council

In 2003 a Sentencing Guidelines Council was set up under the Criminal Justice Act 2003. This Council issued guidelines on any aspect of sentencing. However, in 2010 both the Sentencing Guidelines Council and the Sentencing Advisory Panel were replaced by the Sentencing Council. The Sentencing Council has responsibility for:

- developing sentencing guidelines and monitoring their use;
- assessing the impact of guidelines on sentencing practice; and
- promoting awareness amongst the public regarding the realities of sentencing and publishing information regarding sentencing practice in Magistrates' and Crown Courts.

The Sentencing Council has more powers than the previous Council. In particular, the courts are now under a duty to impose a sentence which is within the offence range set out by the Council. The courts should only depart from the range when it is in the interests of justice to do so.

A survey of Crown Court sentencing in 2011 for assault cases showed that 96 per cent of sentences were within the guidelines range for the offence. One per cent were below the range and 3 per cent were above the range. This shows that guidelines can help produce consistent sentencing.

14.4 Powers of the courts

As already indicated, the courts have several different types of sentences available to them. There are four main categories: custodial sentences, community sentences, fines and discharges. The courts also have the power to make additional orders such as compensation orders, and, in motoring offences have other powers such as disqualification from driving.

14.4.1 Custodial sentences

A custodial sentence is the most serious punishment that a court can impose. Custodial sentences range from prison for a few days to life imprisonment. They include:

- mandatory and discretionary life sentences
- fixed-term sentences
- suspended sentences.

Custodial sentences are meant to be used only for serious offences. Section 152 of the Criminal Justice Act 2003 says that the court must not pass a custodial sentence unless it is of the opinion that the offence (or combination of offences):

'was so serious that neither a fine alone nor a community sentence can be justified'.

The age of the offender is also important as young offenders should only be given a custodial sentence as a last resort. Where a young offender is given a custodial sentence they are always held in separate units from adults.

The court must state its reason for imposing a custodial sentence, and in the case of the Magistrates' Court, that reason must be written on the warrant of commitment and entered in the court register.

Mandatory life sentences

The only sentence a judge can impose for murder is a life sentence. However, the judge is allowed to state the minimum number of years' imprisonment that the offender must serve before being eligible for release on licence. This minimum term is now governed by s 269 Sched 21 to the Criminal Justice Act 2003. This gives judges clear starting points for the minimum period to be ordered. The starting points range from a full-life term down to 12 years. A whole-life term should be set where the offence falls into one of the following categories:

- the murder of two or more persons, where each murder involves a substantial degree of premeditation or planning or the abduction of the victim or sexual or sadistic conduct
- the murder of a child if involving the abduction of the child or sexual or sadistic motivation
- a murder done for the purpose of advancing a political, religious or ideological cause, or
- a murder by an offender previously convicted of murder.

Cases which have a starting point of 30 years include where the murder is of a police or prison officer in the course of his duty, or a murder using a firearm or explosive or the sexual or sadistic

murder of an adult or a murder that is racially or religiously aggravated. For any offence of murder which is not specifically given a starting point of a whole-life term or 30 years, a starting point of 15 years is given. Where the offender was under the age of 18 at the time of the offence this period is 12 years. Once the judge has decided on the starting point, any aggravating or mitigating factors must then be considered.

Aggravating factors which can increase the minimum term ordered by the judge include the fact that the victim was particularly vulnerable because of age or disability, or any mental or physical suffering inflicted on the victim before death. Mitigating factors include the fact that the offender had an intention to cause grievous bodily harm rather than an intention to kill, a lack of premeditation or the fact that the offender acted to some extent in self-defence (though not sufficient to give him a defence). Where there are mitigating factors the judge can set a minimum term of less than any of the starting points.

A sentence of life imprisonment has normally to be imposed where an offender over the age

Inside a prison

of 18 is convicted of a second serious sexual or violent offence. The judge can set an appropriate minimum time to be served in prison. Where there are 'exceptional circumstances' the judge does not have to impose a life sentence.

Discretionary life sentences

For other serious offences such as manslaughter, rape and robbery the maximum sentence is life imprisonment, but the judge does not have to impose it. The judge has a discretion in sentencing and can give any lesser sentence where appropriate. This can even be a fine or a discharge.

Fixed-term sentences

For other crimes, the length of the sentence will depend on several factors, including the maximum sentence available for the particular crime, the seriousness of the crime and the defendant's previous record. Imprisonment for a set number of months or years is called a 'fixed-term' sentence.

Prisoners do not serve the whole of the sentence passed by the court. Anyone sent to prison is automatically released after they have served half of the sentence. Only offenders aged 21 and over can be given a sentence of imprisonment.

Home detention curfew

The Crime and Disorder Act 1998 introduced early release from prison on condition that a curfew condition is included. The period of curfew is increased with the length of sentence. There is no automatic right to be released on curfew; each prisoner is assessed to see if he or she is suitable. If a home detention curfew order is not made, then the prisoner must serve half the sentence before release on licence.

The reason for introducing such home detention curfews is to encourage recently released prisoners to structure their lives more effectively as well as prevent reoffending. Also, by releasing

prisoners early in this way the prison population is reduced.

Dangerous offenders

The Criminal Justice Act 2003 made special sentences available to the Crown Court when the offender is a dangerous offender. The first is an indeterminate sentence for public protection. This is imposed where the court is of the opinion that there is a significant risk to members of the public of serious harm through the offender committing further offences. In these circumstances the court can impose a life sentence.

The second type of sentence is an extended sentence. This allows the court to impose a custodial sentence up to the normal maximum for the offence, plus an extension period during which the offender is subject to a licence. It can only be used where the court is of the opinion that there is a significant risk to members of the public of serious harm through the offender committing further specified offences.

Minimum sentences

There is a minimum sentence of seven years for anyone aged 18 or over who is convicted of dealing in Class A drugs. There is also a minimum sentence of three years for those convicted of burglary of a residential building for a third time. In both these cases judges can impose a lesser sentence if there are exceptional circumstances.

Suspended prison sentences

A suspended sentence of imprisonment is one where the offender will only serve the custodial period if he breaches the terms of the suspension. The prison sentence can only be between 14 days and 2 years. The period of suspension can be between six months and two years. The idea is that the threat of prison during this period of suspension will deter the offender from committing further offences. If the offender complies with the requirements of the suspended sentence he will not serve the term of imprisonment.

The suspended sentence can be combined with any of the requirements used in a community order (see section 14.4.2). If the offender fails to meet the requirements the suspended sentence may be 'activated'. This means that the offender will be made to serve the term of imprisonment.

A suspended sentence should only be given where the offence is so serious that an immediate custodial sentence would have been appropriate, but there are exceptional circumstances in the case that justify suspending the sentence.

Sentences for young offenders

There has been a lot of debate as to whether young offenders, particularly those under the age of 15, should be given custodial sentences. Government policy on this point has changed frequently during the past few years. It is argued that many young offenders need help rather than punishment and that this is best provided by sentencing orders which keep the offender in the community. Custodial units for young offenders have often been called 'universities of crime'. However, there are at the moment several different types of custodial sentence which can be given, depending on the type of offence, the age of the offender and whether he or she has offended before.

Young Offenders' Institutions

Offenders aged 15 to 20 can be sent to a Young Offenders' Institution as a custodial sentence. The minimum sentence is 21 days and the maximum is the maximum allowed for the particular offence. If the offender becomes 21 years old while serving the sentence, he will be transferred to an adult prison.

Detention and training orders

The Crime and Disorder Act 1998 created a new custodial sentence, called a detention and training order, for young offenders. The sentence must be for a specified period with a minimum of four months and a maximum of 24 months. Half of the period is spent in custody and half in the community.

A detention and training order can be passed on offenders from the age of 12 to the age of 21, but for those under the age of 15 this order can only be made if they are persistent offenders.

Detention for serious crimes

For very serious offences, the courts have additional power to order that the offender be detained for longer periods. For 10- to 13-year-olds this power is only available where the crime committed carries a maximum sentence of at least 14 years' imprisonment for adults, or is an offence of indecent assault on a woman under s 14 of the Sexual Offences Act 1956. For 14- to 17-year-olds, it is also available for causing death by dangerous driving, or for causing death by careless driving while under the influence of drink or drugs. The length of detention imposed on the young offender cannot be more than the maximum sentence available for an adult.

Originally, 10- to 13-year-olds were not included in these provisions, but the law was amended in 1994 to include them, after a court had been unable to give a custodial sentence to a 13-year-old boy who had been found guilty of raping a 12-year-old girl.

Detention at Her Majesty's Pleasure

Any offender aged 10–17 who is convicted of murder must be ordered to be detained during Her Majesty's Pleasure. This is an indeterminate sentence which allows the offender to be released when suitable. The judge in the case can recommend a minimum number of years that should be served before release is considered, and the Lord Chief Justice will then set the tariff.

If an offender reaches 21 while still serving a sentence he or she will be transferred to an adult prison.

Read the following article and answer the questions following it.

> ### 'Tougher jail terms DO deter criminals, admits Home Office'
>
> A Home Office report has concluded that stiffer prison sentences deter crime . . . the study found that convicts jailed for less than a year are almost 50 per cent more likely to commit a fresh crime within two years of their release than those locked up for between one and four years.
>
> And they are twice as likely to break the law as those jailed for at least four years.
>
> The report is embarrassing for the government. Only this month [May 2007], Lord Falconer, newly created Justice Secretary, announced that tens of thousands of burglars and other thieves would receive community punishments instead of jail sentences under plans to ease chronic prison overcrowding.
>
> In March [2007] the Prime Minister signalled that there should be greater emphasis on rehabilitating offenders, tougher community sentences and crime prevention . . .
>
> Figures show that 70 per cent of convicts jailed for under 12 months reoffended within two years, compared with 49 per cent of those convicted to between one and four years and 36 per cent of those serving at least four years.
>
> The report said prisoners released from longer sentences were less likely to reoffend because they were older, had time to be rehabilitated and had been convicted of more serious 'one-off' offences.
>
> Taken from an article by Ian Drury in the *Daily Mail*, 19 May 2007

Questions

1. What sentencing aim does this article suggest that stiffer prison sentences promote?
2. What sentencing aim did the Prime Minister want emphasised?
3. What sentencing aim does the Home Office report say had an effect on longer-term prisoners?
4. Name and explain two other sentencing aims.

14.4.2 Community orders

Prior to the Criminal Justice Act 2003, the courts had individual community sentences which they could impose on an offender. They could combine some of these sentences, in particular unpaid work with a supervision order. Also, they could add requirements about treatment and residence to a supervision order, but they could not use a whole range of orders.

The Criminal Justice Act 2003 created one community order under which the court can combine any requirements they think are necessary. These requirements include all the previous existing community sentences which became available as 'requirements' and can be attached to the sentence. There are also new 'requirements' available. The sentencers can 'mix and match' requirements allowing them to fit the restrictions and rehabilitation to the offender's needs. The sentence is available for offenders aged 16 and over. The full list of requirements available to the courts is set out in s 177 of the Criminal Justice Act 2003. This states:

'177(1) Where a person aged 16 or over is convicted of an offence, the court by or before which he is convicted may make an order imposing on him any one or more of the following requirements:

(a) an unpaid work requirement
(b) an activity requirement
(c) a programme requirement
(d) a prohibited activity requirement
(e) a curfew requirement
(f) an exclusion requirement
(g) a residence requirement
(h) a mental health treatment requirement
(i) a drug rehabilitation requirement
(j) an alcohol treatment requirement
(k) a supervision requirement, and
(l) in the case where the offender is aged under 25, an attendance centre requirement.'

Each of these is defined within the Criminal Justice Act 2003. Most are self-explanatory from their name, such as drug rehabilitation and alcohol treatment. Much crime is linked to drug and alcohol abuse and the idea behind these two requirements is to tackle the causes of crime, and hopefully prevent further offences. Mental health treatment is also aimed at the cause of the offender's behaviour. The main other requirements are explained briefly below.

Unpaid work requirement

This requires the offender to work for between 40 and 300 hours on a suitable project organised by the probation service. The exact number of hours will be fixed by the court, and those hours are then usually worked in eight-hour sessions, often at weekends. The type of work involved will vary, depending on what schemes the local probation service has running. The offender may be required to paint school buildings, help build a play centre or work on conservation projects. When Eric Cantona, the French footballer, was found guilty of assaulting a football fan, the court ordered that he help at coaching sessions for young footballers.

One criticism is that the number of hours is not enough – other countries which run similar schemes can impose much longer hours. However, reoffending rates are lower than for other community sentences.

Prohibited activity requirement

This requirement allows a wide variety of activities to be prohibited. The idea is to try to prevent the defendant from committing another crime of the type he has just been convicted of. Often the defendant is forbidden to go into a certain area where he has caused trouble. In some cases the defendant has been banned from wearing a 'hoodie'. In 2006, a defendant who was found guilty of criminal damage was banned from carrying paint, dye, ink or marker pens.

Curfew requirement

Under these, an offender can be ordered to remain at a fixed address for between two and 16 hours in any 24-hour period. This order can last for up to 12 months and may be enforced by electronic tagging (where suitable). Courts can only make such an order if there is an arrangement for monitoring curfews in their area. Such monitoring can be done by spot checks, with security firms sending someone to make sure that the offender is at home, or offenders may be electronically tagged. There are also pilot schemes on using satellite technology to track those who are tagged.

The cost of tagging is quite expensive. However, it is much less expensive than the cost of keeping an offender in prison.

Statistics show that in the first two years of using electronic tagging, a very high percentage (80+) of offenders completed the tagging period successfully.

However, as the use of electronic tagging has increased (its use doubled between 2005 and 2011), the failure rate has increased.

A report in 2012 by the Chief Inspector of Probation showed that over half of offenders ordered to wear an electronic tag broke the terms of their curfew. Twenty per cent were minor violations where the offenders were warned and then successfully completed their order. However, in 37 per cent of cases there was a serious violation which required further action by the courts.

Exclusion requirement

Offenders are ordered not to go to certain places. The order can specify different places for different periods or days. This is intended to keep offenders away from areas where they are most likely to commit crime. For example, a persistent shoplifter could be banned from certain shopping areas. The order can be for up to two years for offenders aged 16 and over, and a maximum of three months for those under 16.

Supervision requirement

For this requirement the offender is placed under the supervision of a probation officer for a period of up to three years. During the period of supervision the offender must attend appointments with the supervising officer or with any other person decided by the supervising officer.

The Criminal Justice Act 2003 states that a supervision requirement may be imposed for the purpose of 'promoting the offender's rehabilitation'.

14.4.3 Fines

This is the most common way of disposing of a case in the Magistrates' Court, where the maximum fine is £5,000 for an individual offender. The magistrate can impose a fine of up to £20,000 on businesses who have committed offences under various regulatory legislation, such as health and safety at work. In the Crown Court only a small percentage of offenders are dealt with by way of a fine.

14.4.4 Discharges

These may be either a conditional discharge or an absolute discharge. A conditional discharge means that the court discharges an offender on the condition that no further offence is committed during a set period of up to three years. It is intended to be used where it is thought that punishment is not necessary. If an offender reoffends within the time limit, the court can then impose another sentence in place of the conditional discharge, as well as imposing a penalty for the new offence. Conditional discharges are widely used by Magistrates' Courts for first-time minor offenders.

An absolute discharge means that, effectively, no penalty is imposed. Such a penalty is likely to be used where an offender is technically guilty but morally blameless. An example could be where the

tax disc on a vehicle has fallen to the floor – it is technically not being displayed and an offence has been committed. So, in the unlikely situation of someone being prosecuted for this, the magistrates, who would have to impose some penalty, would most probably decide that an absolute discharge was appropriate.

ACTIVITY

Look at the bar chart on the opening page of this chapter which shows the types of sentence used in the Magistrates' and the Crown Courts and answer the following questions.

1. What type of sentence are offenders most likely to be given at the Crown Court?
2. What two types of sentence are offenders most likely to be given at the Magistrates' Courts?
3. Why do you think the sentences used most frequently are different for the two courts?
4. Which two types of sentence show the biggest difference in percentages given at the Crown Court and at the Magistrates' Courts?
5. Why do you think the percentages for these two types of sentence are different in the Magistrates' Court and the Crown Court?

14.4.5 Disqualification from driving

Where a defendant is charged with a driving offence, the courts may also have the power to disqualify that person from driving for a certain period of time. The length of the disqualification will depend on the seriousness of the driving offence. Usually the courts will impose a fine as well as disqualification. For a first-time drink-driving offence the courts have to disqualify the defendant for a minimum of 12 months, unless there are very exceptional reasons not to disqualify. If an offender has a previous drink-drive conviction, then the minimum is usually three years' disqualification.

The courts can use this power to disqualify in any other crime where the offender has used a vehicle to commit an offence. For example, a defendant who drives a car in order to do a burglary could be disqualified from driving, but this power is not often used.

14.4.6 Other powers available to the courts

The courts have other powers which are aimed at compensating victims and/or making sure that the defendant does not benefit from his or her crimes.

Compensation orders and restitution orders

Courts can make an order that the defendant pay a sum of money to his victim in compensation.

Both Crown Courts and Magistrates' Courts must consider making a compensation order in all cases where they have power to do so. In the Magistrates' Court the maximum amount of compensation is £5,000.

If the defendant still has the property he obtained from the victim, then the courts can make an order that the property is returned. This is called a restitution order.

Deprivation and forfeiture orders

A court can order an offender to be deprived of property he has used to commit an offence. For example, a person convicted of drink-driving could be ordered to lose his car. There is special power to order forfeiture in drug-related cases. The Proceeds of Crime Act 1995 also gives the courts powers to take from criminals all profits from crime for up to six years before conviction.

Key Facts

Types of sentence	Age limitations
Custodial sentences	• Prison only for 21+ • Young Offenders' Institution for 15–20-year-olds • Detention and training order for 12–20-year-olds • Powers of detention for 10–17-year-olds in serious cases
Community orders	• May 'mix and match' different requirements to suit different offenders' needs for 16+ • Youth Rehabilitation Orders – also mix and match different requirements
Fines	• Over 18s – Magistrates' Court maximum £5,000 (Crown Court no limit) • 14–17 maximum £1,000 • 10–13 maximum £250
Discharges	• Conditional discharge – 10+ • Absolute discharge – 10+
Other powers	• Disqualification from driving – 10+ • Compensation orders – 10+ • Reparation orders – 10–17

Figure 14.5 *Key facts chart on sentencing powers of the courts*

14.5 Young offenders

This term includes all offenders under the age of 21. However, there are considerable variations in the different sentences available for those under 18, under 16, under 14 and under 12. The main aim in sentencing young offenders is reformation and rehabilitation. As already seen in Chapter 13, offenders under 18 years old are normally dealt with in the Youth Court.

14.5.1 Available sentences

As with adult offenders, the courts have, in general, powers to order custodial sentences, community sentences, fines and discharges, but different sentences are available, and also restrictions on what the courts can order (especially for the youngest offenders). The custodial sentences available have already been explained in section 14.4.1.

Youth Rehabilitation Order

For community sentences, there is now the Youth Rehabilitation Order. This was brought in by the Criminal Justice and Immigration Act 2008. It works on the same principle as a community order for an adult offender. The court can 'mix and match' requirements to suit the circumstances.

The requirements which can be attached to a youth rehabilitation order are:

(a) an activity requirement
(b) a supervision requirement
(c) in a case where the offender is aged 16 or 17 at the time of the conviction, an unpaid work requirement
(d) a programme requirement
(e) an attendance centre requirement
(f) a prohibited activity requirement
(g) a curfew requirement
(h) an exclusion requirement
(i) a residence requirement
(j) a local authority residence requirement
(k) a mental health treatment requirement
(l) a drug treatment requirement
(m) a drug testing requirement
(n) an intoxicating substance treatment requirement
(o) an education requirement.

Discharges

These may be used for an offender of any age, and are commonly used for first-time young offenders who have committed minor crimes.

However, the courts cannot conditionally discharge an offender in the following circumstances:

- where a child or young offender who is convicted of an offence has been warned within the previous two years; unless there are exceptional circumstances, which must be explained in open court
- where the offender is in breach of an anti-social behaviour order
- where the offender is in breach of a sex offender order.

Reprimands and warnings

These are not sentences passed by a court, but methods by which the police can deal with offenders without bringing the case to court. For either a reprimand or warning to be given there must be evidence that a child or young person has committed an offence and admits it. In addition, the police must be satisfied that it would not be in the public interest for the offender to be prosecuted. A reprimand or warning can only be given if the offender has never been convicted of any offence.

There is a limit to the number of times and the occasions on which an offender can be 'cautioned'. The first step is the reprimand. This can only be given if the child or young person has not been previously reprimanded or warned. Even then it should not be used where the constable considers the offence to be so serious as to require a warning.

An offender may be warned only if he has not been warned before or if an earlier warning was more than two years before. When warned, the child or young offender must be referred to a Youth Offending Team. This team assesses the case and, unless it considers it inappropriate to do so, arranges for the offender to participate in a rehabilitation scheme.

14.5.2 Parental responsibility

If the parents agree, they can be bound over to keep their child under control for a set period of up to one year. If the child commits an offence during this period the parents will forfeit a sum of money up to a maximum of £1,000. If a parent unreasonably refuses to be bound over, the court has the power to fine that parent instead. Parents can also be bound over to ensure that a young offender complies with a community sentence.

Where an offender under 16 years old is fined or ordered to pay compensation, the court must require the offender's parents to pay, and the financial situation of the parent is taken into account in deciding the amount of the order.

Parenting orders

This is intended to offer training and support to parents to help change their children's offending behaviour. In this way it is more practical than the existing provisions which merely make a parent responsible for their child's offending behaviour. Under such an order a parent can be required to attend counselling or guidance sessions for up to three months on a maximum basis of once a week.

In addition, the parent may be required to comply with conditions imposed by the courts; for example, escort the child to school or ensure that a responsible adult is present in the home in the evening to supervise the child. A court may make a parenting order where:

- the court makes a child safety order
- the court makes an anti-social behaviour order (or sex offender order) in respect of a child
- a child or young person is convicted of an offence
- a parent is convicted of an offence relating to truancy under the Education Act 1996.

An order should only be made if it is desirable in the interests of preventing the conduct which gave rise to the order. Where a person under the age of 16 is convicted of an offence, the court should make a parenting order unless it is satisfied that it is not desirable in the interests of preventing the conduct which gave rise to the order. In this case the court must state in open court that it is not satisfied and explain why not.

14.5.3 Youth Offending Teams

The Crime and Disorder Act made it the duty of each local authority to establish one or more Youth Offending Teams (YOTs) in their area. The main idea in establishing these teams is to build on cooperation between agencies involved, especially social services and the probation service. These teams are to coordinate the provision of youth justice services in the area.

A YOT must include a probation officer, a local authority social worker, a police officer, a representative of the local health authority and a person nominated by the chief education officer. Any other appropriate person may also be invited to join the team.

The role of YOTs is highlighted by the fact that, under s 66 of the Crime and Disorder Act 1998, any offender who is warned must be referred to the local YOT. Youth courts may also refer offenders to the YOT.

14.6 Mentally ill offenders

The law recognises that, so far as possible, mentally ill offenders should not be punished but should receive treatment. Where an offence has been committed by an offender who is mentally ill, the courts have a wider range of powers available to them. In addition to the ordinary sentences which can be given, there are special provisions aimed at treating such offenders in a suitable way.

The main additional powers available to the courts are to: give the offender a community sentence, with a requirement that he or she attends for treatment; make a hospital order or make a restriction order under s 41 of the Mental Health Act 1983.

A community order requiring the offender to have treatment will be made where the court is satisfied that the mental condition is treatable, and that there is no need to make a hospital order. A hospital order will be made if the condition makes it appropriate that the offender should stay in hospital for treatment.

However, there are some cases in which the protection of the public is a key element. Under s 41 of the Mental Health Act 1983 offenders with severe mental problems, who are considered to be a danger to the community, can be sent to a secure hospital such as Broadmoor. Magistrates' Courts cannot make such an order; it can only be made by a Crown Court. The order can be that the offender be detained for a set period or, where necessary, for an indefinite period. If an offender is ordered to be detained for an indefinite period, the hospital can only discharge him with the permission of the Home Secretary or the Mental Health Review Tribunal.

ACTIVITY

Suggest a suitable sentence for the following offenders and explain what the aim of the sentence would be.

Questions

1. Kevin, aged 22, has been found guilty by the magistrates of two charges of criminal damage. The amount of damage involved is estimated at £600. He is single, unemployed and has no previous convictions.

2. Melanie, aged 15, appeared before the local Youth Court and admitted shoplifting on five occasions. She also admitted two offences of taking and driving a car without the owner's consent. She has appeared before the Youth Court on two previous occasions for similar offences.
3. Andrew, aged 26, has been found guilty at the Crown Court of an assault causing grievous bodily harm. He committed this offence while on bail charged with another offence of violence.

14.7 Penal policies and their effects

Sentencing policies have an effect on the number of offenders who are sent to prison. The United Kingdom sends a higher percentage of its population to prison than any other European Union country. The changes in sentencing policy over the last few years are reflected in the changing size of prison population as the government has first attempted to reduce the number of defendants sent to prison for relatively minor offences, and then (to some extent) reversed their policies in an effort to be seen as the party of 'law and order'.

However, under the Criminal Justice Act 2003, the government introduced tougher community penalties to try to avoid using custodial sentences. Despite this, the prison population has continued to increase.

14.7.1 Prison population

There has been concern that the number of people in prison (known as the prison population) has risen rapidly in recent years. In fact the increase has been going on for the past 50 years, as is shown by Figure 14.6.

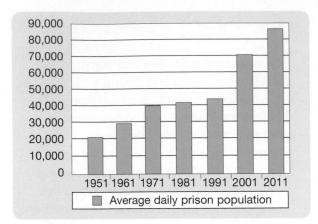

Figure 14.6 *Prison population for England and Wales 1951–2011*

In addition, the government has forecast that the prison population is likely to rise to 93,000 by 2015.

It can be argued that the population of England and Wales has increased during this period and so some increase should be expected. However, the population increase has not been that great and the number of prisoners per 100,000 of the general population confirms that there has indeed been a great increase in the number of people sent to prison. In 1951 there were only 50 per 100,000 of the population in prison; by 2001 this had risen to 136. By 2004 the United Kingdom had the highest rate of prison population per 100,000 in the whole of Europe.

14.7.2 Women and sentencing

Numerically there are far fewer women in prison than men. In 2012 there were 4,100 women in prison, compared to over 85,000 men. It is also true that, for indictable offences, women are more likely to be given a discharge or a community sentence than men, and are less likely to be fined or sentenced to custody.

The Fawcett Society is very critical of the number of women sent to prison. They point out that custodial sentences for women are:

- **inappropriate** – over half of women in prison have suffered domestic violence and one in three has experienced sexual abuse;
- **damaging to the women** – prison causes damage and disruption to the lives of vulnerable women: 70 per cent of women prisoners have mental health problems, and one in three has attempted to commit suicide;
- **damaging to their families** – approximately two-thirds of women in prison have dependent children and over 17,000 children a year are separated from their mothers by imprisonment;
- **ineffective** – prison is an ineffective way of cutting women's offending – the most common offences for which women are sent to prison are theft and handling stolen goods, and 65 per cent reoffend on release.

EXAMINATION QUESTIONS

1. (a) Describe both the aims of sentencing and the factors that are taken into account when sentencing an individual. [18 marks]
   (b) Lewis (aged 25 years) has been convicted of a serious violent offence in the Crown Court. He has three previous convictions for minor violent offences. He has previously been given fines and a community order with a supervision requirement.
   (c) Explain which aims of sentencing are likely to be considered when deciding the sentence for Lewis and suggest two possible sentences. [12 marks]

G151, June 2011, OCR

EXTENSION ESSAY

'The only aim of sentencing should be punishment.' Discuss.

CHAPTER 15

THE LEGAL PROFESSION

INTRODUCTION

In England and Wales there are two types of lawyers (barristers and solicitors), jointly referred to as the legal profession. Most countries do not have this clear-cut division among lawyers: a person will qualify simply as a lawyer, although, after qualifying, it will be possible for them to specialise as an advocate, or in a particular area of law. This type of system is seen in this country in the medical profession, where all those wishing to become doctors take the same general qualifications. After they have qualified, some doctors will go on to specialise in different fields, perhaps as surgeons, and will take further qualifications in their chosen field.

In England, not only are the professions separate, but there is no common training for lawyers, although there have been increasing calls for this. As far back as 1971 the Ormrod Committee was in favour of a common education for all prospective lawyers. Again in 1994 the Lord Chancellor's advisory committee on legal education, under Lord Steyn, recommended that, instead of having separate training for barristers and solicitors, 'the two branches of the profession should have joint training. Neither recommendation was implemented. However, in 2012 another review of legal education and training took place and this may lead to changes (see 15.6).

15.1 Solicitors

There are over 120,000 solicitors practising in England and Wales and they are controlled by their own professional body, the Law Society. Of these, 87,000 are in private practice and the remainder are in employed work, such as for local government or the Crown Prosecution Service.

15.1.1 Training

To become a solicitor it is usual to have a law degree, although those with a degree in a subject other than law can do an extra year's training in core legal subjects, and take the Common Professional Examination (CPE) or Graduate Diploma in Law (GDL). The next stage is the Legal Practice Course (LPC). This is much more practically based than the previous Law Society Finals course and includes training in skills such as client interviewing, negotiation, advocacy, drafting documents and legal research. There is also an emphasis on business management, for example keeping accounts. The LPC can be done as a one-year full-time course or a two-year part-time course. The part-time course allows students to work part-time as well, thus helping with finances.

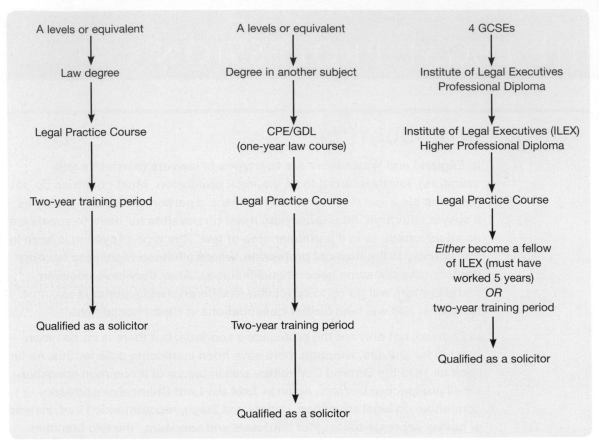

Figure 15.1 *Training routes to become a solicitor*

Training contract

Even when this course has been passed, the student is still not a qualified solicitor. He or she must next obtain a training contract under which they work in a solicitors' firm for two years, getting practical experience. This training period can also be undertaken in certain other legal organisations such as the Crown Prosecution Service, or the legal department of a local authority. During this two-year training contract the trainee will be paid, though not at the same rate as a fully qualified solicitor, and will do his own work, supervised by a solicitor. He will also have to complete a 20-day Professional Skills Course which builds on the skills learnt on the LPC. At the end of the time, the trainee will be admitted as a solicitor by the Law Society and his name will be added to the roll (or list) of solicitors. Even after qualifying, solicitors have to attend continuing education courses to keep their knowledge up to date.

Non-graduate route

There is also a route under which non-graduates can qualify as solicitors by first becoming legal executives. This route is open only to mature candidates and takes longer than the graduate route. The three routes to becoming a solicitor are shown in Figure 15.1.

Criticisms of the training process

There are several criticisms of the training process.

1. The first of these is a financial problem, in that students will usually have to pay the fees of the Legal Practice Course (about £12,000) and

support themselves while doing the course. If they have a degree in a subject other than law and have had to do the CPE/GDL, they will also have had to pay for that course. This problem has arisen because, as the LPC is a post-graduate course, students must pay all the cost. The result of this policy is that students from poor families cannot afford to take the course and are therefore prevented from becoming solicitors, even though they may have obtained a good law degree. Other students may take out bank loans, so that although they qualify, they start the training period with a large debt. In order to overcome this problem a few universities have started offering four-year degree courses, combining a law qualification and a practical course, so students pay only the university fees. This financial problem is also one faced by prospective barristers. The problem has increased since universities have increased their fees to up to £9,000 a year and students are already in debt from their degree course. In order to try to help would-be solicitors, the CPE can be taken as a part-time course over two years, instead of the one-year full-time course. Doing the course part-time allows students to work as well, easing their financial problems. Often this work will be as a para-legal in a law firm, so that the student is also getting practical experience at the same time.

2. A point common to barristers is that non-law graduates do only one year of formal law for the Common Professional Course. The Ormrod Committee which reported on legal education in 1971 thought that the main entry route should be via a law degree, but in practice 25 per cent of solicitors will not have taken a law degree. One critic posed the question of whether the public would be satisfied with doctors who have only studied medicine for one year, concentrating on only six subjects. Yet this is precisely what is occurring in the legal profession.

A solicitor with their client

3. A third problem is one of oversupply, so that not all students who have passed the LPC are able to obtain a training contract.

15.1.2 Solicitors' work

The majority of those who succeed in qualifying as a solicitor will then work in private practice in a solicitors' firm. However, there are other careers available, and some newly qualified solicitors may go on to work in the Crown Prosecution Service or for a local authority or government department. Others will become legal advisers in commercial or industrial businesses. Over 30,000 solicitors are employed.

A solicitor in private practice may work as a sole practitioner or in a partnership. There are some 10,000 firms of solicitors, ranging from the small 'high street' practice to the big city firms. The number of partners is not limited, and some of the biggest firms will have over a hundred partners as well as employing assistant solicitors.

The type of work done by a solicitor will largely depend on the type of firm he or she is working in.

A small high street firm will probably be a general practice advising clients on a whole range of topics such as consumer problems, housing and business matters and family problems. A solicitor working in such a practice is likely to spend some of his time interviewing clients in his office and negotiating on their behalf, and a large amount of time dealing with paperwork. This will include:

- writing letters on behalf of clients
- drafting contracts, leases or other legal documents
- drawing up wills
- dealing with conveyancing (the legal side of buying and selling flats, houses, office buildings and land).

The solicitor may also, if he wishes, act for some of his clients in court. Standing up in court, putting the client's case and questioning witnesses is known as advocacy. Some solicitors will specialise in this and spend much of their time in court.

Specialising

Although some solicitors may be general practitioners handling a variety of work, it is not unusual, even in small firms, for a solicitor to specialise in one particular field. The firm itself may handle only certain types of cases (perhaps only civil actions) and not do any criminal cases, or a firm may specialise in matrimonial cases. Even within the firm the solicitors are likely to have their own field of expertise. In large firms there will be an even greater degree of specialisation, with departments dealing with one aspect of the law. The large city firms usually concentrate on business and commercial law. Amounts earned by solicitors are as varied as the types of firm, with the top earners in big firms on £500,000 or more, while at the bottom end of the scale some sole practitioners will earn less than £40,000.

Conveyancing

Prior to 1985 solicitors had a monopoly on conveyancing: this meant that only solicitors could deal with the legal side of transferring houses and other buildings and land. This was changed by the Administration of Justice Act 1985 which allowed people other than solicitors to become licensed conveyancers. As a result of the increased competition in this area, solicitors had to reduce their fees, but even so they lost a large proportion of the work. This led to a demand for wider rights of advocacy.

Rights of advocacy

All solicitors have always been able to act as advocates in the Magistrates' Courts and the County Courts, but their rights of audience in the higher courts used to be very limited. Normally a solicitor could only act as advocate in the Crown Court on a committal for sentence, or on an appeal from the Magistrates' Court, and then only if he or another solicitor in the firm had been the advocate in the original case in the Magistrates' Court.

Until 1986 solicitors had no rights of audience in open court in the High Court, though they could deal with preliminary matters in preparation for a case. This lack of rights of audience was emphasised in *Abse v Smith* (1986) in which two Members of Parliament were contesting a libel action. They came to an agreed settlement, but the solicitor for one of them was refused permission by the judge to read out the terms of that settlement in open court. Following this decision the Lord Chancellor and the senior judges in each division of the High Court issued a Practice Direction, allowing solicitors to appear in the High Court to make a statement in a case that has been settled.

Certificate of advocacy

The first major alteration to solicitors' rights of audience came in the Courts and Legal Services

Act 1990. Under this Act, a solicitor in private practice had the right to apply for a certificate of advocacy which enabled him to appear in the higher courts. Such a certificate was granted if the solicitor already had experience of advocacy in the Magistrates' Court and the County Court, took a short training course and passed examinations on the rules of evidence. The first certificates were granted in 1994 and by the beginning of 2013 over 6,000 solicitors had qualified to be advocates in the higher courts.

Solicitors with an advocacy qualification are also eligible to be appointed as Queen's Counsel (see section 15.3) and also to be appointed to higher judicial posts (see section 16.1.1).

The Access to Justice Act 1999 (s 36) provides that all solicitors will automatically be given full rights of audience. However, new training requirements to allow solicitors to obtain these rights have not yet been brought in.

Legal Disciplinary Partnerships (LDPs)

Section 66 of the Courts and Legal Services Act 1990 had provisions to allow solicitors to form partnerships with other professions, for example accountants. This would give clients a wider range of expertise and advice in a 'one-stop shop'. At that time the Law Society and the Bar Council had rules which prevented mixed professional practices.

Since then the rules have been changed so that there can be Legal Disciplinary Partnerships and also Multi-Disciplinary Practices. In addition the Legal Services Act 2007 allows Alternative Business Structures (see 15.4).

15.1.3 Complaints against solicitors

A solicitor deals directly with clients and enters into a contract with them. This means that if the client does not pay, the solicitor has the right to sue for his fees. It also means that the client can sue his solicitor for breach of contract if the solicitor fails to do the work.

A client can also sue the solicitor for negligence in and out of court work. This happened in *Griffiths v Dawson* (1993) where solicitors for the plaintiff had failed to make the correct application in divorce proceedings against her husband. As a result the plaintiff lost financially and the solicitors were ordered to pay her £21,000 in compensation.

Other people affected by the solicitor's negligence may also have the right to sue in certain circumstances. An example of this was the case of *White v Jones* (1995) where a father wanted to make a will leaving each of his daughters £9,000. He wrote to his solicitors instructing them to draw up a will to include this. The solicitors received this letter on 17 July 1986

Key Facts	
Original rights	To present cases in County Court and Magistrates' Court, also at Crown Court on committal for sentence or appeal from Magistrates' Court
Practice Direction 1986	Following *Abse v Smith*, allowed to make statement in High Court in cases in which terms had been agreed
Courts and Legal Services Act 1990	Solicitors allowed to apply for certificate of advocacy to conduct cases in the higher courts. Must have experience of advocacy, take course and pass examinations
Access to Justice Act 1999	Solicitors able to have full rights of audience

Figure 15.2 *Key facts chart on solicitors' rights of audience*

but had done nothing about it by the time the father died on 14 September 1986. As a result the daughters did not inherit any money and they successfully sued the solicitor for the £9,000 they had each lost.

Negligent advocacy

It used to be held that a solicitor presenting a case in court could not be sued for negligence. However, in *Hall v Simons* (2000), the House of Lords decided that advocates can be liable for negligence.

Complaints procedure

There have been problems with the complaints procedure operated by the Law Society. One of the main concerns has been that the Law Society's main roles are to regulate the solicitors' profession and to represent solicitors. By operating its own complaints procedure, there was a conflict between the interest of the solicitor and the interest of the client who was complaining.

The other problem for those complaining about poor service by a solicitor was that the complaints bodies run by the Law Society have themselves been frequently criticised for delays and inefficiency.

The lowest point was probably in 1996, when a survey found that two out of every three complainants were dissatisfied with the handling of their complaint.

In an effort to improve both independence and efficiency of its complaints procedure, the Law Society 'rebranded' the body responsible for investigating complaints on a number of occasions during the last 20 years. However, the system was never satisfactory. For example, a report in 2008 found that one out of every three complaints was still not handled satisfactorily. So the Legal Services Act 2007 changed the complaints system and created one complaints body. This is independent of the legal profession and deals with complaints about all sectors of the legal profession, instead of each branch of the legal profession having a separate system, as previously.

The Legal Services Act 2007

The Legal Services Act 2007 created the Office for Legal Complaints. This is completely independent of the Law Society and any other sector of the legal profession. The office has a non-lawyer as chairman and the majority of members must also be non-lawyers. This office deals with complaints against solicitors and also all other sectors of the legal profession. In 2010 it set up the Legal Ombudsman to deal with complaints about poor service by solicitors and other legal professionals.

The Legal Ombudsman

The office started work in October 2010. It is independent and impartial. When a complaint is received, the office will look at the facts in each case and weigh both sides of the story. If the Legal Ombudsman agrees that a lawyer's service has been unsatisfactory, it can ask the lawyer and the law firm to:

- apologise to the client
- give back any documents the client might need
- put things right if more work can correct what went wrong
- refund or reduce the legal fees, or
- pay compensation of up to £30,000.

In 2011–12 the Legal Ombudsman received 7,130 complaints against solicitors. About 20 to 25 per cent of complaints are about costs. Others are about delay, poor advice or poor practice. No statistics are available on the number of complaints which were upheld. There are, however, case studies on the Legal Ombudsman's website showing the type of complaint and stating whether it was upheld.

ACTIVITY

Look at the Legal Ombudsman's website **www.legalombudsman.org.uk** and find a case study of a complaint. You could use this as the basis of a presentation to your class.

Solicitors Regulatory Authority

This deals with complaints about professional misconduct of solicitors. The Authority will investigate the matter. It there is evidence of serious professional misconduct, it can put the case before the Solicitors' Disciplinary Tribunal. If the Tribunal upholds the complaint, it can fine or reprimand the solicitor or, in more serious cases, it can suspend a solicitor from the Roll, so that he or she cannot practise for a certain time. In very serious cases, the Tribunal can strike off a solicitor from the Roll.

A barrister

15.2 Barristers

There are about 12,000 barristers in independent practice in England and Wales. In addition there are about 3,000 barristers employed by organisations such as the Crown Prosecution Service, businesses, local government and the Civil Service.

Collectively barristers are referred to as 'the Bar' and they are controlled by their own professional body – the General Council of the Bar. All barristers must also be a member of one of the four Inns of Court: Lincoln's Inn, Inner Temple, Middle Temple and Gray's Inn, all of which are situated near the Royal Courts of Justice in London.

15.2.1 Training

Entry to the Bar is normally degree-based, though there is a non-degree route for mature entrants, under which a small number of students qualify.

As with solicitors, graduate students without a law degree can take the one-year course for the Common Professional Examination (CPE) (Graduate Diploma in Law – GDL) in the core subjects, in order to go on to qualify as a barrister.

All student barristers also have to pass the Bar Professional Training Course. On this course students study:

- case preparation legal research
- written skills
- opinion writing (giving written advice)
- drafting documents such as claim forms
- conference skills (interviewing clients)
- negotiation
- advocacy (speaking in court).

Students also study specific areas of law related to their future profession, such as civil litigation, criminal litigation and the law of evidence.

All student barristers must join one of the four Inns of Court and used to have to dine there 12 times before being called to the Bar. Students may also attend in a different way, for example a weekend residential course. This helps students on the courses outside London as travelling costs are lower. The idea behind the rule requiring all trainee barristers to dine was that they met senior barristers and judges and absorbed the traditions of the profession. In practice, few barristers dine at their Inns and students are unlikely to meet anyone except other students.

Once a student has passed the Bar Professional Training Course, he or she is then 'called to the Bar'. This means that they are officially qualified as a barrister. However, there is still a practical stage to their training which must be completed. This is called pupillage.

Pupillage

After the student has passed the Bar Professional Training Course there is 'on the job' training where the trainee barrister becomes a pupil to a qualified barrister. This effectively involves 'work shadowing' that barrister, and can be with the same barrister for 12 months or with two different pupil masters for six months each. There is also a requirement that they take part in a programme of continuing education organised by the Bar Council. After the first six months of pupillage, barristers are eligible to appear in court and may conduct their own cases. During pupillage trainee barristers are paid a small salary by the chambers they are attached to.

The various training routes are shown in Figure 15.3.

15.2.2 Barristers' work

Barristers practising at the Bar are self-employed, but usually work from a set of chambers where they can share administrative expenses with

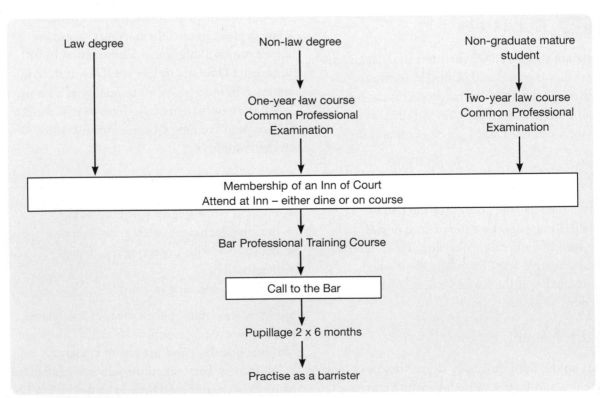

Figure 15.3 *Training routes to become a barrister*

other barristers. Most sets of chambers are fairly small, comprising about 15–20 barristers. They will employ a clerk as a practice administrator – booking in cases and negotiating fees – and they will have other support staff. One of the problems facing newly qualified barristers is the difficulty of finding a tenancy in chambers. Many will do a third six-month pupillage and then 'squat' as an unofficial tenant before obtaining a place. The rule on having to practise from chambers has been relaxed, so that it is technically possible for barristers to practise from home. However, despite the fact that a tenancy in chambers is not essential, it is still viewed as the way to allow a barrister to build a successful practice.

The majority of barristers will concentrate on advocacy, although there are some who specialise in areas such as tax and company law, and who rarely appear in court. Barristers have rights of audience in all courts in England and Wales. Even those who specialise in advocacy will do a certain amount of paperwork, writing opinions on cases, giving advice and drafting documents for use in court.

Direct access

Originally it was necessary for anybody who wished to instruct a barrister to go to a solicitor first. The solicitor would then brief the barrister. This was thought to create unnecessary expense for clients, as it meant they had to use two lawyers instead of one. As a result of criticism the Bar first of all started to operate a system called Bar Direct under which certain professionals such as accountants and surveyors could brief a barrister direct without using a solicitor. This was extended to other professionals and organisations. Then in September 2004 the Bar granted direct access to anyone (business or individual). It is no longer necessary to go to a solicitor in order to instruct a barrister for civil cases. However, direct access is still not allowed for criminal cases or family work.

Cab rank rule

Normally barristers operate what is known as the cab rank rule under which they cannot turn down a case if it is on the area of law they deal with and they are free to take the case. However, where clients approach a barrister direct, the cab rank rule does not apply. Barristers can turn down a case which would require investigation or support services which they cannot provide.

Employed barristers

The employed Bar, which includes those barristers working for the Crown Prosecution Service, can appear in the Magistrates' Court, but used not to be able to conduct cases in the Crown Court, High Court or appellate courts. As these barristers will have done exactly the same training as the independent Bar, this was seen as being unnecessarily restrictive. The Access to Justice Act 1999 allowed barristers working for the CPS or other employers to keep their rights of audience. The Act also allowed barristers who work in solicitors' firms to keep the right to present cases in court.

15.2.3 Complaints against barristers

Where a barrister receives a brief from a solicitor he or she does not enter into a contract with his client and so cannot sue if their fees are not paid. Similarly, the client cannot sue for breach of contract. However, they can be sued for negligence. In *Saif Ali v Sydney Mitchell and Co* (1980) it was held that a barrister could be sued for negligence in respect of written advice and opinions. In that case a barrister had given the wrong advice about who to sue, with the result that the claimant was too late to start proceedings against the right person.

In *Hall (a firm) v Simons* (2000) the House of Lords held that lawyers could also be liable for negligence in the conduct of advocacy in court. This decision overruled the earlier case of *Rondel v*

Worsley (1969) in which barristers were held not to be liable because their first duty was to the courts and they must be 'free to do their duty fearlessly and independently'.

The Law Lords in *Hall (a firm) v Simons* felt that in light of modern conditions it was no longer in the public interest that advocates should have immunity from being sued for negligence. They pointed out that doctors could be sued and they had a duty to an ethical code of practice and might have difficult decisions to make when treating patients. There was no reason why advocates should not be liable in the same way.

They also pointed out that allowing advocates to be sued for negligence would not be likely to lead to the whole case being re-argued. If an action against an advocate was merely an excuse to get the whole issue litigated again, the matter would almost certainly be struck out as an abuse of process.

ACTIVITY

Read the following article and answer the questions below.

Talent, not cash, should open the door to the Bar

The ancient buildings, paved courtyards and well-tended lawns of the Inns of Court shout privilege. But is the privilege of being a barrister one that anyone can attain – regardless of social background or wealth?

Concerns that it is now harder to enter the Bar have grown along with the costs of university and Bar training. Nearly one in three students arrives with debts of £20,000. The one-year vocational course can add another £15,000 – and non-law graduates have to fund an extra year on top of that.

But the barrier is not just financial. Geoffrey Vos, QC, whose father was a Bermondsey leather merchant, identifies other hurdles: lack of contacts or knowledge about the profession; its intimidating en-

vironment; the scramble to find a pupillage, or training place; and then the challenge of securing a seat in chambers. Finally, there is uncertainty of success or earning power.

The profession's entry profile is far more diverse than it was. But then what? Getting in is just the first hurdle. Perceived obstacles once inside can be a further deterrent. At the top the profession is still mostly male, white and privileged: 73 per cent of barristers in eight top commercial chambers went to private schools. At law firms, the proportion of women partners over ten years has risen slowly from 16.55 per cent to 23.2 per cent now. Women in the higher levels of the profession are nowhere near beginning to reflect the level of women entering the profession.

Adapted from an article by Frances Gibb, *The Times*, 3 April 2007 © The Times 2007/nisyndication.com

Questions

1. The article mentions the Inns of Court. Name the four Inns of Court.
2. Briefly describe what the Bar Vocational Course consists of.
3. Why do non-law graduates have to do an extra year?
4. What financial barriers are there to becoming a barrister?
5. What other barriers are there to becoming a barrister?
6. In which area has the legal profession become more diverse?
7. What are the problems at the higher levels of the legal profession?

Bar Standards Board

This is the body which regulates the profession of barristers. It sets training and entry standards. It also sets out a Code of Conduct which barristers should comply with.

The Board investigates any alleged breach of the Code of Conduct. It can discipline any barrister who is in breach of the Code. If the matter is serious it will be referred to the Disciplinary Tribunal of the Council of the Inns of Court. In extreme cases a barrister can be disbarred from practising by the Disciplinary Tribunal.

The Legal Ombudsman

The Legal Ombudsman's office was set up by the Office for Legal Complaints to deal with complaints against the legal profession. As part of its remit it considers complaints against barristers. It has the same powers as for all complaints against solicitors. It can order the barrister to:

- apologise to the client
- give back any documents the client might need
- put things right if more work can correct what went wrong
- refund or reduce the legal fees, or
- pay compensation of up to £30,000.

In 2011–12 there were 212 complaints made about the work of barristers. There are no statistics available to show how many of these complaints were justified.

15.3 Queen's Counsel

After at least ten years as a barrister or as a solicitor with an advocacy qualification, it is possible to apply to become a Queen's Counsel (QC). About

Key Facts

	Solicitors	Barristers
Professional body	Law Society	Bar Council
Basic qualifications	Law degree OR degree in another subject PLUS Common Professional Exam or Graduate Diploma in Law	Law degree OR degree in another subject PLUS Common Professional Exam or Graduate Diploma in Law
Vocational training	Legal Practice Course	Bar Professional Training course
Practical training	Training contract	Pupillage
Number in profession	120,000	12,000
Method of working	Firm of partners OR as sole practitioner	Self-employed, practising in chambers
Rights of audience	Normally only County Court and Magistrates' Court Can apply for full advocacy rights	All courts
Relationship with client	Contractual	Normally through solicitor BUT accountants and surveyors can brief barristers directly
Liability	Liable in contract and tort to clients May also be liable to others affected by negligence (*White v Jones*)	No contractual liability BUT liable for negligence (*Hall v Simons*)

Figure 15.4 *Key facts chart comparing solicitors and barristers*

10 per cent of the Bar are Queen's Counsel and it is known as 'taking silk'. QCs usually take on more complicated and high-profile cases than junior barristers (all barristers who are not Queen's Counsel are known as 'juniors'), and they can command higher fees for their recognised expertise. Often a QC will have a junior barrister to assist with the case.

15.3.1 History

Until 2004 Queen's Counsel were appointed by the Lord Chancellor. However, the Lord Chancellor's criteria for selecting QCs have been criticised as being too secretive. There was also the fact that under this selection process less than 10 per cent of QCs were women and only a very few were from ethnic minorities. In turn, this had an effect on the composition of the judiciary since senior judges are usually chosen from the ranks of Queen's Counsel. The position of women and ethnic minorities in the legal profession is considered in more detail in section 15.7.

Also, in 2003, the Office of Fair Trading (OFT) stated that it thought the position of QC was not of benefit to the public. It said:

- QCs do not necessarily offer a better service.
- The QC title is too generic and does not tell purchasers about the area of specialisation.
- The system focuses on advocacy skills whereas users require a range of skills such as legal advice and case management.
- There is no monitoring of quality or incentive to keep standards high once the title has been conferred.

This led to the Lord Chancellor announcing in May 2003 that the processing of applications for appointment in 2003 would be suspended while the whole system was reviewed. It was followed in July 2003 by the issue of a consultation paper *The Future of Queen's Counsel*.

The Bar wanted the position of QC to be kept, and the Bar Council replied to the consultation paper claiming that the QC system serves the public interest because it:

- is a conspicuous brand that enhances the standing of UK legal services abroad
- is a publicly recognised mark of quality of advocacy
- provides a resource for public inquiries
- promotes competition by supplementing market information
- is a tool for promoting diversity as an increasing number of minority ethnic barristers approach silk seniority.

On this last point, ethnic minority barristers pointed out that the numbers eligible to apply for silk were just about to increase.

Finally, in 2004 the Lord Chancellor, the Bar Council and the Law Society agreed a new system for appointment.

15.3.2 Current appointment system

Selection of who should become a QC is now made by an independent selection panel. Lawyers apply to become QCs. They have to pay a fee of £3,500 or more. Applicants must provide references (these can include references from clients). The applicants are interviewed by members of the independent selection panel. The panel then recommends those who should be appointed to the Lord Chancellor.

The first appointments of QCs under the new system were made in 2006: 443 applied and 175 were appointed. Of these, 33 were women (48.5 per cent of female applicants), ten ethnic minority (41.7 per cent of such applicants) and four solicitors (33.3 per cent of solicitor applicants).

Since then the number of women appointed has been smaller but has reflected the number of women applying. In 2012 a total of 88 new QCs were appointed, some 40 per cent of applicants.

Of these 88, 23 were women from the 40 women who had applied. There were 15 ethnic minority applicants and six of these were successful. Only two solicitors applied and neither of them was successful. Three employed advocates applied and one of them was made a QC.

As a result of the new appointment system, it appears that the diversity of QCs is improving, albeit very slowly.

15.4 Legal Services Act 2007

15.4.1 Background

In 2001 a report by the Office of Fair Trading recommended that unjustified restrictions on competition in the legal profession should be removed.

In 2004 the Clementi Report into the legal profession was published (*Review of the Regulatory Framework for the Legal Services in England and Wales – Final Report*). The main recommendations were that:

- there should be a new complaints body which is independent of the profession
- there should be a legal services board as regulator over all the legal professional bodies
- Legal Disciplinary Practices (LPDs) should be permitted where there are barristers, solicitors and non-lawyers working together in the same practice
- non-lawyers would be allowed to own and manage LPDs, but there would be safeguards to make sure that they were 'fit to own' such a practice.

This report led to the Legal Services Act 2007.

15.4.2 The Legal Services Act

The Act starts by setting out regulatory objectives for legal services. These are:

(a) supporting the constitutional principle of the rule of law

(b) improving access to justice

(c) protecting and promoting the interests of consumers

(d) promoting competition in the provision of services

(e) encouraging a strong, diverse and effective legal profession

(f) increasing public understanding of the citizen's legal rights and duties

(g) promoting and maintaining adherence to the professional principles.

Legal Services Board

The Act provided for the creation of the Legal Services Board. The role of the Board is to have independent oversight regulation of the legal profession. It consisted of a chairman and seven to ten members appointed by the Secretary of State. The majority of members must be non-lawyers.

The Home Affairs Committee reported on the Bill when it was in draft form. The committee was concerned that the Secretary of State was involved in the appointment of the chairman and members of the Board. It felt that this prevented the Board from being independent of the government. The government, however, kept this provision in the final Act.

Complaints about legal services

The Act established the Office for Legal Complaints to handle all complaints in respect of the legal profession. The Office has a chairman and between six and eight members. The chairman must be a non-lawyer and the majority of members must also be non-lawyers.

The Office of Legal Complaints set up the Legal Ombudsman to deal with complaints against the legal profession.

Alternative Business Structures (ABS)

Under the old system there were restrictions on the types of business structures in the legal profession. The main restrictions were:

- barristers and solicitors could not operate from the same business
- lawyers were not allowed to enter into partnership with non-lawyers
- restrictions on non-lawyers being involved in the ownership or management of legal businesses
- legal practices could operate as a companies.

So, generally, barristers and solicitors could not work together, nor could lawyers and non-lawyers work together in legal businesses. The Legal Services Act changed this by allowing:

- legal businesses to include lawyers and non-lawyers
- legal businesses to include barristers and solicitors
- non-lawyers to own legal businesses
- legal businesses to operate as companies.

The Home Affairs Committee Report on the draft Bill pointed out that the provisions in the Bill go well beyond the recommendations of Sir David Clementi. It thought that there may be potential for conflict of interest in ABS firms, both between lawyers and shareholders and between lawyers and non-lawyers. The Committee was also worried about:

- the speed of approach
- the level of uncertainty about the impact of the reforms, particularly on access to justice in rural areas and legal aid provisions.

However, the government chose to go ahead and allow the creation of ABSs. The first three licences were given in April 2012. Two of these were to 'high street' solicitors who wished to bring in a non-lawyer practice manager to their practices. The first 'big name' to be given a licence was the Co-operative Society.

As more ABSs are set up, the style of legal advice and services is likely to change considerably. Traditional solicitors' firms will face competition from commercial firms such as the Co-op.

Internet research **www**

Look up the Legal Services Act 2007 at **www.legislation.gov.uk**.

15.5 Fusion

A major debate used to be whether the two professions should be merged into one profession. The advantages of fusion were thought to be:

- reduced costs as only one lawyer would be needed instead of a solicitor and a barrister
- less duplication of work because only one person would be doing the work, instead of a solicitor preparing the case and then passing it on to a barrister
- more continuity as the same person could deal with the case from start to finish.

The disadvantages of fusion were seen as:

- a decrease in the specialist skills of advocacy
- loss of the independent Bar and the lack of availability of advice from independent specialists at the Bar
- less objectivity in consideration of a case; at the moment the barrister provides a second opinion
- loss of a cab-rank principle under which barristers have to accept any case offered to them (except when they are already booked on another case for the same day). This principle allows anyone to get representation, even if their case is unpopular or unlikely to win.

The argument for fusion is no longer so important since the changes made by the Courts and Legal Services Act 1990 and the Access to Justice Act 1999 mean that barristers and solicitors can take a case from start to finish. Under the Access to Justice Act barristers have the right to do litigation (i.e. the preliminary work in starting a case) which has in the past always been done by solicitors. At the same time solicitors have wider rights of advocacy and may represent clients in all courts.

With the provisions of the Legal Services Act, there is even less need for the professions to be fused. Barristers and solicitors are now able to work together in the same legal business.

The way in which solicitors and barristers can work together now in an ABS is shown by the group Artesian Law. Six of the seven partners are barristers, the other being a solicitor. They also intend to have a non-lawyer practice manager. So the firm can not only do the advocacy in court, but can also do the solicitor's work involved in litigation. It can also bid for legal aid contracts.

15.6 Future reforms

In 2012 the Legal Education and Training Review (LETR) was carried out by the Bar Standards Board, the Solicitors Regulation Authority and ILEX Professional Standards. The report should be published by the beginning of 2013.

This review may well recommend some fundamental changes. Look at the LETR's website (**http://letr.org.uk**) to see their recommendations.

15.7 Women and ethnic minorities in the legal profession

The legal profession has an image of being white male-dominated. In fact this is becoming less and less true as increasing numbers of women and those from an ethnic minority are entering the profession.

Women

Women are forming an increasing number of the entrants to the profession. They now make up over half of new solicitor and half of new entrants to the Bar. As a result of the increasing numbers of women studying law there are now greater numbers of women in both professions: 32 per cent of members of the Bar and 46 per cent of

solicitors are female. Despite this there are very few women at the higher levels in either profession. For example, at the Bar only about 12 per cent of QCs are women although this is slowly increasing. Women solicitors tend to be in junior positions as assistant solicitors or junior partners. Recent statistics show that 45 per cent of women working in solicitors' practices are assistant solicitors. By comparison, only 20 per cent of men are working as assistant solicitors. Women are much less likely to be partners in firms. Only 22 per cent of women are partners. This figure showed some improvement in the first part of this century but it has been fairly static in recent years.

A report, *Obstacles and Barriers to the Career Development of Women Solicitors*, was published by the Law Society in 2010. The following factors were the main reasons why women were less likely than men to progress in the profession:

- lack of flexible working hours
- the organisational culture which was perceived as being traditional, conservative and male-dominated
- the long working hours with the 24/7 mindset
- the fact that the measurement of success was strongly linked to the number of hours billed to clients – measuring quantity rather than quality
- the fact that women are not prepared to challenge the status quo or push themselves forward for promotion.

These factors lead to many women leaving solicitors' firms, often to become an 'in-house' lawyer in another organisation where there is a different work culture.

Ethnic minorities

Proportionate to the composition of the general population, ethnic minorities are well represented at the Bar. At the beginning of 2011, 15 per cent of practising barristers were from an ethnic minority. While they have experienced even more difficulty than women in achieving higher positions, with only 5 per cent of QCs being of black or Asian ethnic minority, this is a great improvement from ten years ago and is likely to increase again in the future.

In the solicitors' profession ethnic minorities are well represented. In the last few years the number of ethnic minority entrants has risen substantially. In 2011, 22.1 per cent of those admitted as solicitors were from ethnic minority backgrounds. Also, 22 per cent of those given a training contract in 2011 were of black or Asian ethnic minority.

Internet research   **www**

Try to find out what the current figures are for entrants to the legal profession. Try the websites for the Law Society and the Bar: **www.lawsociety.org.uk and www. barcouncil.org.uk**.

15.8   Legal executives

Legal executives work in solicitors' firms as assistants. They are qualified lawyers who have passed the Chartered Institute of Legal Executives' Professional Qualification in Law. They specialise in a particular area of law. There are over 22,000 legal executives practising.

Qualification and training

To become a legal executive it is necessary to pass the Professional Diploma in Law and the Professional Higher Diploma in Law. The Professional Diploma is set at A-level standard and can be achieved in two ways:

1. Mixed assessment route: this is by portfolio, case studies and one end-of-course examination which covers the English Legal System and essential elements of law and practice.
2. Examination route: the student has to sit four papers. These are normally taken over a two-year period. They cover the English Legal System, Land Law, Criminal Law and Law of Tort in the first year and Consumer Law, Employment Law, Family Law, Wills and Succession in the second year. There is also an examination on practice and procedures dealing with matters such as conveyancing and procedure in civil and criminal cases.

The Professional Higher Diploma in Law (PHDL) is degree level and students have a choice of areas of law to study. In each area they learn the law and the practice side of that area of law.

As well as passing the PHDL examinations, it is also necessary to have worked in a solicitors' firm (or other legal organisation such as the Crown Prosecution Service or local government) for at least five years. When all the qualifications have been achieved the person becomes a Fellow of the Institute of Legal Executives.

A Fellow of the Institute of Legal Executives can go on to become a solicitor. In order to do this they will have to pass the Law Society's Legal Practice Course, but they may be given exemption from the two-year training contract.

Work

Legal executives specialise in a particular area of law. Within that area of law their day-to-day work is similar to that of a solicitor, though they tend to deal with the more straightforward matters. For example, they can:

- handle various legal aspects of a property transfer
- assist in the formation of a company
- draft wills
- advise people with matrimonial problems
- advise clients accused of serious or petty crime.

They also have some rights of audience. They can appear to make applications where the case is not defended in family matters and civil cases in the County Court and Magistrates' Courts.

Since 2008 legal executives have been able to do a course on advocacy and obtain wider rights of audience. There are three different practising certificates: a Civil Proceedings Certificate, a Criminal Proceedings Certificate and a Family Proceedings Certificate. These will allow legal executives to do such matters as make an application for bail or deal with cases in the Youth Court or the Family court of the Magistrates' Courts.

Legal executives are fee earners. This means that where a legal executive works for a firm of solicitors in private practice, that legal executive's work is charged at an hourly rate directly to clients. In this way a legal executive makes a direct contribution to the income of the law firm. The partners of the firm are responsible for the legal executive's work.

EXAMINATION QUESTIONS

1. (a) Describe the education and training of barristers and how problems that a client has with their barrister are dealt with. [18 marks]
   (b) Discuss whether the 2010 changes have improved the way complaints about barristers and solicitors are dealt with. [12 marks]
   G151, June 2012, OCR

EXTENSION ESSAY

Critically discuss the reforms of the structure of the legal profession made by the Legal Services Act 2007.

THE JUDICIARY

INTRODUCTION

When judges are spoken of as a group, they are referred to as the judiciary. There are many different levels of judges, but the basic function is the same at all levels: judges are there to adjudicate on disputes in a fair, unbiased way, applying the legal rules of England and Wales. There is no clear-cut division between civil and criminal judges, as many judges at the various levels are required to sit for both types of case. This in itself causes problems as, before their appointment, most judges will have specialised in one area of law. The head of the judiciary is the Lord Chief Justice.

When considering judges the first point is that there is a marked difference between what are called superior judges and inferior judges. This affects the method of appointment, the training, the work and the terms on which they hold office, so it is as well to start by understanding which judges are involved at each level.

16.1 Types of judges

16.1.1 Superior judges

Superior judges are those in the High Court and above. Starting from the top and working down these are:

- The Justices of the Supreme Court who sit in the Supreme Court
- The Lords Justices of Appeal in the Court of Appeal
- High Court Judges (known as puisne judges) who sit in the three divisions of the High Court; note that in addition, judges from the Queen's Bench Division also sit in the Crown Court.

16.1.2 Inferior judges

The inferior judges are:

- Circuit Judges who sit in both the Crown Court and the County Court
- Recorders who are part-time judges sitting usually in the Crown Court, though some may be assigned to the County Court
- District Judges who hear small claims and other matters in the County Court
- District Judges (Magistrates' Court) who sit in Magistrates' Courts in London and other major towns and cities
- Judges.

The parade of judges and silks on the first day of the legal year

16.2 Qualifications

To become a judge at any level it is necessary to meet the judicial-appointment eligibility condition relevant to that level. This means the applicant must have the relevant legal qualification and have gained experience in the law for a certain period. The qualifications to become a judge have been widened over the last 20 or so years.

Before 1990 only barristers could become superior judges, although solicitors were eligible for the lower levels of the judiciary. The Court and Legal Services Act 1990 changed this by basing qualifications on the relevant advocacy qualification and allowing for promotion from one level to another. As a result of this, more solicitors became Circuit Judges and solicitors have been promoted from Circuit Judge to High Court Judge. The 1990 Act also allowed academic lawyers to become judges, as it removed the previous need for them to have practised as a lawyer.

The Tribunals, Court and Enforcement Act 2007 changed the qualifications and further widened the pool of potential applicants. This Act states that to apply to become a judge it is necessary to have the relevant legal qualification. This is normally barrister or solicitor, but for some levels the Act has opened up some judicial posts beyond solicitors and barristers for the first time. Fellows of the Institute of Legal Executives (ILEX) and Registered Patents Attorneys and Trade Mark Attorneys may apply for certain lower-level posts.

Gain experience in law

The Tribunals, Court and Enforcement Act 2007 widened the ways in which applicants may have gained experience in law. As well as practising or teaching law, the Act recognises that such activities as acting as an arbitrator or mediator, advising on law or drafting legal documents are also methods by which an applicant can gain experience in law.

The Act also reduced the length of time that a person has to work in the law before they can apply to become a judge. Previously the minimum time was seven years for lower-level posts and ten years for most senior posts. These time periods are now five and seven years respectively.

These changes have all helped to widen the pool of potential candidates for judgeships, and may eventually help to make the composition of the Bench a wider cross-section of society.

The qualifications for each level of judge are set out below.

16.2.1 The Justices of the Supreme Court

These are appointed from those who hold high judicial office, for example as a judge in the Court of Appeal, or from those who have been qualified to appear in the senior courts for at least 15 years. As the Supreme Court is the final appellate court for Scotland and Northern Ireland as well, judges can also be appointed from those who have qualified to appear in courts in Scotland or Northern Ireland for at least 15 years.

16.2.2 Lords Justices of Appeal

These must have been qualified as a barrister or solicitor and have gained experience in law for at least seven years or to have been an existing High Court Judge. In recent times all Lords Justices of Appeal have been appointed from existing High Court Judges.

16.2.3 High Court Judges

In order to be eligible to be appointed as a High Court Judge it is necessary either to have been qualified as a barrister or solicitor and have gained experience in law for at least seven years or to have been a Circuit Judge for at least two years. The vast majority of High Court Judges are appointed from barristers who have been in practice for 20 or 30 years. Deputy High Court Judges, who sit part-time, are also appointed and this is a way of testing the suitability of a person to become a High Court Judge.

16.2.4 Circuit Judges

The applicant can either have been qualified as a barrister or solicitor and have gained experience in law for at least seven years or have been a Recorder. About 13 per cent of Circuit Judges are former solicitors.

The Courts and Legal Services Act 1990 also allows for promotion after being a District Judge, stipendiary magistrate or chairman of an employment tribunal for at least three years. These provisions have widened the pool of potential judges and are gradually leading to a better cross-section among the judges at this level.

The usual route to becoming a Circuit Judge is to be appointed as a Recorder first and then be promoted to a Circuit Judge.

16.2.5 Recorders

This is a part-time post. The applicant must have been qualified as a barrister or solicitor and have gained experience in law for at least seven years. An applicant is appointed as a Recorder in training first and then appointed as a Recorder.

16.2.6 District Judges

At this level an applicant must have been qualified as a barrister or solicitor and have gained experience in law for at least five years or to have been a Deputy District Judge. The vast majority of District Judges in the County Court are former solicitors. District Judges in the Magistrates' Courts need the same qualifications. About two-thirds of these are former solicitors. It is usual to have sat part-time as a deputy District Judge before being considered for the position of District Judge. Under the Tribunals, Courts and Enforcement Act 2007, ILEX Fellows are now eligible to be appointed as a Deputy District

Judges, and by 2013, one had been appointed as a Deputy District Judge in the County Court.

16.2.7 Tribunal Judges

These must have been qualified as a barrister, solicitor or ILEX Fellow and have gained experience in law for at least five years. For the position of Chairman or Deputy Chairman of the Copyright Tribunal, Registered Patents Attorneys and Trade Mark Attorneys are also eligible.

16.3 Selection

16.3.1 History

Until 2005, the Lord Chancellor was the key figure in the selection of superior judges. The Lord Chancellor's Department would keep information on all possible candidates. These files would contain confidential information and opinions from existing judges on the suitability of each person. The contents of these files were secret.

When there was a vacancy for a judicial position in the House of Lords, the Court of Appeal or the High Court, the Lord Chancellor would consider the information in these files and decide which person he thought was the best for the post. That person would then be invited to become a judge.

Not surprisingly, this system of selection was seen as secretive. It was also felt that it favoured white males, as there were few women in the higher ranks of the judiciary.

Matters improved for High Court judgeships as, from 1998, vacancies were advertised and any qualified person could apply. However, even then, the Lord Chancellor continued to invite people to become judges, rather than appoint solely from those who applied.

The major role of the Lord Chancellor in appointment was very controversial as the Lord Chancellor is a political appointment. (See section 16.12 for further information on the Lord Chancellor.) It was thought that the appointment of judges should be independent from any political influence. So the method of appointment was changed by the Constitutional Reform Act 2005.

The following sections will explain how appointments are now made.

16.3.2 Judges of the new Supreme Court

When the Supreme Court took over from the House of Lords, the existing House of Lords Judges became Justices of the Supreme Court. For new appointments, judges for this Court are selected according to the method set out in Part 3 of the Constitutional Reform Act 2005. This states that when there is a vacancy, the Office of the President of the Court must convene a Supreme Court selection commission.

This commission must include the President and the Deputy President of the Supreme Court and one member of the Judicial Appointments Commission. As the Supreme Court is also the final court of appeal for Scotland and Northern Ireland, the commission must also include a member of the Judicial Appointments Board for Scotland and the Northern Ireland Judicial Appointments Commission.

The commission will decide the selection process to be used. It will then use that process to select a candidate and report that selection to the Lord Chancellor.

Under s 29 of the Constitutional Reform Act 2005, the Lord Chancellor can reject that candidate or ask the commission to reconsider. This can only be done if the Lord Chancellor is of the opinion that the person selected is not suitable for the office or that there is evidence that the person is not the best candidate on merit. The Lord Chancellor must give written reasons for rejecting a candidate or asking the commission to reconsider.

Once the Lord Chancellor has accepted the commission's nomination, he then notifies the prime minister and the prime minister must recommend to the Queen that she appoints that person. The prime minister cannot recommend another person for appointment.

The prime minister's role in the appointment has been criticised as it infringes the independence of the judiciary, even though it is now only an administrative role.

ACTIVITY

Opposite is the advertisement of a vacancy which appeared in October 2009. Read it and answer the questions below.

1. Under which section of which Act has a selection commission been established?
2. What is the role of the selection commission?
3. If the candidate has held high judicial office in another court, what is the minimum period of time for which they must have held that office?
4. If the candidate has not held high judicial office, what qualification(s) do they need?

Justice of The Supreme Court

An ad hoc selection commission has been established under section 27 and schedule 8 of the Constitutional Reform Act 2005 to select a candidate to be recommended for appointment as a Justice of the Supreme Court. The vacancy arises as a result of Lord Neuberger's appointment as Master of the Rolls.

The statutory minimum qualification for appointment is to have held high judicial office for a period of at least two years, or to have satisfied the judicial appointment eligibility condition on a 15-year basis or to have been a qualifying practitioner for a period of at least 15 years.

The selection commission invites applications from all eligible candidates who fulfil one of the above statutory requirements.

Additional information on the qualifications, the criteria and the selection process can be found in the Information Pack which is available from Grainne Hawkins (grainne.hawkins@supremecourt.gsi.gov.uk tel: 020 7960 1906).

The closing date for applications is 5pm Monday 26 October.

Applications should be sent to:

Jenny Rowe
Chief Executive
UK Supreme Court
Parliament Square
LONDON SW1P 3BD

16.3.3 The Judicial Appointments Commission

All other judicial appointments are made by the Judicial Appointments Commission. This was created under the Constitutional Reform Act and started work in April 2006. The Commission is responsible for selecting between 500 and 700 people for appointment to judicial posts each year.

There are 15 members of this Commission. There must be:

- six lay members
- five judges – three of these from the Court of Appeal or High Court plus one Circuit Judge and one District Judge or equivalent

- one barrister
- one solicitor
- one magistrate
- one tribunal member.

The key features of the new process for appointing judges are:

- Appointments are made solely on merit.
- The Commission is entirely responsible for assessing the merit of the candidates and selecting candidates for appointment.
- No candidate can be appointed unless recommended by the Commission.
- The Commission must consult with the Lord Chief Justice and another judge of equivalent

experience before recommending a candidate for appointment.

- The Lord Chancellor has limited powers in relation to each recommendation for appointment. He can reject a candidate once or ask the Commission to reconsider once but he must give written reasons for this.

The power of the Lord Chancellor to reject a candidate or ask the Commission to reconsider has been criticised as it infringes the independence of the judiciary.

The Crime and Courts Bill 2012 has provision to transfer the Lord Chancellor's power in respect of all judges below the High Court to the Lord Chief Justice. The Senior President of Tribunals will be given the power to appoint judges for the First-tier and Upper Tribunals. The Lord Chancellor will still be consulted on appointments to the High Court and Court of Appeal. However, for lower court judgeships the process will be completely separate from the government and executive.

The process

Positions are advertised widely in newspapers, legal journals and also online. To encourage a wide range of candidates to apply, the Commission runs road shows and other outreach events designed to communicate and explain the appointments system to potential applicants.

All candidates have to fill in an application form. Candidates are also asked to nominate between three and six referees. In addition, the Commission has published a list of people whom it may consult about candidates. These include existing judges. For lower-level posts, applicants will also be asked to write an essay or do a case study.

A shortlist will then be made of candidates and these will be interviewed. The interview process may include role play or taking part in a formal, structured discussion.

Judicial qualities

The Commission has listed five qualities that are desirable for a good judge. These are:

- intellectual capacity
- personal qualities including integrity, independence of mind, sound judgement, decisiveness, objectivity and willingness to learn
- ability to understand and deal fairly
- authority and communication skills
- efficiency.

More information can be found on the Judicial Appointments Commission's website at **http://jac.judiciary.gov.uk**.

> ### Internet research **www**
> Look at the Commission's website to see if any judicial posts are being advertised.

16.4 Appointment

Once a candidate has been selected and that selection accepted by the Lord Chancellor, then the appointment is made by the Queen for all judicial posts from District Judges up to the Supreme Court.

16.5 Judicial roles

The work that a judge does depends on the level of court in which he or she works.

16.5.1 Justices of the Supreme Court

The judges in the Supreme Court hear about 70 cases each year. These are appeals. They can be in civil or criminal cases. However, there are always far more civil appeals each year. A case can only be appealed to the Supreme Court if there is a point of law involved. Often civil cases involve complicated and technical areas of law, such as planning law or tax law.

The Supreme Court

The Justices of the Supreme Court must sit as an uneven-number panel (minimum three judges) to hear a case. Any decision the Supreme Court makes on a point of law becomes a precedent for all lower courts to follow.

16.5.2 Lords Justices of Appeal

There are some 38 Lords Justices of Appeal. They sit in both the civil and criminal divisions of the Court of Appeal, so they deal with both civil and criminal cases. Their workload is much heavier than the Supreme Court.

On the criminal side, they will hear over 7,000 applications for leave to appeal against sentence or conviction. Each application can be dealt with by one judge. Only about a quarter of these applications get leave to appeal, so the full court then has about 1,800 criminal appeals to hear. In addition, it hears over 3,000 civil appeals. These may be appeals against the finding of liability or an appeal about the remedy awarded, e.g. the amount of money given as damages.

Court of Appeal judges usually sit as a panel of three to hear cases. On rare occasions, in important cases, there may be a panel of five.

Because the workload of the Court of Appeal is so large, High Court Judges are often used to form part of the panel. This means there may be one Lord Justice of Appeal sitting with two High Court Judges.

In law reports Court of Appeal Judges are referred to as Lord Justice or Lady Justice, but when their judgments are being quoted they are usually referred to by their surname followed by LJ, for example, Arden LJ.

16.5.3 High Court Judges

Each judge in the High Court will be assigned to one of the Divisions. There are about 73 judges in the Queen's Bench Division, 18 in the Chancery Division and 19 in the Family Division.

There are also Deputy High Court Judges who sit to help with the workload.

The main function of High Court Judges is to try cases. These are cases at first instance, because it is the first time the case has been heard by a court. They will hear evidence from witnesses, decide what the law is and make the decision as to which side has won the case. If the claim is for damages (an amount of money) the judge decides how much should be awarded to the winning claimant. The type of work dealt with by each Division is described more fully in Chapter 9. When hearing first-instance cases, judges sit on their own. However, in the Queen's Bench Division in some rare cases there may be a jury.

High Court Judges also hear some appeals. These are mainly from civil cases tried in the County Court. The judges in the Queen's Bench Division also hear criminal appeals from the Magistrates' Courts by a special case-stated method. These are appeals on law only. When sitting to hear appeals, there will be a panel of two or three judges.

Judges from the Queen's Bench Division also sit to hear criminal trials in the Crown Court. When they do this they sit with a jury. The jury decide the facts and the judge decides the law. Where a defendant pleads guilty or is found guilty by a jury, the judge then has to decide on the sentence.

In law reports, High Court Judges are referred to as Mr Justice or Mrs Justice, but when their judgments are being quoted they are usually referred to by their surname followed by J, for example, Dobbs J.

Internet research   www

Look up law reports on the Internet. Try **www.bailii.org**.

TRY TO FIND:

1. A law report in which there was a female judge.
2. A report of the Court of Appeal in which at least one of the judges is only of High Court level.
3. A report from the High Court in which the judge sitting is only a Deputy High Court Judge.

16.5.4 Inferior judges

Circuit Judges sit in the County Court to hear civil cases and also in the Crown Court to try criminal cases. In civil cases they sit on their own (it is very rare to have a jury in a civil case in the County Court). They decide the law and the facts. They make the decision on who has won the case.

In criminal cases they sit with a jury. The jury decide the facts and the judge decides the law. Where a defendant pleads guilty or is found guilty by a jury, the judge then has to decide on the sentence.

Recorders are part-time judges who are appointed for a period of five years. They are used mainly in the Crown Court to try criminal cases, but some sit in the County Court to help with civil cases.

District Judges sit in the County Court to deal with small-claims cases (under £5,000) and can also hear other cases for larger amounts.

District Judges (Magistrates' Courts) sit to try criminal cases in the Magistrates' Courts. They sit on their own and decide facts and law. When a defendant pleads guilty or is found guilty, they also have to decide on the sentence.

They may also sit to hear family cases, but this will usually be with two lay magistrates.

16.6 Composition of the Bench

One of the main criticisms of the Bench is that it is dominated by elderly, white, upper-class males. There are very few women judges in the upper ranks of judges, and even fewer judges from ethnic minorities. With the introduction of a younger retirement age, the average age of judges will be slightly reduced, but it is unusual for any judge to be appointed under the age of 40, with superior judges usually being well above this age.

Key Facts

Court	Judge	Qualification	Role
Supreme Court	Justices of the senior court	15-year Supreme Court qualification or hold high judicial office Barrister or solicitor	Hear appeals on points of law Civil and criminal cases
Court of Appeal	Lord Justices of Appeal	7 years' legal experience or be an existing High Court Judge Barrister or solicitor	Hear appeals Criminal cases against conviction and/or sentence Civil cases on the finding and/ or the amount awarded
High Court	High Court Judges Also known as puisne judges	Barrister or solicitor 7 years' legal experience *or* be a Circuit Judge for 2 years	Sit in one of the three Divisions Hear first-instance cases and decide liability and remedy Some appeal work
Crown Court	High Court Judges Circuit Judges Recorders	See above 7 years' legal experience *or* be a Recorder or District Judge for 3 years Barrister or solicitor 5 years' legal experience	Try cases with a jury Decide the law Pass sentence on guilty defendants
County Court	Circuit Judges District Judges	See above Barrister or solicitor 5 years' legal experience	Civil cases – decide liability and remedy District Judges hear small claims
Magistrates' Courts	District Judges (Magistrates' Courts)	Barrister or solicitor 5 years' legal experience NB ILEX Fellows can be appointed as Deputy District Judges	Criminal cases – decide law and verdict Pass sentence on guilty defendants Some family work

Figure 16.1 *Key facts chart of qualifications, selection and appointment of judges*

16.6.1 Women in the judiciary

The number of women in judicial posts is very small, although there has been an improvement in recent years. During the 1990s there was an increase in the number of women appointed to the High Court. The first woman judge in the Queen's Bench Division was appointed in 1992, and the first in the Chancery Division in 1993.

The first woman in the Court of Appeal was appointed in 1988. This was Lady Butler-Sloss. The legal system was so unused to women in the higher levels of the judiciary that when she was appointed she had to be addressed in court as My Lord, and in law reports her title was written as Lord Butler-Sloss!

In 1994 the then Master of the Rolls (the head of the Civil Division of the Court of Appeal) announced that in future she should be addressed as My Lady. However, it was not until the Courts Act 2003 that the official title of women judges in the Court of Appeal became Lady Justice of Appeal.

It was not until 1999 that a second woman was appointed to the Court of Appeal, and a third in 2000. In February 2001 the first all-female Court of Appeal panel sat. The first, and so far only, woman judge in the House of Lords was appointed in 2004. This was Brenda Hale. She is now the only female judge in the new Supreme Court.

By the end of 2012 the total number of women judges in the High Court was 17 out of just over 100 judges. This is the highest number there has been to date. However, there were only four women out of 38 judges in the Court of Appeal.

Lower down the judicial ladder, there are more women being appointed than in the past. By 2012 16 per cent of Circuit Judges and 17 per cent of Recorders were female. The highest percentage of women was for Deputy District Judges (County Courts) where it was 33 per cent.

The Judicial Appointments Commission's annual report for 2012–13 shows that during that period 29 per cent of all appointments were female, although the majority were appointed to lower-level posts.

16.6.2 Ethnic minorities

In 2004 the first ethnic minority judge was appointed to the High Court. Even at the lower levels, ethnic minorities are still poorly represented. In 2012, 2.5 per cent of Circuit Judges and 6.5 per cent of Recorders were from an ethnic minority. These percentages have gradually improved over the past few years.

By 2012 the overall percentage of ethnic minority judges was 4 per cent. This is not representative of the community. However, it is representative of the percentage of black and ethnic minority lawyers who are eligible for appointment. (See figures in the table in the Activity on pages 233–4.)

16.6.3 Educational and social background

At the higher levels judges tend to come from the upper levels of society, with many having been educated at public school and nearly all attending Oxford University or Cambridge University. A survey by the magazine *Labour Research* found that of the 85 judges appointed from 1997 to mid-1999, 73 per cent had been to public school and 79 per cent to Oxbridge.

In 2007, Penny Darbyshire surveyed 77 judges from different levels of the judiciary. She found that there were marked differences in background between superior judges and those at a lower level. For example, none of the District Judges (Magistrates' Court) had been to private school, whilst 11 out of 16 High Court Judges and eight out of the ten Court of Appeal/House of Lords Judges she interviewed had been privately educated.

ACTIVITY

Read the following newspaper article and answer the questions below.

Do you fancy being a High Court judge? Forget the whisper over a drink at your Inn of Court or the traditional 'tap on the shoulder'. Dust off your CV and send in an application. And then prepare yourself for an 'interview' with a selection panel. This is the new world of appointing judges …

The selection process will be undertaken by the Judicial Appointments Commission, the independent body set up under the Constitutional Reform Act in 2005 to take over responsibility for selecting judges from the Lord Chancellor's officials.

There has been advertising for High Court judges before – but they were selected on paper. This time, the candidates will undergo a face-to-face discussion – and that, with references and their own application form, will combine to inform the selection.

Baroness Usha Prashar, who is chairman of the 15 lay and judicial commissioners and 105 staff, will now be responsible for 500 to 700 appointments a year, including the High Court . . .

The aim, she says, is for a much more transparent process that will encourage a greater diversity of candidates. 'Up to now the process was perceived to be very secretive and not very open. There was a view that it was those who you knew who counted – and that probably deterred a lot of people who felt they would not get a fair deal. This will be objective and transparent and hopefully that will encourage more people to apply.'

Taken from an article by Francis Gibb, *The Times,* 31 October 2006 © The Times 2006/nisyndication.com

Questions

1. Who was responsible for appointing judges under the old system?
2. Who is responsible for appointing judges now?

3. Describe the problems with the old system of appointing judges.
4. Describe how the new system operates.
5. Explain whether you think that the new system has encouraged a wider range of applicants for judgeships.

Internet research   **www**

Look up the judicial website **www.judiciary. gov.uk** and look at the section 'About the judiciary'.

1. Look up the biographies of two judges. Find out the following matters:
   (a) Which school did they go to?
   (b) At which university did they get their degree?
   (c) When did they first become a judge?
   (d) What is their current position?
2. Find out how many women judges there are in the Court of Appeal.
3. Find out how many ethnic minority judges there are in the High Court.

University

There was also a major difference in the universities that senior judges had attended compared to judges at a lower level. Ninety per cent of Court of Appeal/House of Lords Judges had been to Oxford or Cambridge, but only one of six District Judges (Magistrates' Court) and four out of thirteen District Judges (County Court) had attended Oxbridge. However, as the judges in the Court of Appeal and House of Lords decide complex cases and law, Darbyshire points out that:

'It would surely be a matter of concern if senior judges were not highly educated and exceptionally intelligent.'

ACTIVITY

The tables below have been adapted from the Judicial Appointments Commission's Report on selections during the period October 2011 to March 2012. Study them and answer the questions below.

Group	Size of eligible pool		Eligible applications		Recommendations for appointment	
	Number	As percentage of total eligible pool	Number	As percentage of total eligible applications	Number	As percentage of recommendations for appointment
Gender	Men: 3,093 Women: 727	81% 19%	Men: 248 Women: 214 Incomplete: 17	51% 45% 4%	Men: 31 Women: 24 Incomplete: 1	55% 43% 2%
Ethnic background	White: 2,270 BAME: 195 Incomplete: 855	73% 5% 22%	White: 395 BAME: 69 Incomplete: 19	82% 14% 4%	White: 51 BAME: 4 Incomplete: 1	55% 7% 2%

BAME = Black and Asian Minority Ethnic

Table 16.1 *District Judge (Civil) appointments*

Group	Size of eligible pool		Eligible applications		Recommendations for appointment	
	Number	As percentage of total eligible pool	Number	As percentage of total eligible applications	Number	As percentage of recommendations for appointment
Gender	Men: 2,869 Women: 737	80% 20%	Men: 107 Women: 18 Incomplete: 1	85% 14% 1%	Men: 23 Women: 2 Incomplete: 0	92% 8% 0%
Ethnic background	White: 2,748 BAME: 139 Incomplete: 721	76% 4% 20%	White: 109 BAME: 16 Incomplete: 1	82% 13% 1%	White: 23 BAME: 2 Incomplete: 0	92% 8% 0%

BAME = Black and Asian Minority Ethnic

Table 16.2 *Circuit Judge (Crime heavyweight) appointments*

Questions

1. How many women were eligible to apply for the post of District Judge (Table 16.1)? And how many of these did apply?
2. Compare these figures with those for men eligible to apply and applying for a post as a District Judge.

3. How many women were eligible to apply for the post of Circuit Judge (Table 16.2)? And how many of these did apply?
4. Comment on the difference in the number of women applying to be a District Judge as against those applying to be a Circuit Judge. What factors might account for the difference?
5. How many from a BAME were eligible to apply for the post of District Judge? And how many of these did apply?
6. How many from a BAME were eligible to apply for the post of Circuit Judge? And how many of these did apply?
7. In the total recommendations for the two posts what percentages were BAME? Using your knowledge of the judiciary, comment on how these percentages compare with the overall totals of BAME in the judiciary.

16.7 Training

The training of judges is carried out by the Judicial Studies Board, which was set up in 1979. Originally, most of the training was, however, focused at the lower end of the judicial scale, being aimed at Recorders. However, training is now given to the newly appointed High Court. Once a lawyer has been appointed as a Recorder in training, they go on four-day residential course run by the Judicial Studies Board. Recorders will then shadow an experienced judge for a week. After this they will sit to hear cases. There is continuation training, one-day courses available from time to time, especially on the effect of new legislation.

Critics point out that the training is very short, and that even if all the people involved are experienced lawyers this does not mean that they have any experience of doing such tasks as summing up to the jury or sentencing. There is also the fact that some Recorders will not have practised in the criminal courts as lawyers, so their expertise is limited and a one-week course a very short training period.

The attitude of the judiciary to training has changed considerably over the last 20 years. Training used to be seen as insulting to lawyers who had spent all their working lives in the courts building up expertise in their field. It was also seen as a threat to judicial independence. However, the need for training is now fully accepted.

Human awareness training

In 1993 the Judicial Studies Board recommended that training should include racial awareness courses. This was accepted by the Lord Chancellor and all Circuit Judges and Recorders now have to attend a course designed to make them aware of what might be unintentionally discriminatory or offensive, such as asking a non-Christian for their Christian name. The Board has also introduced training in human awareness, covering gender awareness and disability issues. The training explores the perceptions of unrepresented parties, witnesses, jurors, victims and their families, and tries to make judges more aware of other people's viewpoints.

Legal research

Another problem that exists is the lack of research facilities for judges at all levels – this is especially true of the appellate courts, where the cases are likely to involve complex legal points. The judges in the Court of Appeal have only four days a month for legal reading, and, unlike many foreign courts, there are no lawyers attached to the court to research the law. In the European Court of Justice there are Advocates-General who are independent lawyers working for the court, whose task is to research legal points and present their findings.

16.7.1 Should there be a 'career' judiciary?

In many continental countries becoming a judge is a career choice made by students once they have their basic legal qualifications. They will usually not practise as a lawyer first, but instead are trained as judges. Once they have qualified as a judge they will sit in junior posts and then hope to be promoted up the judicial ladder. This has two distinct advantages over the system in use in this country:

- The average age of judges is much lower, especially in the bottom ranks. In this country an Assistant Recorder will normally be in their late 30s or early 40s when appointed, and the average age for appointment to the High Court Bench tends to be late 40s/early 50s
- Judges have had far more training in the specific skills they need as judges.

The disadvantage of the continental system is that judges may be seen as too closely linked to the government as they are civil servants. In this country judges are generally considered as independent from the government. This point of judicial independence is explored more fully in section 16.11.

Elected judges

In the USA judges at state and local level are elected to their posts. This may cause pressure groups to canvass voters actively for or against judges, according to the views the judges hold. Judges in the federal courts are appointed by the President but the appointment has to be confirmed by the Senate. Before voting on a new appointee the Senate can question him or her about their background and past life and this is usually

televised. This makes the appointment system very public, but can lead to political overtones in the appointment system, with one political party voting for a candidate and the opposing party voting against that candidate.

16.8 Judges must be impartial

Each judge is meant to conduct proceedings in a fair and unbiased way. An important rule of natural justice is that no person can be a judge in a case in which they have an interest. This has been applied so that it also includes cases where the judge has interest in the promotion of some cause. This was seen in the *Pinochet* case.

16.8.1 Bias and the *Pinochet* case

In December 1998, the judges in the House of Lords heard an appeal by the former head of state of Chile, Ugarte Pinochet, and decided that he did not have immunity from arrest and extradition. The allegations against Pinochet were about torture and deaths which occurred in Chile during the period he was head of state. Amnesty, the human rights movement, had been granted permission to intervene in the appeal and had made written submissions to the House of Lords. One of the judges who heard the case, Lord Hoffmann, was an unpaid director of Amnesty International Charitable Trust.

When the lawyers acting for Pinochet discovered that Lord Hoffmann had this connection, they asked the House of Lords to set aside the decision and have the case reheard by a completely independent panel of judges. The Law Lords decided that the original decision could not be allowed to stand. Judges had to be seen to be completely unbiased. The fact that Lord Hoffmann was connected with Amnesty meant that he could be said to have an interest in the outcome of the case.

This decision upheld the idea that judges must be impartial.

In *Howell v Lees Millais* (2007) Smith J, a High Court Judge, had been negotiating with a firm of solicitors for a consultancy, if he were to retire from the Bench. This negotiation broke down and Smith J sent an acrimonious email to the firm. Soon after this, a disputed case about a trust came before the judge. It involved a partner from the firm of solicitors with whom the judge had been negotiating. The QC representing the partner wrote to the judge asking the judge to step down from the case. The judge refused. There was then an application in court before the case began, asking for the judge to transfer the case to another judge. Again the judge refused and threatened the QC making the application with 'professional consequences'. An application was then made to the Court of Appeal who were very critical of the judge's behaviour. It was a clear case where there was a real possibility of bias.

The judge was referred to the Office for Judicial Complaints for his failure to remove himself from the case and for his behaviour. He was reprimanded.

16.8.2 Bias and human rights

The test for bias has been influenced by the European Convention on Human Rights. In the case of *Re Medicaments (No 2), Director General of Fair Trading v Proprietary Association of Great Britain* (2001) the Court of Appeal followed decisions of the European Court of Human Rights. It said that the test was an objective one of whether the circumstances were such as to lead a fair-minded and informed observer to conclude that there was a real possibility of bias.

16.9 Retirement and dismissal

It is important that judges should be impartial in their decisions and, in particular, that the government cannot force a judge to resign if that judge makes a decision with which the government of the day disagrees. In this country judges are reasonably secure from political interference.

16.9.1 Security of tenure of superior judges

Superior judges have security of tenure in that they cannot be dismissed by the Lord Chancellor or the government. This right originated in the Act of Settlement 1700 which allowed them to hold office while of good behaviour (previously the monarch could dismiss judges at will). The same provision is now contained in the Senior Courts Act 1981 for High Court Judges and Lords Justices of Appeal, and in the Constitutional Reform Act 2005 for the Justices of the Supreme Court. As a result they can only be removed by the monarch following a petition presented to him or her by both Houses of Parliament. This gives superior judges protection from political whims and allows them to be independent in their judgments.

This power to remove a superior judge has never been used for an English judge, though it was used in 1830 to remove an Irish judge, Jonah Barrington, who had misappropriated £700 from court funds.

The Lord Chief Justice can, however, after consulting with the Lord Chancellor, declare vacant the office of any judge who (through ill health) is incapable of carrying out his work and of taking the decision to resign. This power was first introduced in the Administration of Justice Act 1973 and is now contained in the Senior Courts Act 1981.

In fact what has happened on two occasions in the past is that pressure has been put on unsatisfactory High Court Judges to resign. The first of these was in 1959 when the Lord Chancellor asked Mr Justice Hallett to resign; the second in 1998 when Mr Justice Harman resigned after criticisms by the Court of Appeal.

Key Facts

Judges	Court/s	Tenure
Justices of the Supreme Court	Supreme Court	'whilst of good behaviour' (Appellate Jurisdiction Act 1876 s 6)
Lords Justices of Appeal	Court of Appeal	'whilst of good behaviour' (Senior Courts Act 1981 s 11(3))
High Court Judges (puisne judges)	High Court Crown Court for serious cases	'whilst of good behaviour' (Senior Courts Act 1981 s 11(3))
Circuit Judges	Crown Court County Court	Can be dismissed by Lord Chancellor for incapacity or misbehaviour (Courts Act 1971 s 17(4))
District Judges	County Court Magistrates' Court	Can be dismissed by the Lord Chancellor
Recorders	Crown Court Some may sit in County Court	Appointed for period of 5 years; Lord Chancellor can decide not to reappoint NB Under Crime and Courts Bill 2012 this power not to reappoint will be given to the Lord Chief Justice

Figure 16.2 *Key facts chart on judges and their tenure*

16.9.2 Tenure of interior judges

These do not have the same security of tenure of office as superior judges since the Lord Chancellor has the power to dismiss inferior judges for incapacity or misbehaviour. A criminal conviction for dishonesty would obviously be regarded as misbehaviour and would lead to the dismissal of the judge concerned. This has happened only once, in the case of Bruce Campbell, a Circuit Judge, who was convicted of evading customs duty on cigarettes and whisky. Other matters such as drunken driving would probably be seen as misbehaviour, as would racial or sexual harassment.

Under the Constitutional Reform Act 2005, the Lord Chancellor must comply with set procedures and have the consent of the Lord Chief Justice before he can remove any judge from office.

In addition under the Constitutional Reform Act 2005, the Lord Chief Justice has the power to suspend a person from judicial office if they are subject to criminal proceedings or have been convicted. The Lord Chief Justice can only exercise this power if the Lord Chancellor agrees, and must use set procedures. Any judge who is suspended or disciplined in any other way can make a complaint to an Ombudsman if the procedures have not been carried out correctly and fairly.

Complaints about judges

Any complaint about a judge is investigated by the Office for Judicial Complaints, which is overseen by the Judicial Appointments and Conduct Ombudsman. If they find the complaint to be true, the Lord Chancellor and the Lord Chief Justice must also uphold the complaint. If they do, then they have the power to agree to advise, warn or remove a judge. In April 2009, Judge Margaret Short was dismissed in this way for 'inappropriate, petulant and rude' behaviour.

16.9.3 Retirement

Since the Judicial Pensions and Retirement Act 1993 all judges now have to retire at the age of 70, though there are some situations in which authorisation can be given for a judge to continue beyond that age. Prior to this Act judges in the High Court and above could remain sitting as judges until they were 75. The Lord Chancellor may authorise retired senior judges to sit part-time until the age of 75. All inferior judges also retire at 70.

16.10 Doctrine of the separation of powers

The theory of separation of powers was first put forward by Montesquieu, a French political theorist, in the 18th century. The theory states that there are three primary functions of the state and that the only way to safeguard the liberty of citizens is by keeping these three functions separate. As the power of each is exercised by independent and separate bodies, each can keep a check on the others and thus limit the amount of power wielded by any one group. Ideally this theory requires that individuals should not be members of more than one 'arm of the state'.

Some countries, for example the USA, have a written constitution which embodies this theory. In the United Kingdom we have no such written constitution, but even so the three organs of state are roughly separated. There is some overlap, especially in the fact that the Lord Chancellor is involved in all three functions of the state. However, the Lord Chancellor's role in relation to the judiciary is now much reduced.

The three arms of the state identified by Montesquieu are:

1. The legislature
   This is the law-making arm of the state and in our system this is Parliament.

2. The executive or the body administering the law
   Under the British political system this is the government of the day which forms the Cabinet.

3. The judiciary who apply the law
   In other words, the judges.

There is an overlap between the executive and the legislature, in that the ministers forming the government also sit in Parliament and are active in the law-making process. With the exception of the Lord Chancellor, there is very little overlap between the judiciary and the other two arms of the state. This is important because it allows the judiciary to act as a check and ensure that the executive does not overstep its constitutional powers. This is in accordance with Montesquieu's theory. However, it is open to debate whether the judiciary is truly independent from the other organs of government.

16.11 Independence of the judiciary

As already stated, an independent judiciary is seen as important in protecting the liberty of the individual from abuse of power by the executive. Judges in the English system can be thought of as being independent in a number of ways.

16.11.1 Independence from the legislature

Judges are generally not involved in the law-making functions of Parliament. Full-time judges are not allowed to be members of the House of Commons. The rule is not as strict for part-time judges so that Recorders and Assistant Recorders can be Members of Parliament. There used to be judges in the House of Lords when the Appellate Committee of the House of Lords was the final court of appeal. The main reason for the creation of the Supreme Court in 2009 was to separate the judiciary from the legislature. The judges of the Supreme Court are not allowed to be members of the House of Lords.

16.11.2 Independence from the executive

Superior judges cannot be dismissed by the government and in this way they can truly be said to be independent of the government. They can make decisions which may displease the government, without the threat of dismissal. The extent to which judges are prepared to challenge or support the government is considered in section 16.11.4. Judicial independence is now guaranteed under s 3 of the Constitutional Reform Act 2005. This states that the Lord Chancellor, other ministers in the government and anyone with responsibility for matters relating to the judiciary or the administration of justice must uphold the continued independence of the judiciary.

The section also specifically states that the Lord Chancellor and other ministers must not seek to influence particular judicial decisions.

16.11.3 Freedom from pressure

There are several ways in which judges are protected from outside pressure when exercising their judicial functions.

1. They are given a certain degree of financial independence, as judicial salaries are paid out of the consolidated fund so that payment is made without the need for Parliament's authorisation. This does not completely protect them from parliamentary interference with the terms on which they hold office. As already seen, changes can be made to retirement ages and qualifying periods for pensions.

2. Judges have immunity from being sued for actions taken or decisions made in the course of their judicial duties. This was confirmed in *Sirros v Moore* (1975) and is a key factor in ensuring judicial independence in decision-making.

3. As already noted, the security of tenure of the superior judges protects them from the threat of removal.

16.11.4 Independence from political bias

This is the area in which there is most dispute over how independent the judiciary are. Writers such as Professor Griffith point out that judges are too pro-establishment and conservative with a small 'c'.

This view is partly supported by the admission of Lord Justice Scrutton in the 1920s that it was difficult to be impartial, saying: 'I am not speaking of conscious partiality, but the habits you are trained in, the people with whom you mix, lead to your having a certain class of ideas of such a nature that when you deal with other ideas you do not give as sound and accurate judgments as you would wish.'

Pro-government decisions

Griffith cites cases such as the 'GCHQ case' in showing that judges tend to support the establishment. This case, *Council of Civil Service Unions v Minister for the Civil Service* (1984), concerned the minister for the Conservative government withdrawing the right to trade union membership from civil servants working at the intelligence headquarters in Cheltenham. The House of Lords upheld the minister's right, and the decision was seen as anti-trade union. In *Attorney-General v Guardian Newspapers Ltd* (1987) (the 'Spycatcher' case) the House of Lords granted an interlocutory injunction to the government banning the sale of a book about the security services, on the grounds that it was in the national interest of security to do so. This injunction was granted even though the book had already been published in America and Australia.

Anti-government decisions

There is, however, evidence that judges are not as pro-establishment as sometimes thought. Lord Taylor, when giving the Dimbleby Lecture in 1992, pointed out that this could be seen in the case of the Greenham Common women who had camped by an RAF base in protest against nuclear missiles. In *DPP v Hutchinson* (1990) some of the women were prosecuted under a bylaw for being on Ministry of Defence property unlawfully. The case went all the way to the House of Lords, where the Law Lords ruled in the women's favour, holding that the minister had exceeded his powers in framing the bylaw so as to prevent access to common land.

Judicial review

During the 1990s there were several challenges, by way of judicial review, to ministerial actions. In a sizeable number of cases the judges ruled against the minister concerned. This occurred in *R v Home Secretary, ex parte Fire Brigades Union* (1995) in which it was held that the changes to the Criminal Injuries Compensation Scheme made by the Home Secretary were unlawful. Also in *R v Secretary of State for Foreign Affairs, ex parte World Development Movement* (1995) the courts decided that the Foreign Secretary, Douglas Hurd, had acted unlawfully over the development of the Pergau Dam.

Human rights

More recently, the courts have upheld challenges by asylum seekers and by those held under the Anti-Terrorism, Crime and Security Act 2001. In *R (on the application of Q) v Secretary of State for the Home Department* (2003) Collins J in the High Court declared that the Home Secretary's power to refuse to provide assistance to asylum seekers who had not immediately, on their entry to this country, declared their intention to claim asylum was unlawful. The Court of Appeal upheld this decision, although they did suggest how the relevant Act could be made compatible with human rights.

In *A and another v Secretary of State for the Home Department* (2004) the House of Lords declared that the Anti-Terrorism, Crime and Security Act 2001 was incompatible with the European Convention on Human Rights. The Act allowed foreign nationals to be detained indefinitely without trial where here was suspicion that they were involved in terrorist activity. The Lords held that this breached both Article 5 (the right to liberty) and Article 14 (no discrimination on basis of nationality). This decision forced the government to change the law.

With the Human Rights Act 1998 incorporating the European Convention on Human Rights, judges can declare that an Act is incompatible with the Convention. This puts pressure on the government to change the law. The first case in which this happened was *H v Mental Health Review Tribunal* (2001).

So, while it is true that judges are still predominantly white, male, middle-class and elderly, it is possible to argue that they are no longer so out of touch with the 'real world', and that they are increasingly prepared to challenge the establishment.

16.12 The Lord Chancellor

The Lord Chancellor's position, up to 2005, was in direct contradiction to the doctrine of the separation of powers. The position is a political appointment in that he is appointed (and can be dismissed) by the prime minister. He also holds office only while the government of the day is in power: if there is a change of government there will be a new Lord Chancellor.

The Lord Chancellor

Previous role

The Lord Chancellor used to play a role in all three arms of the state as he was:

- The Speaker of the House of Lords when it is sitting in its legislative capacity, and takes part in debates there; he can also introduce new Bills for consideration.
- A member of the Cabinet.
- One of the judges in the House of Lords and the head of the judiciary.

His role was contrary to the doctrine of the separation of powers. He had too much control over the appointment of judges.

Reform of his role

The Lord Chancellor is no longer the Speaker of the House of Lords. In fact he no longer has to be a member of the House of Lords. He can be an MP in the House of Commons. He is no longer a judge, nor is he head of the judiciary: this role has been given to the Lord Chief Justice. The selection of judges is now the responsibility of the Judicial Appointments Commission, but the Lord Chancellor has some limited power to reject their selection or ask them to reconsider.

Lord Chancellor's qualifications

The Constitutional Reform Act 2005 sets out that the Lord Chancellor no longer has to be a

Key Facts

Role in legislature	Role in executive	Role in the judiciary
Was Speaker in the House of Lords	Is Member of the Cabinet	Used to sit as judge in House of Lords, Head of Chancery Division
Takes part in debates on new laws; introduces new Bills on matters connected with justice into the House of Lords (or sits in the House of Commons)	Part of the government of the day; is appointed to this office by the prime minister	Plays limited role in appointment of judges; also has power to dismiss inferior judges

Figure 16.3 *Key facts chart on the Lord Chancellor*

lawyer. The prime minister recommends the Lord Chancellor for appointment by the Queen. The Lord Chancellor has to be qualified by experience and the prime minister can now take into account any of the following:

- experience as a Minister of the Crown
- experience as a member of either House of Parliament
- experience as a lawyer with a senior court advocacy qualification
- experience as a teacher of law in a university
- other experience that the prime minister considers relevant.

The Lord Chancellor has important administrative functions, as he has the responsibility of appointing court staff and providing, equipping and managing the buildings used for court business. In addition the Lord Chancellor oversees the Community Legal Service. He is also responsible for overseeing the work of the Law Commission and the Council on Tribunals, and other bodies including the Official Solicitor's Department, the Land Registry and the Public Trustee Office. He is head of the Ministry of Justice.

16.13 Law Officers

There is also a Law Officers' department within the government for advising on legal matters that affect the government. There are two Law Officers: the Attorney-General and the Solicitor-General. Both are members of the government of the day and are appointed by the prime minister. Both will usually be members of the House of Commons. The Attorney-General appoints the Director of Public Prosecutions, who heads the Crown Prosecution Service.

16.13.1 The Attorney-General

The Attorney-General is the government's chief legal adviser. He or she is not a member of the main Cabinet, though he or she may sit on the Legislation and Home Affairs Committees of the Cabinet. He or she advises the government on legislative proposals and on criminal proceedings which have a political or public element. He or she is also responsible for major litigation which involves the government. At the time of writing, the first woman Attorney-General, Baroness Scotland, is in post.

The Attorney-General is always appointed from those members of Parliament who are barristers and can represent the government in court proceedings. While holding the post of Attorney-General, the Attorney-General cannot practise privately as a barrister. The Attorney-General will sometimes act as the prosecuting barrister in high-profile criminal cases, for example in cases of treason. He or she can also represent the government or government departments in civil cases. This occurred in the case of *Pepper v Hart* (1993) (see section 7.10.2) in which the Attorney-General appeared for the Inspector of Taxes at the hearing in the House of Lords.

The Attorney-General's consent is required before a prosecution can be started in certain cases such as corruption, possessing explosive substances and hijacking. He or she can grant immunity from prosecution and can stop proceedings for any indictable offence by entering a *nolle prosequi* (do not prosecute). This power was used in 1982 when Mary Whitehouse prosecuted the director of the play, *Romans in Britain*, under the Sexual Offences Act 1956 because the play contained a simulated homosexual rape. The Attorney-General prevented the prosecution from continuing. He or she can also instruct the Director of Public Prosecutions to take over any private prosecution.

The Attorney-General also has the right to refer criminal cases to the Court of Appeal (Criminal Division) for a point of law to be considered, following an acquittal in the Crown Court, and can appeal against a sentence which is considered to be too lenient.

16.13.2 The Solicitor-General

The Solicitor-General acts as deputy to the Attorney-General and carries out such functions as are delegated by the Attorney-General.

16.13.3 The Director of Public Prosecutions

The office of DPP was established as long ago as 1879, but the duties have changed with the establishment of the Crown Prosecution Service. The DPP's duties are set out in the Prosecution of Offences Act 1985, which created the Crown Prosecution Service. The DPP must be a barrister or solicitor of not less than ten years' standing. The appointment is made by the Attorney-General to whom the DPP is accountable – the DPP has to make a yearly report to him or her which is then put before Parliament.

The main function of the DPP is to head the Crown Prosecution Service. The other functions are set out in s 3 of the Prosecution of Offences Act 1985. These are:

- To take over the conduct of all criminal proceedings instituted by the police.
- To institute and have the conduct of criminal proceedings where the importance or difficulty of the proceedings makes this appropriate.
- To take over the conduct of binding over proceedings brought by the police.
- To give advice to police forces on all matters relating to criminal offences.
- To appear for the prosecution in certain appeals.

The position of DPP has become much more high profile with the publicity that has been generated by the problems of the Crown Prosecution Service. The Director has had to defend the large number of cases which are discontinued by the Service and has issued the Code for Crown Prosecutors (see Chapter 12).

EXAMINATION QUESTIONS

1. (a) Describe the selection and tenure of the different types of judge. [18 marks]
   (b) Discuss the extent to which judges represent a sufficiently wide cross-section of the population. [12 marks]

   G151, January 2011, OCR

EXTENSION ESSAY

'The current system of appointment of judges is likely to lead to a more diverse judiciary.' Discuss.

CHAPTER 17

MAGISTRATES

INTRODUCTION

There is a tradition of using lay people, i.e. people who are not legally qualified, in the decision-making process in our courts. Today this applies particularly to the Magistrates' Courts and the Crown Court. However, in the past lay people were also frequently used to decide civil cases in the High Court and the County Court, and there are still some cases in which a jury can be used in the civil courts. There are also lay people with expertise in a particular field who sit as part of a panel as lay assessors. This occurs in the Patents Court and the Admiralty Court in the High Court as well as in some tribunals.

17.1 Lay magistrates

There are about 26,000 lay magistrates sitting as part-time judges in the Magistrates' Courts; another name for lay magistrates is Justices of the Peace. They sit to hear cases as a bench of two or three magistrates. The size of panel has been limited to a maximum of three, although before 1996 there could be up to seven magistrates sitting together to hear a case. A single lay magistrate sitting on his or her own has very limited powers. They can, however, issue search warrants and warrants for arrest and conduct Early Administrative Hearings.

There are also District Judges (Magistrates' Courts) who work in Magistrates' Courts. These are not lay people but are qualified lawyers who can sit on their own to hear any of the cases that come before the court. Under s 16(3) of the Justices of the Peace Act 1979 they have the same powers as a bench of lay magistrates. Since the duties of these District Judges are the same as those of lay magistrates and since the history of the

two is linked, details of District Judges (formerly known as stipendiary magistrates) are also included in this chapter.

17.2 History of the magistracy

The office of Justice of the Peace is very old, dating back to the 12th century at least – in 1195 Richard I appointed 'keepers of the peace'. By the mid-13th century the judicial side of their position had developed and by 1361 the title Justice of the Peace was being used. Over the years they were also given many administrative duties, for example being responsible for the poor law, highways and bridges, and weights and measures. In the 19th century elected local authorities took over most of these duties.

The poor quality of the local Justices of the Peace in London and the absence of an adequate police force became a matter of concern towards the end of the 18th century. This led to seven public offices with paid magistrates being set up in 1792 and until 1839 they were in charge of the police as well as hearing cases in court. Outside London the first appointment of a paid magistrate was in Manchester in 1813. In 1835 the Municipal Corporations Act gave a general power for boroughs to request the appointment of a paid magistrate. At the beginning a paid magistrate did not have to have any particular qualifications, but from 1839 they could only be appointed from barristers. Solicitors did not become eligible to be appointed until 1949.

17.3 Qualifications

17.3.1 Lay magistrates

As already stated, lay magistrates do not have to have any qualifications in law. There are, however, some requirements as to their character, in that they must be suitable in character, integrity and understanding for the work they have to perform. In 1998, the Lord Chancellor set out six key qualities which candidates should have. These are:

- good character
- understanding and communication
- social awareness
- maturity and sound temperament
- sound judgement
- commitment and reliability.

They must have certain 'judicial' qualities – it is particularly important that they are able to assimilate factual information and make a reasoned decision upon it. They must also be able to take account of the reasoning of others and work as a team.

Apart from this, there are formal requirements as to age and residence: lay magistrates must be aged between 18 and 65 on appointment. It is rare that a person under 27 will be considered as it is felt they will not have enough experience.

However, with the age for appointment being reduced to 18 in 2003 there is an increased likelihood that young magistrates will be appointed if they are suitable. In 2004 there were at least two

appointments of young magistrates. These were of one aged 21 in Shropshire and another aged 23 in West Yorkshire. Although there have been appointments of some young magistrates, only 4 per cent of magistrates are under the age of 40.

Before 1906 there was a property qualification which meant that magistrates had to be home owners or tenants of property above a certain value. Also before 1919 the Bench was an all-male affair with women becoming eligible for appointment only in that year.

17.3.2 Area

Up to 2003 it was necessary for lay magistrates to live within 15 miles of the commission area for the court which they sat in. In 2003 the Courts Act abolished commission areas. Instead there is now one commission area for the whole of England and Wales. However, the country is divided into local justice areas. These areas are specified by the Lord Chancellor and lay magistrates are expected to live or work within or near to the local justice area to which they are allocated.

17.3.3 Commitment

The other requirement is that lay magistrates are prepared to commit themselves to sitting at least 26 half days each year. This is quite an onerous commitment and does prevent some people from applying to be a magistrate.

17.3.4 Restrictions on appointment

Some people are not eligible to be appointed. These include people with serious criminal convictions, though a conviction for a minor motoring offence will not automatically disqualify a candidate. Others who are disqualified include undischarged bankrupts, members of the forces and those whose work is incompatible with sitting as a magistrate, such as police officers and traffic wardens. Relatives of those working in the local criminal justice system are not likely to be appointed as it would not appear 'just' if, for example, the wife of a local police officer were to sit to decide cases. In addition people whose hearing is impaired or who by reason of infirmity cannot carry out all the duties of a Justice of the Peace cannot be appointed. Close relatives will not be appointed to the same Bench.

ACTIVITY

1. Put the list of six key qualities in 17.3.1 into order, with the one that you think is most important first and the least important last.
2. Compare your list with those of two other people.
3. Explain what other qualities you think magistrates need.

17.3.5 District Judges

These were previously known as stipendiary magistrates. They are only appointed to courts in London or other big cities such as Birmingham, Liverpool and Manchester. They must have a five-year qualification. This means they must be qualified as either a barrister or a solicitor and have gained experience in the law or be a Deputy District Judge. Before becoming a District Judge they will usually sit part-time as a Deputy District Judge to gain experience, and to establish their suitability for full-time appointment.

Fellows of the Institute of Legal Executives can now be appointed as Deputy District Judges, so the pool of potential candidates for District Judges has been widened.

17.4 Appointment

About 1,500 new lay magistrates are appointed each year. The appointments are made by the Lord Chancellor. In order to decide who to appoint, the Lord Chancellor relies on recommendations made to him by the Local Advisory Committees and this method of appointment is much criticised.

17.4.1 Local Advisory Committees

The membership of the committees used to be secret but since 1993 all names must be published. The members tend to be current or former Justices of the Peace and often the Lord Lieutenant of the county is the chairman of the committee. About half the members have to retire in rotation every three years. The committees should have a maximum of 12 members and these should include a mixture of magistrates and non-magistrates.

To try and encourage as wide a range of potential candidates as possible committees have advertised for individuals to put themselves forward, with advertisements being placed in local papers or newspapers aimed at particular ethnic groups, and even on buses! For example, in Leeds, radio adverts have been used and people encouraged to come to open evenings at their local Magistrates' Court in order to get as wide a spectrum of potential candidates as possible.

The intention is to create a panel that is representative of all aspects of society. To achieve this magistrates are matched against a mix of occupational, industrial and social groupings as shown the last census.

17.4.2 Interview process

There is usually a two-stage interview process. At the first interview the panel tries to find out more about the candidate's personal attributes, in particular looking to see if they have the six key qualities required. The interview panel will also explore the candidate's attitudes on various criminal justice issues such as youth crime or drink driving. The second interview is aimed at testing candidates' potential judicial aptitude and this is done by a discussion of at least two case studies which are typical of those heard regularly in Magistrates' Courts. The discussion might, for example, focus on the type of sentence which should be imposed on specific case facts.

The advisory committees will interview candidates and then submit names of those they think are suitable to the Lord Chancellor. He will then appoint new magistrates from this list. Once appointed, magistrates may continue to sit until the age of 70.

17.5 Composition of the Bench today

The traditional image of lay justices is that they are 'middle class, middle-aged and middle minded'. This image is to a certain extent true. Most magistrates are over 50. Magistrates under the age of 40 are still rare, making up only 4 per cent of the magistracy. The majority are supporters of the Conservative party; this is so even in areas where there is a high Labour vote. A report, *The Judiciary in the Magistrates' Courts* (2002), which had been commissioned jointly by the Home Office and the Lord Chancellor's Department found that lay magistrates:

- were drawn overwhelmingly from professional and managerial ranks; and
- 40 per cent of them were retired from full-time employment.

However, in other respects the Bench is well balanced: in 2012 just over 50 per cent of magistrates were women as against 12 per cent of higher level judges. Also, ethnic minorities were reasonably well represented in the magistracy. Eight per cent of magistrates are from ethnic minorities. This compares very favourably to the professional judiciary where only 4 per cent are from ethnic minority backgrounds.

The relatively high level of ethnic minority magistrates is largely a result of campaigns to attract a wider range of candidates. There have been adverts encouraging people to apply placed in some 36 different newspapers and magazines. Adverts appeared in national newspapers and also in TV guides and women's magazines. In an effort to encourage those from ethnic minorities to apply, adverts also appeared in such publications as the *Caribbean Times*, the *Asian Times* and *Muslim News*. This led to an increase in the number of ethnic minority appointments.

The Lord Chancellor has encouraged disabled people to apply to become magistrates. In 1998 the first blind lay magistrates were appointed. Statistics in 2012 showed that about 5 per cent of magistrates were classed as disabled. The magistracy is much more diverse than it used to be.

Internet research www

Look on the Internet for current statistics for gender, age, ethnic background and disability. This can be found on **www. judiciary.gov.uk**. Search for 'Magistrates in post'.

Find the figures for your area.

17.6 Magistrates' duties

Magistrates have a very wide workload which is mainly connected to criminal cases, although they also deal with some civil matters, especially family cases. They try 97 per cent of all criminal cases and deal with preliminary hearings in the remaining 3 per cent of criminal cases. This will involve Early Administrative Hearings, remand hearings, bail applications and committal proceedings. They also deal with civil matters which include the enforcing of debts owed to the utilities (gas, electric and water), non-payment of the council tax and non-payment of television licenses. In addition they hear appeals from the refusal of a local authority to grant licences for the sale of alcohol and licences for betting and gaming establishments.

Youth Court

Specially nominated and trained justices form the Youth Court panel to hear criminal charges against young offenders aged 10–17 years old. These panels must usually include at least one man and one woman. There is also a special panel for the Family Court to hear family cases including orders for protection against violence, affiliation cases, adoption orders and proceedings under the Children Act 1989. This court will become part of the new Family Court which is to be set up under the Crime and Courts Bill 2012.

Appeals

Lay magistrates also sit at the Crown Court to hear appeals from the Magistrates' Court. In these cases the lay justices form a panel with a qualified judge.

17.7 Training of lay magistrates

The training of lay magistrates is supervised by the Magistrates' Committee of the Judicial Studies Board. This Committee has drawn up a syllabus of the topics which lay magistrates should cover in their training. However, because of the large numbers of lay magistrates, the actual training is carried out in local areas, sometimes through the clerk of the court, sometimes through weekend courses organised by universities, with magistrates from the region attending.

Since 1998 magistrates' training has been monitored more closely. There were criticisms prior to then that, although magistrates were required to attend a certain number of hours' training, there was no assessment of how much they had understood. In 1998 the Magistrates New Training Initiative was introduced (MNTI 1). In 2004 this was refined by the Magistrates National Training Initiative (MNTI 2).

The framework of training is divided into four areas of competence, the first three of which are relevant to all lay magistrates. The fourth competence is for chairmen of the Bench. The four areas of competence are:

1. Managing yourself – this focuses on some of the basic aspects of self-management in relation to preparing for court, conduct in court and ongoing learning.
2. Working as a member of a team – this focuses on the team aspect of decision-making in the Magistrates' Court.
3. Making judicial decisions – this focuses on impartial and structured decision-making.
4. Managing judicial decision-making – this is for the chairman's role and focuses on working with the legal adviser, managing the court and ensuring effective, impartial decision-making.

For delivering training there are Bench Training and Developmental Committees (BTDCs) and s 19(3) of the Courts Act 2003 sets out a statutory obligation on the Lord Chancellor to provide training and training materials.

17.7.1 Training of new magistrates

There is a syllabus for new magistrates which is divided into three parts. These are:

1. **Initial introductory training**
   This covers such matters as understanding the organisation of the Bench and the administration of the court and the roles and responsibilities of those involved in the Magistrates' Court.
2. **Core training**
   This provides the new magistrate with the opportunity to acquire and develop the key skills, knowledge and understanding required of a competent magistrate.
3. **Activities**
   These will involve observations of court sittings and visits to establishments such as a prison or a probation office.

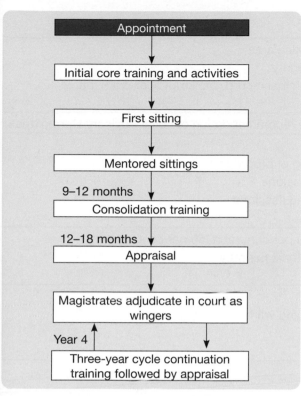

Figure 17.1 *New magistrates' training and appraisal pathway (taken from MNTI 2 handbook issued by the Judicial Studies Board)*

The training programme for new magistrates should normally follow the pattern set out in Figure 17.1.

17.7.2 Mentors

Each new magistrate keeps a Personal Development Log of their progress and has a mentor (an experienced magistrate) to assist them. The initial introductory training is covered before the new magistrate starts sitting in court. They will also take part in a structured courtroom observation of cases on at least three occasions. These should be arranged so that they see different aspects of the work and should include preliminary decisions such as bail, a short summary trial and sentencing.

17.7.3 Training sessions

These are organised and carried out at local level within the 42 court areas. Much of the training is delivered by justices' clerks. The Judicial Studies Board intends that most training should still be delivered locally. However, the Board takes into account the need to collaborate regionally and nationally where appropriate. In particular, the training of Youth and Family Panel chairmen will be delivered nationally for areas which do not have enough such chairmen requiring training to run an effective course locally.

17.7.4 Appraisal

During the first two years of the new magistrate sitting in court, between 8 and eleven of the sessions will be mentored. In the same period the magistrate is also expected to attend about seven training sessions. After two years, or whenever it is felt that the magistrate is ready, there will be an appraisal of the magistrate to check if they have acquired the competencies.

Any magistrate who cannot show that they have achieved the competencies will be given extra training. If they still cannot achieve the competencies, then the matter is referred to the Local Advisory Committee, who may recommend to the Lord Chancellor that the magistrate is removed from sitting.

This new scheme involves practical training 'on the job'. It also answers the criticisms of the old system where there was no check made on whether the magistrate had actually benefited from the training session they attended.

Those magistrates who chair the Bench are also appraised for this role, so that the quality of the chairing in court is improving.

17.8 Retirement and removal

The retirement age is 70, but when magistrates become 70 they do not officially retire – instead

Key Facts

Qualifications	Live or work near local justice area Need common sense, integrity Disqualified for serious criminal record, bankruptcy or work that is incompatible
Appointment	By Lord Chancellor on the recommendation of Local Advisory Committees
Training	Four basic competencies: Personal Development Log of progress Mentors and mentored sessions Attend about seven training sessions Appraisal
Composition of Bench	26,000 lay magistrates, 50 per cent men, 50 per cent women Over 7 per cent from an ethnic minority 5 per cent disabled
Work	Summary trials Ancillary matters, e.g. issuing warrants, bail applications Youth Court Family Court

Figure 17.2 *Key facts chart on lay magistrates*

their names are placed on the Supplemental List. This means that they can no longer sit in the Magistrates' Court. However, they can continue to carry out some administrative functions mainly connected with signing documents. Lay magistrates who move from the commission area to which they were appointed cannot continue as magistrates in that area. If they wish to continue as magistrates their names will be placed on the Supplemental List until there is a vacancy in their new area. Lay magistrates may, of course, resign from office at any time and many will resign before reaching 70.

17.8.1 Removal

Section 11 of the Courts Act 2003 gives the Lord Chancellor the power to remove a lay justice for the following reasons:

- on the ground of incapacity or misbehaviour
- on the ground of a persistent failure to meet such standards of competence as are

prescribed by a direction given by the Lord Chancellor; or
- if the Lord Chancellor is satisfied that the lay justice is declining or neglecting to take a proper part in the exercise of his functions as a Justice of the Peace.

Up to now removal for misbehaviour usually occurs when a magistrate is convicted of a criminal offence. There are about ten such removals each year. However, on occasions in the past there have been removals for such matters as taking part in a CND march or transvestite behaviour. There was considerable criticism of the Lord Chancellor's use of his power of removal in such circumstances and it is unlikely that such behaviour today would lead to removal from the Bench.

17.9 The magistrates' clerk

Every Bench is assisted by a clerk. These are now also referred to as legal advisers. The senior clerk in each court has to be qualified as a barrister or solicitor for at least five years. The clerk's duty is to guide the magistrates on questions of law, practice and procedure. This is set out in s 28(3) of the Justices of the Peace Act 1979, which says:

'It is hereby declared that the functions of a justices' clerk include the giving to the justices …of advice about law, practice or procedure on questions arising in connection with the discharge of their functions.'

The clerk is not meant to assist in the decision-making and should not normally retire with the magistrates when they go to make their decision. In *R v Eccles Justices, ex parte Farrelly* (1992) the Queen's Bench Divisional Court quashed convictions because the clerk had apparently participated in the decision-making process.

Clerks deal with routine administrative matters and in May 1993 were given increased powers so that they can now issue warrants for arrest, extend police bail, and adjourn criminal proceedings. The Crime and Disorder Act 1998 also gives clerks the powers to deal with Early Administrative Hearings.

17.10 Advantages of lay magistrates

17.10.1 Cross-section of society

Lay magistrates provide a wider cross-section on the Bench than would be possible with the use of professional judges. This is particularly true of women, with 50 per cent of magistrates being women compared with 22 per cent of judiciary overall. Also, ethnic minorities are reasonably well represented in the magistracy.

Lay magistrates are more representative than District Judges in the Magistrates' Courts. In 2000 a report, *The Judiciary in the Magistrates' Courts*,

pointed out that in comparison to lay magistrates, District Judges were at that time:

- younger; but
- mostly white and male.

In fact, statistics for 2012 showed that nearly 30 per cent of District Judges were female. Only 4 per cent of District Judges were from an ethnic minority, but the figure was much higher for Deputy District Judges (6.4 per cent). So the composition of District Judges is also gradually becoming more diverse.

17.10.2 Local knowledge

Lay magistrates used to have to live within 15 miles of the area covered by the commission, in order that they would have local knowledge of particular problems in the area. Under the Courts Act 2003 there is no longer a formal requirement that they should live in or near the area in which they sit as a magistrate, although it is intended that normally magistrates will continue to sit in the local justice area in which they reside. However, if there is a good reason to do otherwise, for example, where it is easier for the magistrate to sit in the area where he or she works, then this is allowed.

Even though lay magistrates live or work in the relevant justice area, it is sometimes argued that they do not have any real knowledge of the problems in the poorer areas. This is because most magistrates come from the professional and managerial classes and will live in the better areas. However, their main value is that they will have more awareness of local events, local patterns of crime and local opinions than a professional judge from another area.

Another problem is that during the last ten years, some 150 Magistrates' Courts have been closed. This causes problems of access and attendance as in some areas people have long journeys to their 'local' court. It also means that the advantage of lay magistrates having local knowledge is being lost.

17.10.3 Cost

The use of unpaid lay magistrates is cheap. The report *The Judiciary in the Magistrates' Courts* (2000) found that at that time the cost of using lay magistrates was £52.10 per hour. As against this the cost of using District Judges in the Magistrates' Courts was £61.78 an hour. When this is multiplied by the number of hours' work carried out by lay magistrates in the course of the year, it is obvious that the cost of replacing them with professional judges would be several millions of pounds. In addition, there would also be the problem of recruiting sufficient qualified lawyers.

The cost of a trial in the Magistrates' Court is also much cheaper than a trial in the Crown Court. This is partly because cases in the Crown Court are more complex and therefore likely to take longer, but even so it is clear that the cost both to the government and to defendants who pay for their own lawyer is much higher.

17.10.4 Legal adviser

Since 1999 all newly appointed magistrates' clerks have to be legally qualified. In addition, existing clerks under the age of 40 in 1999 have to qualify within ten years. This brings a higher level of legal skill to the Magistrates' Court. The availability of a legal adviser gives the magistrates access to any necessary legal advice on points that may arise in any case. This overcomes any criticism of the fact that lay magistrates are not themselves legally qualified. In addition, the training of lay magistrates is improving with MNTI 1 and MNTI 2 and the strengthened role of the Judicial Studies Board in their training.

17.10.5 Few appeals

Comparatively few defendants appeal against the magistrates' decisions, and many of the appeals that are made are against sentence, not against the finding of guilt. In most years there are between 5,000 and 6,000 appeals against conviction. Fewer than half of these appeals are successful. There are also about 6,000 appeals each year against the sentence imposed by the magistrates. Again, fewer than half of these are successful. This is from a total workload of about two million defendants dealt with in the Magistrates' Courts. There are also very few instances where an error of law is made. In 2011 there were only 79 appeals by way of case stated to the Queen's Bench Divisional Court. Fewer than half of these appeals were allowed. From this it can be argued that despite the amateur status of lay magistrates they do a remarkably good job.

17.11 Disadvantages of lay magistrates

17.11.1 Middle-aged, middle class

Lay magistrates are often perceived as being middle-aged and middle class. The report *The Judiciary in the Magistrates' Courts* (2000) showed that this was largely true. It found that 40 per cent of lay magistrates were retired and also that they were overwhelmingly from a professional or managerial background. However, as already discussed at section 17.10.1, lay magistrates are from a much wider range of backgrounds than professional judges.

17.11.2 Prosecution bias

It is often said that lay magistrates tend to be prosecution biased, believing the police too readily. One fact supporting this theory is that there is a lower acquittal rate in Magistrates' Courts than in the Crown Court. There is also the fact that they will see the same Crown Prosecution Service prosecutor or designated case worker frequently and this could affect their judgement. However, part of their training is aimed at eliminating this type of bias.

Key Facts

Advantages	Disadvantages
Cross-section of local people Good gender balance Improving ethnic balance Much better cross-section than District Judges	Not a true cross-section 50 per cent are retired people Majority are from professional or managerial background Older than District Judges
Live (or work) locally and so know the area and its problems	Unlikely to live in the poorer areas and so do not truly know the area's problems
Cheaper than using professional judges as they are only paid expenses Cheaper than sending cases to the Crown Court	
Improved training through MNTI 2 and the increased role of Judicial Studies Board	There are inconsistencies in sentencing and decisions on bail
Have legal adviser for points of law	Not legally qualified
Very few appeals	

Figure 17.3 *Key facts chart on advantages and disadvantages of using lay magistrates in the legal system*

17.11.3 Inconsistency in sentencing

Magistrates in different areas often pass very different sentences for what appear to be similar offences. The government's White Paper, *Justice for All*, set out differences found in the Criminal Statistics for 2001 when it gave the following examples:

- For burglary of dwellings, 20 per cent of offenders in Teesside are sentenced to immediate custody, compared with 41 per cent of offenders in Birmingham; 38 per cent of burglars at Cardiff Magistrates' Court receive community sentences, compared with 66 per cent in Leicester.
- For driving while disqualified, the percentage of offenders sentenced to custody ranged from 21 per cent in Neath Port Talbot (South Wales) to 77 per cent in Mid North Essex.
- For receiving stolen goods, 3.5 per cent of offenders sentenced at Reading Magistrates'

Court received custodial sentences compared with 48 per cent in Greenwich and Woolwich (south London) and 39 per cent at Camberwell Green (south London).

Despite the training scheme for lay magistrates, figures for 2010 still show wide-ranging discrepancies in sentencing. Bristol magistrates imposed custodial sentences on 11.1 per cent of defendants whilst Dinefwr magistrates imposed a custodial sentence on only 0.1 per cent of defendants.

Bristol also imposed the highest percentage of community sentences at 32.2 per cent, whilst in Dinefwr it was 6.6 per cent. These figures do not take into account what types of offences were involved, but the figures for Bristol seem to be excessively high. This is so even when compared to other city areas with a similar number of offenders, such as Coventry where 6.8 per cent of offenders were given a custodial sentence and 14.4 per cent a community sentence.

17.11.4 Reliance on the clerk

The lack of legal knowledge of the lay justices should be offset by the fact that a legally qualified clerk is available to give advice. However, this will not prevent inconsistencies in sentencing since the clerk is not allowed to help the magistrates decide on a sentence. In some courts it is felt that the magistrates rely too heavily on their clerks.

EXAMINATION QUESTIONS

Study the tables below and answer the questions based on them.

Region	Gender			Age			
	Total	Male	Female	Under 40	40–49	50–59	60+
Wales	2,014	1,041	973	72	258	643	1,041
England and Wales	29,270	14,472	14,798	1,165	4,287	9,451	14,367
Percentage		49.4%	50.6%	4.0%	14.6%	32.3%	49.1%

Region	Ethnicity							Disabled	
	White	Mixed	Black	Asian	Chinese	Other	Unknown	Yes	No
Wales	1,954	8	34	11		6		106	1,908
England and Wales	27,050	140	1,135	742	49	146	8	1,485	27,785
Percentage	92.4%	0.5%	3.9%	2.5%	0.2%	0.5%	0.0%	5.1%	94.9%

Source: Judicial Statistics (2012) Extract

Magistrates in post (2009)

1. (a) Explain the appointment process of lay magistrates. [14 marks]
   (b) Evaluate the advantages and disadvantages of the lay magistracy in the administration of justice in England and Wales. [11 marks]

   LA2, Summer 2011, WJEC

2. (a) Describe both the selection and the training of lay magistrates. [18 marks]

   (b) Discuss the disadvantages of using lay magistrates to deal with criminal cases. [12 marks]

   G151 June 2011, OCR

EXTENSION ESSAY

Critically discuss whether non-lawyers should have such a major role in the legal system in the Magistrates' Courts.

CHAPTER 18

JURIES

18.1 History of the jury system

Juries have been used in the legal system for over 1,000 years. There is evidence that they were used even before the Norman Conquest. However, in 1215 when trial by ordeal was condemned by the Church and (in the same year) the Magna Carta included the recognition of a person's right to trial by 'the lawful judgment of his peers', juries became the usual method of trying criminal cases. Originally they were used for providing local knowledge and information, and acted more as witnesses than decision-makers. By the middle of the fifteenth century, juries had become independent assessors and assumed their modern role as deciders of fact.

18.1.1 Independence of the jury

The independence of the jury became even more firmly established following *Bushell's Case* (1670). In that case several jurors refused to convict Quaker activists of unlawful assembly. The trial judge would not accept the not guilty verdict, and ordered the jurors to resume their deliberations without food or drink. When the jurors persisted in their refusal to convict, the court fined them and committed them to prison until the fines were paid. On appeal, the Court of Common Pleas ordered the release of the jurors, holding that jurors could not be punished for their verdict. This established that the jury were the sole arbiters of fact and the judge could not challenge their decision. A more modern-day example demonstrating that judges must respect the independence of the jury is *R v McKenna* (1960). In that case the judge at the trial had threatened

the jury that if they did not return a verdict within another ten minutes they would be locked up all night. The jury then returned a verdict of guilty, but the defendant's conviction was quashed on appeal because of the judge's interference.

18.2 Modern-day use of the jury

Only a small percentage of cases is tried by jury today. However, juries are used in the following courts:

- Crown Court for criminal trials on indictment
- High Court, Queen's Bench Division (but only for certain types of cases)
- County Court (for similar cases to the Queen's Bench Division)
- Coroners' Courts (in some cases).

18.2.1 Juries in criminal cases

The most important use of juries today is in the Crown Court where they decide whether the defendant is guilty or not guilty. Jury trials, however, account for fewer than one per cent of all criminal trials. This is because 97 per cent of cases are dealt with in the Magistrates' Court and of the cases that go to the Crown Court, about two out of every three defendants will plead guilty. Also some of the cases at the Crown Court, in which the defendant has entered a not guilty plea, will not go before a jury as the case will be discharged by judge without any trial. This occurs where the Crown Prosecution Service withdraws the charges, possibly because a witness refuses to give evidence. A jury in the Crown Court has 12 members.

Key Facts

Court	Type of case	Role	Number on jury
Crown Court	Serious criminal cases: e.g. murder, manslaughter, rape	Decide verdict Guilty or not guilty	12
High Court	Defamation False imprisonment Malicious prosecution Any case alleging fraud	Decide liability If find for the claimant also decide amount of damages	12
County Court	Defamation False imprisonment Malicious prosecution Any case alleging fraud	Decide liability If find for the claimant also decide amount of damages	8
Coroners' Court	Deaths: • In custody • As the result of an act or omission by a police officer • Where the death was caused by a notifiable accident, poisoning or disease	Decide cause of death	7–11

Figure 18.1 *Key facts chart on the use of juries*

18.2.2 Juries in civil cases

Juries in civil cases are now used only in very limited circumstances, but where they are used they have a dual role. They decide whether the claimant has proved his case or not, then, if they decide that the claimant has won the case, the jury also go on to decide the amount of damages that the defendant should pay to the claimant.

Up to 1854 all common law actions were tried by jury, but from 1854 the parties could agree not to use a jury and gradually their use declined. Then in 1933 the Administration of Justice Act limited the right to use a jury, so that juries could not be used in disputes over breach of contract. The present rules for when juries may be used in civil cases are set out in s 69 of the Senior Courts Act 1981 for High Court cases, and s 66 of the County Courts Act 1984 for cases in that court. These Acts state that parties have the right to jury trial only in the following types of case:

● Defamation, i.e. cases of libel and slander (this is the most frequent use of juries)

● False imprisonment
● Malicious prosecution
● Fraud.

All these cases involve character or reputation and it is for this reason that jury trial has been retained. Even for these cases a jury trial can be refused by the judge if the case involves complicated documents or accounts or scientific evidence and is therefore thought to be unsuitable for jury trial.

Use of juries in personal injury cases

In other civil cases in the Queen's Bench Division of the High Court the parties can apply to a judge for trial by jury, but it is very rare for such a request to be granted. This follows the case of *Ward v James* (1966) where the plaintiff was claiming for injuries caused in a road crash. In this case the Court of Appeal laid down guidelines for personal injury cases. These were:

● Personal injury cases should normally be tried by a judge sitting alone, because such cases involve assessing compensatory damages which have to have regard to the conventional scales of damages.

- There have to be exceptional circumstances before the court will allow a jury to be used in such a case.

The decision in *Ward v James* effectively stopped the use of juries for personal injury cases. The following cases show how the courts have proved very reluctant to let juries be used. In *Singh v London Underground* (1990) a request for a jury to try a personal injury case arising from the King's Cross Underground fire was refused. It was held that the case was unsuitable for jury trial because it involved such wide issues and technical points.

The case of *H v Ministry of Defence* (1991) further reinforced the rule in *Ward v James*; the defendant was a soldier who had received negligent medical treatment necessitating the amputation of part of his penis. He applied for jury trial, but it was held that jury trial for a personal injury claim would only be allowed in very exceptional circumstances and this case was not such a one. The court said that an example of when jury trial might be appropriate was where the injuries resulted from someone deliberately abusing their authority and there might well be a claim for exemplary damages.

Fewer than ten cases are heard by a jury each year, and almost all of these are for defamation.

Trial by jury in the County Court has become very rare, but since 1991 with the changes in the jurisdiction (defamation actions can be transferred for trial to the County Court) there are occasionally cases in which a jury is used. Where a jury is used in the High Court there will be 12 members; in the County Court a jury consists of eight.

18.2.3 Coroners' Courts

In these courts a jury of between seven and 11 members may be used to enquire into deaths. The Coroners and Justice Act 2009 has provision for changes to the use of juries in Coroners' Courts. Under this a jury will be used only if:

(a) there is reason to suspect that the deceased died while in custody and that either:
  (i) the death was a violent or unnatural one, or
  (ii) the cause of death is unknown
(b) the death resulted from an act or omission of a police officer
(c) the death was caused by a notifiable accident, poisoning or disease.

18.3 Jury qualifications

18.3.1 Basic qualifications

The qualifications for jury service were revised in 1972 following the Morris Committee Report on jury service. Before this date there was a property qualification – in order to be a juror it was necessary to be the owner or tenant of a dwelling. This restriction meant that women and young people who were less likely to own or rent property were prevented from serving on a jury. The Morris Committee thought that being a juror should be the counterpart of being a citizen. As a result, the qualifications for jury service were widened in the Criminal Justice Act 1972 and based on the right to vote. The present qualifications are set out in the Juries Act 1974 (as amended) so that to qualify for jury service a person must be:

- aged between 18 and 70
- registered as a parliamentary or local government elector
- ordinarily resident in the United Kingdom, the Channel Islands or the Isle of Man for at least five years since their thirteenth birthday and must not be:
  - a mentally disordered person, or
  - disqualified from jury service.

18.3.2 Disqualification

Some criminal convictions will disqualify a person from jury service. The type of sentence and the length of a prison sentence decide whether the person is disqualified and the period for which that disqualification lasts. Disqualified permanently from jury service are those who at any time have been sentenced to:

- imprisonment for life, detention for life or custody for life
- detention during Her Majesty's Pleasure or during the Pleasure of the Secretary of State
- to imprisonment for public protection or detention for public protection
- an extended sentence
- a term of imprisonment of five years or more or a term of detention of five years or more.

Those in the following categories are disqualified for ten years:

- at any time in the last ten years served a sentence of imprisonment
- at any time in the last ten years had a suspended sentence passed on them
- at any time in the last ten years had a community order or other community sentence passed on them.

In addition anyone who is currently on bail in criminal proceedings is disqualified from sitting as a juror.

If a disqualified person fails to disclose that fact and turns up for jury service, they may be fined up to £5,000.

18.3.3 Mentally disordered persons

A mentally disordered person is defined in the Criminal Justice Act 2003 as:

1. A person who suffers or has suffered from mental illness, psychopathic disorder, mental handicap or severe mental handicap and on account of that condition either:
   (a) is resident in a hospital or similar institution; or
   (b) regularly attends for treatment by a medical practitioner.

2. A person for the time being under guardianship under s 7 of the Mental Health Act 1983.
3. A person who, under Part 7 of that Act, has been determined by a judge to be incapable of administering his property and affairs.

There are criticisms that this definition does not distinguish between those receiving treatment for mild depression from their GP and those sectioned under the Mental Health Act 1983. The definition of a mentally ill person for the purposes of the Juries Act 1974 is likely to be amended in the future in answer to these criticisms.

18.3.4 Lack of capacity

A judge at the court may discharge a person from being a juror for lack of capacity to cope with the trial. This could be because the person does not understand English adequately or because of some disability which makes them unsuitable as a juror. This includes the blind, who would be unable to see plans and photographs produced in evidence. Section 9B(2) of the Juries Act 1974 (which was added into the Act by the Criminal Justice and Public Order Act 1994 s 41) makes it clear that the mere fact of a disability does not prevent someone from acting as a juror. The judge can discharge the juror only if he is satisfied that the disability means that that juror is not capable of acting effectively as a juror.

Deaf jurors

In June 1995 a deaf man was prevented from sitting on a jury at the Old Bailey despite wishing to serve and bringing with him a sign language interpreter. The judge pointed out that that would mean an extra person in the jury room and this was not allowed by law. He also said that the way in which witnesses gave evidence and the tone of their voice were important: 'a deaf juror may not be able to pick up these nuances and to properly judge their credibility'.

In November 1999 another deaf man challenged the ban on him sitting as a juror. The judge in this case felt that there was no practical reason why he should not sit, but the law only allowed the 12 jury members to be present in the jury room. It did not allow a 13th person – a sign-language interpreter – to be present. This made it impossible for the deaf man to be a juror.

18.3.5 The right to be excused from jury service

Prior to April 2004, people in certain essential occupations, such as doctors and pharmacists, had a right to be excused jury service if they did not want to do it. The Criminal Justice Act 2003 abolished this category. This means that doctors and other medical staff are no longer able to refuse to do jury service, though they can apply for a discretionary excusal.

Members of the forces

Full-time serving members of the forces may be excused from jury service if their commanding officer certifies that their absence from duty (because of jury service) would be prejudicial to the efficiency of the service.

18.3.6 Discretionary excusals

Anyone who has problems which make it very difficult for them to do their jury service may ask to be excused or for their period of service to be put back to a later date. The court has a discretion to grant such an excusal but will only do so if there is a sufficiently good reason. Such reasons include being too ill to attend court or suffering from a disability that makes it impossible for the person to sit as a juror, or being a mother with a small baby. Other reasons could include business appointments that cannot be undertaken by anyone else, examinations or holidays that have been booked.

In these situations the court is most likely to defer jury service to a more convenient date, rather than excuse the person completely. This is stated in the current guidance for summoning officers which is aimed at preventing the high number of discretionary excusals. The guidance states that:

'The normal expectation is that everyone summoned for jury service will serve at the time for which they are summoned. It is recognised that there will be occasions where it is not reasonable for a person summoned to serve at the time for which they are summoned. In such circumstances the summoning officer should use his/her discretion to defer the individual to a time more appropriate. Only in extreme circumstances, should a person be excused from jury service.'

If a person is not excused from jury service they must attend on the date set or they may be fined up to £1,000 for non-attendance.

18.3.7 Lawyers and police on juries

There used to be a category of people who were ineligible for jury service. This included judges and others who had been involved in the administration of justice within the previous ten years. This category was also abolished by the Criminal Justice Act 2003. This means that judges, lawyers, police, etc. are eligible to serve on juries. Many people feel that this could lead to bias or to a legally well-qualified juror influencing the rest of the jury.

In *R v Abdroikof*, *R v Green* and *R v Williamson* (2007) the House of Lords considered appeals where a police officer or prosecutor had been one of the jury members. They held that the fact that one of the members of the jury was a police officer did not of itself make a trial unfair. However, a majority of three of the five judges held that in the situation where a police officer on the jury had worked in the same station as a police officer giving evidence for the prosecution in the trial, then there was the risk of bias. The test to be applied in such cases was: 'whether the fair-minded and informed observer, having considered the facts, would conclude that there was a real possibility that the tribunal was biased'.

The House of Lords also quoted from the decision in *R v Sussex Justices, ex parte McCarthy* (1924) where the judge stated that justice must not only be done, but must be seen to be done.

The same three judges in a majority decision also held that the presence of a juror who was a local Crown Prosecutor in the Crown Prosecutor Service meant that justice was clearly not being seen to be done. Lord Bingham stated: 'It is, in my opinion, clear that justice is not seen to be done if one discharging the very important neutral role of juror is a full-time, salaried, long-serving employee of the prosecutor.'

In *Hanif v United Kingdom* (2012), the European Court of Human Rights ruled that having a police officer on the jury was a breach of Article 6(1) of the European Convention on Human Rights – the right to a fair trial. In this case, the police officer juror had immediately alerted the court to the fact that he knew one of the prosecution police witnesses. It was particularly important as the evidence of this witness was crucial to the case against the defendant. However, the trial judge had ruled that this did not matter.

The case continued with the police officer juror being the foreman of the jury and the defendant was convicted. The Court of Appeal, somewhat surprisingly, upheld the conviction. This ruling of the Court of Appeal appears to be contrary to the judgment of the House of Lords in *Abdroikof* as it would appear that a fair-minded person would conclude there was a real possible risk of bias.

Judges on jury service

In June 2004 (just two months after the rules on jury service changed) a judge from the Court of

---

ACTIVITY

Read the following article and answer the questions below.

Why too much legal experience can subvert jury trial

I doubt that many jurors without experience of court understand, before they sit on a jury, that they may well have to listen carefully to oral evidence for hours at a time, over a number of days – or weeks. And that then they are supposed to remember and analyse that evidence after they retire to consider their verdict.

Added to this mix is the new problem of lawyers being allowed to sit on juries. England is not the only country which does this – it is allowed in the United States, for example. But in the US, unlike in England, there is a wide right for peremptory (without having to give a reason) challenges to jurors. And, tellingly, it is standard practice to use those challenges to get rid of lawyers on their juries.

The evidence from the US of what happens when you let lawyers loose in the jury room appears to have been ignored in the rush to end middle-class opt-out on juries. It is not that other jurors will blindly follow the lead of any lawyer on their jury. But the reality is that lawyers have a different approach to assessing evidence. And they know how to argue persuasively for their point of view. It is what they do for a living.

The problem with this is not that it is more or less likely that a jury that includes a lawyer will reach the right decision. Lawyers are no more or less fallible than anyone else. The problem is that randomly assigning lawyers to juries may subvert the whole jury process. Instead of being tried by 12 of your peers, you might in effect end up being tried by one lawyer. It would be possible to devise a system of justice like this – it is called trial by judge alone – but it is not, in any meaningful sense, a jury trial.

Adapted from an Article by Robert Howe, QC, *The Times,* 3 December 2009

Questions

1. What is the role of a jury in a criminal case?
2. What problem does the writer identify in the system regarding evidence?
3. What Act allows lawyers to sit on juries in this country?
4. The article states that lawyers are allowed to sit on juries in the United States. What is different in the US system?
5. Why does the writer think it is not advisable to have a lawyer sitting on a jury?

Appeal, Lord Justice Dyson, was summoned to attend as a juror. This prompted the Lord Chief Justice, Lord Woolf, to issue observations to judges who are called for jury service. These point out that:

- A judge serves on a jury as part of his duty as a private citizen.
- Excusal from jury service will only be granted in extreme circumstances.
- Deferral of jury service to a later date should be sought where a judge has judicial commitments which make it particularly inconvenient for him to do jury service at the time he was called to do so.
- At court if a judge knows the presiding judge or other person in the case, he should raise this with the jury bailiff or a member of the court staff if he considers it could interfere with his responsibilities as a juror.
- It is a matter of discretion for an individual judge sitting as a juror as to whether he discloses the fact of his judicial office to the other members of the jury.

- Judges must follow the directions given to the jury by the trial judge on the law and should avoid the temptation to correct guidance which they believe to be inaccurate as this is outside their role as a juror.

The point about letting the court know when someone involved in the case is personally known to the juror is also relevant to practising lawyers who are called for jury service. It was noticeable that when a Queen's Counsel was summoned for jury service at the Central Criminal Court (the Old Bailey) in the summer of 2004, he was prevented from sitting in each case that he was called for, on the grounds that he knew one or more people involved in each trial.

ACTIVITY

Discuss whether you think the following people should sit on a jury:

1. A woman who was fined for shoplifting a month ago.
2. A man who was fined and disqualified from driving for taking cars without the consent of the owner.
3. A doctor who works in general practice.
4. A doctor who works in an accident and emergency unit of a busy city hospital.
5. A Circuit Judge who frequently tries cases in the Crown Court.

18.4 Selecting a jury

At each Crown Court there is an official who is responsible for summoning enough jurors to try the cases that will be heard in each two week period. This official will arrange for names to be selected at random from the electoral registers, for the area which the court covers. This is done through computer selection at a central office. It is necessary to summon more than 12 jurors as most courts have more than one courtroom and it will not be known how many of those summoned are disqualified – or will be excused. In fact, at the bigger courts up to 150 summons may be sent out each fortnight.

Those summoned must notify the court if there is any reason why they should not or cannot attend. All others are expected to attend for two weeks' jury service, though, of course, if the case they are trying goes on for more than two weeks they will have to stay until the trial is completed. Where it is known that a trial may be exceptionally long, such as a complicated fraud trial, potential jurors are asked if they will be able to serve for such a long period.

18.4.1 Vetting

Once the list of potential jurors is known, both the prosecution and the defence have the right to see that list. In some cases it may be decided that this pool of potential jurors should be 'vetted', i.e. checked for suitability. There are two types of vetting.

Routine police checks

Routine police checks are made on prospective jurors to eliminate those disqualified. In *R v Crown Court at Sheffield, ex parte Brownlow* (1980) the defendant was a police officer and the defence sought

Key Facts

Court	Crown Court
Qualifications	18–70 age Registered to vote Resident in UK for at least five years since age 13
Disqualified	Sentenced to five years' or more imprisonment – disqualified for life Served a prison sentence OR suspended sentence OR a community order – disqualified for 10 years On bail – disqualified while on bail
Excusals	Members of the armed forces Discretionary – ill, business commitments, or other 'good reason'
Selection	A central office selects names from the lists of electors Summons sent to these people Must attend unless disqualified or excused
Vetting	May be checked for criminal record – *R v Mason* (1980) In cases of national security may be subject to a wider check on background subject to Attorney-General's guidelines
Challenges	Individual juror may be challenged for cause, e.g. knows defendant Whole panel may be challenged for biased selection – but no right to a multiracial jury (*R v Ford* (1989)) Prosecution may 'stand by' any juror
Function	Decide verdict – guilty or not guilty Sole arbiters of fact but judge directs them on law
Verdict	Must try for a unanimous verdict BUT if cannot reach a unanimous verdict then a majority verdict can be accepted of 10–2 or 11–1

Figure 18.2 *Key facts chart on the use of juries in criminal cases*

permission to vet the jury panel for convictions. The judge gave permission but the Court of Appeal, while holding that it had no power to interfere, said that vetting was 'unconstitutional' and a 'serious invasion of privacy' and not sanctioned by the Juries Act 1974. However, in *R v Mason* (1980) where it was revealed that the Chief Constable for Northamptonshire had been allowing widespread use of unauthorised vetting of criminal records, the Court of Appeal approved of this type of vetting. Lawton LJ pointed out that, since it is a criminal offence to serve on a jury whilst disqualified, the police were only doing their normal duty of preventing crime by checking for criminal records. Furthermore, the court said that, if in the course of looking at criminal records convictions were revealed which did not disqualify, there was no reason why these should not be passed on to prosecuting counsel, so that this information could be used in deciding to stand by individual jurors (see section 18.4.3 for information on the right of stand by).

Juror's background

A wider check is made on a juror's background and political affiliations. This practice was brought to light by the 'ABC' trial in 1978 where two journalists and a soldier were charged with collecting secret information. It was discovered that the jury had been vetted for their loyalty. The trial was stopped and a new trial ordered before a fresh jury. Following these cases, the Attorney-General published guidelines in 1980 on when political vetting of jurors should take place. These guidelines were revised in 1988 in a Practice Note (Jury: Stand By: Jury Checks) (1988) and state that:

a) vetting should only be used in exceptional cases involving:
   - national security where part of the evidence is likely to be given *in camera*
   - terrorist cases
b) vetting can only be carried out with the Attorney-General's express permission.

18.4.2 Selection at court

The jurors are usually divided into groups of 15 and allocated to a court. At the start of a trial the court clerk will select 12 out of these 15 at random. If there are not enough jurors to hear all the cases scheduled for that day at the court, there is a special power to select anyone who is qualified to be a juror from people passing by in the streets or from local offices or businesses. This is called 'praying a talesman'. It is very unusual to use this power but it was used at Middlesex Crown Court in January 1992 when about half the jury panel failed to turn up after the New Year's holiday and there were not sufficient jurors to try the cases.

18.4.3 Challenging

Once the court clerk has selected the panel of 12 jurors, these jurors come into the jury box to be sworn in as jurors. At this point, before the jury is sworn in, both the prosecution and defence have certain rights to challenge one or more of the jurors. There are two challenges which can be made and, in addition, the prosecution has a special right of 'stand by'. These are:

- to the array
- for cause
- prosecution right to stand by jurors.

To the array

This right to challenge is given by s 5 of the Juries Act 1974 and it is a challenge to the whole jury on the basis that it has been chosen in an unrepresentative or biased way. This challenge was used successfully against the 'Romford' jury at the Old Bailey in 1993 when, out of a panel of 12 jurors, nine came from Romford, with two of them living within 20 doors of each other in the same street. In *R v Fraser* (1987) this method of challenging a jury was also used, as the defendant was of an ethnic minority background but all the jurors were white. The judge in that case agreed to empanel another jury. However, in *R v Ford* (1989) it was held that if the jury was chosen in a random manner then it could not be challenged simply because it was not multiracial.

For cause

This involves challenging the right of an individual juror to sit on the jury. To be successful the challenge must point out a valid reason why that juror should not serve on the jury. An obvious reason is that the juror is disqualified, but a challenge for cause can also be made if the juror knows or is related to a witness or defendant. If such people are not removed from the jury there is a risk that any subsequent conviction could be quashed. This occurred in *R v Wilson* and *R v Sprason* (1995) where the wife of a prison officer was summoned for jury service. She had asked to be excused attendance on that ground, but this request had not been granted. She served on the jury, which convicted the two defendants of robbery. Both defendants had been on remand at Exeter prison where her husband worked. The Court of Appeal said that justice must not only be done, it must be seen to be done and the presence of Mrs Roberts on the jury prevented that, so that the convictions had to be quashed.

Prosecution right to stand by jurors

This is a right that only the prosecution can exercise. It allows the juror who has been stood by to be put to the end of the list of potential jurors, so that they will not be used on the jury unless there are not enough other jurors. The prosecution does not have to give a reason for 'standing by', but the Attorney-General's guidelines issued in 1988 make it clear that this power should be used sparingly.

18.4.4 Criticisms of the selection of juries

Use of electoral register

The method of selecting jurors from the list of registered voters is open to criticism as it does not always give a representative sample of the population. It excludes some groups such as the homeless, who cannot register to vote. Also not everyone who is eligible registers to vote. This is especially true of the young and those who change address frequently.

Random selection

One of the debates has always been whether random selection produces juries which are reasonably representative of the local population. Studies done in the 1970s and 1980s found that juries in some areas were not truly representative in gender (fewer women), age (fewer young people) and race (under-representative of ethnic minorities).

However, a study, *Diversity and Fairness in the Jury System*, published in 2007 and looking at juries in 2003 and 2005, found that juries are now representative in gender, age and race. The only under-representation found by the study was of lower classes and unemployed.

Disqualified jurors

Although some checks are carried out, many disqualified people fail to disclose that they are disqualified and sit on juries. One survey of Inner London juries estimated that one in every 24 jurors was disqualified. In one instance at Snaresbrook Crown Court a man with 15 previous convictions sat as a juror in three cases and was the jury foreman in two of them. He later admitted that as far as he was concerned all defendants were not guilty unless they 'had been molesting kids'.

Excusals

If there are too many discretionary excusals it may lead to an unrepresentative jury. Home Office research in 1999 found that over one in every three jurors was excused from serving. The main reasons for excusal were medical conditions, looking after children or elderly relatives, and business commitments. This widespread use of the discretionary excusal used to prevent juries from being a true cross-section of the local population. Since the Criminal Justice Act 2003, the guidance on discretionary excusals should lead to more representative juries.

Prosecution's right of 'stand by'

The prosecution's right of stand by was kept even when the defence's peremptory challenge was withdrawn. This might be seen as giving the prosecution an advantage in 'rigging' the jury, particularly when combined with vetting. However, even when a jury has been vetted, it does not always give the prosecution an advantage. This was seen in *Ponting's Case*, where the defendant was charged with an offence against the Official Secrets Acts and the jury was vetted. Despite the vetting the jury returned a not guilty verdict (see section 18.6.2 for further comment on this case).

18.5 The jury's role in criminal cases

The jury is used only at the Crown Court for cases where the defendant pleads not guilty. This means that a jury is used in about 20,000 cases each year.

18.5.1 Split function

The trial is presided over by a judge and the functions split between the judge and jury. The judge decides points of law and the jury decides the facts. At the end of the prosecution case, the judge has the power to direct the jury to acquit the defendant if he decides that, in law, the prosecution's evidence has not made out a case against the defendant. This is called a directed acquittal and occurs in about 10 per cent of cases.

Where the trial continues, the judge will sum up the case at the end to the jury and direct them on any law involved. The jury retire to a private room and make the decision on the guilt or innocence of the accused in secret. Initially the jury must

try to come to a unanimous verdict, i.e. one on which they are all agreed. The judge must accept the jury verdict, even if he or she does not agree with it. This long-established principle goes back to *Bushell's Case* (1670). The jury do not give any reasons for their decision.

18.5.2 Majority verdicts

If, after at least two hours (longer where there are several defendants), the jury have not reached a verdict, the judge can call them back into the courtroom and direct them that he can now accept a majority verdict. Majority verdicts have been allowed since 1967. Where there is a full jury of 12, the verdict can be 10–2 or 11–1 either for guilty or for not guilty. If the jury has fallen below 12 for any reason (such as the death or illness of a juror during the trial), then only one can disagree with the verdict. That is, if there are 11 jurors, the verdict can be 10–1; if there are 10 jurors it can be 9–1. If there are only nine jurors the verdict must be unanimous. A jury cannot go below nine.

Majority verdicts were introduced because of the fear of jury 'nobbling', that is jurors being bribed or intimidated by associates of the defendant into voting for a not guilty verdict. When a jury had to be unanimous, only one member need be bribed to cause a 'stalemate' in which the jury were unable to reach a decision. It was also thought that the acquittal rates in jury trials were too high and majority decisions would result in more convictions.

Where the jury convict a defendant on a majority verdict, the foreman of the jury must announce the numbers both agreeing and disagreeing with the verdict in open court. This provision is contained in s 17(3) of the Juries Act 1974 and is aimed at making sure the jury have come to a legal majority, and not one, for example of eight to four, which is not allowed. However, in *R v Pigg* (1983), the Court of Appeal held that, provided the foreman announced the number who had agreed with the verdict, and that number was within the number allowed for a majority verdict, then the conviction was legal. It did not matter that the foreman had not also been asked how many disagreed with the verdict. About 20 per cent of convictions by juries each year are by majority verdict.

18.5.3 Secrecy

The jury discussion takes place in secret and there can be no inquiry into how the jury reached its verdict. This is because section 8 of the Contempt of Court Act 1981 makes disclosure of anything that happened in the jury room a contempt of court, which is a criminal offence. It is a contempt 'to obtain, disclose or solicit any particulars of statements made, opinions expressed, arguments advanced or votes cast by members of a jury in the course of their deliberations in any legal proceedings'. The section was brought in because newspapers were paying jurors large sums of money for 'their story'. This is obviously not desirable, but the total ban on finding out what happens in the jury room means that it is difficult to discover whether jurors have understood the evidence in complex cases.

18.6 Advantages of jury trial

18.6.1 Public confidence

On the face of it, asking 12 strangers who have no legal knowledge and without any training to decide what may be complex and technical points is an absurd practice. Yet the jury is considered one of the fundamentals of a democratic society. The right to be tried by one's peers is a bastion of liberty against the state and has been supported by eminent judges. For example, Lord Devlin said juries are 'the lamp that shows that freedom lives'. The tradition of trial by jury is very old and people seem to have confidence in the impartiality and fairness of a jury trial. This can be seen in the

objection to withdrawing the right to jury trial from cases of 'minor' theft.

18.6.2 Jury equity

Since juries are not legal experts, are not bound to follow the precedent of past cases or even Acts of Parliament, and do not have to give reasons for their verdict, it is possible for them to decide cases on their idea of 'fairness'. This is sometimes referred to as jury equity. Several cases have shown the importance of this, in particular *Ponting's Case* (1985) in which a civil servant was charged under the old wide-ranging section 2 of the Official Secrets Act 1911. He had leaked information on the sinking of the ship, the *General Belgrano*, in the Falklands war to a Member of Parliament. At his trial he pleaded not guilty, claiming that his actions had been in the public interest. The jury refused to convict him even though the judge ruled there was no defence. The case also prompted the government to reconsider the law and to amend section 2.

More recently a jury acquitted a mother of attempting to murder her daughter who committed suicide. Her daughter was aged 31 and had been ill for 17 years. She had injected herself with an overdose of morphine. The mother had given her daughter some medication to ease her suffering in her final hours. She had pleaded guilty to assisting the daughter's suicide, but the prosecution had insisted on continuing to prosecute her for attempted murder.

18.6.3 Open system of justice

The use of a jury is viewed as making the legal system more open. Justice is seen to be done as members of the public are involved in a key role and the whole process is public. It also helps to keep the law clearer as points have to be explained to the jury, enabling the defendant to understand the case more easily. Against this are the facts that the jury deliberate in private and that no one can inquire into what happened in the jury room. In addition, the jury do not have to give any reason for their verdict. When a judge gives a judgment he explains his reasoning and, if he has made an error, it is known and can be appealed against.

18.6.4 Secrecy of the jury room

This can be seen as an advantage, since the jury are free from pressure in their discussion. Jurors are protected from outside influences when deciding on the verdict. This allows juries to bring in verdicts that may be unpopular with the public as well as allowing jurors the freedom to ignore the strict letter of the law. It has been suggested that people would be less willing to serve on a jury if they knew that their discussions could be made public.

18.6.5 Impartiality

A jury should be impartial as they are not connected to anyone in the case. The process of random selection should result in a cross-section of society and this should also lead to an impartial jury, as they will have different prejudices and so should cancel out each other's biases. No one individual person is responsible for the decision. A jury is also not case-hardened since they sit for only two weeks and are unlikely to try more than three or four cases in that time. After the end of the case the jury dissolves and, as Sir Sebag Shaw said, it is 'anonymous and amorphous'.

18.7 Disadvantages of jury trial

18.7.1 Perverse decisions

In section 18.6.2 we looked at the idea of jury equity. That is the fact that the jury can ignore an unjust law. However, in some circumstances this type of decision can be seen as a perverse decision and one which was not justified. Juries have refused to convict in other clear-cut cases such as *R v Randle and Pottle* (1991) where the defendants

were charged with helping the spy George Blake to escape from prison. Their prosecution did not occur until 25 years after the escape, when they wrote about what they had done and the jury acquitted them, possibly as a protest over the time lapse between the offence and the prosecution.

18.7.2 Secrecy

In section 18.6.4 we considered how the secrecy of the jury protects jurors from pressure. However, the secrecy of the jury room is also a disadvantage. This is because no reasons have to be given for the verdict, so there is no way of knowing if the jury did understand the case and come to the decision for the right reasons.

In *R v Mirza* (2004) the House of Lords ruled that it could not inquire into discussions in a jury room. Two separate cases were considered in the appeal. These were *R v Mirza* and *R v Connor and Rollock*.

In *Mirza* the defendant was a Pakistani who settled in the UK in 1988. He had an interpreter to help him in the trial and during the trial the jury sent notes asking why he needed an interpreter. He was convicted on a 10–2 majority. Six days after the jury verdict, one juror wrote to the defendant's counsel alleging that from the start of the trial there had been a 'theory' that the use of an interpreter was a 'ploy'. The juror also said that she had been shouted down when she objected and reminded her fellow jurors of the judge's directions.

In *Connor and Rollock* a juror wrote to the Crown Court stating that while many jurors thought it was one or other of the defendants who had committed the stabbing, they should convict both to 'teach them a lesson'. This was five days after the verdict but before sentence was passed. As in *Mirza* there was a majority verdict of 10–2. The complaining juror said that, when she argued that the jury should consider which defendant was responsible, her co-jurors had refused to listen and remarked that if they did that they could be a week considering verdicts in the case.

The House of Lords held that s 8 of the Contempt of Court Act 1981 made it a contempt to disclose or obtain or solicit information about what had occurred in the jury room even for the purposes of an appeal. They also ruled that s 8 was compatible with Article 6 of the European Convention on Human Rights (the right to a fair trial). They pointed out that:

- confidentiality was essential to the proper functioning of the jury process
- there was merit in finality
- jurors had to be protected from harassment.

Exceptions

There are two exceptions where the courts will inquire into the conduct of the jury in coming to their verdict. The first is where there has been a complete repudiation of the oath taken by the jurors to try the case according to the evidence. In other words, they have used another method to make their decision.

The best-known example of this is the case of *R v Young (Stephen)* (1995) where the defendant was charged with murder of two people. The jury had to stay in a hotel overnight as they had not reached a verdict by the end of the first day of deliberations. At the hotel four of the jurors held a séance using a Ouija board to try and contact the dead victims and ask them who had killed them. The next day the jury returned a guilty verdict.

When the use of the Ouija board became known, the Court of Appeal quashed the conviction and ordered a retrial. The Court also felt able to inquire into what had happened as it had occurred in a hotel and was not part of the jury room deliberations.

The second exception is where extraneous material has been introduced into the jury room. Examples have included telephone calls in and out of the jury room, papers mistakenly included in the set of papers given by the court to the jury and information from the Internet. This last happened in *R v Karakaya* (2005), who was accused of rape. A juror did an Internet search at home and brought into the jury room the printed-out results of the search. The jury convicted Karakaya but this conviction was quashed because of the outside information that the jury had access to during their deliberations. A retrial was ordered and Karakaya was acquitted by the jury in the second trial.

Jurors and the Internet

Judges do direct jurors not to look at the Internet for information, but it seems that the use of Internet research by jurors is getting more common. In Cheryl Thomas's research, *Are juries fair?* (2010), she found that 12 per cent of jurors admitted they had looked on the Internet for information about cases they were trying. The risk of using the Internet is that the information may be prejudicial to the defendant. For example, doing a search on a defendant's name may find newspaper reports of previous convictions, which the jury should not know about. Also defendants have been known to upload highly personal information regarding their own behaviour and even crimes on to social networking sites.

18.7.3 Racial bias

However, although jurors have no direct interest in a case, and despite the fact that there are 12 of them, they may still have prejudices which can affect the verdict. Some jurors may be biased against the police – this is one of the reasons that those with certain criminal convictions are disqualified from sitting on a jury. In particular there is the worry that some jurors are racially prejudiced. This is why the fact that the selection process can produce an all-white jury to try a defendant from an ethnic minority is viewed with suspicion.

In *Sander v United Kingdom* (2000) the European Court of Human Rights ruled that there had been a breach of the right to a fair trial under Article 6 of the European Convention on Human Rights. In the case one juror had written a note to the judge during the trial raising concern over the fact that other jurors had been making openly racist remarks and jokes. The judge asked the jury to 'search their consciences'. The next day the judge received two letters, one signed by all the jurors in which they denied any racist attitudes and a second from one juror who admitted that he may have been the one making the jokes. Despite the discrepancies between these two letters the judge allowed the case to continue with the same jury. The European Court of Human Rights held that in these circumstances the judge should have discharged the jury as there was an obvious risk of racial bias.

A report, *Are juries fair?* by Cheryl Thomas (2010), looked at whether there was bias in cases where a defendant from a black ethnic minority was tried by an all-white jury. This was done by using two main methods:

- case simulations (mock trials) which used 41 juries with 478 jurors
- analysis of over half a million charges tried in the period 1 October 2006 to 31 March 2008.

In the mock trials no racial discrimination was shown. The verdicts from the real cases during 2006–08 showed only small differences based on the defendant's ethnicity. White and Asian defendants both had a 63% jury conviction rate; Black defendants had a 67% jury conviction rate.

18.7.4 Media influence

Media coverage may influence jurors. This is especially true in high-profile cases, where there has been a lot of publicity about police investigations into a case. This occurred in the case *R v West* (1996) in which Rosemary West was convicted for the murders of ten young girls and women, including her own daughter. From the time the bodies were first discovered, the media coverage was intense. In addition, some newspapers had paid large sums of money to

some of the witnesses in order to secure their story after the trial was completed. One of the grounds on which Rosemary West appealed against her conviction was that the media coverage had made it impossible for her to receive a fair trial. The Court of Appeal rejected the appeal, pointing out that otherwise it would mean that if 'allegations of murder were sufficiently horrendous so as to inevitably shock the nation, the accused could not be tried'. They also said that the trial judge had given adequate warning to the jury to consider only the evidence they heard in court.

Another case which highlighted media influence on the jury's decision was *R v Taylor and Taylor* (1993) in which two sisters were charged with murder. Some newspapers published a still from a video sequence which gave a false impression of what was happening. After the jury convicted the two defendants, the trial judge gave leave to appeal because of the possible influence this picture could have had on the jury's verdict and the Court of Appeal quashed the convictions.

The prosecution agencies are aware of the problems that media coverage can cause. This was noticeable in 2006 when five prostitutes were murdered in Ipswich. Prior to anyone being charged with the murders, there was a very high degree of media coverage. Once a man was charged with the murders, a member of the Crown Prosecution Service made a public announcement to the press, reminding them that they must be careful in any further coverage of the case.

18.7.5 Lack of understanding

There are worries that jurors may not understand the case which they are trying. This fear was partly borne out by a survey carried out in 1992 for the Runciman Commission, in which jurors were asked whether they thought they had been able to understand the evidence. Over half (56 per cent) of the jurors questioned thought that the jury as a whole had understood the evidence, with another two-fifths (41 per cent) believing that most of the jury had understood the case. However, just under 10 per cent of jurors admitted that they had had difficulty. When the foremen of juries were questioned on the same point, they thought that a small number of jurors (0.2 per cent) could not understand English sufficiently well to follow a case. The foremen also thought that about 1 per cent of jurors could not understand the details of a case, while another 1 per cent could not understand any case. These may be small numbers, but it is still worrying that in some cases a defendant's future is being decided by some members of the public who do not understand the case. For example, in one case at Snaresbrook Crown Court, the jury after they had retired to consider their verdict sent a note to the judge asking what they had to do! The judge discharged that jury from the case.

Australian research

Research into jury trials in Australia has revealed that some jurors did not know what verdict had been given in the case they had just tried. The research was into 32 trials about child abuse. It involved aspects such as how jurors thought the child witness had been treated in the case.

The jurors were given a questionnaire immediately after the verdict had been given. A total of 277 jurors took part. The first question asked 'What was the verdict in this case?' Only in a quarter of the trials did all the jurors give the correct answer. In the other cases at least one juror gave an incorrect version of the verdict. In one case four jurors said that the accused had been found guilty when he had actually been found not guilty.

The researchers point out that it is possible that jurors were expressing their own view of what they thought the verdict should have been. However, they go on to state that it seems some jurors

were confused, unclear or uncertain about the verdict. If jurors do not know what the verdict was immediately after that verdict has been given, then it creates doubts about how much of the case the jurors had understood.

English research

The report, *Are juries fair?* by Cheryl Thomas, which was published in 2010, looked at various aspects of the use of juries. One area was jurors' understanding of cases. In order to test understanding, a series of simulated trials were used. A total of 797 jurors in three different areas all saw the same simulated trial and heard exactly the same judicial directions on the law.

The jurors were first asked whether they thought they had understood the directions In two of the areas, Blackfriars, London and Winchester, over two-thirds of the jurors felt they were able to understand the directions. In Nottingham only just under half of the jurors felt they understood the directions.

The jurors' understanding of the directions was then tested. This discovered that only 31 per cent of the jurors had actually understood the directions fully in the legal terms used by the judge. When the jurors were given a written summary of the instructions, the number who fully understood increased to 48 per cent.

This study shows that, even with a written summary, fewer than half of jurors fully understood the judge's directions.

18.7.6 Fraud trials

Fraud trials with complex accounts being given in evidence can create special problems for jurors. Even jurors who can easily cope with other evidence may have difficulty understanding a fraud case. These cases are also often very long, so that the jurors have to be able to be away from their own work for months. A long fraud trial can place a great strain on jurors. Such cases also become very expensive, both for the prosecution and for the defendants.

The Roskill Committee in 1986 suggested that juries should not be used for complex fraud cases. There have recently been two provisions made in Acts of Parliament for this to happen.

The Criminal Justice Act 2003 had provision for the prosecution to apply for trial by a judge alone in complex fraud cases. However, this provision was repealed without being brought into effect.

In 2006 another Bill, the Fraud (Trials without a Jury) Bill, was introduced into Parliament to try to implement trial of fraud cases without a jury. This Bill was defeated. As a result, fraud trials are still heard by juries.

However, in the Domestic Violence, Crime and Victims Act 2004 there is a special provision for cases where there are a large number of counts on the indictment. This allows a trial of sample counts with a jury and then, if the defendant was convicted on those, the remainder could be tried by a judge alone. This provision balances the defendant's right to jury trial against the difficulty of a jury having to deal with large numbers of fraud allegations. A jury will try some charges only, making that trial simpler. If the defendant is found guilty, then the remaining charges will be dealt with by a judge alone.

18.7.7 Jury tampering

In a few cases friends of the defendant may try to interfere with the jury. This may be by bribing jury members to bring in a not guilty verdict or by making threats against jury members so that they are too afraid to find the defendant guilty. In such cases police may be used to try to protect the jurors but this may not be effective and is also expensive and removes the police from their other work.

To combat this, s 44 of the Criminal Justice Act 2003 provides that where there has already been an effort to tamper with a jury in the case,

the prosecution can apply for the trial to be heard by judge alone. The first trial without a jury was approved in *R v Twomey and others* (2009). In this case the defendants were charged with various offences connected to a large robbery from a warehouse at Heathrow. Three previous trials had collapsed and there had been a 'serious attempt at jury tampering' in the last of these. The prosecution applied to a single judge for the trial to take place without a jury. The judge refused but the Court of Appeal overturned this decision, ordering that the trial should take place without a jury.

However, in other cases the Court of Appeal has not granted trial by judge alone. In *KS v R* (2010) there had been several trials on various allegations of fraud committed by the defendant. It was not until the tenth trial that jury tampering occurred. It occurred because jurors and members of the public who wished to smoke during breaks were directed to the same area. During one of these breaks, a friend of the defendant approached a juror. The Court of Appeal refused an application for trial by judge alone. They pointed out that the casual arrangements at the Crown Court which had allowed the contact would not be repeated. Also the approach had been opportunistic rather than a deliberate targeting of jurors. For these reasons there was no need to order trial by judge alone.

Also the Criminal Procedure and Investigations Act 1996 allows for a retrial to be ordered if someone is subsequently proved to have interfered with the jury.

18.7.8 High acquittal rates

Juries are often criticised on the grounds that they acquit too many defendants. The figures usually quoted in support of this are that about 60 per cent of those who plead not guilty at the Crown Court are acquitted. However, this figure does not give a true picture of the workings of juries as it

ACTIVITY

Read the following extract from *Diversity and Fairness in the Jury System (2007)* and answer the questions below.

The Criminal Justice Act 2003 removed ineligibility and the right of excusal from jury service for a number of groups (those aged 65 to 69, MPs, clergy, medical professionals and those in the administration of justice). But summoned jurors may still be disqualified or excused from jury service (due to age, residency, mental disability, criminal charges, language, medical or other reasons).

- The study found that the most significant factors predicating whether a summoned juror will serve or not are income and employment status, not ethnicity. Summoned jurors in the lower-income brackets and those who are economically inactive are far less likely to serve than those in medium- to high-income brackets and those who are employed.
- In 2005, of all those who replied to their summons, 64 per cent of jurors served, 9 per cent were disqualified or ineligible, 27 per cent were excused. Of those excused, most were for medical reasons that prevented serving (34%) or childcare (15%) and work reasons (12%). Fifteen per cent of all the summons in the survey were either returned as undeliverable or not responded to, which occurred most often in areas of high residential mobility.
- The report established that most current thinking about who does and does not do jury service is based on myth, not reality.

Myth: Ethnic minorities are under-represented among those doing jury service.

Reality: Analysis showed that, in almost all courts (81 of the 84 surveyed), there was no significant difference between the proportion of black and ethnic minority jurors serving and the black and ethnic minority population levels in the local juror catchment area for each court.

Myth: Women and young people are under-represented among serving jurors, and the self-employed are virtually exempt from jury service.

Reality: The study establishes that jury pools at individual courts closely reflected the local population in terms of gender and age, and the self-employed are represented among serving jurors in direct proportion to their representation in the population.

Questions

1. What are the age limits for jury service?
2. What is the residency requirement to qualify for jury service?
3. What categories of people are disqualified from doing jury service?
4. What categories of people are less likely to serve on a jury?
5. What percentage failed to reply to their summons to do jury service?
6. For what types of reason were people excused from jury service?
7. What does the study show about the representative nature of juries?

includes cases discharged by the judge and those in which the judge directed an acquittal.

The judicial statistics show that in most years more than half of acquittals are ordered by the judge without a jury even being sworn in to try the case. This happens where the prosecution drops the case at the last minute and offers no evidence against the defendant. Usually about 10–15 per cent of acquittals are by a jury but on the direction of a judge. This occurs where

Key Facts

Advantages	Disadvantages
Public confidence Considered to be a fundamental part of a democratic society New qualifications for jury service mean that almost everyone can serve on a jury	High acquittal rates undermine confidence in the criminal justice system Doing jury service is unpopular
Jury equity *Ponting's Case*	Perverse verdicts *Randle and Pottle*
Open system of justice Involves members of the public	Media influence Reporting may influence the decision *Taylor and Taylor*
Secrecy of the jury room protects jurors from pressure	Secrecy means that: • the reasons for the decision are not known • the jury's understanding of the case cannot be checked *Young (Stephen)*
Impartiality Having 12 members with no direct interest in the case should cancel out any bias	Bias In some cases there has been racial bias *Sander v UK*

Figure 18.3 *Key facts chart of advantages and disadvantages of jury trial*

the judge rules that there is no case against the defendant; it might be because of a legal point or because the prosecution evidence is not sufficient in law to prove the case. When these decisions are excluded from the statistics it is found that juries actually acquit in about 30 per cent of cases.

18.7.9 Other disadvantages

The compulsory nature of jury service is unpopular, so that some jurors may be against the whole system, while others may rush their verdict in order to leave as quickly as possible. Jury service can be a strain, especially where jurors have to listen to horrific evidence. Jurors in the Rosemary West case were offered counselling after the trial to help them cope with the evidence they had had to see and hear.

The use of juries makes trials slow and expensive. This is because each point has to be explained carefully to the jury and the whole procedure of the case takes longer.

Use of a jury in cases involving dishonesty may lead to inconsistent verdicts between different juries. This is because jurors in dishonesty cases are directed to consider whether the defendant's behaviour was dishonest according to the standards of ordinary people. Finch and Fafinski carried out online research into people's ideas of dishonesty. They gave a series of situations and asked people to state whether they thought the behaviour involved was dishonest. They found that people's perception of what was dishonest varied widely.

18.8 Special problems of using juries in civil cases

18.8.1 Amount of damages

Juries in civil cases decide both the liability of the parties in the case and the amount of damages that will be awarded. The awards vary greatly as each jury has its own ideas and does not follow past cases. The amount is, therefore, totally unpredictable, which makes it difficult for lawyers to advise on settlements. Judges look back to past awards when deciding awards of damages in personal injury cases, and then apply an inflation factor so that there is consistency between similar cases. Juries in defamation cases cause particular problems with very large awards; one judge called it 'Mickey Mouse' money. In 1989 Lord Aldington was awarded £1.5 million; this is the highest award to date. If the amounts in personal injury cases are compared to this, it can be seen that this size of award would only be given to a very severely injured person who had been permanently disabled.

Until 1990 the Court of Appeal had no power to correct awards which were thought to be far too high. They could only strike out the award and order a retrial. This was both time-consuming and expensive and rarely happened. As a result of cases in which there were overgenerous awards, Parliament enacted s 8 of the Courts and Legal Services Act 1990 which gives the Court of Appeal special powers in such cases. This allows the Court of Appeal to order a new trial or substitute such sum as appears proper to the court, if they feel the damages were excessive or inadequate. This power was first used in a case brought by the MP Teresa Gorman where the Court of Appeal reduced the damages awarded to her by the jury from £150,000 to £50,000. It was also used in *Rantzen v Mirror Group Newspapers* (1993) when the award to Esther Rantzen, the founder of 'Childline' (a charity set up to help abused children) over allegations that she had deliberately kept quiet about the activities of a suspected child abuser, was reduced from £250,000 to £110,000.

18.8.2 Unreasoned decision

The jury does not have to give a reason either for its decision or for the amount it awards. A judge always gives a judgment; this makes it easier to see if there are good grounds for an appeal.

18.8.3 Bias

The problems of bias in civil cases is different from that encountered in criminal cases. In some defamation cases the claimants and/or the defendants may be public figures so that jurors will know and possibly hold views about them. Alternatively there is the fact that the defendant in a defamation case is often a newspaper and jurors may be biased against the press or may feel that 'they can afford to pay'.

18.8.4 Cost

Civil cases are expensive and the use of a jury adds to this as the case is likely to last longer. At the end of the case the losing party will have to pay all the costs of the case, which may amount to hundreds of thousands of pounds. As a result of this, the Lord Chancellor has introduced some reforms so that defamation actions will be less costly. Firstly, with the increase in County Court jurisdiction, parties can now agree that their case should be transferred to the County Court. Here a jury of eight may be used and the trial is likely to be less expensive than one in the High Court. Secondly, the parties may also agree to the case being tried by a judge alone without a jury. The Defamation Act 1996 allows the claimant to seek a limited sum (up to £10,000) in a quick procedure dealt with by a judge. This allows those who want to clear their name and get immediate compensation at a lower cost to do so.

18.9 Alternatives to jury trial

Despite all the problems of using juries in criminal cases, there is still a strong feeling that they are the best method available. However, if juries are not thought suitable to try serious criminal cases, what alternative form of trial could be used?

18.9.1 Trial by a single judge

This is the method of trial in the majority of civil cases, which is generally regarded as producing a fairer and more predictable result. Trial by a single judge is also used for some criminal trials in Northern Ireland. These are called the Diplock courts and were brought in on the recommendation of Lord Diplock to replace jury trial because of the special problems of threats and jury nobbling that existed between the different sectarian parties.

However, there appears to be less public confidence in the use of judges to decide all serious criminal cases. The arguments against this form of trial are that judges become case-hardened and prosecution-minded. They are also from a very elite group and would have little understanding of the backgrounds and problems of defendants. Individual prejudices are more likely than in a jury where the different personalities should go some way to eliminating bias. But, on the other hand, judges are trained to evaluate cases and they are now being given training in racial awareness. This may make them better arbiters of fact than an untrained jury.

18.9.2 A panel of judges

In some continental countries cases are heard by a panel of three or five judges sitting together. This allows for a balance of views, instead of the verdict of a single person. However, it still leaves the problems of judges becoming case-hardened and prosecution-minded and coming from an elite background. The other difficulty is that there are not sufficient judges and our system of legal training and appointment would need a radical overhaul to implement this proposal. It would also be expensive.

18.9.3 A judge plus lay assessors

Under this system the judge and two lay people would make the decision together. This method is used in the Scandinavian countries. It provides the legal expertise of the judge, together with

lay participation in the legal system by ordinary members of the public. The lay people could either be drawn from the general public, using the same method as is used for selecting juries at present or a special panel of assessors could be drawn up as in tribunal cases. This latter suggestion would be particularly suitable for fraud cases.

18.9.4 A mini-jury

Finally, if the jury is to remain, then it might be possible to have a smaller number of jurors. In many continental countries when a jury is used there are nine members. For example in Spain, which reintroduced the use of juries in certain criminal cases in 1996, there is a jury of nine. Alternatively a jury of six could be used for less serious criminal cases that at the moment can have a full jury trial, as occurs in some American states.

EXAMINATION QUESTIONS

1. (a) Describe the different roles juries have in criminal and civil cases. [18 marks]
   (b) Discuss the advantages of using juries in both criminal and civil cases. [12 marks]
   G151, January 2011, OCR

2. (a) Explain the different types of jury trial in England and Wales. [14 marks]
   (b) To what extent is trial by jury reliable? [11 marks]
   LA1, Winter 2011, WJEC

EXTENSION ESSAY

'The advantages for the accused of jury trials over Magistrates' Court trials are so obvious that any proposals to abolish the defendant's right to elect jury trial in "either-way" criminal cases, such as theft, are doomed to failure.' Discuss.

CHAPTER 19

LEGAL AID AND ADVICE

INTRODUCTION

When faced with a legal problem, the average person will usually need expert help from a lawyer, or from someone else with expertise in the particular type of legal difficulty. Most often the need is just for advice, but some people may need help in starting court proceedings and/ or presenting their case in court. For the ordinary person seeking legal assistance there are three main difficulties:

1. **Lack of knowledge.** Many people do not know where their nearest solicitor is located or, if they do know this, they do not know which solicitor specialises in the law involved in their particular case.
2. **People often have a fear of dealing with lawyers; they feel intimidated.**
3. **The final difficulty is one of cost.** Solicitors charge from about £100 an hour for routine advice from a small local firm, to over £500 an hour for work done by a top city firm of solicitors in a specialist field.

19.1 Access to justice

Where a person cannot get the help they need, it is said they are being denied access to justice. Access to justice involves both an open system of justice and also being able to fund the costs of a case. There have been various schemes aimed at making the law more accessible to everyone – for example, the national network of Citizens Advice Bureaux was started in 1939 and now operates in most towns. More recently the Law Society has relaxed the rules so that solicitors are allowed to advertise and inform the public of the areas of law they specialise in.

However, the problem of cost still remains a major hurdle. A judge, Mr Justice Darling, once said: 'The law courts of England are open to all men like the doors of the Ritz hotel.' In other words, the courts are there for anyone to use but cost may prevent many people from seeking justice. The cost of civil cases in the High Court will run into thousands of pounds. Even in the cheaper County Court the cost will possibly be more than the amount of money recovered in damages. There is the additional risk in all civil cases that the loser has to pay the winner's costs. In criminal cases a person's liberty may be at risk and it is essential that they should be able to defend themselves properly.

19.2 History of legal aid and advice schemes

A system of government-funded legal aid and advice began after the report by the Rushcliffe Committee in 1945. This was the era of the development of the Welfare State and access to legal services was viewed as being as important as access to medical services.

The government accepted the proposals in principle and this led to the Legal Aid and Advice Act 1949. The initial scheme covered only civil cases. It was not until 1964 that the scheme was extended to criminal cases. Other parts of the scheme were gradually set up. The main areas of advice came from the Green Form scheme of advice which was set up in 1972. Then, following the Police and Criminal Evidence Act 1984, duty solicitor schemes in police stations and Magistrates' Courts were established. The entire system was consolidated in the Legal Aid Act 1988, when the handling of civil legal aid was taken from the Law Society and given to a specially created Legal Aid Board.

Eligibility

When the scheme started in 1949, about 80 per cent of the population were eligible. This was in line with the idea of the Rushcliffe Committee that the scheme should be available not only to the poor but also to those of moderate means. Because the financial limits for qualifying did not keep pace with inflation, the number qualifying gradually went down to about 48 per cent by 1978. In 1979 the limits were revised upward and once more nearly 80 per cent of the population qualified. This did not last long and in 1993 there were severe cuts to the limits so that only 40 per cent qualified and many of these had to pay large contributions towards their funding.

19.3 The Access to Justice Act 1999

The cost of funding cases under the legal aid scheme was very expensive. There were also criticisms that advice was not available to those who really needed it. In its White Paper, *Modernising Justice*, which preceded the Access to Justice Act, the government stated that it needed to tackle the following problems:

* inadequate access to good-quality information and advice

* the inability to control legal aid
* the need to target legal aid on real legal needs, within a budget the taxpayer can afford.

The advice sector was described as 'fragmented and unplanned' with the result that providers of legal services could not work together to achieve the maximum value and effect.

Under the Access to Justice Act the previous legal aid scheme was replaced by two new schemes. These are the Community Legal Service for civil matters and the Criminal Defence Service for criminal cases.

19.3.1 The Legal Services Commission

Section 1 of the Access to Justice Act 1999 set up the Legal Services Commission.

In March 2010, the House of Commons Committee of Public Accounts criticised the Legal Services Commission for its financial management. As a result the government decided to abolish the Legal Services Commission and manage legal aid through the Ministry of Justice. This was done by passing the Legal Aid, Sentencing and Punishment of Offenders Act 2012.

19.4 The Legal Aid, Sentencing and Punishment of Offenders Act 2012

The Legal Aid, Sentencing and Punishment of Offenders Act 2012 abolished the Legal Services Commission. The administration of legal aid since April 2013 is operated by the Legal Aid Agency and comes under the umbrella of the Ministry of Justice.

An independent civil servant is the Director of Legal Aid Casework, and the decisions on granting legal aid will be made by him and his team.

19.4.1 Service providers

The system works by the Government making contracts with providers of legal services so that the providers can do legal work and be paid from government funds. Providers include law firms and not-for-profit organisations, such as the Citizens Advice Bureaux, offering advice on legal matters.

19.4.2 Criteria for funding civil cases

The Act gives the Lord Chancellor the power to set criteria for making civil legal aid services available. It also sets out the factors the Lord Chancellor must consider when setting the criteria. These factors are set out in s 10(3) of the Act. They include:

- the likely cost of providing the services and the benefit which may be obtained by them
- the availability of resources to provide the services
- the importance for the individual of the matters in relation to which the services would be provided
- the availability of other services, such as mediation
- where the services are sought by an individual in relation to a dispute, the individual's prospect of success in the dispute
- the public interest.

19.4.3 Availability of legal aid

Under previous legal aid systems, aid was available for all cases except those specifically excluded. There always were certain types of case excluded, for example small claims.

Under the new system, the starting point is that legal aid is not available for civil cases unless it is a category specifically mentioned in the Act or other regulations. The types of cases for which it is allowed include those involving children's rights and those involving liberty of the individual. This includes cases being heard at Mental Health Tribunals, as these are about whether a person should continue to be detained in a mental hospital, and cases involving claims for asylum.

The result of this change to the availability of legal aid means that it is no longer granted for those injured through medical negligence. Also removed from legal aid are claims for trespass to the person, to land or to property. These previously were eligible for legal aid.

19.5 Government funding in civil cases

The funding for legal aid comes from the government's budget. This means that a set amount is made available each year. Also, the amount set has to be considered against all the other claims on the budget, such as hospitals, health care and education. As a result, the government cannot afford to make legal aid available to everyone. In order to qualify there is a strict means test.

19.5.1 Means testing

Funding of civil cases has always been means tested. The first test is whether the person's gross income is below a set limit. If it is not, then they cannot receive any public funding. If it is below, then two matters have to be considered. These are the person's disposable income and their disposable capital:

Disposable income

Disposable income is calculated by starting with the gross income and taking away

- tax and national insurance
- housing costs
- childcare costs or maintenance paid for children
- an allowance for each dependant
- a standard allowance for employment (where the person is employed).

People receiving Income Support or Income Based Job Seeker's Allowance automatically qualify, assuming their disposable capital is below the set level.

Key Facts

Managing body	Legal Aid Agency
Different levels of help and representation available	• advice only • Legal Representation – covers all aspects of case • Support Funding – partial funding of a very high-cost case
Means test	Strict means test on gross income, disposable income and disposable capital for all services
Merits test for Legal Representation	Whether the case has a reasonable chance of success and the damages will be worth more than the costs. Other criteria including: • can the matter be funded in another way? • are there funds available?
Problems	• number of solicitors is decreasing • financial level of eligibility excludes people of modest means • capping of fund together with increasing criminal expenditure means that less is available for civil cases • only available for specified types of cases NOT available for PI cases and medical negligence or employment tribunal cases

Figure 19.1 *Key facts chart on public funding in civil cases*

There is a minimum amount of disposable income below which the applicant does not have to pay any contribution towards their funding. For income levels above this minimum level, a monthly contribution has to be paid. The more in excess of the minimum the greater the amount of the contribution. Monthly disposable income is graded into bands. Those bands are:

Monthly disposable income	Monthly contribution
Band A	¼ of income in excess of the band
Band B	+⅓ of income in excess of the band
Band C	+½ of income in excess of the band

There is also a maximum amount above which the person will not qualify for help. This idea of minimum and maximum levels is shown in Figure 19.1. The precise limits for disposable income are usually increased each year.

Disposable capital

Disposable capital is the assets of the person, such as money in a bank or savings account, stocks and shares or expensive jewellery. For Legal Help, Help at Court and representation in immigration matters the maximum limit for disposable capital is £3,000. Funding is not available if the person has assets worth more than this.

For the other publicly funded services there is a minimum limit for disposable capital of £3,000 and a maximum of £8,000. If the assets are below £3,000, then no contribution is payable. If the person has over £3,000 but under £8,000 they will have to pay the extra above £3,000 as a contribution towards their funding. If they have more than £8,000 they must use their own money to fund any legal case, although once they have spent the money in excess of £8,000 they can become eligible for funding.

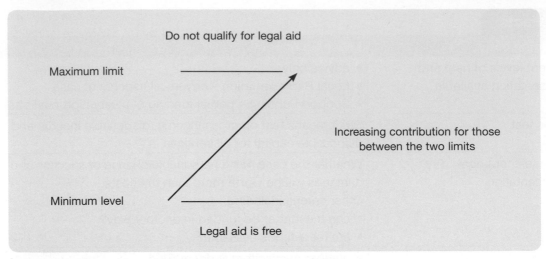

Do not qualify for legal aid

Maximum limit

Increasing contribution for those
between the two limits

Minimum level

Legal aid is free

Figure 19.2 *Minimum and maximum limits for legal aid*

Where a person owns a home the value of that home is taken into account in deciding the disposable capital. This is done by deducting the amount of mortgage, but only up to £100,000, from the current value of the property. If the amount left after this exceeds £100,000 then all the excess is counted as disposable capital.

Example:

House current market value	£220,000
Mortgage £140,000 – can only	
deduct £100,000	£100,000
	leaves £120,000
Deduct allowance of	£100,000
from the value	= £20,000

So this remaining amount of £20,000 is counted as disposable capital. Clearly this is over the maximum limit allowed for disposable capital and, therefore, the person would not qualify to receive funding.

19.6 Providers of legal services

Legal services are provided by a wide range of people and organisations. Local solicitors are a main source of legal services, but there are also advice agencies, welfare associations and consumer protection groups who can offer help and advice. The government intended to extend the range of bodies that provide legal services and to make sure that services were more evenly distributed through the country. In fact there are still problems of being able to access services.

19.6.1 Contracts

The Legal Service Commission granted contracts to services providers. The numbers of contracts decreased steadily. At the start in 2000 there were about 5,000 solicitors' firms with civil contracts. This was lower than the number who used to deal with legal aid cases under the previous system. The number has continued to decrease. By 2006 some 3,600 firms of solicitors had contracts. By 2012 only 1,711 firms had contracts. In addition, 265 not-for-profit agencies had contracts.

This diminishing number of solicitors and other agencies with contracts means that many people will have difficulty accessing publicly funded lawyers. It is likely to cause most problems in rural areas, where clients will have to travel long distances to find a legal aid firm.

This problem is not likely to be resolved by the new system.

19.7 Problems with funding of civil cases

19.7.1 Advice deserts

There is evidence that not enough legal service providers have contracts.

The problems of 'advice deserts' was considered by the Constitutional Affairs Select Committee as long ago as 2004. In the evidence to the Committee, even the Legal Services Commission acknowledged that:

'It is clear that there are parts of England and Wales in which the need for publicly funded legal services is not currently being met.'

In its report the select committee gave the position in Northumberland as an example. There were no housing law advisers and no one with a contract for immigration law in Northumberland. Furthermore, there were only two contracts for employment law in the area.

With the continued decrease in providers there are now even fewer legal service providers in certain areas. People who want help may have to travel long distances to find it.

19.7.2 Eligibility levels

Even where there are enough legal services providers in an area, only people with very low levels of income and capital can qualify for help. As far back as 2004 the Select Committee on Constitutional Affairs which investigated the adequacy of the provision of civil legal aid pointed out that:

'At present, the legal aid system is increasingly being restricted to those with no means at all. There is a substantial risk that many people of modest means but who are home owners will fall out of the ambit of legal aid. In many cases this may amount to a serious denial of access to justice.'

The system has not improved since. In fact the changes proposed by the Legal Aid, Sentencing and Punishment of Offenders Act 2012 may make matters worse.

19.8 Conditional fees

A major problem in taking a civil case to court is that it is not possible to know in advance exactly how much that case will cost. This is because it is not known how serious the other party is about defending the case. It may be that, once a court case is started, the other side will admit liability and the case will not actually go to court; it will be settled quickly and comparatively cheaply. However, if a case is defended then costs start to rise. Apart from lawyers' fees, there will be expenses of getting evidence, perhaps the cost of an expert's report on the matter, as well as the court fees to pay. In big cases in the High Court, the costs of a case can run to hundreds of thousands of pounds.

If the claimant wins then they should be able to get most of the costs, if not all, back from the defendant. But there is the risk that if the claimant loses the case, then they will have to pay the defendant's costs as well as their own. This uncertainty about the actual cost of a case means that for most people taking a court action is too risky, even though they may be advised that they have a very strong case.

Conditional fees agreements were developed in order to help people in this situation. They were first allowed by s 58 of the Courts and Legal Services Act 1990 in personal injury, insolvency and human rights cases. By 1998 the use of conditional fees was extended to all civil cases except family cases.

19.8.1 How conditional fees work

The solicitor and client agree on the fee which would normally be charged for such a case. The agreement also states what the solicitor's 'success fee' will be. This could be an 'uplift' of up to 100 per cent of the agreed normal fee. Under the provisions of the Legal Aid, Sentencing and Punishment of Offenders Act 2012, the Lord Chancellor will be able to set a limit on the maximum percentage for the success fee. If the solicitor does not win the case, then the client pays nothing. If the solicitor is successful then the client pays the normal fee plus the success fee. Most solicitors will also include a 'cap' on the success fee, which means that it cannot be more than 25 per cent of the damages which are awarded to the successful claimant. This is easier to understand by looking at an example.

As the success fee is an extra fee, it used not to be possible for the successful party to claim this from the other side as part of the normal costs of the case. However, the Access to Justice Act 1999 did allow courts to order that the losing party paid the amount of the success fee to the winning party. This has been changed again by the Legal Aid, Sentencing and Punishment of Offenders Act 2012, which states that:

'A costs order made in proceedings may not include provision requiring the payment by one party of all or part of a success fee payable under a conditional fee agreement.'

So now the position is that a winning claimant will have to pay any success fee themselves.

Figure 19.3 shows an illustration of conditional fees.

19.8.2 Insurance premiums

There is still the problem that a person who loses the case will normally be ordered to pay the costs of the other side. To help protect against this it is possible to insure against losing a case. The insurance premium will have to be paid in advance of the case even if the case is eventually won. This can cause problems to people who cannot afford the cost of the premium. This premium cannot under the Legal Aid, Sentencing and Punishment of Offenders Act 2012 be claimed as part of the costs of the case from the other side.

19.8.3 Are conditional fees working?

Conditional fee agreements (CFAs) have helped thousands of people to bring cases to court and obtain justice. One area in which they have been particularly useful for claimants has been in defamation cases. Legal aid has never been available for such cases and only the rich could risk pursuing defamation claims. CFAs have enabled ordinary people to take such cases.

However, there are problems with CFAs. Low-value cases are not attractive to lawyers who need to be able to make a profit for their legal business to survive. Lawyers are also more likely to take on cases where there is a very high chance of success.

The Legal Aid, Sentencing and Punishment of Offenders Act 2012 has made CFAs less attractive for two reasons:

Normal fee	£2,000	
Success fee	£1,000	
Cap on success fee	25%	
Result of case	**Client pays**	
Case is lost	Nothing	
Case is won: Client gets £20,000 damages	£3,000	£2,000 + £1,000
Case is won: Client gets £2,000 damages	£2,500	£2,000 + £500*
*This £500 is because the success fee cannot be more than 25 per cent of the damages.		

Figure 19.3 *illustration of conditional fees*

1. The cost of after-the-event insurance can no longer be claimed back from the defendant by a claimant who wins the case.
2. Success fees can no longer be claimable from the defendant by a claimant who wins the case.

These two points mean that a winning claimant will have to bear more of the cost of taking a case. As a result a large proportion of the amount of damages they receive may well be used up by their costs.

19.9 Advice agencies

A number of different advice schemes are available. The main ones are Citizens Advice Bureaux and law centres. They can apply for contracts to do government-funded work. However, there are other agencies which offer specialist advice on certain topics, for example the RAC and the AA offer members some help in traffic matters, while trade unions will help members with legal problems, particularly in work-related matters. There are also charities, such as Shelter which offers advice to people with housing problems. About 360 not-for-profit agencies have contracts to do Community Legal Service work (this will drop to approximately 115 in April 2013).

The legal profession offers assistance with schemes run by solicitors which provide cheap or free advice. In addition solicitors are now allowed to offer a 'conditional fee' service under which they will agree a set fee for a court case, but are entitled to an increased fee if they win.

Another way of funding a court case is by legal insurance. Most motor insurance policies offer cover (for an additional small amount) for help with legal fees in cases arising from road accidents, and there are policies purely for insurance against legal costs.

19.9.1 Citizens Advice Bureaux

These were first set up in 1939 and today they give advice in over 3,000 locations throughout the country, with a bureau existing in most towns. They give general advice free to anyone on a variety of issues mostly connected to social welfare problems and debt, but they also advise on some legal matters. They can provide information on which local solicitors do legal aid work or give cheap or free initial interviews. Many have arrangements under which solicitors may attend at the bureau once a week or fortnight to give more qualified advice on legal matters.

The Benson Commission in 1979 emphasised the importance of CAB as a first-tier legal advice service and recommended that they should be staffed by 'para-legals' (people who have had some legal training but who are not qualified lawyers) and given more government funding. This has not happened so far – funding is still patchy and Citizens Advice Bureaux rely heavily on volunteers. However, there is a training system for these volunteers and many become quite expert in certain fields. The Legal Services Commission has awarded contracts for some Citizens Advice Bureaux to provide government-funded advice.

Citizens Advice Bureau
Licensed by kind permission

19.9.2 Law centres

These offer a free, non-means-tested legal service to people in their area. The first law centre opened in North Kensington in 1970. This stated its aims as providing 'a first class solicitor's service to the people . . . a service which is easily accessible, not intimidating, to which they can turn for guidance as they would to their family doctor, or as someone who can afford it would turn to his family solicitor'. Their aim is to provide free legal advice (and sometimes representation) in areas where there are few solicitors.

Role

Law centres have played a pioneering role in identifying previously unrecognised areas of need and are orientated to the needs of the particular community they serve. The most common areas of work include housing, planning and environment, welfare, problems connected with employment, discrimination, immigration and children's rights. Some centres have set up duty solicitor schemes in the local County Court to deal with housing cases and try to help prevent evictions.

Many of their clients are disadvantaged.

Funding

Law centres have always struggled to secure enough funding. Recent cuts by local authorities in their budgets have meant the withdrawal or reduction of funding from this source. As a result some law centres have had to close. Funding also comes from the Legal Services Commission (when the Ministry of Justice takes over legal aid, it is to be hoped this funding will continue). Some centres have received funds from the Big Lottery Fund where the law centre is part of a community project.

As at the beginning of 2013 there were 55 law centres operating.

> ### ACTIVITY
>
> Look at the website of the Law Centres Federation at **www.lawcentres.org.uk**. This should give you the present number of law centres. It will also give information about the work they do.

19.9.3 Schemes run by lawyers
Cheap/free interviews

Some solicitors offer an initial interview of about half an hour either free or up to a maximum of £25 on a non-means-tested basis. Many solicitors run such a scheme and advertise the fact, both at their offices and in the press and even on the radio. The local CAB will have a list of solicitors who offer this service and can refer people to these solicitors.

ALAS

This is the Law Society's free Accident Legal Advice Service which is aimed at helping accident victims claim compensation. Solicitors in the scheme will give a free initial interview to advise whether a person has a case worth pursuing. In addition the Law Society has an Accident Line – a freephone telephone service to put accident victims in contact with solicitors who do legal aid personal injury work.

Bar Pro Bono Unit

Since 1996 volunteer barristers have staffed the Bar Pro Bono Unit. This unit gives free advice to those who cannot afford to pay and who cannot get legal aid. They will give advice on any area of law and will also where necessary represent the client in court proceedings.

Free Representation Unit (FRU)

This is also staffed by volunteer barristers. It was founded in 1972 and provides representation for:

- cases in the employment tribunals
- social security appeals, and
- claims for criminal injury compensation.

These are areas of law where legal aid is not available.

Until recently the FRU operated only in London. However, it is trying to set up units in Nottingham, Birmingham and Manchester.

19.10 Legal aid in criminal cases

From 2013, criminal legal aid services are under the Legal Aid Agency in the Ministry of Justice. The Director of Legal Aid Casework will supervise criminal legal aid as well as civil legal aid. The Agency will make contracts with law firms to provide legal services to people charged with criminal offences.

19.10.1 Advice and assistance for individuals in custody

Section 13 of Legal Aid, Sentencing and Punishment of Offenders Act 2012 states that:

'Initial advice and initial assistance are to be available . . . to an individual who is arrested and held in custody at a police station or other premises if the Director has determined that the individual qualifies for such advice and assistance . . .'

The Director must have regard to the interests of justice when making that determination. There will be regulations setting out more precisely what is to be considered in making determinations under s 13.

Telephone advice

One of the problems in the 1990s with duty solicitor schemes was that, in many cases, the solicitor did not attend at the police station but merely gave advice over the telephone. Although this was viewed as a defect in the scheme, telephone advice has now become the government's preferred method of action for duty solicitors. Since 2004 solicitors cannot claim for attending at the police station unless they can show that attendance was expected to 'materially progress the case'.

19.10.2 Representation

In order to get representation, the defendant has to qualify under the 'interests of justice' test. There is also a means test.

19.10.3 Interests of justice

A defendant will only get help with legal funding for representation in court if he can show that he comes within at least one of the five 'interests of justice' factors. These factors are:

- whether, if any matter arising in the proceedings is decided against him, the individual would be likely to lose his liberty or livelihood or suffer serious damage to his reputation
- the case will involve consideration of a point of law
- the individual is unable to understand the proceedings in court or to state his own case
- the case may involve the tracing, interviewing or expert cross-examination of witnesses
- it is in the interests of another person that the individual be represented (such as in a rape case).

19.10.4 Magistrates' Court means testing

As well as having to qualify under the 'interests of justice' test, defendants who are being tried in the Magistrates' Courts are also means tested.

Those who are on income support, defendants under the age of 16 and those under 18 in full-time education automatically pass the means test. For everyone else, the test starts with a first-stage simple means test which is calculated on gross annual income. If their income is too high on this test then the defendant does not qualify for legal aid. If a defendant's income is below a certain level, they qualify. For those in the middle bracket, they are further means tested to calculate their disposable income.

The levels allowed are very low. This means that about three-quarters of adults do not qualify for legal aid in criminal cases in the Magistrates' Courts.

19.10.5 Crown Court means testing

This was gradually introduced during 2010. The main difference from the Magistrates' Courts is that there is no upper limit on disposable income. All defendants can receive legal aid. It is free for those on low incomes.

Where a defendant has to pay, then the higher their income, the higher the contribution they will have to pay towards the case. The maximum amount they have to pay through contributions from their income is set by the type of case.

If a defendant is found guilty, they may also have to pay extra from their capital. This only applies where their capital is over £30,000.

If a defendant is found not guilty, any contributions paid will be normally be refunded.

19.11 Problems with funding of criminal cases

19.11.1 'Interests of justice' test

This test is applied very strictly. Even where a defendant is charged with an offence for which a prison sentence can be given, for example, theft, it does not necessarily mean that they will pass the 'interests of justice' test. The rule is that there must be a real risk of imprisonment.

This has the effect that a defendant who has several previous convictions for theft will qualify for legal help as they are likely to be imprisoned. However, someone with no previous convictions is not likely to be sent to prison. So, if they are pleading not guilty they will have to represent themselves or pay for private legal help.

19.11.2 Means test

In the magistrates' courts this is a strict test. The levels of income allowed are very low. About three-quarters of adults do not qualify for legal aid in criminal cases.

The limits are less severe in the Crown Court, but even here some defendants do not qualify for legal aid. As the cases are more serious and it is

Key Facts

Managing body	Legal Aid Agency
Different levels of help and representation available	• duty solicitor at the police station • advice and assistance • legal representation
Merits test for representation	Whether it is in the interests of justice • defendant at risk of losing liberty, livelihood or reputation • substantial point of law involved • defendant unable to understand proceedings • involves tracing, interview or expert cross-examination of witnesses • is in the interests of another person
Means test	Duty solicitor free of charge and not means tested Means testing for representation in court
Problems	• strict application of 'interests of justice' test • strict means test so that three-quarters of adults cannot qualify in Magistrates' Courts • lack of solicitors doing publicly funded criminal law work

Figure 19.4 *Key facts chart on public funding in criminal cases*

more expensive to defend a case, there is a real risk of injustice due to lack of availability of legal help.

19.11.3 Lack of lawyers

The Government has cut the fees paid to lawyers for criminal cases. Fixed fees are being brought in which do not take account of the true amount of work that may need to be done. As a result, fewer solicitors are taking on government-funded legal work. This makes it more difficult for defendants to find a local solicitor to take their case. The annual reports for the Legal Services Commission emphasise the decrease in solicitors doing legal aid work. Prior to the year 2000 there were over 5,000 law firms doing criminal legal aid work, but by 2012 there were only 1,640 firms.

19.11.4 Budget

The budget given by the government for legal funding has not risen in line with inflation. This means that there is less money to allocate for funding.

EXAMINATION QUESTIONS

1. (a) Explain the sources of funding available to access justice in England and Wales.
      [14 marks]
   (b) Discuss the extent to which there are unmet legal needs in England and Wales.
      [11 marks]

   LA1, Winter 2011, WJEC

EXTENSION ESSAY

'The help provided by publicly funded legal aid for civil cases is insufficient to allow access to justice for the majority of the public.' Discuss.

CHAPTER 20

HUMAN RIGHTS

20.1 The European Convention on Human Rights

Up to 1998 the United Kingdom did not have a Bill of Rights giving its citizens the right to certain basic freedoms. However, as early as 1950 the United Kingdom government signed the European Convention on Human Rights. This Convention was drawn up after the Second World War in order to try to protect people's rights from the abuses that had been seen during the Holocaust under Hitler's rule of Germany, and followed the Universal Declaration on Human Rights made by the General Assembly of the United Nations in 1948. The Convention in its Articles sets out the rights and freedoms that the people of Europe are entitled to expect.

The Convention was adopted by the Council of Europe in 1950. The Council of Europe was formed in 1949 and is not part of the present European Union, but a separate international organisation – it has a bigger membership than the European Union, covering most European countries. During the 1990s the membership has grown rapidly, with countries from Eastern Europe joining. There are now 47 Member States.

Although the United Kingdom signed the Convention in 1950, it was not part of our law until October 2000 when the Human Rights Act 1998 came into effect.

20.2 The Human Rights Act 1998

This Act incorporates the European Convention on Human Rights into British law and makes it unlawful for a public authority to act in a way which is incompatible with a Convention right.

This appears very wide-ranging protection as 'public authority' is defined as including courts as well as any person who has some public functions. However, there is a major limitation since 'public authority' does not include either House of Parliament or a person exercising functions in connection with proceedings in Parliament. This appears to mean that Parliament and government ministers may disregard the Convention.

20.2.1 Effect of the Act on interpretation of the law

When judges are deciding cases in which a question about a Convention right has arisen, s 2 of the Human Rights Act 1998 states that the court must take into account any judgment, decision, declaration or advisory opinion of the European Court of Human Rights. This means that the court must follow decisions of the European Court of Human Rights instead of a conflicting decision by a UK court.

This was seen in the case of *Re Medicaments (No 2), Director General of Fair Trading v Proprietary Association of Great Britain* (2001) where the Court of Appeal refused to follow the decision of the House of Lords in *R v Gough* (1993) on the test for bias because it was slightly different from decisions of the European Court of Human Rights.

The Act also states that, so far as it is possible, courts in England and Wales have to interpret legislation in a way that is compatible with the Convention. This can mean that the courts read the provisions of an Act in a very broad way in order to make it comply with the European Convention.

This occurred in *Mendoza v Ghaidan* (2002) when the Court of Appeal 'revisited' a decision made by the House of Lords in *Fitzpatrick v Sterling* (2001).

The case involved the transfer of a statutory tenancy to a same-sex partner. In *Fitzpatrick v Sterling* the House of Lords ruled that a statutory tenancy could not be transferred because the Rent Act 1977 used the words 'wife or husband'. The House of Lords had held that a same-sex partner could be classed as a member of the family and was therefore entitled to an assured tenancy, but could not have the tenancy transferred to them because they were not the 'wife or husband' of the deceased tenant.

In *Mendoza* the Court of Appeal held that this provision of the Rent Act infringed Article 14 of the Convention (discrimination). The court pointed out that it must, if it can, read the Rent Act so that its provisions are rendered compatible with the Convention. This could be done by reading the words 'as his or her wife or husband' to mean 'as *if they were* his or her wife or husband'. By doing this a same-sex partner was entitled to have the tenancy transferred to them.

The fact that judges are required to interpret legislation in a way which is compatible with the rights set out in the European Convention on Human Rights has had an impact on statutory interpretation in this country. This was pointed out by Lord Woolf in *R v A* (2001) when he said:

'Section 3 places a duty on the court to strive to find a possible interpretation compatible with Convention rights. Under ordinary methods of interpretation a court may depart from the language of the statute to avoid absurd consequences: s 3 goes much further. Undoubtedly, a court must always look for a contextual and purposive approach: s 3 is more radical in its effect . . . It will sometimes be necessary to adopt an interpretation which linguistically may appear strained.'

So in human rights cases a judge may interpret an Act in a very wide manner, in order to make the Act compatible with the rights given by the Convention.

20.3 Declarations of incompatibility

Although courts have to read legislation and give it effect in a way which is compatible with the rights set out in the European Convention, the Act recognises that some legislation may be worded in such a way that it is impossible to give effect to the Convention. If this is so the court must apply the legislation as it stands but may make a declaration that the legislation is incompatible with the Convention.

Section 10 of the Act gives government ministers the power to amend the legislation to bring it into line with the Convention. Any such amendment must be approved by Parliament. This, of course, will not help the person who is complaining that their rights have been breached, though it does mean that in the future other people's rights will not be breached.

The first case in which an Act was declared incompatible with Convention rights was *H v Mental Health Review Tribunal* (2001). This case concerned the fact that the burden of proof was on a patient making an application for release rather than being on the state to justify the continuing detention of the patient. As this involved the liberty of the subject it was a breach of Article 5. However, the domestic law was incompatible with the Convention and so the court could not give effect to the rights. It could only declare that the law was incompatible.

20.3.1 Government's response to declarations of incompatibility

After a declaration of incompatibility the government will usually change the law. However, there is no need for the government to do so. In fact, if Parliament wishes it can deliberately pass new legislation which contravenes the Convention. However, the government has usually changed the law following a declaration of incompatibility.

This can be done by a new Act of Parliament which replaces the incompatible one or, where only a small part of an Act is incompatible, it can be done by a remedial order. A remedial order is a statutory instrument which amends the incompatible provision in order to comply with the Convention rights.

An example of the law being changed was following the House of Lords decision in *A and another v Secretary of State for the Home Department* (2004). In this case the House of Lords declared that the Anti-Terrorism, Crime and Security Act 2001 was incompatible with the Convention. The Act allowed foreign nationals to be detained indefinitely without trial where there was suspicion that they were involved in terrorist activity. The Lords held that this breached both Article 5 (the right to liberty) and Article 14 (no discrimination on basis of nationality). This decision forced the government to change the law and release the detainees. However, they were not given full liberty but released on strict conditions.

Remedial orders

An example of a remedial order being used to amend an Act occurred as a result of the case of *B and L v UK* (2006). In this case a woman had married a man but later divorced him and had a relationship with his father. Although it was perfectly legal for the woman to live with her father-in-law, the Marriage Act 1949 prohibited them from getting married while the woman's first husband was still alive. The only way they could legally marry was to apply for private Act of Parliament giving them permission to marry.

They argued that the prohibition on their marriage was a breach of Article 12 of the Convention which

gives a right to marry. The European Court of Human Rights held that there was a breach of Article 12. Following this the Marriage Act 1949 (Remedial) Order 2006 was passed. This order removed the prohibition on in-laws marrying.

Joint Committee on Human Rights

There is a Joint Committee on Human Rights in Parliament which scrutinises all government draft legislation and picks out those with significant human rights issues for further examination. It will then report on whether, in their view, that legislation is compatible with European Convention Rights. The Committee also looks at government action to deal with breaches of human rights which have been identified by the courts. This includes looking at proposed remedial orders.

20.4 Bringing a case

The Act provides that a person whose rights are violated by a public authority may bring proceedings against that authority. Where an individual establishes that one of their rights has been breached, the court is able to make any order it considers just and appropriate. However, a court can award damages only if it is satisfied that it is necessary 'to afford just satisfaction'.

Decisions have been made on human rights in a number of different areas of law. Two main areas in which human rights points have been raised are criminal law and immigration law, but there have also been issues in many other areas, for example housing law, planning law, consumer credit law and even ecclesiastical law.

20.5 Convention rights

20.5.1 The right to life and liberty

Article 2 of the Convention states that everyone's right to life shall be protected by law, although it does recognise that states have the right to impose the death penalty for those convicted of certain crimes. Article 3 states that no one shall be tortured, or suffer inhuman or degrading treatment or punishment. The United Kingdom has been found to be in breach of this Article in respect of the way that prisoners in Northern Ireland were treated during interrogation. Article 4 declares that slavery is not allowed.

Article 5 sets out that everyone has the right to liberty and that no one shall be deprived of his liberty, except where the law allows arrest or detention. Even in these cases, the arrested person has the right to be told of the reason for the detention. Article 5(4) provides that 'everyone who is deprived of his liberty by arrest or detention shall be entitled to take proceedings by which the lawfulness of his detention shall be speedily decided by a court'. This includes those who have been given a custodial sentence, and in most cases this right is satisfied by the fact that there is the possibility of an appeal against conviction and/or sentence. However, the United Kingdom was held to be in breach of this article because the date of the release of young offenders convicted of murder used to be decided by the Home Secretary and not by a court.

20.5.2 The right to a fair trial

Article 5 is backed up by Article 6 which states that people have the right to a fair and public hearing within a reasonable time (this is so for both civil and criminal cases). On the reasonable time element the European Court of Human Rights in *Darnell v United Kingdom* (1993) held that the United Kingdom was in breach of the Article. The case involved a question of whether a doctor had been unfairly dismissed. The dismissal had taken place in 1984 and proceedings started soon afterwards, but the final decision of the Employment Appeal Tribunal on the case had not been made until 1993.

In *Sander v United Kingdom* (2000) the European Court of Human Rights ruled that a defendant had not had a fair trial and there was a breach of Article 6. During the trial one of the jurors had written a note to the judge raising concern over the fact that other jurors had been making openly racist remarks and jokes. The judge asked the jury to 'search their consciences'. The next day the judge received two letters, one signed by all the jurors in which they denied any racist attitudes and a second letter from one juror who admitted that he may have been the one making the jokes. The judge allowed the case to continue with the same jury.

The European Court of Human Rights held that the facts should have alerted the judge to the fact that there was something fundamentally wrong and he should have discharged the jury. Allowing the trial to continue in the circumstances was an infringement of the right to a fair trial.

The European Court of Human Rights also ruled that there was a breach of Article 6 in the case of *Hanif v United Kingdom* (2012). At *Hanif*'s trial there had been a police officer on the jury. This officer knew one of the police witnesses whose evidence was crucial to the case against *Hanif*. The juror officer had alerted the court to this fact but the judge ruled the trial should continue. This decision was upheld by the Court of Appeal. The European Court of Human Rights held that the presence of the police juror on the jury meant that the trial had not been fair.

Article 7 states that no one shall be found guilty of a criminal offence if his act was not a crime at the time he committed it. This means that the law is not allowed to change retrospectively; in other words, the law may be altered so as to make future acts of the type prohibited criminal offences, but it cannot look back to acts that have already been committed and declare that those are now criminal. However, in *R v R* (1991) a man was convicted of marital rape when the House of Lords overruled a previous precedent which had held that this was not a crime. R challenged this decision in the European Court of Human Rights, but that court decided that there had not been a breach of Article 7 because the law had changed in an earlier case to allow a man to be convicted of raping his wife when they were legally separated.

20.5.3 The right to privacy

Article 8 states that every person has a right to respect of his private and family life, his home and his correspondence. English law has given some protection to homes under the law of tort, and there is also protection of correspondence, but prior to the Human Rights Act there was no general right in English law to privacy. In the past there have been many incidents where people with a high public profile, such as the royal family, sports personalities, film and television stars have suffered from media intrusion into their private lives.

Since the Human Rights Act has come into force, courts in the United Kingdom have taken a more positive attitude towards the right to privacy. In *Douglas and others v Hello! Ltd* (2001) the Court of Appeal had to consider whether there was a breach of Article 8 when *Hello!* magazine published unauthorised pictures of the wedding of Michael Douglas and Catherine Zeta-Jones. The court stated that there was a right to privacy but it had to be balanced against the right to freedom of expression under Article 10. However, the court refused to make an injunction preventing *Hello!* from publishing the pictures. This refusal was mainly because Douglas and Zeta-Jones were prepared to have publicity of their wedding and had actually agreed that another magazine could publish pictures.

Article 8 can be quite wide in its application, as seen in *Hatton v United Kingdom* (2001). In this case the European Court of Human Rights ruled that the increase in the level of noise caused by aircraft using Heathrow airport was a breach of the right to respect for the applicants' private and family lives.

20.5.4 Other freedoms

Under Article 9 everyone has the right to freedom of thought, conscience and religion, while Article 10 states that everyone has the right to freedom of expression (this is the principle of freedom of speech). Article 11 also states that people have the right to freedom of peaceful assembly, and to freedom of association with others. This right includes the freedom to join trade unions.

Article 12 states that everyone has the right to marry.

Article 14 says that all the rights and freedoms should exist without any discrimination on any ground such as sex, race, colour, language, religion, political or other opinion, national or social origin, national minority, property, birth or status.

20.6 European Court of Human Rights

The European Court of Human Rights was established in 1959, in order to protect the rights set out in the European Convention on Human Rights. This court must not be confused with the European Court of Justice, which is one of the institutions of the European Union. The European Court of Human Rights sits at Strasbourg and deals only with breaches of the European Convention on Human Rights.

20.6.1 Procedure

Member States can report another Member State to the court for apparent breaches of the Convention, though this has only happened on a handful of occasions.

Individuals have the right to make an application to the court. However, an application is only admissible if the applicant has exhausted the effective remedies in the country in which the breach of rights is alleged to have occurred. For example, in the case of *S and Marper v UK* (2008)

The European Court of Human Rights

the applicants complained that their DNA samples were being retained indefinitely on the police database, even though they had not been found guilty of any offence. They took a case for judicial review of this, alleging a breach of their right to privacy under Article 8 of the Convention.

The case started in the High Court; there was then an appeal to the Court of Appeal and a further appeal to the House of Lords. The House of Lords ruled that there was no breach of Article 8. At this point the applicants had exhausted their rights within our legal system, so they then applied to the European Court of Human Rights. This application was admissible and the European Court of Human Rights ruled that there was a breach of Article 8 as keeping samples indefinitely was not a proportionate action where a defendant had not been charged or had been found not guilty.

Up to November 1998, there was a separate Commission on Human Rights which investigated the complaint and decided if the case should go to the court. With an increase in cases, this became too slow a process, so the Commission was abolished and the court became larger. The court

now has 47 judges (one for each Member State) and sits full-time in Strasbourg.

Under the present system, individuals who feel that their rights have been breached by their state apply direct to the court. Administrators check each application to decide if it is admissible. If there is still a doubt about admissibility, the case may then be sent to a Chamber of the Court, consisting of a committee of three judges, to decide if the complaint is admissible. If it decides that it is, the government of the state concerned is asked for its comments. There is then the possibility of the state and the complainant coming to a friendly negotiated settlement, but if this does not occur, then the court will hear the case in full and give a judgment on it. As well as deciding whether a state has breached the Convention, the court has the power to award compensation or other 'just satisfaction' to a successful complaint.

Some cases may go straight to a Chamber of seven judges to decide both the admissibility and the merits. In exceptionally important cases, a Grand Chamber of 17 judges will hear the case.

If the court upholds a complaint and rules against a state, that decision is final, but there is

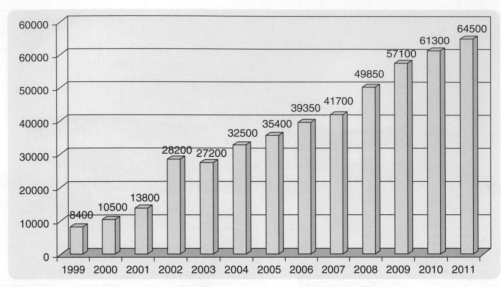

Figure 20.1 *Applications to the European Court of Human Rights*

no method of forcing the Member State to comply with that ruling. However, most states tend to accept the rulings. In an extreme situation it is technically possible for the Council of Europe to expel members who breach the Convention.

20.6.2 Case load

Since 2000 there has been an increasing number of cases being taken to the European Court of Human Rights. This is causing a backlog of cases, with over 151,600 cases waiting to be dealt with in 2011. More than half of these applications had been lodged against one of four countries: Russia 26.6 per cent, Turkey 10.5 per cent, Italy 9.1 per cent and Romania 8.1 per cent.

EXAMINATION QUESTIONS

Study the text below and answer the questions on it.

'The year saw the first occasion since the coming into force of the Human Rights Act 1998 in 2000 when a decision of the House of Lords on the interpretation of the European Convention on Human Rights was overturned by the European Court of Human Rights. In *S and Marper v UK* (decision of 4 December 2008) the Strasburg court disapproved of the House's decision in *R (S) and Marper v Chief Constable of the South Yorkshire Police* [2004] UKHL 39 and held that English law's blanket policy of retaining fingerprints and DNA samples taken from persons who were not later convicted of the offence being investigated was a breach of the right to a private life guaranteed by Art 8 of the European Convention.'

Source: Dickson, *New Law Journal* 23 January 2009

1. (a) Explain the impact of the Human Rights Act 1998 on English and Welsh Law. [14 marks]

   (b) Evaluate the role of the European Court of Human Rights in English and Welsh Law. [11 marks]

   LA2, Summer 2010, WJEC

EXTENSION ESSAY

Critically discuss the ways in which the Human Rights Act 1998 has had an effect on the way judges decide cases.

APPENDIX 1

Hints on some of the activities

This appendix gives help with the activities on pages 5 and 88.

Distinguishing between civil and criminal cases (page 5).

Question 1 (Answers)
Sources A, B and D are civil cases. Sources C and E are criminal cases. This information helps with the remainder of the questions in the activity.

Statutory interpretation and the case of Fisher v Bell (page 88).

The court used the literal rule in coming to the decision in this case. The court considered the technical legal meaning of 'offer for sale' and said that this was the correct literal legal meaning. This meant that displaying knives in the window was not offering them for sale, so it was decided that the knives in the window were not 'offered for sale', neither were they actually sold or hired or lent, so the shopkeeper had not committed an offence and was found not guilty.

APPENDIX 2

Glossary of Latin terms

audi alteram partem – a rule of natural justice that each side must be given the opportunity to put their case and be heard by the court or tribunal involved

certiorari volumus – literally 'we wish to be informed' (usually shortened to *certiorari*) – an order used by the High Court to quash a decision by an inferior court or tribunal

ejusdem generis – 'of the same kind' – a rule used in statutory interpretation where a list of words followed by general words will be taken to include items of the same kind

ex parte – without the other side (or party) to a case – some applications may be made to a court without informing the other party; this may be for emergency injunctions or in an application for leave to apply for judicial review. Since the Woolf reforms of civil procedure this is usually put in English – without notice. However, when looking at pre-1999 cases the Latin phrase will be used

expressio unius est exclusio alterius – the express mention of a person or thing excludes, by implication, other persons and things not mentioned; a rule used in statutory interpretation

locus standi – standing or right to take an action, especially in judicial review proceedings

mandamus – 'we command' – a command issued in the name of the Crown by the High Court ordering the performance of a public legal duty; used in judicial review proceedings

nemo judex in causa sua – 'no one [may act as] a judge in his own case'; a rule of natural justice

nolle prosequi – 'do not prosecute' – the order used by the Attorney-General to stop a prosecution from taking place

noscitur a sociis – a word is known by the company it keeps; a rule of statutory interpretation in which words are looked at in their context

obiter dicta – 'things said by the way' – the non-binding part of a judgment; a legal observation by a judge that is not part of his reason for the decision in the case (can be a persuasive precedent)

per incuriam – by mistake, carelessly or without taking account of a legal rule

prima facie – at first sight; on the face of it

quamdiu se bene gesserint – 'whilst of good behaviour' – this phrase is used to explain the right of a superior judge not to be dismissed without a good reason

ratio decidendi – the legal reason for a decision – the binding part of a judgment

stare decisis – 'stand by the decision' – the fundamental principle of judicial precedent; the full version of the maxim is *stare decisis et non quieta movere* which means, 'stand by the decision and do not disturb that which is settled'

ultra vires – beyond or outside the powers – a concept used in deciding whether delegated legislation or the decision of an inferior court of tribunal or administrative body is legal; if the act done was *ultra vires* it will be declared void

APPENDIX 3

Tips on exam success

There are three main ways in which you can maximise your chances of success in examinations. These are:

- by having good notes
- revising thoroughly
- having good examination technique.

1 Notes

Making notes

During your course you should be making your own notes on each topic. Some of these will be notes written in class, other notes will be from reading. Ideally, as you finish each topic, you should rewrite your notes. This means that the topic is fresh in your mind and, if there are any points that aren't clear or something that you missed, you can sort it out straight away.

When rewriting your notes, put them into a clear format which you find easy to understand. Use lots of headings and highlight case names and Acts of Parliament in different colours.

Cases

Cases are important in law for the legal points they decide. So, when making notes on cases make sure that you note down the point of law. You need only put very brief facts down. As well as your main notes, it is also a good idea to have a revision list of cases. A three-column chart is one method. Put the name of the case in the first column, the facts in the second and the point of law in the third.

2 Revision

Law is a very factual subject, so it is one which requires a considerable amount of learning. It is not possible to do well in law exams if you do not know the important points. The first way to help yourself is by learning each topic immediately after you have finished it during the course. Sometimes your lecturer or tutor may give you a test or a timed essay to do, so this gives an incentive to learn. But even if you have no test on a topic, it is sensible to learn it as you go through the course rather than leave everything to the end. You may feel that this is too far ahead of the exams and a waste of time as you will only forget it. But it is worth doing: some of the topic will 'stick'. You will find that when you do your revision before the exams it will be easier.

Revision before the exam

Be well organised for this. Set yourself a timetable listing which topics you will learn each day. Don't be too ambitious in your timetable. Break each topic up into manageable chunks. Allow yourself short breaks between revising topics. Try different ways of learning. Find out what works best for you. Here are some ideas for varying revision methods:

- Read out loud.
- Write brief notes from memory (especially cases).
- Dictate your notes on to a cassette and listen to them (you can do this on your way to school or college).
- Revise with a friend and test each other.
- Write essay plans.
- Do timed exam questions.

3 Exam technique

Before the exam

This starts before you sit the exam. First of all make sure that you know the topics covered by the exam. Also make sure you know the format of the exam. This includes how many questions you have to answer and whether you have a choice of questions. Get familiar with the types of question that have been asked on past exam papers. There are examples of past questions at the end of each chapter in this book, but you can get past papers from OCR and WJEC. Look up www.ocr.org. uk or www.wjec.org.uk for information on this. If you are doing a degree or other course ask for past papers so you can practise doing past questions.

But remember that this year's questions will have a different focus or emphasis from previous years, even though they are on the same topics. Learning an essay to a past question is NOT recommended.

In the exam

- In the exam, even though time is limited, read the questions carefully.
- Underline or highlight key words in questions.
- Do a brief plan before you start on your answer and then check back to the question to make sure you are keeping focused on the specific demands of the question.
- Look at the number of marks allocated for each question or part of a question. This helps you know how much detail you are expected to give in your answer. It also makes sure that you allocate your time properly and allow time for all your answers.
- If you are running out of time for the last question, then use note form for the last part of your answer. Normally you should not use note format (such as bullet points) in an exam, but if you are running out of time, it is important to get as many points down as possible.

INDEX